Political Will and Personal Belief

Political Will and Personal Belief

THE DECLINE AND FALL OF SOVIET COMMUNISM

Paul Hollander

YALE UNIVERSITY PRESS | NEW HAVEN AND LONDON

To Mina, Sarah, Laura, Sophie, and Lily

Published with assistance from the foundation established in memory of Philip Hamilton McMillan of the Class of 1894, Yale College.

Designed by Rebecca Gibb. Set in Baskerville type by Integrated Publishing Solutions, Grand Rapids, Michigan. Printed in the United States of America by Edwards Brothers, Inc., Ann Arbor, Michigan.

Library of Congress Cataloging-in-Publication Data
Hollander, Paul, 1932–
    Political will and personal belief : the decline and fall of
Soviet communism / Paul Hollander.
        p.   cm.
    Includes bibliographical references and index.
    ISBN 0-300-07620-7 (alk. paper)
    1. Soviet Union—Politics and government.   2. Communist
leadership—Soviet Union.   3. Communism—Soviet Union—History.
4. Communist leadership—Europe, Eastern.   5. Communism—Europe,
Eastern—History.   6. Defectors—Soviet Union.   7. Defectors—
Europe, Eastern.   I. Title.
DK266.H477   2000
321.9'2'094'09048—dc21   99-31370
                                                                    CIP

A catalogue record for this book is available from the British Library.

The paper in this book meets the guidelines for permanence and durability of the Committee on Production Guidelines for Book Longevity of the Council on Library Resources.

10   9   8   7   6   5   4   3   2   1

Contents

Preface

More than any other of my writings, this book is a product of plain curiosity and a desire to better understand something important. There was no particular point I wished to prove, no belief to vindicate, no polemics to pursue or wrongheaded worldview to expose. If such a thing is possible, I approached the topic with a largely open mind, although I am not sure that such approaches are necessarily superior to those that entertain some preconception to be proved or disproved. The only predisposition relevant to the thrust of the book is a general inclination to take ideas and beliefs seriously as factors to be reckoned with in social, political, and historical matters.

As much as I rejoiced in the collapse of Soviet communism, it took me by complete surprise, nor did I find the rising tide of explanations and interpretations quite satisfying. It was puzzlement and unappeased curiosity that led to this attempt to better understand why and how the collapse happened. In exploring the question I tried to follow a path of inquiry not embarked upon by other authors, to focus on the attitudes and beliefs of individuals who were instrumental in both the maintenance and the disintegration of the communist system in the Soviet Union and two of its East European allies, Hungary and Czechoslovakia.

Even aside from such curiosity, it is not difficult to explain why, after an interval of many years, I returned to the topic of Soviet communism, albeit at its terminal stage. Biographical factors discussed elsewhere explain a great deal (see the epilogue in my *Survival of the Adversary Culture* [1988] and my essay in *Red Star, Blue Star* [1997]). The communist system in Hungary, where I grew up, made a substantial and lasting impact on my life. Consequently I became engaged from my early teens until ripe middle age in discussion and debate, both public and personal, over the nature of communist systems and the ideas that inspired them.

Communism, like Nazism, cast a long, dark shadow over much of the twentieth century; it has been a social-political force difficult to ignore for a social scientist or for an intellectual (though many managed to do so) or for anybody interested in the varieties of political repression and the relation between ideological commitments and the exercise of political power, between political ideals and realities, between noble intentions and bad results. By now both Nazism and Communism are largely matters of historical interest, although the ideals that inspired communist systems and movements seem less moribund than those that inspired "national socialism." This is not to suggest that communist systems were lacking in nationalistic components.

Communist systems made an especially deep impression on me (as they did on others who lived under them) on account of the remarkable discrepancy between their idealistic goals and the dismal realities that they perpetuated. They gave virtuoso displays of the unintended consequences of various social-political intentions and actions. Of further interest has been the great contrast between their enormous, concentrated power and their unexpected, rapid, and dramatic disintegration. They seemed formidably strong, yet most of them collapsed like the proverbial stack of cards, confounding all of us grimly contemplating their stubborn persistence despite their unpopularity, inefficiency, and amorality.

In much of my earlier work I tried to understand the attraction that communist systems and ideologies held for groups of people (mostly intellectuals) who were not obliged to live under them. *Political Pilgrims* (1981) was the major product of these efforts. I also pursued the topic in each new introduction to subsequent editions of the book (1984, 1990, and 1997) and in parts of *The Survival of the Adversary Culture* (1988) and *Decline and Discontent* (1992). In the present undertaking I am asking, among other questions, why and how these ideals and systems became finally discredited even by those who exercised power on their behalf and were rewarded by a privileged life. I also hope to shed further light on the more general political-psychological shifts from belief to disbelief and from the lust for power to a diminished will to power.

The reader will notice that the longest chapter (6) deals with "leading specialists in state security," or political police. There are two reasons for the extended treatment accorded this group and the part played by coercion and political violence (or its threat) in the preservation of Soviet communism. On the one hand, I want to acquaint the American reader with some of the figures who played important roles in the apparatus of repression, for little is known about them by the wider public. On the other hand, I wish to draw attention to the decline of the ruthless and determined use of force, a decline that was an important factor in the unraveling of Soviet communism, and at the same time find out why such decline occurred.

Another, more unusual feature of the book is the use of the writings of some famous defectors as source materials. Their accounts of the flaws of Soviet communism and the discontents that communism generated among members of the elite (to which they belonged) anticipated the critiques and discontents that became widespread and public during the years of glasnost. A deeper understanding of the fall of communist systems compels an awareness of these accounts and the long-standing discontents that they reflect. As is explained more fully in the book, this source of information has been neglected by Western social scientists and deserves rehabilitation.

The reader will also note the large number of direct quotations, which I prefer to paraphrases or summaries in order to convey as directly as possible the feelings, states of mind, and beliefs of the protagonists. All translations from the Hungarian are mine.

Nothing in this book was intended to shed light on what happened after the collapse of the Soviet bloc. I made no attempt to predict developments in the years immediately following 1989 and 1991 or in those still ahead. The book is concerned solely with the collapse, its better understanding, and what led up to it. To what extent the events unfolding since 1991 (in the former USSR and Eastern Europe) could be explained with reference to the character of the political system, or the efforts to reform the system, or the Western responses to the collapse is another topic, which would require a different study.

I started working on this study a long time ago, in the fall of 1991, when I made the first round of interviews in what was then postcommunist Czechoslovakia and Hungary. More interviews were carried out in 1992 in the same countries and Slovenia and in 1994 some more in Hungary (see the Appendix). Years of library research followed, as did some interviews in this country with some Soviet émigrés. In the summer of 1996 I did a few more interviews in Hungary and Romania. I should point out that the interviews are by no means the major foundation of the study; rather, they supplement the printed sources.

My work was supported throughout its different stages by research grants from the Earhart Foundation, a longtime generous supporter of my work. The International Research and Exchanges Board gave a grant for the interviews and associated travel in the fall of 1991. The Bradley Foundation provided financial assistance during the 1992–1993 academic year that allowed full-time work on this project as well as travel to and within Europe. The same period coincided with a sabbatical leave from the University of Massachusetts at Amherst, my employer since 1968. I was a visiting scholar at the Hoover Institution and the University of California, Santa Cruz, in the winter and spring of 1993; both institutions provided office space and access to their libraries. At Hoover I also had the opportunity to meet and exchange ideas with many specialists in the study of communist systems. I am grateful to each of these institutions for their help.

My old friend Peter Kenez (University of California, Santa Cruz) read the entire manuscript and offered numerous helpful comments. Richard Pipes read the entire manuscript at a crucial stage; his judicious assessment helped to resolve problems of length. Parts of the manuscript were read by Charles Fairbanks (Nitze School of Advanced International Studies, Johns Hopkins University), Sergei Grigoriev (Kennedy School, Harvard University), Jiri Hochman (translator and editor of the Dubcek autobiography), Rudolf Tokes (University of Connecticut at Storrs), Otto Ulc (State University of New York at Binghamton), Adam Ulam and Janet Vaillant (Russian Research Center, Harvard). Each of them gave good advice. Those listed above include two natives of Hungary, two of the former Czechoslovakia, two of Poland, and one of the former Soviet Union. Janos Kenedi, writer, journalist, and former Hungarian dissident, provided much help and excellent advice about people to be interviewed in Hungary. Michaela Freiova, member of the Czechoslovak Parliament at the time, helped to find appropriate subjects for interviews in Prague; Gyorgy Konrad, another very old friend, provided contacts with several Slovenian writers and with Ivan Klima, the Czech writer. Alexei Koltakov, a native of Russia and at the time a graduate student in history at the University of Massachusetts at Amherst, conducted the Soviet interviews discussed in the Appendix. Denis Kozlov, another native of Russia and a graduate student in history at the same institution at the same time, helped with library research, especially Soviet source materials. Alexander Yakovlev kindly agreed to meet me on his visit to Washington, D.C., in September 1998 and responded to scores of questions. Mary Pasti of Yale University Press provided conscientious and competent editorial assistance. My wife, Mina Harrison, contributed to the completion of this study—as she has to all others during the past twenty-two years—in many indirect ways and, above all, by sharing her life with mine.

I am also thankful to all those (discussed in the Appendix) in the former Czechoslovakia, Hungary, Romania, Russia, and Slovenia who were willing to respond to my questions and exchange ideas on the topic of this book.

Intellectuals and people of higher education have a recurring hope that the accumulation and analysis of information and an expanded understanding of human and social affairs will make some difference to the conduct of human beings and the functioning of social and political institutions. Perhaps a better understanding of the dissolution of the Soviet empire, sought in this volume, will make it a bit more difficult to embrace the kinds of beliefs and delusions that facilitate the rise of repressive political systems such as Soviet communism used to be.

CHAPTER 1

The Human Factor in the Failure of Communism

"Reviewing the history of international affairs in the modern era . . . I find it hard to think of any event more strange and startling, and at first glance inexplicable, than the sudden and total disintegration and disappearance . . . of the great power known successively as the Russian Empire and then the Soviet Union."
GEORGE F. KENNAN

"Regimes can . . . disappear because their ruling groups lose their commitment to the values and institutions that sustain them. The Soviet elite lost confidence in Marxist-Leninist predictions and infallibility, then confidence in the rectitude of their own monopoly of power, and then they abandoned power." JEANE J. KIRKPATRICK

At a time when communist systems[1] have become things of the past, there are especially good reasons for trying to understand not only the political and economic forces that undermined them but also the part played by particular human beings and their beliefs in their decline and fall. Unlike most studies of the collapse of communist systems, which focus on institutional, economic, and political failures, the present one proceeds from individual human beings—their beliefs, aspirations, illusions, and disappointments—to institutions and systems of government.[2]

The erosion of belief central to the discussion that follows is not that of ordinary citizens, whose belief in the system was always questionable and, in any event, largely irrelevant to the survival of the political order. What mattered for the maintenance of a communist system were the beliefs and

1

attitudes of the political elite, especially the leaders. The key question is, as the historian Charles Maier puts it, "How does the determination to rule falter among the ruling elite of an imperial system?"[3]

In this study I will examine individuals who held power or assisted in the exercise of power and who used to believe (to varying degrees) in the ideals that these systems attempted to realize. While a great deal is known about the failures of communist systems and the discontent of the people who had to live under them, there have been virtually no attempts to gauge the disaffection of those who held power and to compare the dynamics of disillusionment in elite groups in various communist states.[4]

Ideology and the beliefs that it entailed were important determinants of the thinking and acting of communist leaders. Correspondingly, the erosion of beliefs, however fragmentary they might have been, was more consequential in the Soviet communist case than it would have been in political systems whose maintenance and legitimacy had less to do with the ideologically derived beliefs of (elected) leaders and more with institutional supports and other bases of legitimacy, including expressions of popular consent (or its absence).[5]

HUMAN PURPOSE AND SOCIAL FORCES

In this book I will explicate the somewhat mysterious process whereby, in the words of a former Soviet author, "the sense of conscience that Bolshevism trampled underfoot gradually revived in all of society, including among people who were destined to rise to the supreme echelons of power."[6] It is those in "the supreme echelons of power" whose attitudes are of prime concern in this study. This group includes people who entertained doubts while holding high office but stifled them for lengthy periods of time; they sought to balance belief and disbelief, old certainties and new doubts, the enjoyment of a privileged way of life and pangs of conscience about it.

Of further interest are those among the political elite whose disaffection led to their departure: defectors, who voted with their feet and subsequently chronicled their disenchantment with the communist system. Their discontent and critiques often anticipated by decades the sentiments expressed during glasnost and in conjunction with the collapse of Soviet communism. This group is much neglected by Western scholars of communist systems.[7]

Instead of focusing on the impersonal forces of history and politics (as is customary among authors addressing the topic), I am seeking to understand the eclipse of communist systems with reference to those who were most intimately involved with their maintenance and legitimation. In doing so, I am guided by the advice of Isaiah Berlin, the English social philosopher who favored "viewing human beings as creatures with purposes and motives" rather than assuming that "the behavior of men is . . . made what it is by causes largely beyond the control of individuals." I also share his conviction that "those who are concerned with human affairs are committed to the use of moral categories and concepts, which normal language incorporates and expresses."[8]

None of the foregoing is to deny that the severe and growing economic difficulties played an important part in the demise of the Soviet Union and Soviet communism. The unrelieved economic failures of the system provide the background of both the critical loss of popular legitimacy and the drastically weakened political will of the leaders that led to the unraveling of the system. Since much has already been written about these failures and weaknesses of the Soviet economy and its impact on the political system, I will not dwell on them and will focus instead on the human beings who had to confront and deal with these problems and whose inability to do so was the most direct cause of the collapse.

Unlike other authoritarian regimes in history, communist states were not defeated in war or overthrown in bloody internal revolution; they expired from internal pressures and defects despite their huge agencies of control, coercion, and propaganda. Valery Boldin, Gorbachev's chief of staff, writes: "The term 'victory in the cold war' is hardly strong enough to convey . . . what really happened . . . it was a total rout of the . . . USSR and the moral devastation of a once powerful adversary. But this rout was not the work of American military and technological might . . . It resulted from . . . internal capitulation."[9] The collapse was probably accelerated by the burden of the costly arms race, especially its high-tech variety, initiated by the United States under the presidency of Ronald Reagan.[10]

I will be looking for connections between change in communist systems (focusing on the Soviet Union, Hungary, and Czechoslovakia) and the transformation of the outlook of key figures who supported those systems. In doing so, I seek a better understanding of several phenomena, each of which, though far from disconnected, could merit an inquiry of its own.

Above all else, I would like to shed light on the connections between institutional decay and the disillusionment of leaders and political elites, including Party intellectuals. How did the loss of faith evolve? How did it undermine the political will, sense of legitimacy, and sense of entitlement to power? Did the loss of political will contribute tangibly to institutional malfunctioning? There is also the problem of deciding what came first: Did disillusionment contribute to the decay of institutions, undermining government and policymaking, or did the realization that institutions and policies did not work lead to disillusionment with the system as a whole?[11] I am not arguing that political systems survive only when the beliefs of the citizens converge with governmental policies; however, attitude change among the political elites is far more consequential.

Though often forgotten by social scientists, individual personality can be an important determinant of the political process, especially in systems where power is concentrated in a few hands and where "the character, intelligence and relative open-mindedness of the person at the apex becomes crucially important," as Archie Brown, the English political scientist, has argued.[12] Two younger Russian scholars, Vladimir Zubok and Konstantin Pleshakov ("products" of both the Brezhnev era and glasnost), similarly emphasize "the role of personality in Soviet policy-making," "the human factor."[13] It is among the ironies of history that political systems inspired by Marxism—which minimizes the importance of the individual in the historical process—turned out to be singularly marked by the personality and mindset of particular individuals, among them Lenin, Stalin, Khrushchev, and Gorbachev.

The emphasis on human beings and their animating beliefs gains further importance from the fact that the Soviet Union began as a political system self-consciously committed to the realization of certain beliefs and theories. It was what Raymond Aron calls an "ideocracy," which legitimated itself by Marxist doctrines.

Almost to the very end, the importance of ideology for the maintenance of the communist system remained a matter of dispute in the West. The part played by ideology involves two questions: Did the rulers retain important doctrinal beliefs? and Did it matter for the survival of the system whether they did retain such beliefs? The importance placed on ideology is, among other things, suggested by the concealment by the regime—even during the "stagnant" Brezhnev era—of the full extent to which old beliefs were being abandoned. Ernest Gellner wrote: "Appearances were maintained and society functioned on the surface *as if* it still were a charismatic community, bound by a messianic faith. Individuals may have noted that their own faith had vanished, but they did not probe into the fidelity of others. So the assumption that the Founding Faith was upheld continued, in a vague general kind of way, to pervade the atmosphere."[14]

In a society of this kind it is hard to gauge popular dissatisfaction, because there are profound differences between private and public opinion, making the prediction of radical change difficult and leading to a form of behavior Timur Kuran has called "the act of misrepresenting one's preferences under perceived social pressure"[15] (let alone very real pressure). Even observers well aware of the lack of popular support for communist systems could not tell (until glasnost) how strong the dissatisfaction with these systems was.

Even when the extent of the unpopularity of a political systems is revealed and widely perceived, a revolutionary upheaval is far from imminent. as long as the ruling elites' determination to stay in power is unshaken. By the same token, it may also be argued that the ruling elite with an unshaken will to power does not allow public reflections of its unpopularity to emerge; we learn about widespread public dissatisfaction only when the will and entitlement to power is weakened. Clearly, in the Soviet Union and the communist states of Eastern Europe this was the case by the 1980s. At the same time, as Adam Ulam has observed, the leaders probably believed that, whatever their true feelings, "an ideological veneer was a necessary condition of the political security of the . . . regime."[16]

Unlike many observers of the Soviet system, I have always believed that there was, even recently, some degree of ideological commitment on the part of the political elite, that the love of power and privilege did not adequately explain their behavior. Arkady Shevchenko, a former high-ranking Soviet diplomat, agrees: "Men do not reach the pinnacle of Communist power without . . . an abiding commitment to the rightness of the Soviet system . . . they base their conduct on a blend of ideological and pragmatic motives."[17]

Even in the post-Stalin and post-Khrushchev era, ideology or at least certain key beliefs remained important influences. Zubok and Pleshakov write: "The Kremlin statesmen inherited the Soviet revolutionary-imperial paradigm in the form that was bequeathed by Stalin . . . The transformation of the world under the aegis and with the assistance of the Soviet Union remained a powerful raison d'être for the . . . Soviet power elites, however cynical they became . . . [T]he messianic prescriptions of revolutionary-imperial ideology loomed large in the political environment in which Soviet leaders struggled, rose and fell. Ideology . . . was . . . the core of the regime's self-legitimacy, a terrifying delusion they could never shake off."[18]

The key political institution of this system, the Communist Party, "could be defined as the disciplined association of those committed to the implementation of the truth."[19] If Ernest Gellner's definition holds, it may also be possible that in some instances, "the disillusioned were driven into opposition to the Stalinist Party leadership by the same spiritual factors, the same humanitarian passions, that had, once upon a time, made them join the ranks of Stalin's followers."[20] Although the latter point was made with reference to some Hungarian communist functionaries in the mid-1950s, it may also apply to the "humanitarian passions" of Soviet reformers such as Gorbachev, Yakovlev, and Shevardnadze.

One further reason should be noted for undertaking this study. At a time when new discontents have emerged in most former communist societies, it is worthwhile to recall the shortcomings of communist systems before awareness of them is submerged in the more recent dissatisfactions. The personal experiences, accounts, and chronicles of disenchantment—including those of people who rejected these systems well before their collapse—provide vivid and memorable inventories of the fatal flaws of the undertaking aimed at creating vastly improved human beings and institutions.

TAKEN BY SURPRISE: WESTERN SCHOLARS AND THE COLLAPSE
The fall of Soviet communism was among the major historical events of modern history that few anticipated, including myself; although it might have been "rationally predictable," it was "neither emotionally nor instinctively awaited," as two Hungarian social scientists put it.[21] Even after the fact, I found most of the explanations put forward unconvincing or incomplete.

I fully agreed with Strobe Talbot that "most of us who tried to understand the USSR were profoundly wrong about it in one crucial respect. We believed that bad as it was in so many ways, the system was good at one thing— its own preservation . . . Therefore the system would surely last for a very long time." In a similar vein Alexander Dallin wrote: "What we are really puzzling over is how as thoroughly controlled, as tightly disciplined and as heavily indoctrinated a system as the Soviet Union managed to fall apart, unravel so easily and so completely."[22] Few even among the specialists sensed the impending end of the Soviet empire, a circumstance that lends further justification to this enterprise aimed at achieving a better understanding of how and why it happened.

Riszard Kapuscinski, the Polish author, has observed that "just before the breakup of the USSR, the view of that country as a model of the most stable and durable system in the world had gained wide acceptance among Western Sovietologists . . . there was not one American political scientist who predicted the collapse of the USSR."[23] Robert M. Gates, former head of the CIA, confessed that "he was amazed by the breakdown of the USSR and rests his defense on the entirely fair observation that virtually no one in the defense or intelligence business predicted that the Soviet Union was bound for the dustbin of history until it hit bottom."[24] Walter Laqueur reminds us that "the general view in the West during most of the 1960s and 1970s was that the Soviet Union had no monopoly on serious economic problems, which seemed by no means incurable . . . With a few exceptions Western experts grossly overrated the Soviet GNP and thus underrated per capita arms spending and thus the defense burden for the population . . . According to a study published as late as 1988 by a well-known Western economist [E. A. Hewett] specializing in the Soviet Union, Soviet citizens enjoyed 'massive economic security.'"[25] Severyn Bialer, another well-known specialist in Soviet affairs, wrote in 1982 that "the Soviet economy . . . administered by intelligent and trained professionals will not go bankrupt . . . like the political system, it will not collapse."[26] Jerry Hough, a prominent Soviet specialist, argued in 1991 that "economic reform in the Soviet Union was going ahead with amazing speed and that Soviet political problems had been grossly exaggerated." He also wrote, shortly before the historical events of the summer and fall of 1991: "The belief that the Soviet Union may disintegrate as a country contradicts all we know about revolution and national integration throughout the world," and "Anyone who sees him [Mikhail Gorbachev] as a tragic transitional figure has little sense of history."[27] Moshe Lewin, the historian, in 1988 saw the Soviet Communist Party as "the main stabilizer of the political system" and could not conceive of conditions under which any group "would back measures likely to erode the integrity of the entire union or the centralised state. The party . . . is the only institution that can preside over the overhaul of the system."[28]

Senator Daniel Moynihan was among the handful who envisioned the eventual disintegration of the Soviet Union, and not merely for economic reasons but resulting from a profound malaise of the entire system. Richard Pipes was another observer who had few illusions about the long-term stability of the Soviet system, noting in 1984 that it was in "crisis" and "has outlived its usefulness and that the forces making for change are becoming well-nigh irresistible."[29]

Western specialists as well as Western political elites were susceptible to impressions of Soviet strength and self-assurance that the regime projected, often by means of coarse and primitive propaganda.[30] For many decades the regime succeeded in covering up or distracting attention from its underlying weaknesses. Martin Malia wrote in 1990 that "the world in fact was being hoodwinked by the assertion of efficacy and power in just one domain": heavy industry and military production.[31] John Lewis Gaddis notes that "nuclear weapons preserved the image of a formidable Soviet Union long after it had entered into its terminal decline."[32]

Why was it so widely believed that the Soviet Union was virtually indestructible or, at any rate, stable and durable? Possibly the reluctance to pay attention to the attitudes and beliefs of particular human beings contributed to this state of affairs.[33]

Seymour M. Lipset and Gyorgy Bence have suggested that the failure to anticipate the collapse was more common among scholars than among journalists and politicians. By the 1970s and 1980s "most of the Sovietologists . . . were left-liberal in their politics, an orientation that undermined their capacity to accept the view that economic statism, planning, socialist incentives, would not work."[34]

Of all the reasons for the Western failure to anticipate the unraveling of the Soviet empire the belief in the superpower symmetry and moral equivalence were probably the most important. Numerous ancillary beliefs rested on the "two superpowers" scenario. It was, for instance, widely believed that global stability required an equilibrium between these powers. Critical views of the United States were also bolstered by the seemingly objective equation of its shortcomings with those of the Soviet Union; the somewhat cynical, hence apparently impartial wisdom used to be that neither of the superpowers inspired much respect and that each used the other for nefarious purposes (to bloat defense budgets and to establish unseemly domestic policies, among others). After the late 1960s these viewpoints became conventional wisdom among influential American journalists, academic intellectuals, many politicians in the Democratic Party, and the liberal middle classes. Even when the domestic weaknesses of the Soviet Union were noted, its successes abroad seemed impressive, its superpower status resting on its spreading influence abroad, especially in the Third World.[35]

Another important force contributing to the Western belief in the durability of the Soviet Union was the antinuclear/peace movement. All those convinced of the imminence of nuclear holocaust who dedicated their lives, at least their public lives, to averting the disaster and for whom the cause of peace and nuclear disarmament (unilateral, if necessary) became an important source of identity had a vested interest in the persistence of the Soviet Union. The peace movement could not flourish without the cold war. The former needed the latter at least as much as the CIA and the KGB needed one another (another item in the inventory of "superpower symmetry," part of the conventional wisdom of the period).

Another group, not large but influential, consisted of academics and other intellectuals who quietly harbored the hope, after the rise of Gorbachev, that the Soviet Union might yet realize the great aspirations of the October Revolution, reclaim its founding ideals, and become at last a democratic socialist society. They also tended to believe that on the whole the Soviet Union was successful in modernizing.

There were also those—usually critics of the United States—who were deeply (and hopefully) committed to the idea that the "late capitalist" United States was in decline and was in fact the most decadent society around: surely the Soviet Union could not overtake the United States in its rate of decline. In this view, American decadence was caused by, or associated with, capitalism; a socialist (even a semi- or quasi-socialist) society such as the USSR was expected to have a greater staying power and a better chance to solve its problems. Critics of capitalism could not anticipate or entertain the prospect of the Soviet Union breaking into its constituent parts and scrambling to create a market economy, thus reversing the Marxian principles of historical development. Even as "actually existing socialism" was collapsing in the Soviet Union and Eastern Europe some American intellectuals entertained hopes of its rebirth.[36]

Some critics of the United States, at home and abroad, believed that the Soviet Union was a crucial counterweight to the United States and predatory imperialism and did not wish to contemplate a world without it. Such wishful thinking also contributed to a belief in the durability of the Soviet Union.

For the most part, the conservative critics of the Soviet empire were no more farsighted in predicting its collapse than were those less averse to its prolonged existence. The "cold warriors" and unembarrassed critics of the Soviet Union (myself among them) had few illusions about the virtues and advantages of Soviet-style socialism over the depravities of capitalism and were never tempted to consider the Soviet Union a successful, modernizing society. Their belief in the durability of the Soviet system did not depend on overlooking its moral, political, or economic flaws; they were not under the impression that it had enjoyed a high degree of legitimacy in spite of its shortcomings (as many on the left believed); they did not believe in an implicit social contract between the rulers and the ruled. The anticommunist critics thought that the system was durable because it seemed to them— wrongly, as it turned out—that the communist states had succeeded in building institutions of control that would keep them going regardless of their economic inefficiency and minimal legitimacy and because the USSR had managed to offset domestic stagnation by expansion abroad and was capable of producing an abundance of modern weaponry to remain a formidable power.

In retrospect, it is clear the conservative critics overestimated the efficiency of the apparatus of control, the political cohesion of the Soviet ruling elite, its commitment to power, and its ability to manipulate the citizenry regardless of their growing discontents. These views were influenced by the theories or models of totalitarianism that used to be helpful in grasping the character of the Soviet system but were far less useful in stimulating realistic anticipations of its end.

The conservative (or anticommunist) critics of the Soviet system also underestimated the long-term subversive impact of increased information about and contact with the West that began in the 1970s.

ANTICIPATION IN THE SOVIET BLOC

Insiders, products of Soviet communism, failed as well to anticipate the unraveling of the Soviet system. Two émigré Soviet historians who had no illusions about the severe domestic situation and believed that the system had "shown itself incapable of resolving economic, social or nationality questions" nonetheless suggested that the system could perpetuate itself through foreign policy successes: "The Soviet Union finds life-giving energy only in expansionism and an aggressive foreign policy. Thus expansion is becoming the only form of life for mature socialism." By the same token, "communism threw in the towel the moment its expansion was finally brought to a halt," Milovan Djilas observed in retrospect.[37] Arkady Shevchenko, quoted earlier, believed (in 1984) that "it is very important . . . to understand the built-in continuity and momentum of the Soviet system . . . the faltering economy and other afflictions should not mislead anyone about the durability of the regime. There is no doubt that the USSR is experiencing serious domestic and other difficulties. But it has overcome worse troubles in the past."[38] Jan Sejna, a former Czech general and high-ranking Party official (discussed in Chapter 2), believed that the Soviet Union had a grand design for global domination, hence the dire title of his book, *We Will Bury You*. He also claimed that Brezhnev himself, notwithstanding his tendency toward personal corruption and high living, believed that "the only way for Communism to triumph [was] by the destruction of Capitalism" and that détente was merely a tactical ploy to advance this goal.[39] Zubok and Pleshakov regarded Brezhnev as "the incarnation of the post-revolutionary new elites whose expansionism was driven by great power commitments . . . [t]hough the revolutionary-imperial paradigm was still alive."[40]

Valentin Turchin, a prominent Soviet dissenter, observed in the early

1980s that "the basis of the social order [in the Soviet Union] is considered by the citizens as absolutely immutable . . . They consider it as a given, as Newton's Law. When you fall you don't blame gravity." Natan Sharansky, another leading dissident, wrote in 1988: "Not only the authorities consider citizens cogs in the wheel of the state, the people so consider themselves too."[41] Alexander Zinoviev, another prominent dissenter, thought that the system had become "essentially unshakeable," that "Homo Sovieticus" was entrenched.[42] Vassily Aksyonov, the Soviet émigré writer wrote: "All of our lives, if we ever dreamed of the demise of totalitarian Communism, it was assumed that the monster would never surrender without a devastating fight . . . Then the wildest dreams of my generation of Russians came true."[43]

If belief in the durability of the Soviet system on the part of its critics was rooted in a pessimistic overestimation of the powers of coercion, of popular inertia, and of apathy, there were also those in the West who credited its prolonged survival to its material accomplishments, overlooking what a more knowledgeable commentator called "the Soviet planner's habitual contempt for social needs." Some of these recent sanguine assessments resembled the colorful Western misperceptions of the Soviet Union dating back to the 1930s. Many of them persisted, remarkably enough, to the very end of the system. Paul Samuelson, the famous American economist, wrote in 1976 that it was "a vulgar mistake to think that most people in Eastern Europe are miserable." John Kenneth Galbraith, another well- known economist, wrote in 1984 that the Soviet economy had made "great material progress in recent years . . . one sees it in the appearance of solid well-being of the people on the streets."[44] These observations were reminiscent of those made by G. B. Shaw in the early 1930s, when he commented on, and freely generalized from, the abundance and excellence of meals he consumed in certain restaurants in Moscow where he was taken by his attentive hosts.

The misconceptions of visitors diligently fostered by the authorities help to explain both the belief in the prolonged survival of the Soviet system and the surprise upon its abrupt collapse. Steven Solnick accurately labeled it "a system . . . complacently accepting of its own artificial reality." He also writes: "Just as artificial 'Potemkin villages' hid the squalid countryside from traveling tsars, plan fulfillment reports obscured the true state of Soviet economic social relations from Moscow planners. General Secretaries [of the Party] determined to make their own observations found contemporary versions of Potemkin villages thrown up for their benefit."[45]

If in retrospect "it seems a marvel that a system so complacently accepting of its own artificial reality could have survived," the most obvious explanation of the inability to foresee its demise was the facade of strength, unanimity, and stability the system managed to project almost to the very end (or at least until the intensification of glasnost). Much of this rested on "preference falsification" and "the imperfect observability of private preferences" on the part of the masses. Timur Kuran writes: "The system and its instruments of violence were supported by a pervasive culture of mendacity. Individuals routinely applauded speakers they disliked, joined organizations whose mission they opposed, ostracized dissidents they admired, and followed orders they considered nonsensical, unjust or inhuman."[46]

Anticipating radical change was also difficult in Eastern Europe. Eugen Loebl, a surviving victim of the major Czech show trial (of the Slansky "conspiracy"), recalled that "most of the people I met in civilian life [that is, outside prison after his release] did not believe that things could change or that those in power could be overwhelmed."[47] Gyorgy Konrad, the Hungarian writer and social critic, noted: "Two months ago I spoke to a distinguished Czech writer of the opposition who said that one cannot expect any significant change, the standard of living is quite high . . . the working classes are not discontented, the students are not active and the Party is not split! . . . And then we saw the pictures on TV, the hundreds and thousands of demonstrators in the streets of Prague and Bratislava." Even in retrospect, when the temptation to correct for past error is great, a survey, conducted in March 1990, found that 76 percent of the East Germans were "totally surprised" by the collapse of the East German communist regime.[48]

The unanticipated disintegration of communist states provides new opportunities for addressing the connections between shifts in individual belief and institutional change. "Objective" factors such as economic decline make a difference to the survival of political systems only insofar as people, especially those in power, recognize and respond to them. Arguably, the Soviet system had confronted more serious difficulties in the past, yet it survived.[49]

The tolerance of deprivations of any kind depends on prevailing expectations; information about socioeconomic problems or malfunctioning institutions may be brushed aside, rationalized, or taken seriously, depending on the disposition of the leaders; popular discontent can be ignored, repressed, or paid attention to by the powerholders. Systems do not radically change or unravel merely because of economic difficulties but because rulers come to see the difficulties in a new light, as profound, systemic, or intractable. Economically weak political systems are often capable of staying in power as long as the will to power remains intact at the top and the personnel of coercive institutions are ready to perform their duties, as in Cuba and North Korea.[50] Before the 1980s the Soviet Union repeatedly experienced severe economic difficulties, which it managed to survive. It was the economic difficulties combined with other setbacks (for example, Afghanistan, NATO's introduction of intermediate missiles into Western Europe) *and* the changed attitude on the part of the rulers that together led to the familiar outcome. Domestic reform under Gorbachev went hand in hand with a far less aggressive foreign policy—with pulling out of Afghanistan and giving up Eastern Europe—as if the diminished self-assurance of the rulers had found expression in hesitation about imposing their will abroad.

The self-assurance and sense of legitimacy of the ruling political elite provide the key to system maintenance in highly authoritarian states such as the former Soviet Union and its allies. Such self-assurance and the associated will to power must in turn be nurtured by deeply held political beliefs, as well as by the material advantages that the beneficiaries enjoy and believe they deserve. If in earlier times "the official ideology . . . functioned to give the ruling elite an inflated self-confidence and legitimacy,"[51] this was no longer the case by the mid 1980s. By then, ideology had become, in George F. Kennan's words, "a lifeless orthodoxy . . . [Though] Still able to command a feigned and reluctant obedience, it had lost all capacity to inspire."[52] Lost inspiration contributed to the decline of ruthlessness the preservation of the system required. Alexander Dallin referred to the same phenomenon as "an unadvertised but far-reaching crisis of identity and self-doubt . . . a decline . . . in the rulers' self-confidence concerning their right to rule . . . [and a] newly perceived challengeability of the Soviet system."

General Leonid Shebarshin of the KGB summed it up: "The decisive factor . . . was a lack of political will at the centre."[53]

The self-assurance of the Soviet leaders and the leaders of other communist states in Eastern Europe which allowed them to preside for decades over a wasteful, inefficient economy, a system of politically allocated privileges, and the untroubled repression of dissent was apparently lost by the end of the 1980s. Although there was an awareness, especially on the part of the hardliners, that the system was in danger of collapse, the leaders failed to act expeditiously to prevent this from happening. Vladimir Kryuchkov, head of the KGB, said in a televised speech in 1990: "'A danger has developed that the Soviet Union might disintegrate . . .' But the KGB would fight 'with all the means at their disposal' against 'anti-Communist' elements inside the country and abroad that threaten the state. 'To be or not to be,' that is the choice for our great state."[54] The awareness of impending doom did not lead to effective countermeasures.

As David Remnick describes it, "The men of the Communist Party, the Army and the KGB who had tried to seize power [in August 1991] in the name of Leninist principles and imperial preservation betrayed their weakness before the cameras: their hands trembled, they drank themselves senseless, they could not bear to pull the trigger."[55] The attempted coup failed "because of divisions and hesitation among the plotters." The intervention in the Baltics "was almost a caricature" compared to earlier interventions in Czechoslovakia and Hungary, characterized as it was by "inefficiency and half-heartedness."[56] The forces with which to crush these challenges to the regime were available, but the political will to make use of them was lacking.[57] It is also noteworthy that the conspirators made no reference whatsoever to Marxism or socialism in their manifesto, speaking instead of maintaining order and the national boundaries. [58]

A circumstance that may help to explain the lack of reflexive and requisite ruthlessness in the last crop of Soviet leaders is that they largely lacked the traumatic experience of personal political insecurity of the earlier generations of leaders; they were pampered members of the nomenklatura, exercising power in relative security. Past suffering and personal hardship had not hardened their attitudes or help them justify the infliction of suffering on others. Nor did experiencing spectacular social mobility, as the earlier generation of leaders had, deepen their sense of legitimacy and self-assurance. By contrast, Khrushchev had believed that "the dispossessed of the world would inevitably prevail; he himself had been a miner . . . Mikoyan added that he had been a plumber, Gromyko that he had been the son of a beggar and . . . Frol Kozlov that he had been a 'homeless waif.'"[59]

Experiences of suffering and insecurity, rather than creating a greater capacity for empathy, often lead to the opposite—ruthlessness, presumably because adversaries are presumed to be implicated in the suffering that the revolutionary politician experiences. Suffering, then, may not improve character; rather, it creates a sense of entitlement to compensatory power and privilege, a sense of grievance, and a readiness to seek retribution for wrongs suffered. The generation of Soviet leaders in power during the 1980s had no such experiences or background; for the most part they had no bitter store of memories of personal suffering to call upon to justify crushing opposition and taking any measures to preserve the system.[60] This is not to say that such memories and experiences are the only basis of moral indifference to suffering; the capacity to inflict pain and deprivation, especially on a large scale, has a variety of sources, as will also be discussed in Chapter 6.

MORAL BANKRUPTCY AND POLITICAL DECLINE

What is puzzling about the collapse of communist systems, the Soviet Union in particular, is not the failure of an extraordinarily inefficient, rigid, and repressive political-economic system to endure. Rather, the mystery is that political systems that amassed historically unprecedented powers and created huge institutions of coercion failed to employ them to prolong their existence.[61]

Powerful empires do collapse, but rarely so abruptly and without efforts to save themselves. Powerholders in communist states were steeped in an ethos (for which Lenin should take most of the credit) that emphasized the singular importance of holding on to power. And yet, as Martin Malia puts it, "the whole Leninist edifice imploded without any of its guardians offering serious resistance . . . The most militant political movement of the modern age, which in its time had made a career of armed insurrections and minority coups d'etat, at the end proved capable only of the pitiful farce of August 1991."[62]

In communist systems, official mendaciousness and the ubiquitous dissemination of its products were central to both day to day functioning and the final disintegration. This is exactly what John Clark and Aaron Wildavsky meant when they proposed that the collapse of communism was above all "a moral collapse."[63] As the time of the collapse approached, both the leaders' capacity to generate falsehood and public toleration of official propaganda diminished. Kennan suggests that it may be considered "a firm law of political life that when a given regime is no longer able to carry on without accommodating itself to a wide-ranging pretense that it shares with its subject people . . . then its ultimate fate must be considered as inevitable and probably imminent."[64] That is what happened in the communist states as they approached their fall.

Many scholars overestimated the political cohesion, staying power, and coercive skills of communist regimes; we believed that proven techniques of intimidation would preserve them as long as the subservient majority internalized its powerlessness and the ruling elites did not hesitate to cling to power. None of these assumptions turned out to be correct. A likely source of error was the overestimation of the sense of legitimacy and entitlement to power on the part of the rulers. Events of the late 1980s and early 1990s and the behavior of the rulers during those years suggest that their sense of legitimacy rested on shakier ground than was earlier believed.

If an understanding of the fall of communist systems is linked to the decline and loss of the sense of legitimacy of the powerholders, it is important to understand both the roots of the earlier sense of entitlement to power and the reasons for its erosion over time. It is possible that at some point the protagonists in power were caught in situations reflecting the unanticipated consequences (and the havoc) that their policies wrought, and began to feel uneasy in the face of them. Orlando Figes's conclusion goes to the heart of the matter: "One final reason for the absence of repression stands out. Most of the intelligent party leaders had long ceased to believe in the Communist system; it was not worth a fight in their view. This slow inner death had transformed the party into an empty shell."[65] It is the particulars of this "slow inner death" of belief that will be at the heart of this study.

It has been written of the Soviet general Dmitri Volkogonov, who used to be head of the army's department of psychological and ideological warfare and who wrote a demythologizing biography of Lenin, that "even as he was indoctrinating troops in Communist orthodoxy . . . [he] was struggling with private doubts based on the horrors he discovered hidden in the archives."[66] Apparently, access to information was a crucial factor in his case: "The more he studied the historical sources, the more his disillusionment grew: his unfailing loyalty to the Communist cause ultimately turned into passionate hatred. In his last years he acted like a man awakened from a long hypnotic sleep." Volkogonov readily acknowledges that "I was a Stalinist. I contributed to the strengthening of the system that I am now trying to dismantle." Like many other Soviet intellectuals, he came to see "the roots of catastrophe in the ideology itself, in Leninism: 'Abstract ideas give rise to fanatics . . . The utopianism, the ferocity, of Bolshevism gave rise to the totalitarian state.'"[67] Under what conditions communist leaders and Party intellectuals arrived at the same juncture as General Volkogonov did is a major question pursued in this book.[68]

The faith of the Soviet political elites also diminished for more prosaic reasons: their growing realization of the inefficiency, backwardness, and inability of the regime to deliver in comparison to Western societies, of which they became more knowledgeable during the 1970s and 1980s. Vassily Aksyonov, a Russian writer who chose exile during the Brezhnev era, writes: "Undoubtedly, long before perestroika, a profound discontent was growing in the party's ranks. Despite being a self-proclaimed 'Vanguard of the Soviet People,' party members felt oppressed and humiliated by their pathological regime. They didn't have enough Western goods, they didn't have enough dollars, they couldn't take Canary Islands vacations . . . The Communist system was doomed because of its inability to meet the ever-growing demands of its own ruling elite."[69] Elsewhere Aksyonov writes: "A handful of dissidents challenged the system openly, but there were millions . . . of Party members whose souls . . . became impregnated with discontent, disappointment, bitterness and despair. The seeds of this unique revolution of the presumed rulers against their own rule were sown and grew in these souls."[70] If so, the morale of the political elites and their unwavering support for the system was eroded by both moral and material factors.

Changes in the outlook of the elite groups during the 1970s and 1980s (well before perestroika) were also stimulated by the growth of contacts with the West and the resulting comparisons that were not to the advantage of the "Socialist Commonwealth." Exposure to the West was subversive even if the effects took a long time to manifest themselves.[71] Although these contacts were largely a product of the desire to catch up in scientific and technological fields, they contributed to the undermining of political stability. As Christopher Andrew and Oleg Gordievsky explain it, in aspiring to and maintaining superpower status the Soviet Union "steadily built up a huge army of diplomats, intelligence officers, journalists and academics who gradually assembled a critical mass of information on the West, which eventually undermined some of the certainties of a system already decaying from within."[72]

The pervasive awareness of decay during the Brezhnev period is vividly conveyed in the recollections of Valery Boldin, Gorbachev's chief of staff.

> The economic situation was further aggravated by a loss of faith in the political leadership . . . Labor discipline was extremely poor: every day hundreds of thousands of people failed to show up at work . . . the quality of goods produced deteriorated . . . Agricultural machinery arrived on the farm in such abominable condition that it could not be used . . . This in turn meant that one-third of the food harvest was lost.
>
> Shortages of goods . . . meant that workers . . . spent more time hunting for goods in short supply than actually producing anything . . .
>
> Brezhnev and his entourage were increasingly helpless. An atmosphere of alcoholic indulgence was pervasive . . .
>
> . . . the trouble started with the loss of authority at the highest level of leadership . . . The virus of dishonesty gravely impaired the Party's immune system and wrecked its stability . . .
>
> Corruption was not the Party's only ailment. The sense of purpose that brought it to power and sustained it during industrialization and the heroic defense against Hitler . . . began to lapse in more peaceful times. Members were joining for the wrong reasons; the leadership was now dominated by old men, and the party began to lose touch with the people.[73]

Leonid Brezhnev's niece Luba Brezhneva recalls that "during my uncle's tenure as general secretary, theft flourished as never before. It became so much a part of our life that no stigma was attached to it."[74]

Commentators on Soviet affairs in the United States paid insufficient attention to corruption and moral corrosion as significant factors in the collapse. Apparently, corruption was both a contributor to the collapse and, more important, an indication of the loss of ideological beliefs. Corruption spreads when beliefs no longer sustain and discipline the individual, when it becomes a secure means to material advantage and improved social status. At the same time, the determination to stamp out corruption flags when a strong conviction that the cause is good atrophies.

There were many indications of corruption in the ruling strata, some of which came to light only after the regime fell. The personal lives of many leaders and their families were marked by self-indulgence, drunkenness, and the unembarrassed maximization of the privileges that their position yielded. Memoirs such as that of Luba Brezhneva depict a group of rulers remote from their subjects and increasingly preoccupied with their own material welfare and worldly pleasures. She writes:

> The elite and the common people scarcely crossed paths . . . the members of the elite had their exclusive food stores, medical clinics and pharmacies, their own motor pools, gas stations and telephone booths . . . schools, institutions of higher learning . . . their own dressmakers and tailors . . . even their own cemeteries.
>
> Each member of the party elite was surrounded by an ever-expanding octopus: his own family, the relatives of his wife and his girlfriends, his illegitimate children, the friends of his children and grandchildren . . .
>
> I never saw any of the elite wearing Soviet-made clothes . . .
>
> State dachas [vacation homes] . . . were . . . reserved for the elite . . . with stables, orchards and conservatories. My uncle had pheasants and peacocks strutting about . . . The quiet, secluded park on the property was a place for the general secretary, believing . . . that he had been chosen by his nation to express its will and its interests, to stroll in peace . . .

> . . . the nomenklatura's wives rated one another by the quality
> and quantity of their coats, the number and price of one's furs
> serving as an indicator of social status.[75]

Brezhneva was one of the children of the elite who came to view their elders with contempt and displayed the kind of rebelliousness more typically encountered in the generational conflicts of the upper classes in the West. She found her father's "blind faith [in communism] . . . infuriating and endlessly frustrating" and notes that "as my uncle consolidated his power, all the Brezhnevs became increasingly out of touch with real life, " She also recalls "fall[ing] into a dull stupor during lectures on political subjects." In turn, her parents and others bemoaned the ways of the young people. Brezhneva was regarded as an ungrateful misfit by the KGB in part because of her "spiritual kinship" with the dissidents. She even had the nerve to ask her uncle whether he ever read Solzhenitsyn. "Highly offended, he answered with pride that he never read anti-Soviet trash. 'But even Lenin read all the bourgeois literature. He said that we must know the enemy's face,'" she taunted him. "During one of our meetings . . . I asked him why I had to defend the right to read, why reading sounded like such a subversive idea to him. 'Because,' he said, 'if everyone started doing what they feel like, there won't be any order in our country.'"[76]

Yakov Brezhnev, her father (Leonid's brother), "himself a party member who believed dogmatically in the official line, asked his brother, general secretary of the Communist Party, 'What do you think Lyonya, will communism ever come?' Leonid laughed without mirth. 'Oh, for heaven's sake, Yasha, what are you talking about? All that stuff about communism is a tall tale for popular consumption. After all, we can't leave the people with no faith. The church was taken away, the czar was shot, and something had to be substituted. So let the people build communism.' My father came away from this conversation deeply disappointed."[77]

The official interpreter of both Gorbachev and Shevardnadze notes matter-of-factly that "the system under which the country was operating was outdated and the ideology on which it was based not even worth discussing. It was a waste of time."[78]

The moral dissolution of these communist societies was also apparent to dissidents in Eastern Europe. Ivan Klima, the well-known Czech writer, recalls that "for years I watched as dishonesty grew around me. I associated it . . . with the system that called itself socialist. In this country, everyone felt cheated and therefore justified in cheating others."[79] Adam Michnik, the Polish dissident, links coercion to this phenomenon:"An intimate bond exists between force and deception. This concept . . . is exceptionally valid in . . . the totalitarian world in which it has been our fate to live . . . Deception becomes a method of self-defense."[80]

The theory-practice gap became especially devastating during glasnost, when awareness of the defects of the system abruptly surfaced, allowing them to be compared to the official verities and versions of the way things were supposed to be.[81] By contrast, in the past, as Boris Pasternak writes, "to conceal failure people had to be cured, by every means of terrorism, of the habit of thinking and judging for themselves, and forced to see what didn't exist, to assert the very opposite of what their eyes told them."[82]

Under Gorbachev, the leaders no longer had the will and power to impose their vision of communism, nor the self-assurance to insist on reality-denying, reality-defying propaganda. They, Gorbachev in particular, misread the power of free, even partially free, expression; glasnost amounted to ideological disarmament, which the system could not afford if it were to endure.

Anatoly Dobrynin, former ambassador to the United States, also alludes to the lack of political will; he believes that economic factors, especially the strain of the arms race, were far from decisive in the disintegration: "The Politburo under Gorbachev or anybody else who advocated a tough, militaristic policy would have had no lack of support from the military-industrial complex and, more important, from the whole country . . . If the leaders of the Soviet Union had pictured the American military buildup as a threat to the existence of the nation, the Soviet people would have responded . . . The Soviet Union was a totalitarian state, and it is unrealistic to believe that any political opposition would have been able to stage, let alone win, a debate over the relative merits of military versus civilian spending."[83] Dobrynin firmly believes that "the fate of the Soviet Union was decided inside our country" and that Gorbachev played a great part in determining that fate: "The roots of the demise of the Soviet Union must be found mainly at home, in our political struggles, in our incompetent but highly ambitious leaders."[84]

PERSONAL EXPERIENCE AND POLITICAL WILL

At the heart of this study are questions of political morality and its relation to the decline and fall of the Soviet empire. Over time it became increasingly apparent to members of the political elite that the moral foundations of the social order they maintained had become seriously weakened.

What chain of events led to this realization? What specific experiences or events tilted the scales between belief and disbelief? Was recognition of the moral flaws of the system a component of the changing attitude of the political elite that led to the erosion of their political will? Did specific incidents spark a moral revulsion, as happened with a former Viennese admirer of Hitler? Hans Fantel writes: "A few weeks later [after the Nazi invasion of Austria in March 1938] the Gestapo came to arrest our neighbor . . . When they pushed him along the driveway, his dog came to his defense. One of the arresting officer shot the dog dead. I did not care about Herr Eisler one way or another . . . But the killing of the dog rankled . . . I liked playing with her. I was upset. Mitzi [the housekeeper] offered reassurance. 'It doesn't matter' she explained. 'It's a Jewish dog . . .' I knew something was wrong. I didn't believe there were Jewish dogs . . . Besides even if the dog was Jewish . . . that didn't seem sufficient reason to kill him . . . Without knowing it, I had begin to distrust the Fuehrer."[85]

Another example of a dramatic break prompted by a specific event was the impact of the 1939 Nazi-Soviet Pact on the French fellow traveler Paul Nizan: "When the newspapers, with their astonishing headlines reached them [he was in the company of Sartre and Simone de Beauvoir], Nizan stood on their summer terrace, so much in shock that the paper rattled in his hands . . . he stood speechless and overwhelmed . . . For Nizan it was the end of innocence . . . [he] broke with the Party that week."[86]

An incident that may or may not have meant "the end of innocence" for Nicolai Bukharin occurred in 1930 when he was traveling through the Ukraine and came upon "children begging for alms at the little local [train] stations, their stomachs swollen from hunger." Back in Moscow he cried out: "'If more than ten years after the revolution one can see such things as this, what was the point of doing it?'"[87]

More recently, Yuri Afanasyev, an important Party intellectual, a prominent reformer, and head of the Historical Archive Institute under Gorbachev, was among those who could also recall a transformative incident. After Stalin's funeral in 1953, as he walked away from the crowds " he could hear some drunks singing in an alleyway. He had never heard such joyous singing. The drunks were celebrating the death of Stalin. 'I suppose once or twice in a lifetime you have those moments when you see or hear something that tilts your life . . . When I heard those men . . . suddenly the purity of my political consciousness was stained . . . I felt the first moment of doubt. It wasn't until Khrushchev's speech three years later that I really started to rethink things more thoroughly but it was this drunken celebration in the dark corners of Moscow that made me start to doubt. I was never quite the same.'"[88]

People hardened by ruthless power politics probably do not often have such experiences, and if they did, they would not readily disclose them. Those at the top in the Soviet Union were, especially before the 1980s, generally insulated from the morally disturbing aspects of social reality that could have undermined their beliefs and confidence in the system. It was said of Stalin that his knowledge of the state of collectivized Soviet agriculture rested on Soviet socialist-realist movies produced to glorify the collective farms. The most recent generation of communist leaders were less insulated from the difficulties and contradictions of their social-political system and from the outside world. Several of them had taken trips abroad or served for extensive periods in diplomatic positions in the West.

The leaders' loss of political will, intertwined with their eroding sense of legitimacy, appears to be the crucial factor in the unraveling of the communist systems. In Hungary, for instance, at the outbreak of the Revolution of 1956, the Party leaders met endlessly and wavered back and forth between allowing or banning mass rallies and meetings. One participant in these proceedings recalls: "This body [the Politburo of the Hungarian Communist Party] was no longer the leading collectivity of the country but a group of confused individuals who were making diametrically opposed decisions every half hour."[89] The same process apparently unfolded in Moscow in August 1991, when the leaders of the aborted coup against Gorbachev were incapable of taking decisive action against those they wished to oust. By contrast, the Chinese communist leaders ordered their elite troops to crush (literally, with tanks) the young rebels in Tiananmen Square in June 1989, and the commanders of the troops executed their orders without perceptible difficulty.

The declining convictions and concomitant weakene ! will to power can also be measured by looking at the promptness or hesi .tion with which the Soviet leadership responded to challenges to its rule within the Socialist Commonwealth. As time went by, each military intervention became less prompt and decisive. The East German uprising in 1953 was instantly and brutally put down by Soviet troops; the Hungarian Revolution of 1956 was crushed after some hesitation, being allowed to persist for two weeks. The reform government of Dubcek in Czechoslovakia in 1968 lasted for eight months before the massive Soviet (Warsaw Pact) intervention. The defiance of Solidarity in Poland was tolerated for well over a year, and the Soviet Union let its Polish ally do the job of destroying the movement (which it did half-heartedly and with limited success). The invasion of Afghanistan in 1979 was more decisive and, as such, was an exception to this pattern, but in 1988 the Soviet Union withdrew, admitting failure.

By contrast, despite initial hesitation, decisive force was used to preserve the empire in 1956 and 1968, even after the shock of the death and discrediting of Stalin. A former Hungarian communist intellectual observes: "The Soviet leaders . . . are fully convinced of the importance of keeping Stalin's empire intact. Since they believe in the superiority of their system, they would regard it as betrayal if even a small piece of the Soviet sphere became detached, let alone drawn into the sphere of interest of 'the other side.'"[90]

As has become clear, by the late 1980s the Soviet rulers' belief in the superiority of their system was eroded to an extent that interfered with the preservation of the empire. The collapse was brought about not merely by economic difficulties and general institutional malfunctioning but also by a grudging recognition among those who held power that the system was not merely inefficient but morally flawed, that their ideals (or past ideals) were not approaching realization, and that the proverbial gulf between theory and practice, ideal and reality, was not narrowing and could not be bridged. Such presumed shifts in elite attitudes provide the best explanation of why the leaders' response to economic difficulties was different than at earlier times.

THE PROTAGONISTS AND THEIR CHARACTER

Deciding who and how many individuals should be the subjects of this study was not easy. I was engaged in neither an attitude survey nor a series of biographies but something in between: learning about the political attitudes of a small group of people who were products of their political culture and who played important roles in the maintenance and legitimation of communist systems.

I selected case studies using the following criteria: (1) undisputed political importance; (2) availability of biographical or autobiographical information or personal access for an interview; and (3) Soviet, Hungarian, or Czechoslovak national background (as this was to be a study of the dynamics of the decomposition of the Soviet empire in different settings). I also wanted to be sure to include (4) "occupational" types representing the three groups most vitally engaged in the maintenance of political power in the communist systems: (a) political leaders and high-ranking Party functionaries; (b) high-ranking officials in the political police (state security); and (c) Party intellectuals. In some instances, the categories overlap or their clarity may be disputed. For example, Alexander Yakovlev was both a politician-functionary and a Party intellectual. Similarly, Andras Hegedus was prime minister of Hungary, then something of a Party intellectual, and later a non-Party intellectual and full-time sociologist.

I included more Soviet than Eastern European figures because of the greater importance of developments in the Soviet Union, which were the precondition for the political transformations in Eastern Europe.

I have also incorporated information provided by prominent defectors and exiles, mostly former functionaries or Party intellectuals. This group is included because it represents a huge and largely untapped source of information about discontent with communist systems and because the authors were anxious to trace in detail the growth of their disillusionment with the system. The information and insight yielded by this group adds a historical dimension, showing the roots of discontent, which, in more recent times, encouraged by glasnost, broke through to the surface and undermined the political will of the rulers, thereby hastening the fall of Soviet communism.

Much remains to be learned about the personality and mentality of those who played key roles in controlling, maintaining, and legitimating communist systems and about the reasons that many of them ceased to be capable of or willing to perform these tasks. Rarely has it been asked if there were distinct personality types attracted or recruited to positions of power in these systems. Were they people who (as one stereotype has it) loved mankind but cared little about real human beings? Or were they, to the contrary, people who loved their families and friends and could be moved to tears by the music of Beethoven (a tendency that Lenin specifically deplored) but who were able to compartmentalize their life between work and politics on the one hand and family and private pursuits on the other?[91] Lenin need not have worried about classical music subverting political will. Lavrenti Beria, head of the political police under Stalin, loved music and had a huge collection of classical records. Reportedly, upon listening to the preludes of Rachmaninov he often burst into tears.[92]

Some of my chosen cases probably belong to a larger group (better known in the Nazi context) personifying the "banality of evil." They routinized their commitments and were moved more by habit and obedience than by a stern and fanatical idealism or by some personal aberration that let them take pleasure in the ruthless exercise of power. By contrast, Stalin took great pleasure in plotting and anticipating the destruction of his political enemies.[93]

Numerous inquiries have been made into the psychology and personality of Nazi leaders and activists, but few to probe the personality of communist leaders and activists (with the exception of Lenin and Stalin). This is owing in part to the apparent strength and durability of communist systems, an apparent source of vindication which foreclosed the kinds of questions historians and social scientists were eager to raise in relation to the relatively short-lived Nazism. Both social scientists and the Western public at large have tacitly assumed that attributing psychopathology to Nazi leaders and activists was more appropriate than doing the same to their communist counterparts.

Whereas Nazism was indisputably delegitimated by the Holocaust and by military defeat, communist states not only persisted for much longer periods but were legitimated by an ideology or belief system with far broader appeal than Nazism had.[94] The responsibility of communist systems for mass murders remains to this day poorly known in the West, perhaps in part because little photographic documentation of such atrocities, which is conducive to moral indignation, has been available (unlike in the Nazi case).

Until recentlyWestern intellectuals also widely believed that while an "authoritarian personality" type might have been the key explanation for the character of the Nazi movement and regime, the concept had little relevance or applicability to communist movements, regimes, or activists, because such personalities were neither attracted to nor played any part in them.[95] As such examples show, the moral frameworks in which Nazi and communist systems were viewed and studied were fundamentally different, calling for different questions, concepts, and theories.

Thus scholars were not advised to restrain their moral indignation or revulsion while studying Nazism, whereas those writing about communist systems were regularly admonished to curb their moral impulses and were often rebuked when they allowed them to intrude on their analyses. Nor were students of Nazi Germany warned against imposing their own values (that is, against being ethnocentric), or urged to refrain from becoming judgmental—warnings regularly sounded in discussions of the study of communist systems. There were few, if any, researchers and writers who felt compelled to silence their belief that Nazi leaders and functionaries were deeply flawed human beings and that their misdeeds warranted probes of their deformed psyches.[96]

I believe that, as with the Nazi leaders, it is of interest to know what kind of people the communist leaders and functionaries were and how their personalities and attitudes contributed both to the persistence and to the decay of their systems. It is worth knowing whether they relinquished or relaxed their grip on power because they realized that "the system did not work," or because they suffered a genuine moral dilemma, trauma, or ideological conversion. Were they pragmatists or converts, opportunists or moralists? Did they reach the conclusion that the system was incapable of realizing their ideals or—more painful to behold—that the legitimating theories themselves were of little use in realizing their ideals?

Personality may have contributed to the substantial range of variation in the responses to and interpretations of the collapse of the Soviet bloc among different communist leaders and functionaries inside and outside the former Socialist Commonwealth. Molotov, foreign minister under Stalin and his lifelong loyal associate. continued to view the Purges and the massacres linked to them as morally unproblematic even as he was approaching death in the 1980s: "[The Purges of] 1937 were necessary . . . there were all manners of enemies around and we were faced with the dangers of fascist aggression . . . In 1937 we had to make sure there would be no fifth column in the war . . . I don't think we should have rehabilitated many of the military people who were repressed in 1937."[97] A true believer to the end of his days, Molotov "could sign the death sentences of 3,187 people in just one night and then watch Western movies with Stalin with a pure conscience."[98] Along with Andrei Gromyko, another pillar of the system and foreign minister for decades, Molotov was among the Soviet powerholders to whom George Kennan's observation fully applies: "Many foreigners would be amazed . . . to learn with what self-satisfaction and complacency . . . a great many senior Soviet statesmen have come to look back upon their own part in the dramatic, and so often terrible, events of their own time."[99] Lazar Kaganovich, one of the last survivors among Stalin's close associates, revealed toward the end of the Gorbachev era that despite his poor health, his belief in socialism kept him going: "Socialism will be victorious. Of this I am sure . . . I believe in the strength of our Party."[100]

In communist China, Wang Li—described as one of "the most ardent firebrands of the early Cultural Revolution . . . [who] inspired fear and awe among millions of Red Guards"—"had no regrets about [his] actions. 'I made mistakes. It was all right to make mistakes in those times.'"[101] Georges Marchais, head of the French Communist Party, reached the reassuring conclusion that "during our century, next to the good things, one did many bad things in the name of communism . . . But this does not condemn the objectives of Socialism and Communism."[102] Van Huu Ngoan, deputy director of the Marxism-Leninism Institute in Hanoi, shared this conviction: "I don't believe the doctrine has collapsed; the collapse of the [European Communist Bloc] proves that the principles are right and they applied them wrongly."[103] Nguyen Van Linh, leader of the Vietnamese Communist Party until 1991, though acknowledging the crisis of socialism, "charged that 'imperialist forces' were behind the events in Eastern Europe . . . 'Socialism is the only right decision. For our country there is no other way to have freedom and happiness for the people.'"[104] Gus Hall, the venerable leader of the American Communist Party, when commenting on the August 1991 events in Moscow, maintained that "socialism was not dead, just resting," and recommended North Korea both as a vacation spot and as an exemplar of socialism. Elsewhere he avers that the CIA "was very much involved in the events in the Soviet Union."[105] Of Erich Honecker, former head of the East German communist regime, it was noted that "neither old age nor years of authority seem to have altered . . . [his] ideals."[106] As late as January 1993 he insisted that "socialism is not only not dead, but is in fact the only alternative for the future." Honecker also remained unwavering in his support of the Berlin Wall, the building of which he called a "'historic event' [which] was correct and remains correct"[107] and which had averted nuclear war.[108]

Boris Yeltsin came to the conclusion that "this experiment which was conducted on our soil was a tragedy for our people . . . It would have been better if this experiment had been conducted in some small country, at least, so as to make it clear that it was a utopian idea . . . I think gradually this will come to be understood by other countries where supporters of the idea of Communism still exist."[109] In a similar spirit, Günter Schabowski, who headed the Communist Party in East Berlin at the time of the collapse, did not flinch from making a connection between the nature of the system and those who died trying to escape from it: "Those who died at the wall are part of the burden we inherit from our misguided attempt to free humanity from its plagues . . . Our search for utopia led us to lay everyone on a Procrustean bed in which the individual was cut to what was thought to be the ideal size."[110]

Todor Zhikov, the former dictator of Bulgaria also made a sweeping reassessment after his loss of power. He was facing corruption charges and under house arrest at the time. "If I had to do it over again, I would not even be a Communist . . . we started from the wrong basis . . . The foundation of socialism was wrong . . . We should have gone back to the original Marxist sources and had socialism developed within a highly developed capitalist world." When reminded of a typical declaration that he had made while in power—that Bulgaria and the Soviet Union "act as a single body, breathing with the same lungs, and nourished by the same bloodstream"—he dismissed it. ""That was just an image, just rhetoric,' Mr. Zhikov said, waving his hand. 'Those were different times.'" He "said he knew of the . . . labor

camps and of political killings carried out in Bulgaria and elsewhere in Eastern Europe" but "could do nothing to stop the terror."[111] He further claimed
that he had disapproved of the invasion of Czechoslovakia in 1968, done
with Bulgarian participation, but "he and Bulgaria had no choice but to go
along because the Kremlin had Bulgaria's economy in a stranglehold."[112]

As these examples suggest, the response of former communist leaders to
the collapse of their regimes ranges from deep regret to opportunistic reassessment and genuine soul-searching.

REVISITING *THE GOD THAT FAILED*

Given the periodic, massive eruptions of discontent within communist systems[113] and their rapid, unexpected collapse in recent times, it is a matter
of historical and social-psychological interest to recall what attraction they
initially exercised and how this attraction was replaced for many by doubt,
rejection, or revulsion. Given the focus on political disaffection and its role
in the fall of communist systems, this study touches on some of the questions memorably raised by the contributors to the classic *The God That Failed*,
a volume that presented the political-ideological self-scrutiny and chronicle
of disillusionment of famous Western writers: Louis Fisher, André Gide,
Arthur Koestler, Ignazio Silone, Stephen Spender, and Richard Wright.[114]
Among the old but still pertinent questions, the most important remain: Why
are some people (usually intellectuals) drawn to communist ideologies, movements, and systems in the first place? and Under what circumstances do they
abandon their convictions and commitments? Although this study deals with
communist powerholders and functionaries and not Western intellectuals,
the dynamics of disillusionment—especially those aspects linked to the divergence between theory and practice—are likely to be shared.

In this study, a central question is, At what point did the communist elites,
including the Party intellectuals, sense or acknowledge the vast divergence
between theory and practice? Did they become disillusioned with their
ideals before or after they were threatened by the loss of power? Most important, what impact did the exercise of power have on belief? Was the
gradual disillusionment of political elites the first link in a chain of events
that eventually led to the complete loss of legitimacy of these systems and
their disintegration? Or was disillusionment irrelevant or coincidental to

other processes—for example, the economic crisis or the withdrawal of Soviet military support for the communist governments in Eastern Europe?

As far as the political role of intellectuals is concerned, it is to be recalled that in Eastern Europe many intellectuals helped communist movements both to gain power and to consolidate it, as well as to pursue legitimacy. They advised communist governments on devising educational and cultural policies, propaganda campaigns, and economic plans.[115] It may be argued that by doing so, intellectuals ceased being "true" intellectuals. On the other hand, it may also be suggested that to be an intellectual need not mean that the preoccupation with ideas (even with social justice and the definition of a meaningful existence) must always remain untainted by considerations of power, status, and material interest.

If a commitment to free expression is the touchstone of the true intellectual, then Party intellectuals clearly do not qualify.[116] At the same time, we must remember that it was not only the Party intellectuals in communist societies who provided elaborate justifications for curtailing free expression; many Western intellectuals who admired communist systems from afar argued that the limits placed on free expression were fully justified by the lofty values and goals of these systems.[117]

Although intellectuals often faithfully served the communist systems for lengthy periods of time, most of them ultimately became disillusioned and either fled the country, withdrew from politics, or performed their political roles without enthusiasm or commitment. This was true virtually everywhere (Cuba, Eastern Europe, the Soviet Union, and China) that communist systems were established. Thus intellectuals who had been drawn to communist movements and systems and initially contributed to their legitimation were also prominent in their terminal delegitimation.

Closer examination of the historic relation between intellectuals and communist systems reveals certain basic patterns. There are those (in the West) whose sympathies thrived on distance and ignorance and those (in communist states) whose idealism did not survive the encounter with reality or else proved compatible (opportunistically or not) with the attempted realization of the official ideals. The latter were intent on participating in the creation of the new society and were willing to accept the moral-ethical sacrifices entailed.

Whereas the relationship between Western intellectuals of the fellow-traveler variety, and communist movements and systems (at least the older, pro-Soviet kind) has been reasonably well explored, much less has been written about the motives and attitudes of intellectuals who became Party functionaries and participated in the exercise of power in existing communist systems. In this group of Party intellectuals (or quasi-intellectuals) one may include Castro, Che Guevara, Stalin, Mao, and Ho Chi Minh, as well as some of the former *commandantes* in Nicaragua. Each of them displayed substantial intellectual (sometimes artistic) pretensions and aspirations and thought himself to be both a great theoretician and benefactor of his nation. In their attitudes, idealism and the love of power and privilege were fused in ways that are hard to separate and that invite inquiry.[118]

By examining the sources of personal disillusionment this study may provide insight into the deepest flaws shared by communist systems and may illuminate what made these systems unsatisfactory in the final analysis even for those who used to invest much of their lives in their support. Further light may also be shed on some unresolved and controversial issues regarding the relations between personality and politics that have always intrigued psychologists, moral philosophers, and writers of good fiction: the swings between idealism, integrity, high-mindedness, and lofty moral values on the one hand and cruelty, cynicism, fanaticism, and love of power on the other.

CHAPTER 2

Defectors and Exiles

Disillusionment Before the Fall

"Such a decision is the outcome of a painful process extending over years—years taken up with doubts and recantations and pangs of conscience and fabricated theories to set conscience at rest. But once this process has begun there is no going back." WOLFGANG LEONHARD

"It isn't money or comfort . . . we have anything we want . . . a dacha, a country place . . . We have plenty of money . . . in exchange I have to be as obedient to the system as a robot to his master—and I no longer believe in the system." ARKADY SHEVCHENKO

The earliest accounts of disaffection with communist systems have been provided by defectors and exiles. Given the interest in tracing the roots of discontent and the lengthy process of disillusionment—and in discovering how far into the past they extend—the testimony of defectors is an essential source of information. Their accounts are also helpful for learning about the differences and similarities among the discontents that different communist states generated. It is of further interest to compare the expressions of discontent of the defectors with the critiques of those who stayed. Since the goal of this project was to learn about attitude change among the Soviet communist political elite, I focus attention on the defectors who belonged to elite groups.

High-level defectors could be viewed as the predecessors of the people— dissenters and assorted functionaries with a shaken faith—whose dissatisfaction eventually engulfed the communist systems. Admittedly, the dissatisfaction of defectors had no direct connection with the decay of these systems, because, having removed themselves physically, they were not in a position to undermine them.[1] Nonetheless, articulate defectors helped to discredit these systems abroad (insofar as attention was paid to them), and the dissatisfaction they chronicled anticipated the discontents that more directly undermined these systems later on.

The cases discussed below may also shed light on how the growth of political disillusionment was affected by the possession of idealistic beliefs. One may argue that the greater the idealism, the more likely the believer is to become disappointed, for high ideals rarely measure up to reality. On the other hand, a high degree of idealism that leads to a deep and durable commitment often exerts pressure on the believer to ignore flaws and imperfections that could lead to disillusionment; the greater the idealism and the corresponding moral-emotional investment in a cause, the greater the reluctance to abandon it, the greater the pressure to stay the course and to rationalize any cognitive dissonance.[2]

DEFECTORS AS A SOURCE

Generally speaking, three major groups among the disillusioned elites may be distinguished. In the first are those in or near positions of power—leaders, functionaries, Party intellectuals—who, as their doubts grew, either performed their tasks without much conviction or hoped to improve the system from inside. It was the loss of *their* political will that most directly undermined the communist systems. Second, there are the outspoken dissidents who made their estrangement from and critique of the system publicly known and who were ready to face the consequences; this group emerged gradually from the 1960s on. Third, there were the defectors, discussed in this chapter, whose unqualified rejection of the systems led them to flee. Opportunity, knowledge of a Western language, family ties, and other personal variables helped determine whether a politically estranged person stayed or became a defector or an exile. Beginning in the 1970s some well-known dissenters, such as Alexander Solzhenitsyn, were expelled.

Upon reaching the West many of the escapees and exiles put their experiences and critiques into writing. The defectors who published their personal histories were anxious to reveal and clarify the reasons for their departure; their accounts often represent the most focused and clearly articulated inventories of the flaws of communist systems. Their disillusionment was highly authentic: they had voted with their feet, facing considerable dangers and difficulties in doing so. Often they left their families behind. If they were better known, their reputations were smeared by communist propaganda. Sometimes they were threatened by kidnaping or assassination abroad, even by the possibility of being returned by the governments whose hospitality they had sought.[3] Few of them left purely or mainly for personal reasons (for example, to escape a bad marriage or career problems) or economic reasons, especially given their relatively privileged position.

There is a crucial difference between the discontent of the defectors and the discontent of those who stayed, in particular the dissidents and disillusioned Party intellectuals: the defectors had no interest in improving the system or did not think that it was possible.

Although there are many individual accounts of defections, such works and their authors have received little attention as source material for better understanding the discontents that communist systems generated.[4] The lack of social scientific attention paid to such writings was in part due to the presumption that they were too subjective and therefore unworthy of serious scholarly attention. Numerous Western intellectuals used to feel a measure of antipathy toward these messengers with the unwelcome message that the social system in which they had invested various degrees of hope was deeply flawed. Frederick L. Schuman's 1946 review of Kravchenko's *I Chose Freedom* is a fine example of this attitude. Besides calling Kravchenko, among other things, a "Soviet renegade" and a "socially myopic and politically unworthy careerist," Schuman writes: "The latest spicy dish from the Red-baiters kitchen purports to be the autobiography of Victor Kravchenko . . . the book conforms . . . to the prescribed formula, including melodramatic flights of the author from the secret agents of the NKVD [People's Commissariat of Internal Affairs] bent upon his liquidation, the usual array of slanders and the customary framing, poisoning and butchering of all good people by fiendish Stalin."[5] But as Walter Laqueur observes, "If those who left had been submitted to thorough and systematic debriefing, an interesting picture of the state of Soviet society would have emerged . . . Those who left Russia were considered unreliable sources by many Western experts. They obviously did not like the Soviet system . . . The judgement and even observations of such disaffected people could not be trusted."[6]

The importance of defections can also be measured by the extraordinary efforts that communist states made to prevent them from occurring and by the venom they poured on those who succeeded.[7] The most abhorrent aspect of defections for these regimes was symbolic: the defector rejected what was supposedly the most advanced and just social system that ever existed. When a privileged or well-known member of society defected, the symbolic damage was all the greater—as was the vitriolic response.[8]

Given the abundance of such writings, it was not easy to decide what to select. I based the selection on several criteria, such as the recognized importance of the author and his former position in a communist hierarchy. I looked for writings that reflected different periods or stages in the evolution of communist systems and for ones that were not limited to the Soviet experience. Lucidity of style and the quality and substance of information were also major considerations. In all these respects and especially the last, subjective judgments were unavoidable.

VICTOR SERGE (1890–1947)

Victor Serge was one of the first generation of idealists dedicated to the Soviet Revolution and the system that emerged from it. His idealism and commitment also led him to become one of its early critics. After becoming a member of the Left Opposition in the late 1920s, he was spared arrest for several years, though kept under intense surveillance. Imprisonment and exile followed, and finally expulsion from the Soviet Union.

Serge was born in Belgium, son of earlier revolutionaries in exile from the tsar. ("I grew up among Russian revolutionary exiles . . . they taught me to have faith in mankind and to wait steadfastly for the necessary cataclysms. They waited for half a century, in the midst of persecution.")[9] In Belgium and France he moved in the circles of revolutionary idealists and anarchists, attended study groups, participated in working-class politics. As a young man, he was imprisoned in France for his political associations and activities, then interned with other leftists and early supporters of the Russian Revolution of 1917. His desire to offer tangible support to the Revolution was fulfilled when he and other detainees were exchanged for French officers who had been arrested in Russia. Of the fifty-seven years of his life he spent ten "in various forms of captivity" and another ten in exile in Mexico.

Serge, like other defectors from the Soviet Union—especially those who left during the 1930s and 1940s—was the subject of a well-orchestrated campaign of vilification by Western leftists, particularly members of communist parties. While in Belgium, he could not find work as a printer (the craft of his youth) owing to the communist union. He was denounced in communist and communist-influenced publications and was in danger of assassination, so he often changed his address.

Unlike many of those in the political hierarchy who became disillusioned at later stages in their career, Serge's commitment to the system did not yield any material or status benefits and played no part in prolonging his attachment to the system, nor did the return to the West promise improvements in his way of life. He had great difficulty in publishing his writings. In his words: "In the United States, with only two exceptions, conservative publishers considered my work too revolutionary, and left-wing publishers too anti-totalitarian, that is, too hard on the Stalin regime."[10] This was during World War II, when publishers were anxious not to offend the Soviet ally. Serge died as a penniless exile in Mexico City.

Serge was one of a handful of people who actually moved to a communist state on account of their beliefs, rather than as a last resort to evade capture for spying (like Kim Philby and a few others) or to avoid persecution by their government. Serge personified, in a somewhat old-fashioned way, the selfless idealist whose life was dominated by public-political concerns but who lacked a brutal, intolerant streak and a sense of entitlement to use any means to attain the great goals. He writes: "Early on I learned from the Russian intelligentsia that the only meaning in life lies in conscious participation in the making of history."[11]

This background helps to explain the first sentence of his memoirs: "Even before I emerged from childhood . . . I felt repugnance, mingled with wrath and indignation, towards people whom I saw settled comfortably in this world. How could they not be conscious of their captivity, of their unrighteousness? All this was the result, as I can see today, of my upbringing as the son of revolutionary exiles."[12]

These youthful attributions of false consciousness did not endure; as it turned out, unlike many of his fellow idealists turned revolutionary activists and functionaries, Serge had a limited capacity to rationalize political violence in order to make history. Unlike other committed supporters of the same cause, Serge recognized its flaws early on. He succeeded for a long time in balancing these insights and critiques against other considerations: "I immediately discerned within the Russian Revolution the seeds of such serious evils as intolerance and . . . the persecution of dissent. These evils originated in the absolute sense of possession of the truth . . . What followed was contempt for the man who was different, of his arguments and way of life. "[13]

In his early hopes he was badly disappointed, along with many other Soviet citizens who had hoped during World War II that repression would diminish and life would become easier after the war; they, too, were seeking plausible explanations for the harshness of the system in the external threats that it faced at the time.

Serge's arrival to the Soviet Union in 1919 suited his attitude and the historical circumstances: "We crossed the Soviet border at dead of night, in the middle of a forest. Our progress was painful, blocked by snow. The sharp cold bored through our thin Western clothing and our teeth chattered . . . Men with lanterns, standing on a little white bridge in the misty moonlight counted us as we passed. Choked with joy, we shouted, 'Greetings, comrade!' to a Red sentry; he nodded and then asked if we had any food. We had. Here, take it. The Revolution is hungry."[14]

As a veteran of Western working-class movements who was well connected to their leaders, Serge was initially welcomed, and he became familiar with such major political figures as Bukharin, Kamenev, Radek, Trotsky, and Zinoviev and the writers Andrei Bely, Maxim Gorky, Boris Pasternak, Boris Pilniak, and Alexei Tolstoy. Undoubtedly, the friendly attitude of the Soviet leaders was related to their early hopes for Western working-class support for the Revolution and the new Soviet state.

Serge was offered work in the Universal Literature publishing house. He was also on the staff of the Petrograd Soviet (city council), worked as an instructor in public education clubs, as inspector of schools, and as lecturer to the Petrograd militia, and later he "ran the Romance-language section and publications of the Communist International." He also organized weapon smuggling from Finland to Russia. At one point, he and his friends, not having "the slightest desire to enter the ruling bureaucracy," attempted to found, north of Petrograd, near Lake Ladoga, "an agricultural colony in the heart of the Russian countryside . . . [where] we would live close to the earth, in the wilds." Unhappily, "in three months hunger and weariness forced us to abandon the project."[15]

His memoirs suggest—as far as his years in the Soviet Union were concerned—a constant oscillation between repugnance toward the system and a sense of obligation to support it. It was, after all, the only socialist system in existence, the only revolutionary country, and on these grounds alone it deserved support.

Repeatedly Serge writes as if the Cheka (the first incarnation of the Soviet political police) was an organization that the leaders of the regime could not fully control; thus he was able to divorce its brutality from that of the system as a whole. Reflecting on a massacre carried out by the Cheka in 1920 (the shooting of imprisoned suspects who would have been spared by the impending abolition of the death penalty), he writes: "The Chekists presented the Government with a fait accompli. Much later I became personally acquainted with one of those responsible for the Petrograd massacre . . . 'We thought,' he told me, 'that if the People's Commissars [who passed the decree abolishing the death penalty] were getting converted to humanitarianism, that was their business. Our business was to crush the counter-revolution forever . . .' It was a frightful and tragic example of occupational psychosis."[16]

Lev Kopelev, who belongs to a later generation of defectors, also attempted in his youth to come to terms with the repression:

> It was a shame that many innocent people had to suffer [in the 1930s] . . . But surely Japanese spies and saboteurs had infiltrated the region [the Far East] . . . This was a threat to the entire country . . . So it was necessary to clamp down on hundreds of thousands. In those same years they resettled Poles, Estonians and

> Finns from the western territories. And again it seemed unfortu-
> nately severe, but necessary in order to 'clean up the rear lines of
> the future front' . . .
>
> Our leader and mentors . . . our talented writers . . . demon-
> strated to us that the old Bolsheviks, former friends of Lenin him-
> self, out of their urge for power, or out of avarice, had become
> traitors [This is in reference to the accused in the show trials of
> the 1930s] . . .
>
> What did we have to counter this? What could we use to hold
> together yesterday's wobbly ideals?
>
> They offered us . . . *rodina* and *narod* [fatherland and nation].
> And we gratefully accepted the refurbished ideals of patriotism.[17]

The crushing of the Kronstadt uprising of sailors, who had earlier been
among the vanguard of the Revolution, jolted Serge and distanced him
from the system. ("The worst of it all was that we were paralysed by the official falsehoods. It had never happened before that our Party had lied to us
like this.") The sailors demanded elections by secret ballot, free expression
for all revolutionary parties and groups, freedom for trade unions, an end
of requisitioning, in the countryside, and similar measures to revitalize the
Revolution. Nonetheless, "after many hesitations and with unutterable anguish," Serge finally supported the Party: "This is why. Kronstadt had right
on its side. Kronstadt was the beginning of a fresh, liberating revolution for
popular democracy . . . However, the country was absolutely exhausted,"
and it seemed to him that groups hostile to the Revolution "could come back
to life in a matter of weeks." Moreover, "if the Bolshevik dictatorship fell, it
was only a short step to chaos . . . and in the end . . . another dictatorship."[18]

Thus, up to a point, despite all his misgivings, Serge embraced the rationalization widely used by people in similar circumstances: "Expulsion from
the Party, as we repeated often enough, amounted to our 'political death.'
How could living people, full of faith, ideas and devotion, be turned into
political corpses?"[19] Serge was nonetheless among the handful of early critics of the regime (along with Rosa Luxemburg and Bertrand Russell) who
were not willing to excuse the political violence and repression as an acceptable price paid for material progress: "We could not, like so many for-

eign tourists and bourgeois journalists . . . fail to note that the cost of industrialization was a hundred times multiplied by tyranny. We remained
convinced that the achievements of Socialist democracy would have been
. . . infinitely better and greater, with less cost, no famine, no terror and
no suppression of thought."[20]

As his objections to the unfolding polices of the regime became more
vocal, his personal life became difficult. His writings were not published. and
the head of a publishing house told him: "You can produce a masterpiece
every year, but so long as you are not back in the line of the Party, not a
line of yours will see the light!" Several neighbors in the communal apartment
spied on him. His wife suffered a nervous breakdown requiring hospitaliza-
tion, partly on account of the persecution of her father, an old revolutionary
worker.

As Stalin's power expanded, Serge's life deteriorated: "From . . . 1928 on-
wards, the ring closes in relentlessly. The value of human life continuously
declines, the lie in the heart of all social relationships becomes even fouler
and oppression ever heavier . . . I asked for a passport for abroad." He did
not get it. In 1933 he was arrested and exiled, this comparatively mild treatment due to influential voices of protest abroad raised by people whom the
regime wished to impress, such as the French author Romain Rolland.[21]
Serge was allowed to leave in 1936 "after seventeen years' experience of
victorious revolution."[22]

An idealist like Serge could not indefinitely retain his allegiance to a
political system that so spectacularly abandoned its original, idealistic programs but not its idealistic rhetoric.[23] He was among many idealists who
could not accept the immense gulf between theory and practice, promise
and fulfillment. He writes: "I began to feel, acutely . . . this sense of a danger
from inside, a danger within ourselves, in the very temper and character of
victorious Bolshevism. I was continually racked by the contrast between the
stated theory and the reality, by the growth of intolerance and servility
among many officials and their drive towards privilege."[24]

Serge also had reason to be disappointed in some of his fellow intellectuals who turned out to be spineless supporters of the increasingly repressive
system that persecuted some of the best writers. Thus, for example, "when
the [Soviet] Press denounced Zamyatin and Pilniak as public enemies . . .

my author friends voted everything that was expected of them against their two comrades . . . When at the time of the technicians' trial the Party organized demonstrations in favor of the execution of the culprits . . . the writers voted and demonstrated like everybody else; this although they numbered men who knew what was going on and were troubled by it, such as Konstantin Fedin, Boris Pilniak, Alexei Tolstoy, Vsevolod Ivanov and Boris Pasternak."

Famous Western intellectuals and prominent fellow travelers of the period, such as Henri Barbusse and Paul Vaillant-Couturier, also impressed Serge with their (far less excusable) cowardice. Of the former he observes: "He was concerned above all to disguise opinions he could no longer express openly . . . all with the real aim of making himself the accomplice of the winning side! Since it was not yet known whether the struggle had been definitely settled, he had just dedicated a book . . . to Trotsky, whom he did not dare to visit for fear of compromising himself." Serge came to despise Barbusse for allowing himself to be used for spreading official falsehoods abroad to discredit the Left Opposition.[25]

Another example of questionable integrity among intellectuals was provided by the Hungarian philosopher George Lukacs, whom Serge knew quite well: "I was to meet George Lukacs and his wife . . . in 1928 or 1929 in a Moscow street. He was then working at the Marx-Engels Institute; his books were being suppressed . . . Although he was fairly well disposed towards me, he did not care to shake my hand in a public place, since I was expelled as a well-known Oppositionist. He enjoyed physical survival and wrote short, spiritless articles in Comintern journals." On another, earlier occasion in Vienna, Lukacs had told him: "Don't be silly and get yourself deported for nothing, just for the pleasure of voting defiantly [in the Comintern]. Believe me, insults are not very important to us. Marxist revolutionaries need patience and courage; they do not need pride. The times are bad, and we are at a dark cross-roads. Let us reserve our strength: history will summon us in its time."[26] The remark illuminates the beliefs and attitudes of a prominent committed Party intellectual who succeeded in salvaging his faith by hope in a future that would redeem the sordidness of the present, including his own lack of integrity.

The confessions and recollections of Serge show that what Raymond Aron

calls the "myth of the revolution" was the key factor in his tortured, ambivalent, yet supportive attitude toward the Soviet system. His loyalty was
based on a generalized attraction to the Revolution, always appealing to
intellectuals seeking fundamental and radical change not merely of social
institutions but of the human condition itself. Serge was susceptible to the
myth of the revolution precisely because, in the words of Aron, "it fosters
the expectation of a break with the normal trend of human affairs . . . provides a welcome break with the everyday course of events and encourages
the belief that all things are possible."[27] This is not to suggest that Serge
had anything in common with the Western intellectuals of more recent times
whom Hans Magnus Enzensberger has called "tourists of the revolution."[28]

By the time Serge was in exile in Orenburg, on the border between European and Asiatic Russia, the mystique of the revolution was tarnished,
and he was no longer in a position to try to help move it in a more humane
direction. In Orenburg he was, while hospitalized, once more assailed by
the painful divergence between theory and practice. As a privileged exile,
he was allowed to buy butter, sugar, and rice: "I shall never forget the way
in which some of the sick people gazed at me when I was brought such
food, or their deference when they took their share of it. Nor, for that matter,
shall I forget how on the most wretched of our days of misery we all heard
a radio broadcast from a regional meeting of *kolkhoz* workers. Passionate
voices went on endlessly thanking the leader for 'the good life we lead'; and
twenty or so patients tormented by hunger, half of them *kolkhoz* workers
themselves, listened to it all in silence."[29]

Serge died a believer in the possibility of renewing socialism "through the
jettisoning of the authoritarian, intolerant tradition of turn-of-the century
Russian Marxism."[30] His account of his life and experiences in the Soviet
Union remains an outstanding and moving testimonial to what Trotsky called
"the revolution betrayed."

VICTOR KRAVCHENKO (1905–1966)

Victor Kravchenko, largely forgotten today, might be considered one of the
most famous Soviet defectors because of the controversy his defection and
public statements generated. His revelations came at a time when Western
public opinion was unprepared for them. Not only the Soviet government

but Western and especially French leftists also accused him of being a liar. He sued the last in a French court in 1946 and won. His idea to defect to the United States "began to take shape in January 1943, and a passport for the journey was actually issued in July. During those six months I felt like a rare beetle on a pin in a huge laboratory where legions of entomologists, zoologists, chemists and other scientists studied the specimen from every possible angle . . . All the energies of an omnipotent state seemed centered on the job of exploring my humble person."[31]

He arrived in the United States in 1943 as a representative of the Soviet government and defected in 1944, dying in the United States in 1966. The official cause of death was suicide, but there had been earlier assassination attempts.[32]

Kravchenko easily meets the criteria proposed earlier: he was a member of the Soviet elite (Party member, highly placed engineer, industrial admin-istrator), he used to be a believer in the system and its ideals, and he pro-vided a lengthy and detailed account of the sources of his disaffection. His disillusionment, as was often the case, germinated for many years before prompting him to take action: "For a long time I had known that this deci-sive hour was inevitable. For months I had planned the flight. I had looked forward to it as a release from the maze of hypocrisies, resentments and con-fusions of spirit in which I had wandered for so many years. It was to be my expiation for the horrors about which, as a member of the ruling class . . . I felt a sense of guilt."[33]

Though by no means the first to report the existence of Soviet forced labor camps and other unappealing features of the Soviet system, prior to Kravchenko's revelations, information of this nature was largely ignored and neutralized, as it were, by World War II.[34] Following his arrival in the United States, Kravchenko noted that "the prevailing American notions about the wonders of Sovietism in practice were truly extraordinary. Great chunks of Communist reality—like slave labor, police dictatorship, the mas-sive periodic purges, the fantastically low standards of living, the great famine of 1932–33, the horrors of collectivization . . . [seem] to have completely es-caped American attention."[35] It was in part for that reason that his dis-closures appeared shocking and even questionable. Serious critiques of the Soviet Union—of Western or, especially, of native origin—were hard to find during World War II and its immediate aftermath, when the wartime sufferings of the Soviet people (confused with the strength of the system) were still vividly recalled. The Cold War had not yet begun, and casting aspersions on the wartime ally of the United States appeared to be in bad taste.

At the time of Kravchenko's defection few Soviet citizens entertained the possibility of defecting, and even fewer had succeeded; controls over the freedom of movement of Soviet citizens were extremely tight, and opportunities for escape were virtually nonexistent except for those taken as prisoners or slave laborers by the Nazis.

Kravchenko had his share of almost every disillusioning experience that life in the Soviet Union under Stalin could provide: firsthand knowledge of the forced collectivization of agriculture and the sufferings it led to, as well as the fear that the Purges created (he came close to being arrested himself). As a high-ranking industrial administrator, he learned about the wastefulness and irrationality of Soviet planning and the hardships it imposed on the people; as a member of the elite, he knew about privileges, which contrasted sharply with both the impoverished condition of the masses and the rhetoric of the regime; he was also in a position to observe the contributions that political prisoners made to the "building of socialism," because they were often provided to the enterprises he directed. He had ample contact with the political police (GPU at the time) and learned of its methods; he knew highly placed officials and became familiar with their character and attitudes. He was in an excellent position to experience the pervasive, institutionalized discrepancies between theory and practice, promise and reality. To be sure, countless other Soviet officials had similar experiences and opportunities for becoming disaffected, yet they did not defect and did not seek to expose the inequities of the system. What made Kravchenko different?

Three factors stand out in his biography, and their combination helps to explain the path he took. Throughout his youth he was a highly committed, idealistic supporter of the system. As noted earlier, the greater such idealism, the greater the possibility, indeed probability, of disappointment and estrangement as reality fails to measure up to the ideals. Second, he himself suffered indignities (short of arrest) at the hands of the GPU as a suspect during the Purge period. Third and perhaps most important, his father, a member of the pre-revolutionary working class and a fighter for the October

Revolution, became a critic of the system and shared his disillusionment with his son, although for many years, while the son's devotion to the system was unwavering, father and son disagreed about politics. His mother was equally vocal in communicating her critiques of the system. Kravchenko's disillusionment was emotionally legitimated and given moral support by parents he was close to.

There are also, as always, the intangibles of personality. Evidently Kravchenko had a greater capacity for moral indignation and lesser tolerance of injustice, repression, and institutionalized lying than had many of his contemporaries in similar positions. Perhaps in the more tolerant Brezhnev era he would have become a dissenter instead of a defector. Under Stalin, options were scarce. Kravchenko's case was unique only insofar as he managed to escape and describe his beliefs and experiences on paper; in all probability, hundreds of thousands, if not millions, of Soviet citizens of similar levels of education, socioeconomic position, and experience harbored similar feelings without being able to express them publicly. Kravchenko, having pondered why he defected, offered this answer: "Mine was not a step any Soviet Russian, especially a Communist of long standing and fairly advanced in the ranks of the bureaucracy, took frivolously . . . It was an act that had its beginnings somewhere far down in the substratum of my mind . . . I was moved by a childhood pervaded by the robust idealism of my father, the profound religious faith of my mother. Their goodness, their love of humanity, were different in kind, but somehow identical at the core. And it was this core, no doubt, that remained also in me."[36]

Kravchenko's youthful enthusiasm was similar to the feelings of other committed supporters of communist movements and systems in other places and at other times:

> I felt myself part of something new, big, exciting . . . There were
> many defects, extensive suffering. But there was also the lift of
> terrific excitement, and inflamed hopes . . . I belonged to the mi-
> nority that was stirred by the ideas behind the great effort . . .
> today's pain seemed only a necessary payment for the glorious
> future . . .
>
> The shadows of the GPU, the state political police, did not

touch me; besides, it seemed to me quite natural that at such a critical, strained moment in the life of the country everyone should be carefully checked and controlled . . .

In the middle of 1929 I was admitted to the Party. It seemed to me the greatest event in my life.[37]

The collectivization campaign was the first important personal experiences that, with others to follow in their wake, undermined his beliefs:

Rumors of incredible cruelty in the villages in connection with the liquidation of the kulaks [more prosperous peasants] were passed from mouth to mouth. We saw long trains of cattle cars filled with peasants . . . presumably on their way to the tundras of the North . . .

The railroad stations of the city were jammed with ragged, hungry peasants fleeing their homes . . . homeless children . . . were again everywhere. Beggars, mostly country people . . . again appeared on the streets . . .

Which was the reality, which the illusions? The hunger and terror in the villages, the homeless children—or the statistics of achievement?[38]

The importance of directly experienced details was conveyed to him by his former mentor, a lower Party functionary, who told him: "You see I've just returned from the Ukraine . . . My job was to put through the collectivization in one region . . . Comrade Molotov called the activists together and he talked plainly, sharply. The job must be done, no matter how many lives it cost, he told us . . . There was no room for softness or regrets."[39] Subsequently Kravchenko himself was sent to the countryside to assist in the collectivization. He and other activists were briefed by a Party functionary: "The class struggle in the village has taken the sharpest form. This is no time for squeamishness or rotten sentimentality . . . What is required from you is Bolshevik alertness, intransigence and courage. I am sure you will carry out the instructions of the Party and the directives of our beloved Leader."[40]

These warnings and pep talks were reminiscent of the disquisition that

Himmler gave to the SS officers engaged in even more unappealing tasks. In both cases, the leaders seemed aware of the necessity to bolster the determination of their subordinates so that they could perform duties that could have inspired massive revulsion even in ardent supporters of the system. Kravchenko witnessed what an abstraction such as "the liquidation of kulaks as a class" precisely meant and how it was carried out:

> What I saw that morning making the rounds of houses was inexpressibly horrible. On a battlefield men die quickly, they fight back, they are sustained by fellowship and a sense of duty. Here I saw people dying in solitude by slow degrees, dying hideously without the excuse of sacrifice for a cause. They had been . . . left to starve, each in his home, by a political decision made in a far-off capital . . .
>
> The most terrifying sights were little children with skeleton limbs . . . Starvation had wiped every trace of youth from their faces . . . Everywhere we found men and women lying prone, their faces and bellies bloated, their eyes utterly expressionless.

The idea "that the horrors were not accidental, but planned and sanctioned by the highest authorities," began to "sprout" in his mind. He joined those "Communists who had been directly immersed in the horrors of collectivization [and who] were thereafter marked men. We carried the scars. We had seen ghosts . . . we shrank from discussion of the peasant front . . . We found it hard to justify the agrarian terror."[41]

Moreover—and contrary to many Western intellectuals' beliefs at the time—the hardships of collectivization were not part of the sacrifices all had to bear. While millions starved, a minority, including some in the countryside, were well provided for. Politically determined privileges and inequalities were an important characteristic of the Soviet system that was unknown to outsiders. Kravchenko recalls: "In bed that night I thought of the new privileged class in the village—the Party and Soviet [local council] functionaries who were receiving milk and butter and supplies from the cooperative shop while everyone else around them starved. Slavishly they obeyed orders from the center, indifferent to the suffering of common people. The corruption of character by privilege was fearsome to behold."

This was the time when, "in the secret recesses" of his being, his break with the Party began: "The village horrors left psychological lesions which never healed." But to survive physically "one had to come to terms with a reality from which there was no escape." Hence, "it was imperative to squelch those emotions, to drive them into the underground of my mind. I labored to repair my loyalties. With the purge in the offing this urgency was even greater."[42]

Another traumatic experience was finding out that his girlfriend "belonged to the legion of spies operating in all crevices of our Soviet society! . . . Theoretically, as a Communist I could hardly condemn the pervasive GPU espionage. It was no news to me that thousands of persons seemingly engaged in other activities actually were devoted to spying. Yet the discovery that the woman I loved was . . . a GPU agent shocked me deeply."

He was distressed and humiliated when the police searched the belongings of two American engineers whom he had been instructed to house and who worked at his plant: "You understand, of course, comrade Kravchenko, that not a word of this must be ever known." He was asked to sign a "voluntary" pledge to keep his mouth shut. "When the men left I wandered through the house, depressed, stranger in my own home. I was ashamed to face the Americans when they returned."[43]

This was also the time when "jittery Party men went to bed in their clothes 'just in case.' Like nearly everyone else, I had a small suitcase packed with the things a man could use in prison." At a Party meeting he was severely criticized for sabotage and for concealing the political past of his father, who used to be a Menshevik (member of a moderate, non-Leninist faction of the Russian Socialist Party) prior to the Revolution. Kravchenko also learned about the specifics of torture inflicted by the political police from an old friend who held a high government post but had earlier "confessed" to sabotage.[44]

Inequality—a recurring theme in these recollections—was a major source of embittered disillusionment. Among the incidents that Kravchenko recalls was his mother's visit to one of his places of work, the metallurgical plant in Nikopol. She was impressed by his elegant house "and especially the fact that I had five rooms all to myself." But after looking around the factory, its housing, clubs, and childcare facilities, she was "shocked" by what she saw:

"I see you have a lovely white bath all for yourself. But the workers, thousands of them, have only a vile hole that doesn't deserve the name of bath—and even that is not working. In a project like this, costing tens of millions, why no decent bathhouses . . . ? And here is another example: the crèches. Not enough linen, not enough medicine, not enough anything."[45]

On another occasion he took his mother to the Agricultural Exposition in Moscow, but she was not impressed: "It all seems a masquerade . . . If there are so many cows in the country, why is there no meat in Dniepropetrovsk? If there is so much cotton, why can't I buy a shirt for your father?"

At a steel mill in Taganrog, he was once more "assigned to a comfortable apartment in the administration compound where the elite residences were located." He asked himself: "Had the planners been intent on dramatizing the contrast between the upper and lower classes in the Soviet world? I doubt it. Yet the contrast was there, it shrieked at you, made you uncomfortable. Beautiful shade trees shut out the sight of the factory structures and barracks. Gravel walks flanked by lilac bushes led to a swimming and bathing strip (reserved for officialdom . . .) on a well-combed beach."[46]

There were also the special stores and the shoemaking and tailoring establishments for the elite. "Not one Russian in a thousand suspected that such abundant shops existed, and, indeed, the authorities operated them discreetly."[47]

Almost daily he saw forced laborers under guard—"as tragic looking a group of human creatures as I had ever seen. Their unsmiling silence was more terrible than their raggedness, filth and physical degradation." The presence of forced laborers at or near the various industrial projects he directed was an especially stark reminder of the distance between those at the top and those at the bottom. They were "haggard, scarcely human creatures, in their filthy rags . . . work[ing] ten to twelve hours a day under armed surveillance." It was no different at a job near Sverdlovsk, where he had at his disposal both a limousine and a smaller Ford and an income about ten times that of the workers. On the way to the plant he "saw the barbed wire fence of a concentration camp a few hundred meters off the road." When he inquired about it, his companion told him, "I see you are new to the Urals. You'd better get accustomed to the prisoners everywhere."[48]

On another occasion in the Sverdlovsk area he came upon hundreds of women working in "a dismal stretch of marshes . . . indescribably dirty and grotesquely clad . . . many of them stood up to their knees in the muddy water. They worked in absolute silence, with the most primitive tools." During the war, when visiting an underground munitions factory "deep in Moscow province," he came upon forced laborers who looked even worse than those encountered earlier in the Urals and Siberia: "They were walking corpses . . . poisoned by the chemicals with which they worked."[49]

Even when he was traveling by train, scenes of starvation intruded. In his first-class compartment and in the well-stocked dining car he was "startled by several little faces peering through the window with sad, hungry envious eyes. These were . . . homeless boys and girls in motley rags. They were staring at one of their 'socialist uncles' . . . This in the Ukraine, which once upon a time provided food not only for all its population but for a large part of Europe!" At a stop he went out for a walk only to witness "a uniformed Chekist [political policeman] shooing off a peasant family . . . 'You belong over there, citizens, in the third-class waiting room,' he said, and they walked off meekly."[50]

During the war he discovered that the waitress serving him abundant meals in his Moscow office was starving and ate the leftovers. On a visit to a wood product plant he learned that workers were, even during the war, making "elegant furniture" for "top Party, government and Red Army officials."[51]

It was also during the war, when he "sat near the pinnacle of power" (in a war production office in Moscow), that he learned more of the mindset of the rulers and "the complacency with which these people used human life . . . like so much inert raw material for their plans, experiments and blunders. Suddenly I found myself among men who could eat ample and dainty food in full view of starving people not only with a clear conscience but with a feeling of righteousness." It was also during the war when he was pleading for better food supplies for the workers of a particular plant that "the head of the Sovnarkom [Council of People's Commissars] looked at me with unconcealed irritation. 'Kravchenko, look here. Are you a social worker or a Bolshevik? Humanitarianism is a bad guide in making state decisions. Learn from Comrade Stalin—love the people but sacrifice their needs when essential!"[52]

The appearance-reality gap made many appearances in Kravchenko's world. One notorious issue was that of production norms, or piece rates, whereby a particular amount of work (for example, stamping out X number of metal parts) was declared to be the "norm" (or 100 percent) and anything above it would warrant extra pay. Kravchenko writes:

> Orders arrived to revise 'norms' . . . upward by 10 to 20 per cent. It was nothing more than a roundabout order to exact 10 to 20 per cent more work for the same wage . . . To add insult to injury the new norms had to be presented and accepted by the workers 'themselves', not only 'voluntarily' but enthusiastically . . . It was no different when the new labor book was issued without which no worker could obtain employment or change his job and which also carried a record of reprimands or punishments for various infractions such as being late: . . . in the usual Soviet fashion, the victims were forced to accept their new chains not merely 'willingly' but 'with enthusiasm' . . . at staged mass meetings . . . selected Party people rhapsodized about the new blessings . . . shrill resolutions of approval . . . were adopted unanimously.[53]

He himself was not spared from contributing to the make-belief:

> It fell to me to deliver a "lecture" on . . . Party history to responsible Party members of the Pervouralks district . . . My specific subject was "The Communist Party in the Struggle for the Collectivization of Agriculture." I crammed my mind with the appropriate passages from the official history . . . then stood in an auditorium filled with people and lied . . .
>
> And all the time, as I spoke, I had no doubt that my listeners, too, knew I was lying . . . we were so many actors going through our prescribed parts in a tragic political comedy.[54]

Lying was also endemic in the production reports. At his plant "not a word was said about the fact that some days more than 25% of the claimed output was fraudulent." Elsewhere he notes that "properly indoctrinated" communists had little trouble with the gap between propaganda and reality, treating it as would "a general in the field who misleads and disorients the enemy."[55]

His response to the new Soviet constitution, introduced in 1936, illustrates the struggle that people of his type waged within themselves to salvage their faith: "Like millions of others, I reached out for the promise of human rights for the ordinary citizens [offered by the constitution]. We grasped at the straw of hope."[56]

For those in high positions, a major technique for living with doubt was immersion in work: "In drugging my mind with immediate worries about business details I succeeded in blotting out disturbing thoughts about the larger national picture. The more deeply I hated the whole regime . . . the more loyally I focussed my energies on the job in hand."[57]

Meanwhile his own impressions and unexpressed critiques were reinforced by his father (who remained a worker) during visits home. His father told him about workers they both had known who disappeared from the factory and about the miserable living conditions of the proletariat. "I felt as if he were holding me personally responsible, as a Party member, for every injustice." The father wondered if his son was "as content as the rest of the bureaucrats to be one of the bosses over the miserable Russian people." For his father it was small consolation that everything was done in the name of the workers.[58]

The best summary of Kravchenko's discontent and alienation is at the end of his book: "Nowhere in the world was there such a fearsome concentration of wretched suffering and political despotism, nowhere else was misery so cynically disguised with 'advanced' slogans."[59]

In one respect, Kravchenko's account is strikingly similar to those of various leaders and high-level functionaries of later periods (examined in subsequent chapters): they too lived for years, if not decades, with doubts and anguished questions, yet continued to perform their duties and to wear "the Party mask," the facade of unflinching loyalty and dedication to the system. At the same time, the possibility cannot be ruled out that all those who *in retrospect* dwelled on their misgivings and moral agonies had fewer and less intensely experienced feelings of this kind when the morally unsettling events and experiences took place, when they were part of the system.

ARKADY SHEVCHENKO (1930–1998)

Arkady Shevchenko was, according to his publisher, "the highest ranking Soviet official ever to defect." An adviser to Foreign Minister Gromyko and the undersecretary-general of the United Nations, among other positions, he was indisputably a member of the political elite and a beneficiary of its privileges. He was regarded "as an orthodox Soviet functionary, obedient, loyal, a hard-line Communist. The fact that I was one of the USSR's youngest ambassadors was cited, along with my service as adviser to Gromyko, as proof not only of my 'brilliant career' but also of my political reliability." It is a testimony to his skills of simulation that even at the United Nations in New York, while he was hatching schemes of defection "my U.N. colleagues regarded me as a hard-liner, an orthodox guardian of Soviet interests in the Secretariat."[60]

Like Kravchenko, Shevchenko took advantage of being posted to the United States, and he, too, wrote a book about what had led to his decision to defect. But unlike Kravchenko, he never had any brushes with the system. He was not under suspicion nor had been criticized at Party meetings or otherwise. His career was not declining or endangered by bureaucratic infighting or losing favor with higher-ups. He was of a younger generation and thus had no personal experience of collectivization or the Purges.

Why did he come to reject the Soviet system and even to work with the CIA? It was certainly not because of any disadvantage or deprivation—political or economic—that he or his family suffered under the Soviet system, including the days of Stalin. He writes:

> I should not have had any real reason to hate or even dislike the Soviet system. It had given me its best: a high position in the ruling class, complete financial security, privileges and the prospect of still further advancement . . .
>
> I did not suffer during the Stalin period; on the contrary, I had everything I could want . . . I had plenty of hope . . . I would be graduating from the prestigious diplomatic institute with many opportunities ahead of me.
>
> Occasionally, one or another dark side of Soviet life irritated me or aroused indignation at the gap between theory and practice, words and deeds. But there were always sufficiently convincing explanations for all the shortcomings: the Soviet Union was the brave land where a golden age was being built, and the new is

never born without struggle and errors that are the result of
human nature.[61]

The theory-practice gap loomed large in his disillusionment too. Upon
his defection he wrote to Brezhnev: "The betrayal of the ideals of the October Revolution which is taking place now in the USSR and the monstrous
abuses carried out by the KGB compel me to take the decision to renounce
my membership in the CPSU [Communist Party]." His final confrontation
with the gap between ideals and realities was revealed memorably in the personal hypocrisy of Dobrynin, the Soviet ambassador to the United States.
According to diplomatic ritual, he was supposed to tell the ambassador of
his decision to defect on the premises of the U.S. State Department: "Em-
ploying the intimate form of 'you' that Russian friends normally use with
one another, he expressed only concern for me, bewilderment at my action.
'Arkady, we have known each other for many years. I don't believe that all
these years you have acted contrary to your convictions . . . How can it be
explained?' . . . The hypocrisy in Dobrynin's question was tiresomely familiar . . . millions upon millions of Soviet citizens conceal their feelings
about the Party line and policy. I knew that many officials . . . held deviant
opinions hidden for years, lifetimes. Anyone foolish enough to voice such
thoughts risked losing not only his position and privileges but perhaps his
life."[62]

Shevchenko had entered service in the Ministry of Foreign Affairs in
1956 and was inspired by the policies of Khrushchev. Gradually, as he rose
he "acquired a deeper understanding of Soviet society . . . and the life of the
elite." The latter he found unappealing: "While condemning consumerism
. . . the privileged valued above all else the consumer goods and comforts
of the West. I was not immune. The gulf between what was said and what
was done was oppressive." The elite privileges included "high salaries,
good apartments, dachas, government cars with chauffeurs, special railway
cars and accommodations, VIP treatment at airports, resorts and hospitals
off limits to outsiders, special schools for their children, access to stores
where consumer goods and food are available at reduced prices . . . They
[the nomenklatura] live a rarefied existence far removed from the common
man . . . When we became part of this class, we regarded the luxuries and

special courtesies accorded us with delighted wonder. All too soon the garnering of more and the deference by others became something that we treated as if it were our birthright."[63]

Such feelings and experiences were also reported by other former leaders, functionaries, and members of the Party intelligentsia. But initially and often for lengthy periods of time, the acceptance and enjoyment of these privileges was not problematic, not seen as one of the numerous instances of the gap between theory and practice but rather as a just reward for service, dedication, and commitment. In retrospect, these inequalities and politically earned privileges were almost invariably deplored. Rarely did any of the authors cited here claim that the privileges themselves prompted instant distaste or disillusionment or were the *initial* source of questioning; more typically it was in light of the loss of ideological conviction, stemming from other sources, that the privileges and inequalities came to be seen as unfair, as a major departure from the ideals supposedly pursued by the system. The privileges, which had earlier helped to solidify already existing loyalties, later became a liability, eventually undermining the sense of legitimacy that the political elites possessed.

Shevchenko explains his progressive disillusionment as a result of his promotions, which allowed him to get to know the highest echelons of the nomenklatura, including Brezhnev and Gromyko. He found these people personally, politically, and morally repugnant, hypocritical, corrupt, resistant to new ideas, and completely isolated from ordinary people. Gromyko, for example, "had not set foot in the streets of Moscow for almost forty years." Shevchenko also believed that his own work at the United Nations expanded his "philosophical horizons"—presumably it was not just the United Nations but the whole experience of being in the United States that had this effect. Among other things, he mentions being deeply impressed by "the wealth and volume of every imaginable kind of newspapers, magazines, books, television and radio."[64]

Like other Soviet citizens, he had learned since childhood the necessity of simulation, the careful separation of the private from the public self. At age ten, after the German invasion of Russia, he raised questions in school about the poor performance of the Red Army. Upon learning of this, his father told him: "It doesn't matter what the truth is. It matters what people think. You cannot go around saying whatever comes into your smart-alecky little head. People will say you are a defeatist. They will think you picked up your ideas from me or your mother. Do you want us to be denounced?" As a child he also learned about the deportation of the Crimean Tatars, for he had Tatar schoolmates. Later, in early 1953, the so-called doctors' plot came as a shock; he (and his wife) found it hard to believe that "Jewish doctors injected their patients with cancer-causing agents . . . [or] syphilis, or that Jewish pharmacists . . . gave people pills made of dried fleas." Stalin's death was still a blow to him.[65]

Khrushchev's famous revelations in 1956 created great confusion. Not only was Stalin delegitimated and denounced, but the event made the young Shevchenko wonder how and why his trusted collaborators—"Zhdanov, Malenkov, Molotov, Kaganovich, Bulganin and Khrushchev himself—didn't know what was going on and were not accomplices." Whatever the twinges of doubt, the "heady excitement of work" and the company of "some of the country's more important figures" mattered more. Khrushchev was at the height of his powers when he visited the United States in 1960: "To travel with him and other senior figures . . . was an extraordinary opportunity."[66]

As the recollections of other highly placed officials also suggest, it was not too difficult for Shevchenko to live with his doubts as long as he was part of a cohesive group or community in which everybody seemed to believe the official verities and worked for their realization and in which his talents were rewarded by recognition and privilege.

The case of Shevchenko exemplifies the growth of disaffection during the long Brezhnev era, one of widespread corruption and increasingly apparent loss of idealism. Shevchenko certainly gained little in terms of status, recognition, or material benefits by defecting. One cannot help but believe that he sought satisfaction in the types of freedom that only open societies can provide: "To this day I cannot get over the real satisfaction of being able to say something freely for the first time in my life without the necessity of remembering constraints on what was politically or ideologically acceptable."[67]

Shevchenko's defection suggests certain sources of the vulnerability of the Soviet system and its ultimate brittleness. In a system that compelled members of the ruling elite to wear a tight-fitting mask of unconditional loyalty, there was no way to know and test the depth of their loyalty; it was hard to distinguish genuinely committed supporters from opportunists who would desert the regime once conditions allowed them to do so without risk. Increasingly during the Gorbachev era, this conformity revealed its hollowness and contributed to the unexpected unraveling of the system.

PETRO GRIGORIENKO (1907–1987)

General Petro Grigorienko was another highly placed member of the Soviet elite whose loyalty toward the system was for decades unshaken. Nonetheless, he ended up in a "psychoprison" and later in exile. As noted in his obituary, "little in his early life suggested that he would become a dissident."[68] In a preface to his memoirs he writes: "Born into a working family, from my childhood onward I believed in communist ideas and later served them fanatically. I took a leading place among the ruling hierarchy and worked successfully in my chosen field . . . And all of a sudden I embarked on a road of struggle, something that not only deprived me of all my privileges but led me into hostile relations with the authorities . . . How does one explain this kind of phenomenon? The authorities gave it a very simple explanation—lunacy."[69]

Grigorienko was Ukrainian and his a sense of ethnic identity is affirmed early in his autobiography. He was also a man of humble social origins. His father was a hired farm laborer; his mother had died when he was three. There was one unusual circumstance in his father's background: he worked for German settlers whose agricultural competence was far superior to that of native-born population, and he remembered all his life what he saw on the German-run farms. Undoubtedly these experiences played a part is his critique of the collectivization of agriculture in later years.

In 1922, at age fifteen, he received, as a member of Komsomol (the Party youth organization), a copy of Bukharin's *The ABC of Communism.* A Komsomol functionary gave it to him with the comment "This contains all the wisdom of humanity. You must study it from cover to cover," and he did so. It was a time, he recalls, when "we failed to ask who gave us, a minority of the people, the right to reeducate the rest and to suppress those who refused to be reeducated." When he was a teenager, he helped collect a new tax imposed on the peasants "who had nothing with which to pay the new tax. Still, we Komsomols went from hut to hut, taking everything of any value."[70] Subsequently he attended a vocational and technical school, then worked as a skilled worker in a locomotive depot and, later, as a political instructor in the Komsomol. He became a Party member in 1927, when he was passionately enthusiastic about the goals of industrialization and collectivization. Later he was sent to the Kharkhov Technical Institute as a promising young worker.

In those years he knew or cared little about the man-made famine in the Ukraine and the violence associated with collectivization. But in retrospect he did not "accept the justification of ignorance. We were deceived because we wanted to be deceived. We believed so strongly in communism that we were ready to accept any crime if it was glossed over with the least bit of communist phraseology . . . Confronted with something unpleasant, we compelled ourselves to believe that it was an isolated phenomenon."[71] These were time-honored ways of dealing with policies and actions that could cast doubt on the principles in whose name they were carried out.

Early in his life he learned from his father about the collectivization of agriculture and its consequences. His father, who worked on such a farm, had firsthand knowledge of what was going on and told his son about it in no uncertain terms. "Yet I did not turn away from communism. Instead, the facts angered me and compelled me to search for refutations."[72] But his father's words stayed with him and apparently confirmed his subsequent disillusionment, although he himself did not assign great importance to them as contributors to his loss of belief.

Time and again, while his commitment was solid, observable realities mattered less than cherished beliefs in whose light these realities could be redefined or dismissed. For instance, "in 1930–31 the Soviet Union had a totally ruined agricultural system and disorganized transport system. Yet people like me continued to be hypnotized by the old ideals and the new construction projects . . . I saw many negative things but *I was unable to generalize from what I had seen*" (my emphasis).[73]

The last point captures a crucial aspect of the mindset of the true believer: the inability or refusal to connect particular phenomena or events to broader, underlying patterns, beliefs, and generalizations, and a determination to dispute the relevance of such supposedly dissonant phenomena or details to the *fundamentals* of belief. This determination in turn hinges on a highly subjective or arbitrary definition of what is fundamental, typical, or systemic as opposed to the atypical and isolated phenomena that need not be given serious moral attention.

In this manner Grigorienko was capable of digesting or assimilating the arrest of his uncle and, later, numerous fellow officers whom he knew to be innocent. In 1931, while already a student at the Military Engineering Academy, he rushed to visit his ailing father in the old village and saw "the station packed with half-dressed adults and children who literally besieged the railway car chanting: 'Bread, bread, bread!'"[74] At the time and for years later he was under the illusion that the higher authorities were unaware of what had gone wrong in the countryside and were generally ill informed about the abuses of power at the local level. In other words, his thinking was still dominated by the conviction that good intentions and well-meant policies mattered more than the errors in their implementation.

A young and competent military engineer, Grigorienko dutifully partici- pated in what he later saw as "one of the most flagrant instances of barbarism of our age—the destruction of the most important historical monuments of the Byelorussian and Russian peoples, their churches." He managed at the time to take professional pride in a job well done as he "admired the pile of bricks that remained where the cathedral has been."[75]

During the Purges of the 1930s, as the ranks around him thinned out, "frankness and openness disappeared. People looked at me suspiciously . . . The number of the enemies of the people multiplied." People were arrested for knowing somebody who had earlier been arrested. Grigorienko, a well- trained and highly motivated professional military man, often encountered the incompetence of the political leadership as it managed the affairs of the country and dictated policy for the military. The Purges decimated the ranks of the professional military men and elevated political above professional criteria.

In 1938, Grigorienko's older brother, arrested and later released, pro- vided firsthand information about conditions in the prisons and about the people held there. He also described the tortures inflicted on his cellmates. Still believing that the higher authorities had no knowledge of such outrages, Grigorienko sought to inform Andrei Vyshinsky, the procurator general of the USSR, who was among those masterminding the show trials and who delivered the most vicious and absurd accusations against the defendants subjected to public trial. Grigorienko succeeded in meeting Vyshinsky and "left [him] . . . with a feeling of deep gratitude and respect. He seemed to have taken to heart the violations of legality recounted by Ivan [his brother] and wanted to take decisive action to bring them to an end. This appointment convinced me that tortures were local abuses."[76]

On the other hand, the disclosures of a woman (who later became his second wife) about her imprisonment and of other imprisoned women deeply disturbed him: "I wondered again and again why these women had been punished so horribly. From time immemorial a person has been held responsible only for his crimes. But our humane government had managed to think up the concept of punishing an entire family . . . for the crime of one man."

As Grigorienko learned more about these outrages he also began "to realize that one or two men could not successfully attack the awful machine of suppression. Thus I began to suppress my own feelings of outrage, to seek justification for any atrocities I heard about and to struggle, not against evil as a whole, but against its particular, partial manifestations only."[77] This was the counsel of fear, as he himself acknowledged.

Grigorienko "had not been brought up to criticize. To me the words of the Party leadership, especially those of the 'great leader,' were the height of wisdom." He revered Stalin despite the disastrous mistakes he had made at the time of the German attack on the USSR:

> Though I had begun the war with doubts about the 'wisdom' of
> Stalin's leadership, I ended it believing that we had been very
> lucky, that without Stalin's genius, victory would have taken much
> longer to achieve . . .
>
> . . . I was not a protestor, a critic of the system . . . but a man
> who was dedicated to and loved his work . . . Without hesitation
> I accepted everything that was said about Stalin, about the party,
> about the country, as truth . . . Were people starving in the coun-
> try? Well, that was natural—we had just come through a terrible
> war . . . Were trainloads of Soviet prisoners being sent to camps?
> Why not—if they had betrayed the motherland in a critical

hour? Were they arresting civilians who had remained on occupied territory? Naturally . . . they would release the innocent.[78]

Grigorienko records an even more astonishing instance of confidence in
the system in the face of experiences totally at odds with such trust:

> My father-in-law . . . had been a typical idealist . . . He joined the
> revolutionary movement in 1904 and after the October Revolu-
> tion continued as a rank-and-file communist party member . . .
> His two sons and his four daughters all joined the party. And the
> party "rewarded" their father richly. His elder son was shot in
> 1934 . . . His younger son was forced into hiding during the mass
> arrests in 1936–38. Two of his sons-in-law were arrested in 1936.
> One was killed during interrogation and the other was shot. His
> eldest daughter perished in camp. Another daughter languished
> for months in prison. Despite all this he kept right on idealizing
> the party.[79]

World War II and the attendant rallying of the nation by the Party and
Stalin to the common struggle helped to diminish the memory of the Purges
and allowed hope for a better future after the war. But the war also allowed
Grigorienko to learn about life and standards of living outside the Soviet
Union. Thus, upon entering what used to be a part of Czechoslovakia, in
the Carpathian region, "we were astonished by the enormous, full wine
cellars, by the piles of fruit and vegetables and by the abundant poultry
in the homes."[80] The area was annexed by the Soviet Union after World
War II.

Even during the war symptoms of corruption among the leaders were
apparent, as in the case of Bulganin's "harem" at the front and his drunkenness, which Grigorienko personally witnessed. He also had opportunity
to meet the young Leonid Brezhnev during the war and to note his obsequiousness and servility, including adjustments of his facial expressions for
the benefit of higher-ups: "The artificiality of his facial expressions and his
voice caused people to think of Brezhnev as a lightweight, a dullard, a
simpleton." Twenty years later he came to be portrayed "as a great strate-
gist and . . . [was] ascribed an almost decisive role in the victory over Hitler's

Germany"—a development that led Grigorienko to remark on "the rotten-
ness of a system that permits such utter lies."[81]

Recollecting a particularly successful operation during the war led to
reflections that highlight the human capacity to divorce means from ends and
the ease with which empathy can be turned off:

> I walked among the corpses [of German soldiers] and felt noth-
> ing but satisfaction. The thought never entered my mind that
> these were human beings, that they had mothers, wives, and
> children . . . dreams and expectations . . . I did not see the faces
> frozen by horror, torment and pain . . . For me these were name-
> less, faceless units of production . . . as logs would have been to a
> woodcutter. And I felt the same as a woodcutter who had man-
> aged to cut an enormous quantity of wood. I was proud of my-
> self and . . . about what I had accomplished.[82]

But these thoughts apparently came to him many years later; on balance,
World War II helped to restore his faith in the system and Stalin, who became once more the "great infallible leader."[83]

Toward the end of the war the heavy losses depleted the ranks of those
who could be enlisted hence "the lack of manpower was so acute that mo-
bilization became like hunting and trapping, like the work of slave traders
in Africa. Voluntary enlistment was organized in more or less the same way
as a one hundred percent turnout of Soviet citizens at Soviet elections is
organized."[84]

In 1945 he began teaching at the Frunze Academy of Military Science,
an occupation that was to last for 16 years. Later Grigorienko thought that
living with ordinary Soviet people (while teaching at the military academy)
rather than being segregated in a compound for the privileged military men
also contributed to becoming critical of the system: "If I had accepted an
appointment as division commander . . . my wife, children and I would have
gone to a military cantonment where we would have had more than enough
of everything we needed. We would never have known how ordinary Soviet
people were living. The Soviet system was set up so that a man worked only
among people of his particular social group, lived only among them, shopped
only among them, and socialized with no one else."[85]

Learning about anti-Semitism and its official tolerance after World War II was another source of misgivings about the system, and he considered writing a letter to the Central Committee and Stalin himself: "This encounter with anti-semitism dealt a blow to my sociologically naive views . . . Until then the world had seemed simple . . . The worker was the ideal, the repository of the highest morality. The kulak was a beast, an evil-doer . . . The capitalist was a bloodsucker . . . The communist party was the one and only repository of the new morality . . . Even though I witnessed many deviations from these ideal rules, in my heart I was convinced that they were only accidents and that in reality life was the way I wanted it to be."[86]

Grigorienko's *Memoirs* do not make entirely clear when and how Grigorienko lost his ability to rationalize the outrages experienced and silence his moral indignation. But it was the Twentieth Party Congress and its revelations that consolidated the isolated insights and experiences about the moral and institutional failures of the system; it was, as he puts it, "the real turning point in my thinking." He realized at last that the matters that had disturbed him earlier were neither accidental nor isolated. But he resisted even the revelations of the Congress: "I was horrified and revolted, but my party indoctrination was so strong . . . that although I did not argue against the evaluation of events, for a long time I continued to affirm that the Central Committee did not have right to make its accusations public."[87]

Grigorienko's critiques of the system intensified in the post-Stalin period, at a time when great improvements took place. For instance, he admitted that when Stalin devalued the currency in an "openly extortionate" way, he had not protested, but he did protest when Khrushchev did the same. In the same (Khrushchev) period he became disturbed by the government's resistance to innovation, by instances of "inefficiency, illegality, bureaucracy and stupidity," none of which had been in short supply in earlier years. It is likely that he had found all such matters more acceptable under Stalin, when the policies of the system had a more heroic cast, when the ruthlessness appeared to serve lofty goals. In responding to the posthumous revelations of Stalin's abuse of power he was more irritated by the hypocrisy of his successors (who had gone along with abuses while Stalin was alive) than scandalized by the new information. Nonetheless, it was in the years after these revelations that he came to the decision to become an outspoken critic of the system. It was in September 1961 at a district Party conference, at which he was a delegate of the Frunze Academy Party organization, that Grigorienko mounted his first public critique of the system by raising the question of the political-institutional conditions that allowed Stalin's cult of personality to arise and would not preclude the repetition of similar cults in the future. He also said: "I consider that the principal paths along which the development of the personality cult took place were, in the first place, the abolition of the party maximum [income], and that very few people returned to work at production, that they became bureaucrats, that they allowed the struggle for the purity of the ranks of the party to weaken."[88] His words went well beyond the permissible limits of criticism even under Khrushchev, and Grigorienko became increasingly penalized by the authorities, which in turn led to his full-scale assumption of the dissident role. Grigorienko gradually lost his privileges—his job, Party membership, pension, even the opportunity for an occupation commensurate with his training.

Initially as he wrestled with the question of what had gone wrong with the system he "went to Lenin for answers," that is, he reread the major works of Lenin to get to the bottom of the problem. For the first time (apparently after his iconoclastic speech in September), "the idea entered my head that the social structure created in our country was not a socialist one, that the ruling party was not communist." Eventually he found contradictions in Lenin's writings, "things did not seem to 'add up' in Lenin." From then on, his dissident activities took on a desperate and somewhat quixotic character. He decided, for instance, to write lengthy letters to the Central Committee further explaining his position, and he pondered "creating a revolutionary organization whose theoretical basis would be selected opinions and teachings from Lenin." Such actions and attitudes lent, in the Soviet context, a certain plausibility to the official claim that he was deranged and to his detention in a psychiatric hospital for political dissidents.[89]

By the summer of 1963, "having completed . . . [his] ideological and theoretical work," he was fully persuaded of the need "to battle the leadership of the CPSU and not try to propitiate it with loyal requests." In this spirit he began distributing leaflets in Moscow—among other places, at the entrances of the Hammer and Sickle factory. His naivete is further illustrated in his recollection that while being detained and interrogated "I did not restrain myself and set forth everything I thought and dreamed about. I saw my interrogator not as an enemy but as soldier who was sincerely confused and whom I must help to see the truth." One of his interrogators (in the psychiatric hospital) was genuinely incapable of understanding what motivated him: "Dozens of times she asked: 'But just what was it you needed—given your high salary and your special privileges?'"[90] After his stay in a psychoprison he was deprived of his citizenship and exiled. He died in the United States.

The trajectory of Grigorienko's disillusionment was similar to that for other highly placed figures who either defected or chose exile. For much of his life and especially in his youth, he was a dedicated, idealistic supporter of the system and a dutiful professional soldier. This idealism gradually became incompatible with the policies and practices of the system and at last fell apart—or, rather, took a new form, that of public dissent. His account does not make clear which experiences were the most traumatic and decisive in estranging him from the system.

WOLFGANG LEONHARD (B. 1921)

Wolfgang Leonhard was raised largely by the Soviet authorities rather than by parents or other kin; from age fourteen he had an institutionalized upbringing. German by birth, he arrived in the Soviet Union in 1935 at the age of fourteen with his mother, to whom he was deeply attached. She was a German communist who was escaping to the Soviet Union from Hitler's Germany. Like many such refugees, she was dispatched to a Soviet labor camp, where she spent twelve years. Leonhard makes no reference to his father in the autobiographical volume discussed below.

Even while in Germany, Leonhard attended a communist school and belonged to the Communist Party's organization for children. After his mother's arrest he was taken care of by the Soviet state and trained to be a Party functionary. In 1945, at the age of twenty-four, he was the youngest member of the first group of German émigré communists (led by Walter Ulbricht) sent back to East Germany from the Soviet Union with the explicit purpose of establishing a pro-Soviet regime. In 1949 he defected to Yugoslavia, via Prague. Eventually he found his way to West Germany.

Leonhard used to make a sharp distinction between the theories of

Marxism-Leninism and the practices of the Soviet system; he was above all a critic of Stalinism and believed that "the real communists are those who are fighting against subjection to the Soviet Union";[91] he counted himself among them. At the time of his break he was still searching for a socialist system closer to the original ideals and theories. He defected as a committed Marxist-Leninist and felt at the time that he was choosing a more authentic socialist system, Tito's, over one that had betrayed the socialist ideals, the Soviet Union.

Leonhard's case is one of the best examples of the prolonged survival of commitment and disciplined loyalty in the face of doubt and adversity—adversity that included the arrest of his mother when he was fourteen. He was among those who knew the morally problematic features of the system they served. He and others like him remained loyal because of a core belief that somehow the fundamentals or essentials of the system—the key values, animating beliefs, and validating intentions—remained intact despite the various departures from the ideals, justifying the ethical-moral compromises made and the distasteful means used to attain the worthwhile goals.[92] Moreover, there are always greater evils elsewhere, in past history, or in the contemporary world, or in one's mind, which puts the evils of the system, here and now, in the proper perspective and makes them tolerable up to a point. Even the children whose parents had been arrested learned this reasoning:

> Each of us knew from the first that his mother or father was innocent of the charges. But our Soviet indoctrination had progressed so far that we did not base our judgment on the fate of individuals, even when those individuals were our parents . . . Not one of the ten or so of us [who were together in the Children's Home for German and Austrian children] whose parents had been arrested allowed this cruel personal blow to lead us directly into opposition against the system. We instinctively recoiled from the thought that what was happening . . . was in diametrical opposition to our Socialist ideals. We still went on trying to convince ourselves that what was happening was no more than an exaggeration of measures which were in themselves both necessary and justified.

Or, as one of them put it at the time: "This is certainly very unpleasant for the individuals, but looked at it from the standpoint of principle, it is justified, considering that what is at stake is to preserve the only Socialist state in the world." Given this attitude toward their own parents, it is not surprising that they could find justification for the mistreatment of the multitude of strangers during the Purges: "To many of us, these events had the appearance of historical necessity—perhaps serving purposes which were unknown to us, but which were so important that they could not be sacrificed by those in positions of higher authority."[93] Here we find familiar echoes of the attitude of the religious believer who disclaims the capacity to understand divine purpose and dispensation when confronted with troubling or disastrous experiences.

Leonhard repeatedly tries to explain his attitudes at the time: "A Western reader may possibly find this peculiar. My mother had been arrested, I had witnessed the arrest of my teachers and friends, and . . . I had long ago realized that reality in the Soviet Union was completely different from the picture presented in Pravda. But somehow I dissociated these things, and even my personal impressions and experiences, from my fundamental political conviction."[94]

As a teenager (and later as an adult), Leonhard often felt critical of "everyday events and experiences" while regarding "the great Party line" as correct. The attitude persisted until his defection. His recollections illuminate with exceptional clarity how a person can live with unanswered questions for many years without allowing them to undermine the fundamentals of a belief system or interfere with the political roles he played. Undoubtedly the training he received in the various Soviet institutions made it easier to compartmentalize and contain the questions and contradictions he observed: "We learned to form radically divergent judgments on developments and phenomena . . . which at first sight appeared similar. All depended on whether the context was capitalist or Soviet society.[95] . . . A rise in the price of food in capitalist countries was assessed as 'fresh evidence of the intensified exploitation of workers' but a rise in the price of food in the Soviet Union was an 'important economic contribution to the construction of Socialism.' Dilapidated housing in the West was . . . 'proof of the miserable standard of living of the workers' but dilapidated housing in Moscow was a 'relic of the past.' We learned to condemn or approve of any event with-out hesitation by observing where it had taken place."[96]

Nonetheless, Leonhard did notice some of the flaws of the system at an early age: "At the age of fourteen I had already experienced the beginning of a gigantic wave of arrests, which separated me from my mother; by the time I was fifteen there had followed the arrest of my teachers . . . the trials, the savage attack on personalities who had been held up to us only a few months before as examples to model ourselves on. At the age of sixteen I had witnessed the arrest of a pupil in the dormitory of our Children's Home."[97]

It may well be that for Leonhard and the other youths it was the arrest of their parents, the only people close to them in a strange country, that made them all the more dependent on the authorities, on the "mothering" of the Party, whose policies therefore had to be defined as sacrosanct, or at least reasonable. They were not in a position to bite the hand that fed them both literally and figuratively.

Also important for understanding Leonhard's attitude is that it was a time when the unusual and horrific became mundane and ordinary. He writes: "I no longer found it extraordinary when I visited a friend to find the door sealed, or another family installed since my last visit . . . Only a few years before, the idea of being under arrest had meant something exceptional and terrible. Now it was commonplace. Almost every day on my short journey to school, I used to see the familiar green lorry carrying away those who had been arrested."

Nonetheless, these events and experiences implanted the first seeds of doubt: "They had somewhat shaken my faith and diminished my enthusi-asm, but had no yet brought my inner self to the point of rupture with the system. These were my first serious doubts, but my breach . . . had to wait more than another ten years."[98] Later, while a student at the Moscow Acad-emy of Foreign Languages, he learned that one of his fellow students whom he liked was an informer." His response was typical of that period in his life: "An uneasy feeling came over me. Every single political statement, however trivial, was perhaps being taken down in writing and sent in a weekly report to the NKVD. I was myself not opposed to the system, but did I not occa-sionally say something which did not exactly correspond to the party line? . . . I resolved to be even more cautious . . . about keeping to the party line in any political conversation and to get away from political subjects as quickly as possible."[99]

The abandonment of belief and the political system at the time was not a realistic option for those in the political elite or in training to become its members; they had little choice but to live with their doubts until and unless exceptional circumstances allowed them to physically remove themselves from the system. This was especially true for Leonhard, homeless and, for all practical purposes, orphaned.

Leonhard recalls another occasion that raised questions in his mind: his first experience of criticism–self-criticism in the Comintern school that he attended during World War II.[100] He was accused (on the basis of trivial incidents) of "arrogant personal opinions," individualism, and frivolousness (he had made remarks about some pretty girls). Although the inquisitorial proceedings made him feel guilty (and also revealed how carefully his behavior had been monitored), they also raised new doubts: "Without any intention on my part, my thoughts went further: . . . Was it really necessary to use such methods to train party officials? . . . Would it not have been possible to do it differently and give me some friendly advice from time to time? I recoiled from my own thoughts but it was now impossible to suppress them . . . I made up my mind in the future to be much more cautious in what I said . . . I would think out every sentence and every word before I uttered it. But again there came doubt. Must it be so?"

At the time and for years to come, Leonhard could still retreat to a position that allowed the recognition of flaws to be balanced against loyalty to the fundamentals: "I still believed firmly that Socialism had been realized in the Soviet Union, and that such of its manifestations as were unattractive to me personally were not the result of the system, but were explicable by the fact that it was in such a backward country . . . that the Socialist order had first been established. I already saw these . . . defects quite clearly, but I did not yet see that they were linked . . . To me, they were still lapses by local officials: the childhood diseases of a new society."[101] This was precisely what Arthur Koestler calls "the doctrine of unshaken foundations."[102] But these foundations cracked after many years of intense regimentation, thought control, and suppression of spontaneity in personal relations, as Leonhard experienced at the Comintern school and elsewhere.

The many shifts and inconsistencies in the Party line also played a part in undermining belief. Leonhard lived during the Purges, when old and revered Bolsheviks and revolutionaries were suddenly declared spies and traitors and vilified accordingly. He saw the abrupt shift from antifascist policies to a close alliance with Nazi Germany in 1939; from the glorification of the Comintern to its unexpected dissolution in 1948; from the promise of a more independent road to socialism for the East European parties after 1945 to a rigid adherence to the Soviet mode. Although each of these shifts was given elaborate justification, they demanded too much suspension of disbelief.

Leonhard's decisive political estrangement occurred after his return to East Germany. He was among other East European communists who had two expectations thwarted. One was that after the war the repression and regimentation in the Soviet Union would be lifted; the second was that in Eastern Europe the building of socialism would be different than in the Soviet Union: more humane and more closely tailored to the traditions and local conditions of the individual countries. Neither of these expectations was met: domestic repression continued in the USSR after the war, even intensified, , as millions of returning soldiers and former prisoners of war were put into camps as unreliable. Nor did the East European countries occupied by the Red Army achieve greater autonomy. Rather, they were forced to imitate slavishly every Soviet social, economic, political, and cultural arrangement and institution, from the design of army uniforms to the style of architecture, the organization of show trials, the setting up of collective farms, and the cult of local leaders in addition to that of Stalin.

It was also upon his return to East Germany that Leonhard's ability to tolerate and rationalize the officially sanctioned inequalities and politically determined privileges came to an end. While in Karaganda (in Central Asia) during the war he was astonished to see poverty that he could not have conceived of earlier, including accommodations consisting of "holes in the ground covered over with cardboard or wood and a layer of earth . . . with a few poles to support the roof." Appalled as he was, he managed to comfort himself "with the thought that these were only relics of the past, inevitable in an industrial town which had developed so quickly, and impossible with the best will to eliminate while the war was on." He was nonetheless struck by the contrast between such dwellings and "the tall office buildings which looked by comparison so splendid in these surroundings." There were also the "reserved" shops, restaurants, and distributors: "Everyone knew . . . that even in times of difficulty such as these . . . every kind of food was to be found in abundance in the 'reserved' restaurants and shops . . . But the 're-served shops' . . . this was a subject about which one did not talk."[103]

The awareness of such privileges grew when he became a member of the nomenklatura upon entering the Comintern school: "This was the pe-riod in which I was admitted to the official class . . . I was now released from all the burdensome difficulties and adversities I had experienced before. No more sleepless nights at railway stations . . . No more starvation."

These privileges, though welcome at the time, were not as important in cementing his loyalties as was the trust that the system seemed to place in him. The sense of becoming gradually initiated into an esoteric political environ-ment and the corresponding sense of belonging were the most important: "This gradual division between those who knew nothing, those who knew more, and those who knew a great deal, with the corresponding careful gra-dation of the doses in which information was given to the population, was an important and distinctive feature of the Stalinist system. Thanks to these gradations, being well informed gave one the feeling of 'belonging.'"[104]

Becoming, while at the Comintern school, a recipient of the secret in-formation bulletins that incorporated Western sources was proof of such belonging: "I remember very well the feelings with which I held one of these secret information bulletins in my hands for the first time. There was a sense of gratitude for the confidence placed in me and a sense of pride at being one of those officials who were sufficiently mature politically to be trusted with the knowledge of other points of views."[105]

During his years in East Germany a number of factors converged to un-dermine these attitudes and precipitate his break with the system. Upon ar-riving he learned from ordinary Germans about the atrocities committed by the Soviet troops, their mistreatment of the civilians, the widespread rape of women ("It was a story which I was to hear repeated in dozens and hundreds of different versions and variants . . . Could such things have really happened? I was shaken but I firmly believed that these could only be regrettable isolated cases.") He witnessed the refusal of Walter Ulbricht to discuss the problem of the women who had been raped and impregenated by Soviet soldiers and who were seeking abortions; this was a matter of profound indifference to the leadership. It also made a poor impression on him that hunting down the remaining Trotskyites appeared to be an urgent task of the Soviet occupiers and their German allies: "If anyone had to be ferreted out I would have preferred it to be Nazi leaders rather than Trotskyites."[106]

It became clear that the East European communist states, including East Germany, were not to be significantly different from the Soviet Union—his hopes for a more humane and independent socialist system were unsupported. There was one apparent exception: Tito's Yugoslavia. The Soviet condemnation of Yugoslavia in 1948 made it clear that Stalin would not tolerate any independence in his empire.

Matters that he had been able to rationalize before now became morally unacceptable, among them the privileges of the nomenklatura and their finely calibrated nature: "One of the outstanding evils . . . was that of the privileges enjoyed by officials. My friends and I who had grown up in the Soviet Union had never known it otherwise and at first we saw no problem . . . It was true that as long ago as 1942 in Karaganda I had thought it not altogether right that there should be such a vast difference in time of war between the great mass of the working class . . . who were, in the literal sense of the word, starving, and a small number of Party officials who never knew what it was to have the least material anxiety; but then it was only the degree of the officials' privileges that I regarded as excessive, not the fact itself. A single event changed my mind."

The incident occurred when he encountered a visiting West German Communist Party official in the Central Committee building. The official was looking for the dining room. Leonhard responded to his inquiry.

"That depends on what sort of ticket you have . . ."

It was Category III—a ticket for the less important members of the staff. I showed him the way.

"But tell me—are the meals different for different members of the staff in the Central Committee?"

"Yes, of course. There are four different kinds of ticket, according to the class of work one is doing . . ."

"Yes, but . . . aren't they all members of the Party?"

"Yes, of course . . ."

He looked at me in astonishment and said: "Different tickets—different meals—and they are all members of the Party!"

He turned and went without another word . . .

For the first time I had an uneasy feeling as I opened the door into the dining room reserved for our category. Here, at a table covered with white cloth, the senior members of staff enjoyed an excellent meal of several courses. Curious, I thought, that this had never struck me before.[107]

After this incident Leonhard also became bothered by the housing privileges of the nomenklatura:

My thoughts turned to the luxurious villas . . . where Pieck, Grotewohl, Ulbricht . . . and the others lived . . . The whole quarter was fenced off . . . exits were guarded by Soviet sentries.

"Well, I agree," I said to one of the senior officials who lived there. "I understand the need for security measures, but do they have to . . . be Soviet soldiers? And of course you need plenty of room to live in; but does it have to be a palatial villa? It is not a question of principle, but at a time when everything is short, preferential treatment may well provoke bitter feelings among the population."

The man I was talking to grew serious.

"I should never have expected such antiquated ideas from you . . . it's nothing but reversion to petit bourgeois egalitarianism. Why shouldn't our leading comrades live in these villas? . . . Sometimes I have the impression that in spite of your responsible position you are something of a starry-eyed revolutionary idealist." . . . I said no more.[108]

None of this should have surprised him. While at the Comintern school in the Soviet Union he observed that "the standard of living of the staff of the Comintern was as discriminatory as their accommodation. All officials who were directly employed in the Comintern took their meals . . . in the office building . . . The most senior officials, apart from living in splendor in the Bashkiria Hotel, also had large parcels . . . brought to their homes . . . packets of food over and above the normal ration. Other members of the Comintern were provided from a 'reserved' shop . . . Thus all Comintern workers were graded according to their political usefulness in a carefully calculated hierarchical system."

At that time Leonhard could digest such matters without strong moral indignation. Years later, these and similar experiences coalesced and obliterated the "fundamentals" of his commitment when it became clear that his vision of an independent road to socialism "free of the features which had so often worried me in the Soviet Union" would not be realized in East Germany.[109]

It was also in East Germany that at last he reunited with his mother, released from Soviet captivity—a matter of incalculable emotional importance, especially since she no longer had even residual commitment to or trust in the Soviet system. Although Leonhard does somewhat play it down, his mother's reappearance must have been a decisive factor in the break. Even her appearance testified to her sufferings: "She had a haggard look and it was easy to see the signs of years of deprivation . . . All through our first conversation I was more and more struck by her bewildered, intimidated air. 'Is that all right? Can I do that? Where might I report to?' she asked anxiously time and again . . . At first we could hardly find a common language, so different had been the twelve years which we had passed, she in a concentration camp, and I in the Komsomol and Party. At first, I sharply rejected the expressions of opposition to the regime which she brought out in our earliest conversation. I was determined in no circumstances to allow my mother's fate to influence my political reasoning."

It took another week for him to confide in her his own misgivings and his support for Yugoslavia in the conflict with the Soviet Union. But mother and son still differed in the origin and extent of their opposition: hers was rooted in her experiences in the camps, in the death and pain of former revolutionaries, in her having witnessed flagrant distortions of the original ideals. She had reached the conclusion that the Soviet Union was not a socialist country. "This was going too far for me at the time. My opposition still turned on the question of an independent road to Socialism and equality among the socialist countries. I was still convinced that the Soviet Union *was* a Socialist country."[110]

The growth of Leonhard's disillusionment was accelerated, possibly even brought to fruition, by the public rebuke that he received while an instructor at the Party school in East Germany on account of his hesitation to fully embrace the Soviet line regarding Yugoslavia. There was the possibility that "further measures would be taken against me."

It should also be noted that in the course of his training as a functionary Leonhard had occasion to read unorthodox and, from the regime's point of view, highly subversive materials, including old Trotskyite newspapers that he found in some Party archives in Karaganda, as well as extracts from Arthur Koestler's "Soviet Myth and Reality" (from his *Yogi and the Commissar*), which made a deep impression on him. He also read the Yugoslav rejoinders to the Soviet accusations. Leonhard writes that it was the realization that "the creation of a Socialist society independent of Moscow" was not in the cards that led most directly to his decision to make the break: "The last link that still bound me to the Party was snapped—the theory of a separate German road to socialism."[111]

As is evident in this statement, being German also loomed large in Leonhard's disaffection from the Soviet Union. His homecoming in 1945 at once raised his expectations, exposed him to a new set of discrepancies between ideals and realities (including the Soviet mistreatment of the German civilians), and probably strengthened his inner resources in more intangible ways: he was now in his own country, speaking his native language, surrounded by other Germans, and reunited with his mother, whose fate had most unequivocally reminded him of the inequities and absurdities of the system.

JAN SEJNA (1927–1997)

Jan Sejna, who defected in 1968, achieved a distinguished career in the Czechoslovak communist political-military hierarchy. Coming from a poor peasant family, he joined the Communist Party as a young man after World War II and rapidly advanced in the hierarchy. As one of the few people in his area with a secondary education, he quickly became district chairman and propagandist for the Communist Youth Organization, later a member of its regional committee and a commissar of the local militia. (Commissars were

military officers in charge of political matters, including political training.)
He "was an enthusiastic supporter of Marxism-Leninism, regularly attended
Party lectures and studied hard to master the theory and doctrine. Soon I
was ready and eager to pass on my knowledge and convert others." In the
years before the Communist Party took over the government in 1948, he was
seeking to widen popular support for the Party. One of his tasks in 1947 "was
to disrupt the meetings of other parties . . . We would pack the hall with our
own supporters and as soon as the speaker opened his mouth we would
shout him down and pelt him with eggs and tomatoes." In 1948, at the age
of twenty-one, he became the District Party Committee's secretary for
agriculture. At that time there were waves of arrests of "bourgeois elements,"
that is, "non-Communists who enjoyed more influence at the local level
than party representatives [did]. My committee had to prepare lists of such
people; they were arrested and held for three or four years without trial in
a prison camp." He participated in these activities

> without a twinge of conscience, for I was a convinced Commu-
> nist and regarded these unfortunates as enemies of the revolu-
> tion. People may understand my attitude if they remember that
> I was born in extreme poverty and . . . always admired my uncle
> and other relatives who had been communists before the war and
> many of whom died in Nazi hands . . . I also attributed our es-
> cape from poverty to the influence of the Communist Party, which
> was now offering me a chance to play a leading part in the com-
> munity's affairs. As I studied Marxism-Leninism, it seemed to
> provide me with the chance of a new life and a new purpose . . .
> And so the Party's cause became my cause, its enemies mine. But
> I like to think that I never wholly lost my humanity, and at least I
> can say that on my way up the Party ladder I trod on no bodies.[112]

There is a discrepancy between the last sentence and one quoted a few lines
above where he reported his committee's involvement in, and his whole-
hearted support for, the arrest and detention of totally innocent people
defined as enemies by the Party.

After being drafted into the army he was appointed company propagandist, because of his Party background, and sent to a school for political

commissars. The transfer to the school for commissars was especially welcome, for he felt that "the School would help to compensate for my lack of formal education."[113] For Sejna, mobility aspirations and dedication to the Party and its political values were intertwined from the beginning of his career. In 1953 he was promoted to lieutenant colonel, and he continued his rise. "At the age of twenty seven I found myself a Colonel, a Commissar and M.P. and a member of the Central Committee of the Czech Communist Party."[114] He became a general at age forty. All over Eastern Europe zealous young people of talent and approved political beliefs were advancing rapidly.

Following the death of Stalin in 1953, Sejna had an opportunity to meet Khrushchev when Khrushchev visited and addressed the Czechoslovak Party Congress. This could have been the beginning of his disaffection from the system. He was favorably impressed by Khrushchev, who was unlike "the typical Soviet bureaucrat"; the speech struck him as "gust of fresh air."[115] At the time, it needs to be pointed out, the Czech communist regime was not anxious to de-Stalinize and was far from receptive to Khrushchev's ideas.

Sejna's reservations about the system were initially mild. He wished, in the spirit of Khrushchev, to see it modernized and somewhat liberalized; he claimed to favor de-Stalinization even before Khrushchev's famous "secret speech" at the Twentieth Soviet Party Congress in 1956. He was impressed by Khrushchev's observation at the same conference that "Socialist ideas . . . can only triumph when the peoples of Eastern Europe eat like the delegates at this Congress." He agreed with Khrushchev that "good party activists" who had been arrested "for no other reason than that the KGB denounced them as traitors" deserved to be released.[116]

It is not clear from these recollections exactly how and when Sejna's reservations about the system began or whether any of them preceded the influence of Khrushchev. Sejna writes that after the secret speech he was among the vocal critics of the Stalinists in the army, especially of Alexei Cepicka, then minister of defense and earlier (during the Czech Purges) minister of justice. He was critical of Cepicka for carrying out "the dirtiest job of all in the period," the Purges, as well as for imposing Soviet military codes on the Czech military. Cepicka also hungered for luxuries and veneration. He was almost a caricature of the power-hungry, ruthless, and corrupt communist official. His wife, Sejna writes, owned seventeen mink coats. On maneuvers, whenever he got out of his car, an enormous red carpet was laid out for him to walk on. At a high-level Party meeting in 1956, Sejna openly criticized him—an unusual step at the time. Given the direction of the political winds, Sejna was rewarded by an appointment as chief of staff to the new minister of defense when Cepicka was removed. In 1956, Sejna's career was still in the ascendant: he became secretary of the Military Committee of the Central Committee.[117]

Sejna's disillusionment had a nationalistic component resulting from witnessing Soviet arrogance: high-ranking Soviet officers and officials were rude and condescending as they instructed and supervised the Czechs in virtually every walk of life in their capacity as "advisers." Sejna recalls: "Even I had no idea of the degree to which the Russians controlled my country until I became Chief of Staff to the Minister of Defense."[118]

He also recognized the proverbial inefficiencies and bureaucratic malfunctioning of the socialist economy. When he was chairman of the Agricultural Committee of the Parliament, he uncovered "wastage . . . [that] would have made Lenin weep." There was the case of a steel foundry for agricultural machinery where no roof was put over the compressors to save money, which resulted in their rusting; he was told that the official concerned acted in accordance with Politburo instructions to save money, and was warned against "intemperate" criticism. Upon discovering "500 brand new balers rotting in a field" Sejna was told by the local chief of agricultural machinery that the balers had not worked to begin with, but the chief had "to accept them under the current Five Year Plan; he was waiting for them to rust a bit more before taking them to the scrapyard." The minister of heavy industry told Sejna that thousands of such machines around the country were not working. Sejna asked, If so, why were they were produced? The answer was, "I have to meet my target under the Five Year Plan." By the early 1960s the country was "choking in bureaucracy because our centralized administration gave powers of decision over the smallest units of production to anonymous Party officials in Prague."[119]

Until 1956 Sejna's commitment and service to the Party seems largely untroubled, although he notes that around 1954, when he was placed on the Central Committee, he learned that "there were two Marxisms: one for the Party leaders . . . the other for the rank and file." What he meant was, as he explained, that the Marxism of the leaders was compatible with "the bourgeois life of enjoyment," that the leaders managed to reconcile their Marxist beliefs with the enjoyment of their numerous privileges. He was especially shocked when in the course of his numerous official visits to the Soviet Union he discovered that the lifestyle of the political and military leaders "was the same as that of the nobility in Tsarist days. I am sure that they treated the poor worse, and spent money with more abandon than in the West. This was a genuine shock to me, for I had always thought that the Soviet leaders lived as simply as the workers."[120]

Probably no official who had defected from any communist country ever failed to register his objections to the unfair material privileges of the power-holders and their untroubled enjoyment of them while the system proclaimed its egalitarian policies. Sejna, like others similarly disenchanted, managed for lengthy periods of time to accept and avail himself of these privileges and the official, insiders' rationalizations to justify them. Indignation over the privileges did not start the process of disillusionment; rather, it emerged after disaffection began for other reasons. Sejna explained his choices after he lost belief in the system:

> Either I could quit, in which case not only would I myself be fin-
> ished but so would my family . . . or I must lead a double life—
> on the surface, the official Party life, but privately the life of a
> pleasure-seeking bourgeois. I chose the second alternative, the
> double life . . .
>
> The further I advanced in the Communist party, the more I
> understood that the Communist system was a self-serving bureau-
> cracy designed to maintain in power a cynical elite. During my
> early years of struggle for the party I firmly believed in Marxism-
> Leninism and closed my eyes to practices which later became
> abhorrent.[121]

It is exactly this ability to close one's eyes to what is morally abhorrent that enabled highly placed supporters of these systems to continue working for them. It was not the loss of innocence or new revelations that led to their breaks with the system; the people here discussed knew what was wrong with the systems but decided to overlook the flaws. The reasons included their and their families' safety and the hope that the flaws would eventually be corrected by the system itself (a more realistic hope after Stalin's death or after Brezhnev's); in other instances, the hope took the form of a residual, if vague, conviction that, despite defects, the system as a whole somehow retained legitimacy, that the whole, in some mysterious way, was different from and superior to the parts that constituted it.

Sejna's innocence, or "rustic naivete," as he put it, survived a number of experiences that could have proved devastating. But in 1955 his beliefs "received the first series of shattering blows." The occasion was his criticism of the closing down of sugar refineries, which forced peasants "to transport their [sugar] beets to distant mills for processing." These peasants were his constituents, for he was at the time a member of Parliament. He was severely reprimanded by a superior: "Your job is not tell the Party what the masses want but to explain the Party's policy to the people." The remark summed up the unshakeable and ingrained elitism of the regime and its functionaries, the serene conviction that the wishes and desires of actually existing human beings were of no consequence or relevance to the historic mission being carried out by the Party. Sejna throughout his career must have encountered that attitude innumerable times, so it is not clear why this particular incident was especially subversive of his idealism.

Among the incidents recalled by Sejna (but evidently morally unproblematic at the time) was the brutal assassination of a Colonel Vasek in 1949 by military counterintelligence. After his murder by beating, a military tribunal sentenced him to death! His wife was told that he had defected to West Germany.[122]

After 1956, experiences and discoveries multiplied which gradually undermined his idealistic support for the system. For example, Sejna as a member of a parliamentary commission charged with overseeing prison conditions was able to learn about the Purges carried out a few years earlier. He also "saw the cream of Czech intelligentsia in the prisons at Jachymov, where they excavated uranium for the Soviet Union, and at Pankrac [a major prison near Prague]." He reports that on these tours of inspection he "found it difficult to talk to the political prisoners in our jails because of my embarrassment at their obvious innocence." Sejna also learned of the conditions that prevailed in the prisons, including torture to induce political prisoners to "confess."[123]

The major, transforming revelations apparently came when Sejna opened the safe of the former defense minister, the aforementioned Cepicka. "What I found in those safes appalled me. They contained a comprehensive record of Cepicka's involvement in the purges as Minister of Justice ... There were hundreds of letters from the condemned, pleading innocence and asking for the death sentence to be commuted. Each one carried the single word 'execute,' initialled by Cepicka. There were also reports from the Secret Police on the execution of priests and Catholics, and lists of victims . . . No details were given of the charges against any of them." He showed these documents to Novotny, head of the Party, who said: "We already have enough trouble explaining the past . . . after that 20th Congress of the Soviet Party. If I have Cepicka put on trial, the process won't stop there; people will blame the Party and start asking who else was responsible. Go back to your office now, and just forget what you've seen." This incident, Sejna writes, "sowed . . . the first seeds of disillusion with the Communist system." The refusal of Novotny to take action against the archvillain Cepicka was particularly disturbing because Novotny was the highest authority figure, a personification of the system; here was evidence that the system was incapable of major reform.[124]

By 1967 signs of dissatisfaction in the country were increasing (leading up to the "Prague Spring" of 1968) and confirmed Sejna's private doubts. At the Congress of Writers in June 1967 the disaffection of Czech intellectuals with the Novotny regime and with Soviet control over the country was unmistakable.[125] In the same year Dubcek emerged as a voice of moderation and reform.

Sejna defected before Dubcek came to power and before his reform movement was crushed in August 1968. Sejna's most immediate motive was the concern for his personal safety. He felt threatened because of his refusal to "yield to Soviet pressure to submit a pro-Novotny resolution from my Committee." He writes: "I first began to think about defecting in the spring of 1967 after the interview . . . I had in Moscow with General Yepishev . . . The meeting confirmed that the Kremlin was totally opposed to any modernization of the Czech Party . . . the Soviet leadership would not deviate from their commitment to the most dogmatic and incompetent cadres in our Party . . . My twenty years in the Party had left me without confidence in the system; I had lost my idealism as well as my faith in the Party's ability to deal with the problems we were facing and I was thoroughly depressed by the dead hand of Soviet influence on our Government and society."[126]

An article in the official army newspaper suggested that the Party committee that Sejna headed undermined the fighting spirit of the army, which "amounted to a charge of treason." He had grounds to suspect that his arrest was imminent. He no longer had any illusions about the outcome of a struggle against a Soviet-supported faction in the Party and the military. Most decisive, he was warned of the impending loss of his parliamentary immunity.[127]

Would Sejna have defected if he hadn't expected to be arrested? It is difficult to balance the personal threat against the more principled sources of his rejection of the system. If Sejna's memoirs correctly describe the sequence of events, he got into personal danger because of a reformist orientation, because of a diminished subservience to Soviet policies and their Czech executors. Besides his Czech nationalism and belated moral revulsion against the Stalinist repression, he also learned in the course of his service of the system that it was incapable of carrying out the idealistic goals that had attracted him to it in his youth.[128]

This sketch of Sejna's ideological transformation would be incomplete without reference to possible family influences. Early in the book he recalls that in the house where he grew up, Stalin's portrait was, after the war, added to those already hanging there: images of Christ, the Madonna, and President Benes.[129] There were also memories of his father's apprehension of the impending collectivization of the land well before it actually occurred.[130] It is possible that the memory of these parental attitudes planted seeds that later came to life, that his later experiences converged with his father's skepticism, which had been brushed aside in his youth.

A number of basic similarities were noted in the accounts of defectors examined above and their professed motives for breaking with the systems which they had served for much of their lives. Each of them accumulated a large store of experiences that were at odds with the ideals and promises of these regimes; each exhausted their capacity to accommodate to these divergences, to rationalize morally repugnant policies and practices. As subsequent chapters will show, in all these respects their experiences and critiques were quite similar to those of other critics who also belonged to elite groups but did not openly break with the system but instead stayed, often in high positions till the very end. The differences between these groups of critics have their roots in belief or disbelief in the reformability of the system, in the degree of personal threat experienced, and in other personal circumstances that hindered or facilitated a decisive break as a matter of both practical opportunity and emotional disposition. But the basic diagnosis of what was wrong with the system was shared by these apparently disparate groups: defectors and functionaries in power.

CHAPTER 3

Soviet Leaders

The Reformers

"We tend to forget that in 1985, no government of a major state appeared to be as firmly in power, its policies as clearly set in their course, as that of the USSR . . . before perestroika [no one] could readily spot those social and economic weaknesses of the system that, within a few years, would contribute to its crash."
ADAM ULAM

"I have sometimes wondered why he [Gorbachev] ever decided to launch the process of change. Was it because he is still relatively young, and he detests the lies and hypocrisy that have almost totally destroyed our society? Was it because he sensed that there was still a chance to make one last effort to break free of the past and become a civilized society? I cannot find an answer to all these questions."
BORIS YELTSIN

Four aspects of political disenchantment are of particular interest. The first is, What originally gave rise to the commitment? Why was the individual in question attracted to the Party and the ideas it sought to realize? Second, what sustained the initial commitment—sometimes in the face of the many discernible contradictions between theory and practice and the unintended consequences of official programs and policies? Third and most important, what began or contributed to the erosion of belief, the inner conflicts, and the ultimate loss of conviction, culminating in a final disillusionment? Finally, especially given the unraveling of communist states, what impact did the inner conflicts and loss of belief have on the day-to-day political performance of the powerholders? How might the conflicts have impaired their capacity to exercise power and oversee society?

None of these questions is easy to answer, especially the last. To argue that the political attitude of leaders contributed to the collapse of the systems they managed must be reconciled with the probability that signs of impending collapse—the growing inefficiency and malfunctioning of the system— led to the attitude changes. But even if this was the case, and undoubtedly it was, the novel element in the situation was the way the leaders responded to the difficulties of the system.

The discussion in this chapter begins with the Soviet leaders, for it was the changes in their attitudes and policies that were the most consequential and started a chain reaction that spread across the globe, leading to the momentous political changes not only in the neighboring Eastern European members of the Socialist Commonwealth but also in several Soviet-supported Third World countries, as well as in left-wing political movements elsewhere. An American student of Third World revolutions, Forrest Colburn, has argued that " there was a sweeping loss of faith throughout Latin America, the Middle East, Africa and Asia in the promise of revolution and in the dominant revolutionary ideology—socialism . . . For revolutionary regimes in the poorer parts of the world, the dissolution of the Soviet Union was a monumental event."[1]

Unlike at other times in Soviet history, the widely recognized deficiencies of the system under Gorbachev did not lead to either their massive denial or renewed waves of political repression, but rather to reforms that finally undid the system as they unintentionally called its foundations into question. During the latter half of the 1980s the difficulties that the system faced led to a new attitude on the part of the leaders and a weakened grasp on power. There was also greater concern with the attitudes of the ruled and their responses to official policy. The new disposition of the leaders and the reforms of the 1980s may require explanations different from those elicited by the reforms in the past.

Because Gorbachev's reforms have often been compared to those of Khrushchev, it should be recalled that Khrushchev's de-Stalinizing policies coincided with his brutal crushing of the Hungarian Revolution in 1956 and the placing of missiles in Cuba in 1962—neither policy a sign of a weakened will to power, or global retrenchment. By contrast, Gorbachev's attempts at domestic reform were accompanied by withdrawal from Afghanistan as well as from Eastern Europe. Khrushchev showed little hesitation about using force to save the empire. Gorbachev belonged to another generation. One of his Western admirers, Archie Brown, believes that "it was Gorbachev's awareness of the importance of means as well as ends in politics that distinguished him from all his Communist predecessors . . . Gorbachev's mindset was far removed from the Bolshevik psychology of *kto kogo* (who will crush whom)."[2]

Before examining the autobiographies it may be prudent to reflect on the uses and reliability of such writings, which, despite their well-known limitations, remain widely used as a source of information about complex political matters. Rather than dismissing them as insufficiently objective, it is well to bear in mind, as Robert Conquest reminds us, that "individual reminiscences must be treated critically—but so must documents."[3] The latter can as readily be falsified as individual recollections, sometimes in more massive and predetermined ways. On the other hand, these two sources of information may also be mutually supportive; for example, the personal reminiscences of Soviet authors about the prison camps were borne out by archival materials that they became available after 1991.

To be sure, few autobiographies *intentionally* reveal the unfavorable traits of their author or dwell on their author's morally questionable actions; all autobiographies are in the broadest sense (and perhaps by definition) self-serving—they seek to vindicate the personal life and accomplishments of the author. Few of them describe shortcomings in order to live up to Orwell's belief that "an autobiography that does not tell something bad about the author cannot be any good."[4] In some autobiographies and memoirs we do find evidence of self-criticism and self-doubt, even self-flagellation, but rarely in abundance.[5] The memoirs of political figures (and show business celebrities) tend to have the least critically self-reflective qualities, and not only in the former Soviet Union. In the case of politicians and other public figures, there is certainly more to explain and vindicate, a greater need to be "self-serving." Nevertheless, the number of favorable references to the self may vary considerably, and the same may be true of the amount of praise lavished on the author by others who are quoted (a device that some autobiographers prefer to outright self-praise). Thus Gorbachev could not resist including in his *Perestroika* (admittedly, not an autobiography) a reference to a worker writing to him from the Yakut Autonomous Republic whose seven-year-old child was in the habit of "yell[ing] to me whenever he sees you on television: 'Daddy come quick. Gorbachev's speaking.'"[6] The memoir of his wife, Raisa, has an abundance of similar flattering references, while Yegor Ligachev is far more sparing with both types of ego massage; Andras Hegedus of Hungary has hardly any such material in his political autobiography (Ligachev and Hegedus are discussed below).

It is possible to detect and minimize the highly subjective element in such writings. Although no methods are foolproof, those available resemble safeguards used to establish the reliability of literary materials as social-historical documents for a better understanding of a period, social institution, or cultural setting. One may rely on less subjective sources of information against which autobiographical assertions can be checked. There is also the matter of psychological plausibility and congruence—to be sure, a far more elusive standard. Still, whatever we know about human nature from personal experience or scholarly research can be used to test autobiographical assertions.

Four groups of Soviet leaders and functionaries may be identified on the basis of their attitude toward political change in the USSR. The first consists of those at the top who wished to reform, improve, or streamline the system while preserving its essential structure—above all, the monopoly of the Party on power. (They were apparently unaware of, or determined to disregard, the incompatibility of major reform with the survival of the system, especially one-party rule.) They retained—to what degree remains a matter of dispute—certain basic or residual beliefs in Marxism-Leninism. Gorbachev is the prime example. It was his predicament—given his commitment to the fundamentals of the system—that, in the words of Zdenek Mlynar, roommate of Gorbachev's at Moscow University, he had to manage to criticize "the past sixty years of the Soviet system while avoiding the impression that those sixty years were a catastrophe and that the overall balance is a purely negative one."[7] Alexander Yakovlev straddles this category and the next one, for he became progressively more estranged from the system and even its ideals, as will be discussed below.

In the second group we find those who had undergone a genuine and sweeping change of attitude. Their disillusionment with past political practices was profound and uncompromising, and they wished to create an entirely new system modeled largely on Western political and economic arrangements. Boris Yeltsin is the major examplar of these attitudes;[8] so is Yegor Gaidar, who was briefly prime minister under Yeltsin.

Both groups found the system troubled, both were aware of its defects and liabilities, but they drew different conclusions, more far-reaching and uncompromising in the case of Yeltsin than in the case of Gorbachev. It was said of Yeltsin that he "had what Gorbachev didn't, a visceral feel for the politics of the new era. He was surely right, instinctively right, that working within the system was a dead end."[9]

In the third group are functionaries of varying importance who opportunistically served the system till the last moment but were also willing to accommodate to, or cautiously support, reformist policies. Georgi Arbatov is a fine specimen in this group. He is also among those who retroactively identified himself as a closet dissenter at the heart of the system, trying to change it from the inside. In a study of the Soviet intelligentsia, Arbatov was described by the Soviet émigré author as one of those who "have tried to refurbish their past and find actions to help present themselves in a tolerable light."[10] Arbatov was a public figure of great visibility, and his behavior did not bear out his own retroactive reassessments. Dobrynin too belongs to this group, although he was more open about his fondness for the Soviet empire, which provided him with excellent employment.

A fourth group of apparatchiki were opposed to *major* reform, foreseeing—quite correctly, as it turned out—that tinkering with the structure would lead to its collapse. They would have agreed with Yuri Orlov, the dissident, "that not even a single brick could be pulled from the Leninist-Stalinist structure without bringing the whole structure down."[11] Besides Yegor Ligachev, those who sought to oust Gorbachev in the summer of 1991 obviously belong to this group, as does—outside the Soviet Union—Eric Honecker, former head of East Germany. One may add the Ceauscescus of Romania, Fidel Castro, and the leaders of North Korea and, to a lesser degree, those of Vietnam. All of them resisted the kind of reforms associated with both glasnost and perestroika, especially the former.

Those in the first two groups contributed the most, wittingly and unwittingly, to the disintegration of the system. It is for that reason that an examination of the political beliefs and attitudes of Gorbachev, Yeltsin, Shevardnadze, and Yakovlev, the foremost reformers, will yield much information helpful for understanding the unraveling of the Soviet system.

There is an interesting and puzzling similarity between the lives of most of those alluded to so far and others noted below: most of them had some personal experience or knowledge, either as children, young adults, or adults, of the repressiveness of the Soviet system which sometimes had a direct impact on their own family. They include Arbatov, Vadim Bakatin (last head of the KGB),[12] Mikhail Gorbachev,[13] Raisa Gorbachev, Ligachev, Molotov, Shevardnadze, Dmitri Volkogonov,[14] Yakovlev, Yeltsin. The East European leaders and functionaries who had corresponding experiences include Alexander Dubcek, Andras Hegedus, Janos Kadar, Gyorgy Aczel (the cultural commissar under Kadar),[15] former General Jaruzelski of Poland, and Marshal Rokossovsky.[16] Molotov's lifelong loyalty to Stalin was unshaken by the detention and exile of his wife;[17] Kalinin's wife (he was the figurehead president of the Soviet Union from 1938 till 1946) was imprisoned for seven years.[18] Leonid Brezhnev had a "narrow escape from the NKVD" in the fall of 1937.[19]

Pavel Sudoplatov, head of the KGB task force for spying and assassinations, writes that in 1938 both he and his wife (also a high-ranking KGB official) "feared for our lives and faced the threat of being exterminated by our own system. At that time I began to think about the system, which sacrificed those devoted to its service. I accepted the brutality and stern order that characterized our centralized society; it appeared to be the only method of preserving the country when it was surrounded by German, Polish and Japanese enemies."[20]

How was it possible that despite such experiences, often acquired during their formative years, these individuals ended up as pivotal supporters, even leaders of the regime, members of its political elite? Could they have been genuine believers in the rectitude of the system given their personal experiences of terror under Stalin? Sudoplatov gave one answer: it was "the times" in which he lived that made him accept the personal danger and allowed him to regard the threats to his own security as a somewhat unfortunate by-product of historical circumstances. As will be shown later, a greatly expanded notion of collective self-defense goes a long way toward explaining how so many succeeded in rationalizing the use of morally questionable means by the regime or themselves.

Ernest Gellner offered another suggestion or hint as to the peculiar but highly functional way in which "fear and faith" combined to keep the system in place: "Both fear and faith were present and . . . both were indispensable. Fear may have actually confirmed faith: there is a story about a Renaissance visitor to Rome, who came back from the holy city convinced of the truth of Catholicism. He argued thus: nothing but divine favor could explain the survival of an institution quite as rotten as this. Similarly, I suspect that the faith of many was sustained under Stalinism by an analogous reflection: nothing other than the truth of Marxism could account for a terror of such unique scale, pervasiveness and horror."[21]

To amplify the point, it may well be that the scale of suffering was such that many people experiencing it could not bring themselves to conclude that it could be wholly meaningless and purposeless. In such fashion, the immense deprivations and sufferings that the systems inflicted—from the Civil War to forced industrialization, collectivization, the Purges, and the ruthless conduct of World War II, unsparing of the human resources of the nation— became a peculiar source of its legitimacy, both for many ordinary citizens and for the higher-ups.

How did these individuals adapt to the system, let alone develop a strong political commitment to it? Is it possible to become idealistically attached to a political system that threatens one's family and friends and perhaps one's personal well-being as well? Can people develop and maintain genuine political-ideological commitment under such circumstances? Is it possible that this relation to the system was, at least in some instances, similar to what psychologists have designated identification with the aggressor, found among inmates of Nazi concentration camps and among hostages and kidnapping victims in more recent times?

More plausibly, the commitment to the system in many instances amounted to staying out of harm's way; it was part of a quest for personal security combined with upward mobility that over the years and decades became transformed into a taken-for-granted loyalty.

MIKHAIL GORBACHEV (B. 1931)

Few would dispute Zhores Medvedev's proposition that "the Gorbachev succession marks the appearance of a new political generation which differs from the old guard in style, knowledge and historical vision."[22] On the other hand, there is disagreement about Gorbachev's formative early experiences and their long-term impact. Was the deportation of the Kalmuks from Gorbachev's region (of which he must have heard as a child) an event of some importance?[23] What of the imprisonment of family members? Gorbachev disclosed in 1990 that in 1933 his paternal grandfather had been arrested for "failing to fulfill the plan for sowing grain."[24] According to an old friend quoted in one of his biographies, Gorbachev "grew up in the years 1937 and 1938. Although he was still a young child, he saw what was happening to the people around him. To the simple, honest people, who had made the Revolution . . . They had all suffered, though they were innocent." But the biographer himself thought that "it is questionable whether the young . . . Gorbachev, even at the time when he came to Moscow as a student, could have had an idea of what really happened in the time of collectivization and the political purges." The biographer speculates: "Mikhail Gorbachev was a boy when his native village was collectivized, and a little boy when the waves of arrests during the purges swept the land. He must have experienced the atmosphere of oppression and silence at home . . . Perhaps he noticed that his relatives and neighbors were living a kind of double life: public enthusiasm and agreement, and private fear."[25] In a similar spirit Medvedev observes that "Russian rural families have strong links. Their children know the tragedies and problems suffered by their native villages."[26]

After his loss of power Gorbachev ceased to be reticent about these experiences: "It was then that I experienced my first real trauma—when they arrested my grandfather. They took him away in the middle of the night . . . I remember how after Grandfather's arrest our neighbors began shunning our house as if it were plague-stricken. Only at night would some close relative venture to drop by. Even the boys from the neighborhood avoided me . . . All of this was a great shock to me and has remained engraved in my memory ever since."[27] Gorbachev's wife had a similar experience: "Raisa was three when her father was arrested and banished to a prison camp. His offense: speaking on the dire economic and political consequences of collectivization."[28] Nonetheless, she too turned out to be a believer in socialism. Gorbachev married a woman of impeccable political credentials (a teacher of Marxism-Leninism) and apparent ideological convictions. Nobody was compelled even in the Soviet Union to choose such an occupation; even those seeking to live in peace with the system had other avenues for building a career. According to an American academic who read her dissertation: "[She] writes in a decidedly dogmatic and didactic fashion. She wants to prove that the standard of living of the Russian peasant rose constantly since 1917. She mentions in passing collectivization, but does not write a word about Stalin . . . She is undoubtedly ideologically biased . . . she advocates a switch from religious ceremonies to more 'enlightened ones.'"[29]

Boldin also observed that "Raisa's views were those of a dedicated Communist; in fact she frequently upheld her convictions in private and public. She taught hundreds of students in the same spirit, instilling in them a sense of loyalty to Marxism-Leninism. As Gorbachev used to say about his family . . . Raisa was the head of 'our family party cell.'"[30]

It was after the 1991 coup that Gorbachev made an effort to find the records about his grandfather's case, although he could have gained access to them when he occupied various high positions in the Party. David Remnick offers an explanation of Gorbachev's ability to prevent these facts from interfering with his political commitments and obligations: "It was as if Gorbachev's family was a paradigm of the Stalin era: one grandfather was punished for failing to fulfill the absurd and brutal demands of collectivization; the other, a leader of collectivization, suffered for no other reason than . . . Stalin's scheme of organized, random terror . . . Gorbachev made plain that he himself was the leader of a particular generation with a particular vision: a man of late middle age, born into a system that betrayed his family, but one who is convinced nevertheless that 'genuine' socialism was possible . . . The tragedy of the Stalin era and the farce of the Brezhnev period represented for Gorbachev not the failure of ideology, but rather its perversion."[31]

In taking this position Gorbachev (who "could never distance himself enough from a discredited ideology")[32] resembled those Western intellectuals who, following the collapse of Soviet communism, continued to insist that nothing was wrong with the theory and that the defunct system was in no way socialist; hence its fall could not discredit socialist ideals. This position was, it would seem, easier to maintain in Western countries than in those where serious attempts were made to implement at least some of the ideals of Marxism.

Perhaps it is more important for an understanding of Gorbachev's political evolution to know that "he knew the true situation of the kolkhoz farmers, and how it compared to the propagandistic picture drawn in Moscow of socialist country life."[33] Zdenek Mlynar, too, indicated that Gorbachev as a student at the university had personal knowledge of the sorry state of the collective farms.[34] If so, it may well be that the theory-practice gap, glimpsed early in life and widened and deepened after Khrushchev's revelations in 1956, became an underlying factor in Gorbachev's political transformation and desire for radical reform.

His way of life as a young functionary in Stavropol could also have contributed to a more realistic view of the shortcomings of the system: "Our communal apartment was shared by a welder, a retired colonel, a mechanic . . . and their families; an alcoholic bachelor with his mother; and four single women."[35] Nonetheless, Gorbachev admits in his memoirs that he was among the students at Moscow University who, when Stalin died, perceived his death "as a tragedy for the country." He quotes similar feelings expressed at the time by none other than Andrei Sakharov![36]

In 1986 and 1987 Gorbachev sketched the dimensions of the changes (perestroika) he was seeking: "Restructuring is a serious business. Not long ago it was thought that only the upper reaches of society were involved . . . that a change in the leaders' behavior had to take place. Now people know that all of society, each individual citizen, has to be restructured . . . We envisage really revolutionary changes in society in all sectors. Such a radical step is inevitable, simply because there is no other way." But he also introduced (in 1986) some crucial qualifications: "We must not search for answers . . . outside the confines of socialism but within our system . . . This is not to everyone's liking in the West. They always hope over there for signs that socialism will be relinquished, that we bow to capitalism and adopt its ways . . . All solutions of the new problems have to be found within socialism, not outside."[37]

This remained his position to the very end, when he objected to the dissolution of the Party by Yeltsin—a measure he obviously found incompatible with the preservation of socialism. The more puzzling question is what exactly he meant by socialism besides the continued, if more permissive, rule by the Party. According to Archie Brown, as time went by, his conceptions of socialism increasingly resembled Western-style social democracy.[38]

There is little doubt that after 1985 Gorbachev was committed to substantial reform. Less clear are his initial motives and expectations, how completely he grasped the flaws of the system and how far he wanted the changes to go. Much that is contradictory in his attitudes could be explained by what Robert Kaiser has called the unresolved struggle of being both an apparatchik and a reformer. Kaiser believes that Gorbachev changed "in less than six years from a modest reformer to the revolutionary leader who ended seventy-three years of Communist rule in Russia."[39] Archie Brown was convinced that Gorbachev "had consciously rejected from the earliest days of his leadership the *psychology* of Bolshevism—hostility to all compromise and coalition-building except as a temporary expedient; the view that the end justifies the means."[40]

By contrast, Martin Malia believes that "if by perestroika's success we mean effecting a transition from a Party-state and a command economy to democracy and the market . . . such a transition is not the aim of Gorbachev's perestroika; its aim, rather, is to salvage what can be saved of the existing system by halfway-house concessions to economic and human reality."[41]

For Anatoly Sobchak, an outspoken critic of the regime who became mayor of Leningrad, Gorbachev was "a mystery . . . He never bares himself to the person he is talking to, and there has never been an occasion when any one of my fellow deputies to the Supreme Soviet could say: I know what Gorbachev is really like."[42]

Initially Gorbachev rejected the Western view that perestroika "has been necessitated by the disastrous state of the Soviet economy and that it signifies disenchantment with socialism and a crisis for its ideals and goals."[43] In fact, the foregoing was a correct summary of the roots of perestroika, confirmed by subsequent events. In 1987 Gorbachev still felt compelled to argue that "of course perestroika has been largely stimulated by our dissatisfaction with the way things have been going in our country in recent years. But it has to a far greater extent been prompted by an awareness that *the potential of socialism had been underutilized* . . . We have a sound material foundation, a wealth of experience and a broad world outlook with which to perfect our society purposefully and continuously" (my emphasis).[44] The wording suggests that he saw the situation as far from critical, as merely a matter of making better use of potential. Or, as Richard Pipes has suggested, Gorbachev portrayed the system (mostly for the benefit of foreign audiences) "as fundamentally sound and merely fatigued."[45] By contrast, in his *Memoirs* there is full awareness that the flaws of the system were fundamental and reach back to the very beginning. They included "the inability of the Bolsheviks to change their ways . . . [they] continued to act like wartime commissars . . . Command methods, suppression of heterodoxy and repression, which at first were said to be due to the peculiar conditions of capitalist encirclement, became an integral part of the system. A totalitarian regime developed."[46]

Gorbachev's limitations as a reformer were noted by Arkady Shevchenko, the high-ranking defector discussed earlier: "Mikhail Gorbachev is . . . a product of the Soviet system . . . of the party apparatus. One would be absolutely wrong to entertain the idea that he would want to alter substantially the existing system."[47] Admittedly, this was written in 1985, before Gorbachev's rise to power and before his initiatives gathered speed. A Soviet émigré social scientist, Dmitri Simes, has a similar view, which benefited from a longer perspective. In 1995 he wrote: "As great reformers as they were, Gorbachev and Yakovlev were appallingly blind about the very nature of the system that produced them and which . . . they were determined to reform. They failed to see that communist dogma, totalitarian controls, and a police state were not aberrations but the true foundations of the regime. Once these foundations were shattered, the regime was unable to rule." And, according to a Hungarian commentator, Gorbachev "believed till the end in socialism and its reformability and failed to realize that as the system weakened as a military superpower, it was the end . . . After the 17 years of stagnation under Brezhnev . . . he believed that all that was required was to start the engine of economic growth . . . to solve all the problems of the economy. It was a typical Bolshevik, voluntaristic reflex."[48]

In 1988, during the heyday of perestroika, George Kennan also pointed out that Gorbachev was "a true believer—in a dream that he calls socialism. One may think as one likes about the realism of the dream. The faith itself is evident."[49] Against such assessments Archie Brown has argued (somewhat implausibly) that Gorbachev was at first constrained to present his far-reaching plans seeking fundamental changes "as a return to Leninist first principles if they were to get off the ground in the real world of Soviet politics."[50]

The sources (as distinct from the manifestations) of the problems to which glasnost and perestroika were the responses remain elusive in Gorbachev's initial rendering:

> In the latter half of the seventies . . . the country began to lose momentum. Economic failures became more frequent . . . unresolved problems began to multiply. Elements of what we call stagnation and other phenomena alien to socialism began to appear . . . An absurd situation was developing. The Soviet Union, the world's biggest producer of steel, raw materials, fuel and energy, has shortfalls in them due to wasteful or inefficient use. One of the biggest producers of grain . . . nevertheless has to buy millions of tons . . . We have the largest number of doctors and hospital beds per thousand of the population and at the same time there are glaring shortcomings in our health services . . .
>
> . . . side by side with . . . scientific and technological triumphs is an obvious lack of efficiency in using scientific achievements for economic needs . . . A gradual erosion of the ideological and moral values of our people began . . .
>
> Propaganda of success—real or imagined—was gaining the upper hand. Eulogizing and servility were encouraged; the needs and opinions of ordinary working people . . . were ignored . . . a breach has formed between word and deed, which bred public passivity and disbelief in the slogans being proclaimed . . . alcoholism, drug addiction and crime were growing.[51]

In pointing to the breach between word and deed Gorbachev puts his finger on the key weakness of the Soviet system, one however that did not originate in the latter half of the seventies but much earlier. In any event, he was well aware of the widening gap between ideals and actualities: "There was a growing awareness that things could not go on like this much longer. Perplexity and indignation welled up that the great values born of the October Revolution and the heroic struggle for socialism were being trampled underfoot. All honest people saw with bitterness that people were losing interest in social affairs, that labor no longer had its respectable status, that people, especially the young, were after profit at all cost."

These observations are quite different from the earlier, cheerier words about realizing the full potential of socialism. Such swings between fully confronting and denying the crisis presumably had their roots in his clinging to old beliefs and doctrines. If indeed in 1987 he still found "the works of Lenin and his ideals of socialism . . . an inexhaustible source of dialectical creative thought, theoretical wealth and moral sagacity,"[52] then it is not surprising that the causes of the difficulties eluded him. Brown explains such paradoxes by suggesting that "Gorbachev ceased to be a Leninist without consciously rejecting Lenin." As Brown sees it, "Gorbachev was seriously interested in political change as well as economic reform, but . . . in the course of the struggle to introduce it, he came to realize that reform was not enough, and . . . the political system had to be comprehensively transformed."[53]

In weighing these arguments it is important to keep in mind that Gorbachev was in every sense a product and beneficiary of the system, the Party apparatus that he served loyally and apparently without desiring to radically change it. He did not show signs, until embarking on perestroika (when he was well into his fifties), of seriously questioning the system or of having an ideologically unorthodox disposition. Margaret Thatcher recalls that he "insisted on the superiority of the Soviet system. Not only did it produce the highest growth rates, but if I came to the USSR I would see how the Soviet people lived—'joyfully.'"[54]

In 1987 he insisted—in *Kommunist*, the ideological journal of the Party— that "even the grossest mistakes, even the departure from the principles of socialism which have occurred could not deflect our people and our country from the path they entered upon by the choice made in 1917."[55] Did he truly believe this at the time? If so, for how long did he continue to cling to such beliefs?

On the other hand, according to Myron Rush, Gorbachev was precisely the kind of leader the Soviet system of cadre selection meant to keep from rising to the top. Rush believes that Gorbachev succeeded in rising because he concealed from his fellow functionaries "his true beliefs and character. In choosing him "his supporters did not knowingly choose the revolutionary course he would follow."[56] According to Archie Brown, "Gorbachev was selected as a modernizer who would give dynamism to Soviet policy, not radically transform it. His own intentions . . . were reformist rather than transformative at the outset."[57] One may add that Gorbachev himself did not know that he would follow such a course, having been pushed by the forces he himself had unleashed in directions he did not anticipate. He described himself as "a product of the nomenklatura and at the same time . . . its gravedigger."[58]

Gorbachev had several unusual attributes that no other Soviet leader before him had had, as Wolfgang Leonhard has pointed out: he was the first leader "not formed by Stalin"; the first "who did not participate in the 'Great Patriotic War'"; and the first who was not an engineer by early training and who had two degrees—one in law, the other in agriculture.[59]

The forces that exerted pressure for policies of reform included the Western support for these measures and the increasing degree to which Gorbachev validated himself and his policies by the responses abroad, often far more positive than those at home. He rapidly endeared himself to Western elites, including intellectuals and the celebrities of the world of entertainment. In 1988, following a reception at the Soviet embassy in Washington attended by carefully chosen celebrities, Joyce Carol Oates wrote: "There was a murmur of excitement as the Gorbachevs were entering the room, and it was as if royalty had appeared in our midst . . . Shaking Mikhail Gorbachev's hand, looking the man in the eye . . . one comes away with the visceral certitude that this is a person of surpassing integrity, a man of utmost sincerity; somewhat larger than life."[60]

Such "visceral certitudes" of Western intellectuals were often manifest in their past assessments of other Soviet leaders as well, but they rarely endured. In characterizing Gorbachev, *People* magazine referred to the "gusting force of his personality," describing him as a man who "spoke a supple language all men could understand"; "misty-eyed, he can sing a haunting song."[61]

According to Valery Boldin, who worked closely with him physically (but joined the attempted coup against him in August 1991), Gorbachev's vanity and thirst for acclaim shaped his behavior. As support for his policies diminished at home but not abroad, he cut back on his domestic but not his foreign travels.[62]

Trips abroad, especially those undertaken early in his career, were important in shaping Gorbachev's view of the world and may well have laid some of the foundations of his reformist impulses. He went on a trip to France in 1966 while he was still based in Stavropol[63] and to Canada in 1983 (when he visited farms). He also visited Italy with a group of Party workers invited by the Italian Communist Party. Gorbachev himself noted later that these trips brought home to him the discrepancy between the images created by Soviet propaganda and the actual nature of Western capitalist countries.[64] His visit to Czechoslovakia after the 1968 invasion had a different impact: "To say that we felt uneasy and downcast would be an understatement. We felt viscerally . . . that this action was indignantly rejected by the people."[65]

Whatever his eventual historical role, Gorbachev's political beliefs had deep roots. He came from a peasant family that supported the system; his maternal grandfather "led the drive for collectivization and became chairman of the Privolno kolkhoz." Both Gorbachev and his father were awarded the Order of the Red Labor Banner in 1949. He joined the Party in 1952 at twenty-one, an age considered young for this honor and at a time when the cult of Stalin was at a new peak, shortly before the "doctors' plot" was unveiled. He had no apparent trouble following the Party line as a Komsomol leader.[66] More than that, according to Zdenek Mlynar, "Gorbachev took Marxism very seriously . . . [he was] convinced that Marxism was the final answer that would change the world."[67]

From an early age Gorbachev positioned himself for a career in the Party apparatus. In the words of his Soviet émigré biographers: "Gorbachev was frenetically active; he was the youngest Party member at the school, Komsomol Secretary of the Law Faculty and a member of the Party Committee of the entire university! . . . Lev Yudovich recalls that Gorbachev was widely resented by his classmates for his participation in the 'anti-cosmopolitanism' campaign."[68] According to a former fellow student, he was immediately noticeable "because he wore a medal—the Order of Labour. That was unusual."[69] The very choice of a career was revealing of his inclinations and was an unlikely preparation for embarking on reform later in life: "The

Moscow School of Law . . . had nothing to do with the law. As Mlynar notes, instead of teaching young people to think in terms of legality, Soviet law schools weaned them away from it. Students were perceived as the future cadres for the punitive organs—above all, State Security."[70]

Subsequently Gorbachev promoted his career by ingratiating himself with those higher up. As a functionary in an area well endowed with spas (Kislovodsk and Piatogorsk), "he made it his duty to greet his colleagues and superiors in person, to supervise their accommodations and see to their recreation, thereby cultivating useful contacts." He selected Mikhail Suslov and Yuri Andropov, during their Stavropol stays, for special treatment. As has been observed: "Gorbachev was lucky with his bailiwick: it included the country's main resort area, with numerous spas and dachas. It was a unique opportunity for a humble Party Secretary to make friends, or even rub shoulders with the country's masters. It was here, playing host to high Kremlin guests, that Gorbachev won his Kremlin patrons: . . . Kulakov, . . . Suslov, and the most important among them, . . . Andropov, then chief of the KGB." Furthermore, "his willingness to go along was rewarded with trust and influence . . . Everyone was his benefactor: Brezhnev, Andropov . . . and even Chernenko."[71]

Gorbachev's efforts to be in the good graces of his superiors were not limited to the activities noted above. He also went out of his way his way to praise Brezhnev's literary accomplishments: "*The Little Land* [Brezhnev's book] . . . shines by its ideological contents and the breadth of the commentaries and judgments expressed by its author, so that it has become a great event in public life. It has found a warm welcome in Soviet hearts . . . workers of Stavropol express their most heartfelt thanks to Leonid Illych Brezhnev for this literary and Party work which describes with great philosophical depth the courses of the heroic deed of our beloved country, its moral and spiritual strength."[72] In Gorbachev's memoirs a far less charitable view of Brezhnev unfolds, including references to his cunning and vindictiveness.[73]

A more charitable interpretation of Gorbachev's rapid rise in the Party hierarchy is offered by Gavril Popov, an economist: "He didn't drink or join in dacha parties. He worked hard . . . and didn't take part in the complicated power intrigues in Moscow . . . he was modest . . . he was a work-horse."[74] This was said with reference to his career in Stavropol.

Gorbachev seriously misread the relation between perestroika and glasnost, that is to say, the reformability of the system and the compatibility of its survival with free public expression. In doing so he might have been influenced by his political conditioning under Khrushchev. According to Peter Reddaway, he believed, like Khrushchev, "that if one trusted the people, loosened political controls, increased incentives, created opportunities for political participation, strove for social justice and conducted a more peaceful foreign policy, the people would be grateful, would work harder . . . would 'make socialism work' rather than challenge it by supporting nationalism, regionalism, anti-Communism or multiparty democracy. Both leaders failed (or did not want) to see that within Soviet society lay the seeds of potential anti-Russian and anti-Communist revolutions."[75]

Gorbachev seemed genuinely unaware of the intensity of the popular cynicism about the system. If so, this too was at least in part a result of having led, for much of his life, the charmed life of the top-level Party functionary, largely isolated from the bleak realities of Soviet life, a circumstance that had broad implications for the stability of the system. A former high-level functionary writes: "A member of a nomenklatura family can spend his life . . . working, resting, eating, shopping, traveling, talking or being ill without ever coming into contact with the Soviet people, whom he is supposed to be serving." They were, as a group, motivated by "the perfectly conscious need . . . to mark themselves off from the rest of humanity and to have dealings with no one outside the narrow circle of their own social class."[76]

Boldin recalls the way the system insulated high-level functionaries, including Gorbachev, from the bleak realities:

> The general secretary wanted to go to the Likachev car factory, a
> local hospital, a school and a store . . . it was not a surprise visit,
> as he had disclosed his intentions to . . . the secretary of the
> Moscow party *gorkom* [district committee]. Everything . . . was
> ready for the general secretary's visit . . . [in the hospital] The
> side-walks, paths and drive to the main entrance got a fresh coat
> of asphalt . . . on the floor we inspected, patients were not al-
> lowed out into corridors . . . As I later found out from members

of Gorbachev's security detail, in the two or three wards he was supposed to enter, the beds were occupied by healthy, well-fed security officers with closely cropped hair, who warmly commended the medical staff and the hospital food while finding it difficult to be precise about their ailments . . . We got the same "Potemkin village" treatment in a few other places too. For example, we were invited, supposedly at random, into the new apartment of an "ordinary worker" who happened to have on hand some excellent hors d'oeuvres.[77]

These incidents are reminiscent of the treatment accorded to distinguished foreign visitors to the Soviet Union. A case in point is Henry Wallace and his entourage. When they visited the Kolyma labor camps in 1944, healthy guards and administrators replaced the far less presentable inmates to meet the vice president and Owen Lattimore.[78] The institutionalization of Potemkin villages for internal purposes was one of the vulnerabilities of the Soviet system, depriving Soviet leaders of a sound grasp of the condition of their society.

Gorbachev did not foresee that glasnost, that is, the greater and growing freedom to criticize the system, would release pent-up passions and hatreds that were not compatible with its continued or apparent legitimacy and, in the end, survival. Gorbachev did not doubt the basic legitimacy of the system, but he did understand many of its specific ailments; he opened the floodgates of criticism on the assumption that unfettered public discussion would infuse Soviet society with new vitality. This was a profound misjudgment based on the underestimation of popular grievances. As it turned out, the public expression of the wide variety of grievances increased the popular awareness of everything that was wrong with the system and further eroded its legitimacy. De Toqueville's observation in a different historical context (the beginning of the French Revolution) is relevant here: "The evil suffered patiently as inevitable seems unendurable as soon as one conceives the idea of escaping from it. All of the abuses that have been removed seem only to delineate better those that remain and to make one's feelings more bitter."[79]

The dynamics of perestroika were probably also similar to what took place in the United States when at long last the sins and evils of racism came to be publicly acknowledged and denounced beginning in the 1960s: "When the oppressors admit their crimes, the oppressed can give full vent to their long repressed rage because now there is a moral consensus between oppressor and oppressed that a wrong was done."[80]

When the new freedom of expression combined with the greatly lessened fear of punishment for nonconformist behavior, it became impossible to make significant improvements in the system and retain its fundamental structures and policies. Yuri Orlov, a dissident Soviet scientist, writes: "What Gorbachev should really have feared was glasnost . . . Not understanding that democracy and freedom of expression cannot be doled out like doses of medicine, Gorbachev got far more than he expected."[81] The Gorbachev reforms were sufficient to deepen public understanding and apprehension of the flaws and injustices of the system but inadequate to remedy them.

An underestimation of the importance of ethnic hostilities and grievances also contributed to Gorbachev's being overtaken by events. Helen Carrere D'Encausse points out that "he lacked an understanding of the phenomenon of the nation. In this sense he was very much heir to Lenin, for whom the nation . . . had only a strategic interest . . . Gorbachev was reduced to passively witnessing nationalist convulsions that threatened everything he did."[82]

Gorbachev's 1987 comments on the subject substantiate this view: "Comrades, we are entitled to say that we have settled the nationalities question. The revolution paved the way for equality of rights among the national groups . . . The friendship among the Soviet peoples is one of the greatest triumphs of the October Revolution . . . this is a unique phenomenon in world history and, for us, one of the fundamental pillars of the power and solidity of the Soviet state."[83] The limitations of Gorbachev's understanding of ethnic-nationality conflicts were also revealed when in 1987 he advised a group of visiting U.S. congressmen "that the United States solve its race problems by setting up separate states for blacks and other minorities." He suggested that, following the Soviet model, the United States should provide autonomous areas not only for blacks but also for Puerto Ricans and even Polish Americans.[84]

Glasnost further undermined the system by gradually opening up virtually everything for public discussion and inspection, thereby depriving it of many secrets that had been critical for its survival. As Jorge Semprun, a former Spanish communist leader, points out, "This love of secrecy . . . revealed something deeper. It stressed the relationship between the secret and the sacred."[85] Since glasnost arrived in the age of television, visual exposure of the defects of the system and the weaknesses of its leaders accelerated and deepened public disillusionment. Ryszard Kapuscinski writes: "Politics at the highest rungs of power was surrounded here for centuries by an airtight, almost mystical secrecy. The rulers decided about the life and death of people, yet these people were never able to see the rulers with their own eyes. And then suddenly, here they are, the rulers, getting angry, their ties askew, waving their arms around, picking their ears . . . Television gave to perestroika a dimension that no other event in the history of the Imperium had ever had."[86] There was a connection between the diminishing areas of secrecy and the shrinking legitimacy of all communist systems.

When, by the beginning of the 1990s, even Lenin ceased to be immune from criticism—up till then he had been the most sacred icon of the system—it was apparent that nothing was left to protect the system against attacks on its legitimacy.

Insofar as Gorbachev believed in the compatibility of a substantial increase in free expression *and* the continued, unquestioned rule of the Party, he ceased being an orthodox Leninist even while he invoked the spirit of Lenin in support of his reforms.[87] Lenin never wavered in his belief that ideas are weapons, and he had no doubt that their free circulation could loosen the grip on power.

In the end, Gorbachev's determination to push ahead with reforms faltered, and he was undermined by indecisiveness. According to one interpretation, "the will of the country's leader was broken by the merciless force of the nomenklatura."[88] The same analyst, Sobchak, also points out that those among Gorbachev's associates more deeply committed to change— such as Yakovlev, Shevardnadze and Bakatin—abandoned him upon realizing that he rejected "the cause he himself had initiated."[89] Roy Medvedev has summed it up best: "The Soviet system was a dam into which Mr Gorbachev punched some holes to make the water flow better . . . But he found out too late [that] the whole dam was rotten. He didn't understand the huge social, political and nationalistic tensions that had built up over the past 70 years."[90]

Whatever the precise nature of Gorbachev's gradual disaffection from the system, he does not fit the pattern of a former member of the ruling elite who at some point in his life becomes estranged and turns passionately against the system that had nurtured him. As Michel Tatu, among others, has noted, "Gorbachev invoked democracy and glasnost not because of any special longing for liberty but because of the imperatives of economic and chronological realities."[91] Less charitably, Boldin writes: "On the one hand, he could see the absurdity of the existing order and strove to transform society. On the other, he was wedded to the old ways of doing business. Despite all his talk about democratization and glasnost, his alter ego continued to be a crafty, cruel, perfidious prototype . . . Suslov."[92]

If Boldin were to be believed, it was Gorbachev's unappealing character traits that explain his behavior better than would a serious reappraisal of the past. Despite his excellent vantage point, Boldin does not shed much light on the mainsprings of Gorbachev's reformist impulses but makes him responsible for the collapse of the system and the associated social-political pathologies. ("Notwithstanding Gorbachev's good intentions . . . his actions led to the fall of a once united state, industrial paralysis, rising crime, a lower birthrate and a lower standard of living.")[93]

By contrast, Charles Fairbanks sees Gorbachev as one among several high-level Party functionaries who sought not merely to make the system more efficient in a technocratic spirit but also to return it to its original, utopian ideals. He writes: "One of the elements that produced the collapse of communism was the return, in Gorbachev, of the enduring revolutionary desire to re-structure society . . . Gorbachev . . . after all the disappointments since 1985, still believed in the imminent arrival of the New Man."[94] Fairbanks perceives Gorbachev as belonging to the group or generation of "those who in their youth still cherished the 'high' Soviet tradition (Marxist-Leninist ideals) in some sense against those who actually held power during the 1970s but represented Marxist-Leninist principles only in a greatly simplified and debased way." He further argues that the social origins of people who made perestroika places them in the regime's aristocracy or elite.[95] This interpretation is quite different from most others, which do not perceive a revolutionary radicalism in Gorbachev's policy of reform but a far more qualified commitment to social change and social justice that vastly expanded despite the intentions of those who initiated it under the pressure of events and the discontent that glasnost released.

Gorbachev's qualified commitment to change may also be inferred from his reluctance to reduce the material privileges of the nomenklatura and his claim that criticism of such privileges amounted to an attack on incentives and rewards that were well deserved: "Are we to stop encouraging a writer, a talented scientist or any other honest, industrious person? Are we to hold up the flag of the bourgeois concept of social justice and abolish pensions, sanatoria and rest homes . . . This would be yielding to petty thinking and our attempt to fight inequality would make us guilty of a far greater kind of social injustice. Comrades, this must become clear—social justice does not mean levelling."[96]

There is a remarkable resemblance between these words and those of Stalin in the early 1930s, when he justified the reintroduction of substantial wage and salary differentials on similar grounds, caricaturing egalitarian aspirations as "petty bourgeois" and conjuring up the notion of harmful "levelling" as alien to human nature and undermining incentives to excel in production. Gorbachev's attitudes toward the privileges of the nomen-klatura contrast sharply with those of Yeltsin—"the only person who dared to touch the taboo," according to Tatu.[97]

Yeltsin's earlier and deeper estrangement from the system might have originated in and remained bolstered by his sense of indignation over the politically based inequalities, whereas this matter did not disturb Gorbachev, nor lead him to raise broader questions about the legitimacy of the system as a whole. According to the Soviet émigré biographers, "To Gorbachev, nothing was ever enough. He was the one to propose that Politburo members' salaries . . . be almost doubled. He expanded . . . dacha construction for the Kremlin elite . . . He built himself a house in the Lenin Hills and a new dacha outside Moscow, renovated Khrushchev's dacha . . . on the Caucasian Black Sea coast, and erected a supermodern palazzo in Foros in the Crimea . . . Gorbachev was the first Kremlin ruler to order his suits from international couturiers."[98]

By contrast, Ruge, his German biographer, writes that as a provincial functionary, Gorbachev "led a comfortable but not luxurious life. His house was simply furnished . . . One thing that struck . . . [his] colleagues was that unlike his predecessor [in Stavropol], he did not have himself driven to his office in a black limousine . . . but walked . . . Even after [he was] promoted to his job in the Central Committee it was said that he lived simply. He didn't offend the apparatus by pointedly refusing official privileges, but took only what was his due as Central Committee Secretary, asking for nothing extra . . . Unlike other functionaries, they [Gorbachev and his wife] had no foreign refrigerator or imported television." But even Ruge notes that after a move to a bigger apartment, he too acquired a Japanese television set and a bath imported from Scandinavia.[99]

Apparently Gorbachev's taste for a more luxurious lifestyle developed gradually. Presumably his wife's tastes were not in sharp contrast with his. An otherwise highly sympathetic biography of Raisa Gorbachev notes that "she does not travel light." On a trip to Cuba in 1989 she was observed to have on her luggage cart "a white hatbox, nine plastic clothes bags, and five leather suitcases."[100] In light of these observations it is noteworthy how much space Raisa Gorbachev devotes in her self-serving autobiography (published before her husband's loss of power) to the hardships and material deprivations of her life with Gorbachev.[101]

None of the accounts or critiques erase the fact that Gorbachev intentionally and unintentionally made a greater contribution to the unraveling of the Soviet system than any other single, identifiable human being.

BORIS YELTSIN (B. 1931)

Yeltsin's frequently expressed indignation over the privileges of the nomenklatura appears genuine and seems to have been an integral part of his struggle against the power of the Party aristocracy and their resistance to change. He writes in his autobiography:

> A few dozen people live in the ideal conditions that are predicted as universal when we have reached the stage of "full communism," while the population as a whole lives in conditions that are barely tolerable.
>
> . . . if you have climbed all the way to the top . . . then it's full

communism! And it turns out that there was no need of the world revolution, maximum labor productivity, and universal harmony in order to have reached that ultimate, blissful state as prophesied by Karl Marx . . .

In using the word "communism" I am not exaggerating . . . "From each according to his abilities, to each according to his needs" . . . Their needs are so great that so far it has only been possible to create real communism for a couple of dozen people . . . Even at my level as a candidate member of the Politburo, my domestic staff consisted of three cooks, three waitresses, a house-maid and a gardener with his own team of assistant gardeners . . .

When I drove up to the dacha for the first time . . . I had been overwhelmed by the size of the place . . . We were shattered by the senselessness of it all . . . Why was it thought necessary to give expression to such an absurd degree, to the fantasies of property, pleasure and megalomania harbored by the party elite? No one . . . could possibly find a use for so many rooms, lavatories, and television sets.

Yeltsin goes on listing the undeserved privileges of the nomenklatura to which he belonged:

When the elite want to go on vacation, they can choose virtually any warm place in the south. There is bound to be a special dacha there . . .

. . . Do you want a new suit? Precisely at the appointed hour comes a discreet knock on the door of your office. In walks a tai-lor, who takes your measurements . . . Soon you have an elegant new suit.

Do you need a present for your wife . . . No problem: You are brought a catalog with a choice of gifts to satisfy even the most sophisticated taste . . . The attitude toward families is most con-siderate. There is a Volga for their use, bearing prestigious Krem-lin license plates, with drivers working in shifts, taking your wife to work or the children to and from the dacha. The big ZiL . . . is reserved for the father of the family.[102]

Evidently Yeltsin's distaste for the perks of high office waned with his becoming the head of the new Russian Republic (in 1991). David Remnick writes that when he returned to power "he commandeered a splendid dacha, organized a regal caravan of limousines and made a public show of his love for that proletarian game, tennis . . . Yeltsin made his name by mocking the privileges of the Party powerful, but he is doing now a fairly good imitation of Louis XIV. Gorbachev's old arrangement of a cortège of three ZiL limousines did not suffice: Yeltsin travels in a fleet of three or four Mercedes-Benz sedans."[103]

Even if this is the case and even if Yeltsin, too, succumbed to the familiar corruptions of power, his earlier struggle against the privileges of the nomenklatura is a matter of historical record, as is his recognition of the vital connection between privilege and support for the system: "Obsequiousness and obedience are rewarded . . . The higher one climbs up the professional ladder, the more comforts surround one, and the harder and more painful it is to lose them. Therefore the more obedient and dependable you become. It has all been most carefully devised."[104]

If Gorbachev had comparable feelings about the inequities of the system and a sense of its moral failings, they found little expression. This is also apparent in his major attempt to confront the defects of the system in his book *Perestroika*.[105]

Indignation over the privileges of the nomenklatura (and inequality in general), was an important component of Yeltsin's disillusionment. It was linked to the recognition that the system betrayed a major claim to its legitimacy, that the politically determined privileges represented a major instance of the theory-practice gap. Because Gorbachev did not appear disturbed by the privileges of the political elite and by the inequalities that the system had institutionalized, his critiques of the Soviet social order were far more qualified and lacked emotion.

Yeltsin believed that perestroika would not have "ground to a halt" if Gorbachev had confronted the issue of elite privilege. This reluctance, according to Yeltsin, had its roots in Gorbachev's predilection for luxurious living, bolstered by the corresponding tastes of his wife. Yeltsin also accused Gorbachev of insensitivity toward the needs of ordinary people, of being out of touch.[106] By contrast, Yeltsin's refusal to accept these privileges as unproblematic allowed him and his family to share some of the experiences of most Soviet people: "When I refused to accept all those things my family immediately encountered exactly the same problems that confront millions of Soviet families."[107] Reportedly, "whether he was the Party Boss of Moscow or Minister of Construction, or Russian President, his wife always shopped in the regular stores, standing in line with the rest of Moscow."[108] If so, this might have been a source of Yeltsin's more heartfelt rejection of the Soviet system; unlike Gorbachev, he knew from personal experience just how bad things were; he knew the specifics of the malfunctioning of the system and its impact on the daily lives of ordinary people.

I quote at length from Yeltsin's autobiography not merely to illustrate what appears to have been genuine indignation on his part but also to recall the privileges that played an important and paradoxical part in both the perpetuation and the demise of the system. On the one hand, as Yeltsin points out, these privileges created a strong commitment on the part of their recipients to support the social order that so generously rewarded them; on the other hand, they also created the seeds of its destruction by replacing ideological commitment with the enjoyment of privilege. Ideally, the combination of ideological commitment *and* the sense of privilege well deserved constituted the joint pillars of loyalty. (For Stalin it was the combination of privilege and fear, fear of losing not only one's privileges but one's life.)

There remains another question, pursued below: At what point and under what circumstances do such privileges cease to constitute sufficient motivation for the unhesitating support of the system, and when, instead, do they become perceived as the root of its corruption and stagnation? It is of interest to note here that the rulers' children did not enter political careers. For example, Anastas Mikoyan's son was an academic. Khrushchev's son became a rocket engineer, as did Beria's. Gromyko's son was a historian and a corresponding member of the Academy of Sciences, heading its African Institute, his daughter an editor. The children of Pavel Sudoplatov, a high-ranking KGB spymaster and organizer of "special tasks," attended the Institute of Foreign Languages.[109] Oleg Kalugin, a former KGB general, was the son of an NKVD captain; he recalled (in a conversation with the author) that his father had not wanted him to follow in his footsteps by joining the KGB.[110]

In this respect, the Soviet political elite resembled first-generation, self-made capitalists whose children would have nothing to do with running the business and instead became professionals, intellectuals, or artists. The Soviet leaders were anxious to transmit their privileged ways of life to their offspring, but not the risky political positions they occupied.

Yeltsin correctly believed that the success of perestroika was severely circumscribed by the attitudes of the nomenklatura. He viewed them as

> people hopelessly tainted with the Brezhnevite philosophy of stagnation, who perceived the power they were given as nothing but a means of achieving personal prosperity and status . . .
>
> I have always understood why many decent people continued to regard me with suspicion even after I had fallen into disfavor. [This was under Gorbachev between 1987 and 1988.] It is because Yeltsin is still seen as a party functionary . . . It is impossible to attain that position, still less to be promoted to the Central Committee, and remain decent, fair, courageous and independent. To make a career in the party—and this belief is universally held by Soviet people—a person must excel at adapting his personality and convictions to whatever is required by the powers that be . . . He must be dogmatic and learn to do or say one thing while thinking something else . . .
>
> . . . An intelligent and independent-minded official of the Central Committee is a combination of words so paradoxical that one's tongue cannot even utter them.[111]

Yeltsin was the apparent exception to these propositions, and it remains to attempt to explain how and why this came about.

The more one learns about Yeltsin and Gorbachev, the clearer it becomes that what separates them, among other things, is the lack of a strong sense of moral indignation in Gorbachev regarding many of the *moral* defects of the system. There was a "feeling of shame that distinguished Yeltsin from his Kremlin colleagues," observe Vladimir Solovyov and Elena Klepikova, Gorbachev's biographers.[112] Even the language that Yeltsin and Gorbachev used to describe the failings of the system were different. As Martin Malia explains, Yeltsin, unlike Gorbachev, "had never been a classic apparatchik . . . he had not made his career entirely in the apparat."[113]

In comparing the careers of these two, it is also of interest that Gorbachev joined the Party in 1952, when Stalinism was still in full bloom, whereas Yeltsin joined almost ten years later, in 1961, during an era of liberalization. Moreover, Yeltsin's teachers recall that he " shunned ideological, doctrine-laden courses . . . using every means available, mostly excusing himself for team practice."[114] And whereas Gorbachev continued, even after the failed coup in the summer of 1991, to express his faith in socialism,[115] Yeltsin was said to be the first Soviet politician to remove Lenin's picture from his office.[116] It was also Yeltsin's important symbolic gesture to remove the honor guard from Lenin's Mausoleum after the failed rebellion in the fall of 1993. None of this is to deny that Gorbachev whatever his underlying motives—initiated an avalanche of changes that in the final analysis led to the destruction of the entire political order.

Having contrasted Gorbachev's and Yeltsin's political attitudes, one must attempt to explain, first, why and how two highly placed functionaries reached the conclusion that the system had to be changed, and, second, why one of them went much further than the other in the pursuit of change.

Personality clearly played a part. Yeltsin was a far more rebellious, combative human being and had shown signs of this from an early age. He notes that, like his father, he was "rough and quick tempered"; in school he was "a ringleader, always devising some mischief." He was denied his graduation certificate because at his graduation ceremony "while about six hundred people were gathered . . . [and] everyone was solemnly handed his or her diploma . . . I suddenly stood up and asked permission to speak . . . Everyone thought that I would simply say a few gracious words . . . But then I declared that our homeroom teacher had no right to teach children because she crippled them mentally and psychologically . . . I described how she mocked her pupils, destroyed their self-confidence and did everything possible to humiliate us . . . There was an uproar. The whole event was ruined."[117]

This was a promising start for a person who apparently had little hesitation in challenging prevailing beliefs and attitudes, was capable of spontaneous moral indignation, and—unlike Gorbachev—did not seek to further his career by winning the approval and support of his superiors. In the end, the young Yeltsin got a commission of inquiry set up. He received his school diploma, and the teacher was fired.

Yeltsin's fearlessness at an early age had other expressions. At age eleven he lost two fingers from playing with hand grenades that he stole from a local ammunition dump. One summer, after ninth grade, he and his friends undertook an expedition to find the source of a nearby river; they ran out of food and survived on mushrooms and berries, got lost, and were rescued after being found unconscious with typhoid fever. After his first year at the Zaporozhe Polytechnic Institute (where he studied construction engineering) he decided to embark on an exploration of the country, traveling "sometimes on the roofs of [railroad] passenger cars," sometimes hitching rides with truck drivers. He survived along the way by doing odd jobs. Upon arriving someplace, he "would sleep in a park or at a railway station before setting off again on the roof of a passenger car." He returned in rags after two months.

Yeltsin was also an avid athlete, volleyball being his avocation, often while in college training six to eight hours a day. After graduation from the Polytechnic he decided "to spend a year learning the twelve basic trades," such as brick laying, concrete making, and carpentry.[118] This was an unusual aspiration in the Soviet Union when social mobility for many people of similar background meant escaping manual labor for good.

Thus in the young Yeltsin there is evidence of adventurousness, curiosity, courage, and abrasiveness combined in a personality apparently disposed to challenge any "establishment." It was not entirely surprising that after becoming a member of Gorbachev's Politburo, Gorbachev "decided to get me out of his hair. I was too obviously a misfit in his otherwise obedient team."

Though a doer rather than a thinker, Yeltsin began to harbor doubts about the system while trying to make it work better in his capacity both as construction boss and as Party secretary of a huge, remote area in the Urals. He recalls: "Toward the end of my decade in office, it seemed we had stretched ourselves to the utmost, that we had tried every possible method, every conceivable way of getting things done. It became more difficult to find new approaches . . . Yet I nevertheless felt—although never admitted to anyone—that my satisfaction in the job was beginning to diminish. Our stock of ideas and methods had been exhausted."

It is likely that such experiences—combined later with the shock of learning more, in Moscow, about the privileged and corrupt ways of the elite—were major factors in his rejection of the system. Undoubtedly his indignation over these inequities was also reinforced by his childhood experiences of acute deprivation, for he came from a poor peasant family: " [We] lived in near poverty, in a small house with one cow. We did have a horse, but when it died, we were left without an animal to pull the plow. In 1935 the situation became more unbearable—even our cow died . . . my father decided to leave the farm and find work on a construction site." There they lived in one of the "communal huts"; six of them and a goat shared a room, sleeping on the floor. They lived in that crowded wooden hut for ten years.[119]

Some of the hardships that befell the family were politically determined and might have had a long-term, delayed effect on his outlook. Yeltsin's grandfather was classified as a kulak: his possessions were confiscated, and he was exiled with his wife at age seventy to the remote northern forest region. Yeltsin's father's brother was (falsely) charged with sabotage and sentenced to forced labor. In 1937 Yeltsin's father was himself arrested and spent several months in jail.[120] Yeltsin does not dwell on these matters in his autobiography.

The historic role of Yeltsin has been tarnished by his performance during his years in power, when he presided over the war in Chechnia, economic chaos, a substantial decline in the standard of living, and the unchecked power of criminal enterprises. During these years physical infirmities and the dynamics of preserving power played an increasing part in his policies at the expense of principle and integrity.

EDUARD SHEVARDNADZE (B. 1928)

Eduard Shevardnadze is another major Soviet leader who apparently underwent fundamental political conversion and became one of those who directly contributed to the unraveling of the system. He had much in common with Gorbachev as regards understanding the flaws of the Soviet system, but he went much further in renouncing the system and the official beliefs. The two leaders "shared frustration with the inefficiencies and corruption of the communist system they served" and "knew that the Soviet Union was desperately weak economically, that its defense burden threatened to overwhelm it"; they both were skeptical about the decline of the United States and capitalism. In their famous conversation in the winter of 1984–1985 at Pitsunda they concluded that "everything has gotten rotten." In the end, unlike Gorbachev, Shevardnadze completely disavowed the ideological heritage. In 1988 Gorbachev still "spoke of class struggle, denounced imperialism . . . and argued that 'the prestige and role of socialism in world development' were on the rise." By contrast, by October 1989 Shevardnadze ceased to make any references to socialism or Marxism-Leninism; he favored "common human values" as a guide to Soviet policy rather than "Leninist norms."[121]

To realize how far Shevardnadze had traveled from his political past it may be recalled how he characterized Leonid Brezhnev in 1981 at a meeting of Georgian Party activists devoted to the Twenty-sixth Party Congress:

> Comrade Brezhnev's speech opened up to the world a broad panorama of the progress of our country in economics, science and culture. It is as if he gathered unto himself all the power of our Party, its unity and solidarity. We could sense in it the sure footstep of our great homeland into the future, to the shining summits of Communism.
>
> Every proposal and every conclusion of Leonid Ilyich's speech, every word resounds with Leninist professionalism, Leninist purposefulness, Leninist objectivity, self-criticism, a truly Leninist, profoundly scholarly approach to an analysis of contemporary life. On the podium stood Leonid Ilyich Brezhnev, so close and dear to each of us.[122]

Ligachev, who provided the above quote (apparently settling old scores with Shevardnadze), averred that he was "amazed at the elasticity of Shevardnadze's political views, his constant readiness to support the leaders in everything and carry out their orders with dispatch."[123] Adam Ulam, with no axe to grind, also notes that "Shevardnadze had been one of the most assiduous eulogists of Brezhnev and had repeatedly gone beyond the call of duty in extolling Georgia's debt and gratitude to the great Russian nation."[124] Shevardnadze certainly knew what political survival and advancement required and, like Gorbachev in similar circumstances, was ready to pay tribute to his superiors in language that was redolent with the spirit of Stalin's cult of personality.

His American biographers observe that his "career in Georgia was filled with contradictions . . . [he] displayed ambitious careerism and crass opportunism . . . He was responsible for the torture and execution of many innocent people including dissidents . . . [his] views at the beginning of his career had been no different from those of most of his generation of Soviet officials and his hands certainly were not clean."[125] If so, he was among the leaders who has undergone the most striking political transformation. As minister of foreign affairs, he directly contributed to the dismantling of the Soviet empire.[126] Although he rightly calls himself "a creature and guardian of the system . . . who had risen to the top by using it,"he was also a major architect of the shrinking of the Soviet empire and an early ally (and later critic) of Gorbachev and supporter of major reforms.[127]

He joined the Communist Party in 1948 at the age of twenty because he was "attracted to political work, since it gave me an opportunity to fulfill my father's commandment to go among people and work for them." In the same vein he remarked that whereas "the one-party power monopoly had destroyed political life in our country," the Komsomol and the Party "remained the only sphere for political self-expression." He considered himself among the minority who were drawn to the Party not "from an instinct of self-preservation or the realization that there was no other way of finding a place in society worthy of their talents"; rather, they were "prompted by their heart and soul."[128] Elsewhere he writes: "I was raised in a Communist household . . . I didn't pursue my career out of ambition. I really believed in Communism. But during Brezhnev's rule I realized Communism was not working . . . [Gorbachev] was a great reformer, but may be I did foresee what perestroika would do while he did not realize it at all. He did and continues to believe in socialism, while I was no longer a socialist."[129]

Shevardnadze's career included the position of first deputy minister of public order in Georgia and later minister of internal affairs—positions that placed him high in the KGB hierarchy. He was also the first secretary of the Georgian Communist Party.

It is not easy to grasp how the attitudes and activities that such positions required gave way to a realization that the system was deeply flawed and in need of a total overhaul. His own account of such an evolution of attitudes is incomplete; the reader is not given an opportunity to discover when the first questions or disaffection emerged, or what the milestones were in the process.

As a young man, Shevardnadze disappointed his parents by abandoning his studies for a medical career and opting instead for the job of political instructor at the district Komsomol committee. He writes: "My parents never forgave me for this. Many years later, when I was already Minister of Foreign Affairs in Georgia, . . . my mother said: 'You took to curing social ills. It's a hopeless cause. You would have done better to ease my suffering.' Of course she was right. How many times, in despair from the realization that it was impossible to fix anything, improve anything, or restore even a tiny speck of health to an ailing society, I would remember my mother's reproach."[130]

Another potential source of political soul searching might have been the social background and history of his wife and her family, for her father "was arrested as an enemy of the people. I don't even know if he is still alive," she told him. Subsequently Shevardnadze learned that he had been executed by firing squad. This revelation did not deter him from the marriage, nor did it apparently hurt his career, although it might have planted another seed of eventual disaffection.[131]

The case of Shevardnadze once more illuminates the remarkable capacity that people of his type and position apparently possessed to compartmentalize, to cast aside memories or experiences of politically determined misfortunes that befell to people close to them, and to proceed, despite such knowledge, to scale (or stay at) the heights of political power, prestige, and privilege.

In 1951 another event took place that could have contributed to an erosion of his faith in the system, especially given Shevardnadze's ethnic loyalties. It was the expulsion (perhaps more correctly, deportation) of "several thousand Georgian families . . . solely because they had relatives abroad." At the same time, "hundreds of honest Communists were again being persecuted." How did he cope with these events? He writes: "I will allow myself one admission . . . : I was confused by what was happening around me . . . I believed in Stalin . . . The only salvation was the thought that Stalin didn't know about it [i.e., the persecution of innocent Communists]. But there was something else . . . The collectivism that I served with all my might was literally working miracles, transforming barren land, defeating fascism, raising the country from ruins . . . But it was also turning into a horrible, lawless force."[132] Here he seems to suggest that the regime's success in the fight against fascism and its "transformation of barren land" (at horrible environmental costs) helped him to accept the injustices he was aware of.

As must be apparent to the reader by now, Shevardnadze's account is somewhat confusing and contradictory; strands of admiration for the system are interwoven with insight into its fundamental defects. Among the matters upon which little light is shed are the reasons for the initial appeal of the system despite his experiences while growing up in the 1930s. Yet among the "processes and events" that left their imprint he mentions the experience of his family's political persecution:

> The year was 1937. People began to disappear from Mamati and the surrounding villages. They were the most respected and the most authoritative. A day did not go by without a rumor . . . of the arrest of the latest "enemy of the people . . . "
>
> One day my father disappeared. A member of the Party since 1924 . . . he was both an enlightened and respected figure in the village [a teacher of Russian language and literature] . . . Outside my home, I sensed the chill of alienation around me. In school I had been considered a leader . . . but now I was completely alone, no one approached me, no one called me over to play . . . the label "son of the enemy of the people" was already stamped on my chest . . . I learned that I was not accepted for the rural Pioneer camp that summer. This was the first and greatest shock of my childhood . . . Father was released some time later. Only later did I learn that . . . he escaped persecution thanks to one of his former pupils, an officer of the district NKVD.[133]

Shevardnadze does not say with what attitudes his father emerged from this experience. Nor does he reveal what, if any, reflections his father's unjustified arrest inspired in him at the time. He does note that when later contemplating these events and "the repressions of 1937 . . . for the first time

I began to think about the reasons why families were divided and the harmonious choir of the rural community was splintered."[134] Apparently such musings became submerged in later years during his energetic and successful pursuit of a political career.

In the final analysis it is far from clear what effect these difficult experiences had on the political thinking of Shevardnadze. Presumably they were successfully suppressed for a long time, because they did not interfere with his career, which required both the display and the presence of some degree of genuine loyalty to the system.

Shevardnadze's Georgian origin and ethnic loyalty might also have predisposed him to or contributed to his eventual dissidence—not that non-Slavic ethnic roots inevitably led to unorthodox thinking. It is noteworthy that on the first pages of his book explaining his political evolution, Shevardnadze mentions among the errors of the system (already embarked on perestroika) the anti-alcohol campaign, which "threatened to devastate the wine industry [in Georgia], one of the mainstays of our national economy." He also notes in the beginning of the book how Georgian independence was brought to end as early as 1920–1921 "after Red Army detachments marched on Tbilisi."[135]

His love of Georgia was evidently also linked to a nostalgia for traditional rural life. He writes: "The beautiful thing about village life is its openness; the people and their affairs are all out in plain sight . . . My father taught us how to tend the beehives . . . Many years later . . . on a government dacha plot, I planted a few vines and set up four beehives. As First Secretary of the Central Committee of the Georgian Communist Party, I had no need to raise food for myself this way . . . [yet] I was glad that the habits of working the land had not been lost. I could still talk shop on equal terms with a plowman or a shepherd, a winegrower or a beekeeper."[136] He became further estranged from the system (already under Gorbachev) after the bloody attack of Soviet army troops on civilian demonstrators in Tbilisi, capital of Georgia, in April 1989. The civilians killed were his own people.

The death of Stalin and Khrushchev's revelations in 1956 were for him— as for others of his generation and position—the pivotal events that, as it were, permitted him to confront doubts earlier suppressed and to reassess his attitudes toward the system. He admits to being "shaken . . . by the direct connections between the politics of terror and Stalin's activity. It is agonizingly difficult to acknowledge that you have worshipped the wrong god, that you have been deceived. It shattered my life and my faith."[137]

There were additional sources of disillusionment. The so-called Virgin Lands campaign initiated under Khrushchev was one of them. "I was assigned to lead the Georgian Komsomol brigade . . . I can clearly recall this grandiose but poorly organized 'virgin land' era, the stupid decisions, and the ill-conceived strategies that cancelled out many successes. We watched helplessly as equipment brought to the new territories . . . began to break down. Thousands of people worked themselves ragged but failed to gather in the gigantic harvest. The crops rotted in the fields, and there was no place to store the grain. Billions of rubles and vast amounts of equipment and manpower were squandered."[138]

And yet he also remembers that period with nostalgia. It was " good and glorious, because it gave us what . . . youth needs most: the proof that we are capable of building our lives from scratch."[139] Perhaps a key to his disillusionment was a growing recognition, intensifying during the long Brezhnev years, that not only was the system increasingly inefficient, but its errors resulted not from idealistic blundering (as at earlier times) but from corruption at the highest levels and from the loss of a sense of mission. It seems that he could accept the blundering during the Virgin Land campaign as long as it had idealistic origins, but could not accept malfunctioning that was not connected to uncompromising idealism and high-mindedness.

By the end of the 1970s, he reports, he and Gorbachev were friends and shared their discontent: "We no longer held anything back." Evidently what disturbed him the most were not so much the moral issues and abuses associated with the system but the malfunctioning of the economy: "Our economy is rigged in such a way that people often find it unprofitable to work. The pay is not equal to the effort . . . 'You pretend to pay us, and we pretend to work' . . . describes the real state of affairs." This was especially the case in agriculture.

He also came to recognize that "vast expanses have been turned into ecological disaster areas under pressure from irrational centralism . . . Avaricious exploitation—'fulfilling the plan at any price'—has exhausted national resources."[140]

Gradually, it appears, he discerned the systemic roots of what earlier might have struck him as merely local problems or managerial weaknesses: "Work in the Party committees, first in the rural districts, then in the city boroughs, opened my eyes to many things. I did not immediately see a direct link between the flaws of centralized economic management and bureaucratic corruption. For a long time I thought they were unrelated, and for me corruption took top priority . . . The . . . ordinary citizen . . . could not find relief either from the highest echelons or from the law enforcement agencies, because the mafia had penetrated these structures . . . Faith in the authorities was undermined . . . The processes of rot and disintegration were particularly horrifying when contrasted with the rampant exploitation of Communist and patriotic phraseology."[141]

Here we encounter the familiar theory-practice gap. Communist systems created and deepened alienation and public cynicism by their relentless insistence on ritualistic promises and claims and by a vast outpouring of propaganda divorced from reality. Elsewhere Shevardnadze writes: "My knowledge of the true state of affairs in our country has led me to conclude that the root of existing evils is not in the individual people, but in the system." He also recalls: "'Everything is rotten. It has to be changed.' I really did say that to Gorbachev on a winter evening at Pitsunda, and I will not recant those words today."[142]

Intervention in Afghanistan was another policy he deplored, calling it "a fatal error." And, echoing (doubtless unintentionally) some social critics in the United States, he asked what good it does to have a bloated military establishment to protect national security when it remains threatened by the multitude of unresolved domestic problems and the scarcities of basic necessities: "We have captured first place in the world weapons trade . . . But we occupy about sixtieth place in standard of living, thirty-second place in average life expectancy and fiftieth in infant mortality."[143]

In 1989 Shevardnadze supported the Hungarian government's policy of allowing East German tourists in Hungary to defect to West Germany—a major departure from prior Soviet bloc policy. Gyula Horn, Hungarian foreign minister at the time, recalls a conversation with him in New York during the U.N. session in which Shevardnadze asked how many people Horn thought might wish to move from East to West Germany. Horn guessed that it could be as many as one or two million. Shevardnadze's response was: "I believe that anybody who wants to leave must be allowed to do so. People must not be stopped by force."[144] Through much of his political life Shevardnadze was a servant of a political system that did precisely that.

I do not pretend to fully understand the change and evolution of Shevardnadze's political attitudes. Given the available information, it appears that his disaffection from the system resulted more from a pragmatic recognition of its inefficiencies, from its economic malfunctioning, than from deeply felt moral indignation over its inequities.

ALEXANDER YAKOVLEV (B. 1923)

Arguably, no member of the Soviet leadership who contributed to political change under Gorbachev went as far in the repudiation of previously held beliefs as Alexander Yakovlev did. He was a major architect of perestroika and the most liberal of Gorbachev's supporters and advisers. His change of heart and mind is all the more remarkable since Yakovlev was, for long periods of time, the most highly placed ideologue of the system. He worked in the Central Committee between 1953 and 1973 in high positions connected with ideology and propaganda and was head of the Party's propaganda department in 1969. He was ambassador to Canada in 1973–1983. In 1983, under Andropov, he was appointed director of the Institute of International Economy and Relations, and when Gorbachev came to power in 1985, he was restored to his former position as head of the Party's propaganda department; in 1986 he became secretary of the Central Committee in charge of ideological matters; in 1987 he became a member of the Politburo.

Yakovlev came from a poor peasant family; his father had four years' of education at a church school and became the first chairman of the local collective farm. In 1937 he escaped arrest only by being forewarned to disappear for a few days. His mother was an illiterate "downtrodden peasant woman and a religious believer to the end of her days." Yakovlev fought in World War II and was wounded. After the war he attended and graduated from a pedagogical institute; he told interviewers that he aspired to an academic, not a political, career; he applied for postgraduate study but was not initially accepted. Instead, the authorities suggested that he study at the Higher Party School, which he did. (He became a Party member in 1944.)

After handling various party jobs he studied at the Academy of Social Sciences while working for the Central Committee.[145]

Thomas Remington writes that "Alexander Yakovlev belongs to the high priesthood of Marxism . . . he is probably the most highly placed among the intellectuals who have assaulted Marxism from within."[146] Or, as a former Soviet commentator puts it, "All this horrible Soviet truth about Marxism is told by a man who was for years among the 'top guardians of the temple' . . . Yakovlev exposes the amorality of Marxism, which appeals to hatred, envy and malice."[147] It was probably Yakovlev's lengthy involvement with theory and ideology that led him to ponder not merely the practical defects of the Soviet system but those of the ideas that inspired it. Unlike other political figures associated with the Gorbachev reforms, Yakolev came to reject not merely the Stalinist distortions of socialism but their Leninist and Marxist ancestry as well; in doing so, he distanced himself not only from his Soviet colleagues (including Gorbachev) but also from the multitude of Western intellectuals who, to this day, are reluctant to recognize the affinity between Marxism and the practices it has inspired.

Yakovlev was among the handful of writers, including those observing the collapse of the Soviet system from the West, who raised the question, "Why was it that the particular features and peculiarities of Marxism . . . became the basis for Party ideology? Why was this ideology . . . seized upon so passionately by the original fanatics?" Yakovlev had no doubt that there was a connection between the repressions and violence perpetuated by the Soviet system and the "Marxists who sincerely believed that the revolution was the locomotive of history and violence was its midwife." He did not flinch from asking: "What gave the revolutionary class the right to decide the destiny of another class called 'reactionary'? Can everything be justified in the name of progress? And is it really progress? What gives one group of people the right to sentence to death civil society or popular custom, centuries in the making?" Entertaining such questions led him "to reflect on the psychological roots of the doctrine by which the 'new life' was constructed for three quarters of a century."[148]

A conversation he held with two Western interlocutors in 1989 indicates that Yakovlev's views changed slowly from total commitment to reservations to complete rejection of the system and its theoretical foundations. In 1989 his tone was still that of the loyal Party functionary, his speech still sprinkled with the terminology of the old agitprop language (references to the "ruling circles" of the United States, the "smearing with dirt" of the Soviet Union by its enemies, and so forth). He was defensive, evasive, and resentful of the United States; he defended Soviet policies, past and present; especially, he assumed that a reformed Soviet system would emerge and endure. He recalled only the negative aspects of his 1959 stay in the United States (he studied at Columbia University), when Americans' hostility to and ignorance of the Soviet Union "made . . . [his] hair stand on end."[149]

In 1989 he saw perestroika as a continuation of the October Revolution that required "a revival of genuine Leninism." The alternative to perestroika was "the death of socialism," which was not a pleasing prospect for him, because "without socialism there is no other alternative at the present moment or for the foreseeable future." He attacked Stalin for abandoning Leninist principles and practices. He viewed Lenin as "a living adviser in our analysis of present-day problems."[150]

In this conversation his views of collectivization were still relatively benign. As he recalled, in his district there was no "dekulakization" (that is, systematic persecution of the kulaks); many people joined the collective farm voluntarily. He defended the censorship of historical novels (such as Rybakov's *Children of Arbat*) on the ground that there are no historical documents proving that Stalin planned the assassination of Kirov, as was suggested in the book. He also claimed that "censorship in the past and today is concerned only with the protection of military and state secrets."[151]

At the time Yakovlev was somewhat evasive regarding the nature of the forthcoming political reforms, especially those concerning the Party: "The party is reforming itself . . . but at this time it is impossible to answer your questions fully . . . Much will have to be suggested by *life itself* as we go along." For a putative Marxist and believer in planning, this was a strange notion, though conveniently vague. In the same interview Yakovlev favored "a socialist market" instead of a Western-capitalist one that would involve "unlimited competition . . . unemployment and other negative social consequences."[152]

He had no criticism of the Soviet interventions in Hungary in 1956 and Czechoslovakia in 1968, suggesting that "events preceding them" justified such a course of action. The origins of the Cold War were to be found in Churchill's Iron Curtain Speech in 1946, which "convinced us that there was real danger." The United States was "to blame for creating the arms race." Some Soviet mistakes were conceded but in the same breath rationalized: "Remember that we were the first socialist country, and we have had to learn from our experiences."[153]

What, then, were the sources of the uncommonly complete reversal of his beliefs, which apparently occurred sometime between 1989 and 1992? Why was Yakovlev's break with the system and even its proclaimed ideals so radical? What were his specific critiques of Marxism? How did he come to conclude that there was a connections between theory and practice?

In the interview quoted above, Yakovlev made an interesting admission relevant to the halting development of his critiques of the system: "It was not until 1985 that we learned just how bad things really were, particularly in our economic and financial affairs."[154] That is to say, not until Gorbachev rose to power and encouraged free expression did Yakovlev realize how bad things were. High position rather than a source of privileged information isolated him from social realities. The nomenklatura, shielded from any deprivation, did not know how bad things were, which was among the reasons it did little to stave off the unraveling of the system. In my conversation with him, he noted that elite privileges were among the sources of his disillusionment, in particular the nutritional privileges at a time when ordinary people were starving.

Apparently Yakovlev's "first faint doubts" about Stalin emerged when he read his article on linguistics, which, understandably enough, struck him as unscientific nonsense.[155]

Several plausible explanations for Yakovlev's change of heart may be proposed. First, he was of the generation upon which Khrushchev's revelations in 1956 had a particularly strong impact (he was then in his early thirties). Second, Yakovlev spent one year in New York and ten years in Canada. These provided heavy doses of exposure to Western values and institutions, whatever his immediate reaction to them were. He did not seem to enjoy his long stay in Canada and repeatedly requested to be sent home.

Third, experiences long buried or repressed also evidently played a part in what might be called his political awakening, though much later, when numerous personal recollections and external developments began to come together. For example, Yakovlev recalls that he was upset after World War II with the treatment of former Soviet prisoners-of-war, who were put into camps upon their return to the Soviet Union. In an interview with the English author Jonathan Steele he also revealed (unlike in the interview cited earlier) that his experiences in Prague in 1968 (where he was sent "to oversee Soviet journalists who were to cover the event") had a profound effect: "At the time he was deputy head of the propaganda department of the CPSU central committee and this was a vital assignment. Officially the dispatch of troops was described as friendly assistance, but Yakovlev was shocked by what he found. 'I saw gallows with effigies of Soviet soldiers hanging there . . . People were shouting "Fascists, Fascists"' . . . Neither then nor throughout the period of perestroika did Yakovlev make any public mention of his impressions of Prague, and he only felt free enough to divulge them after he had retired. Yakovlev summed up the experience as 'an important school for me . . . It had the greatest sobering effect.'"[156]

In 1979 he disapproved of the Soviet invasion of Afghanistan, though apparently more on prudential than on moral grounds. He also advised Gorbachev to release Sakharov from exile, evidently again less because he was repelled by it than because he wanted to gain the support of the intelligentsia for Gorbachev.

Fourth, it may well be that his very involvement with ideology, with ideas, with questions of theory and practice—combined with the other experiences mentioned earlier—could have been conducive to the kind of reflection and philosophical soul searching that led him to renounce virtually everything he had believed earlier, or, at any rate, that he did not question earlier. A further, more remote possibility is that the kind of common human decency embodied by his parents also contributed in some subterranean way to the emergence of similar impulses later in life, on behalf of which he rejected the politically mandated untruth and deprivations that the system imposed on people.

Finally, there is the possibility that personal injuries suffered during the years of perestroika at the hands of the conservative Party establishment helped cause his profound change of attitude. Yakovlev writes: "A great deal of this attack fell on my head. Someday I will publish the articles, flyers and excerpts from speeches that demonstrate so well the methods of the Bolsheviks."[157]

Whatever the sources, Yakovlev's critique of the Soviet system and its ideological underpinnings has been far-reaching. He rejected Marxism for many reasons but most importantly because he came to regard it as a flawed way of looking at the world, at human beings, their relationships, and conflicts. Similar critiques of Marxism have been put forward before, but never by a man who was a high-level Party functionary in charge of ideology and propaganda in the former Soviet state. The accelerated decay of the Soviet system was an excellent setting for undertaking a thorough critique of Marxism.

Far from revering Marxism as "scientific socialism" or a science of society, Yakovlev, in the wake of the collapse of the Soviet system, ended up perceiving it as a "neo-religion," "a deluded faith" that, like traditional religious beliefs, thrives on "a deeply seated habit of relying on an authority that supposedly knows and understands and . . . is capable of releasing us from responsibility for our own thoughts and actions."[158]

Above all, Yakovlev finds Marx's conception of human nature fundamentally flawed, lacking in psychological depth, unmindful of the complexities of human beings and crudely and simplemindedly optimistic about the prospects of altering and improving it. Yakovlev writes: "Marx . . . had no interest in the psychological realm of people who, as he supposed, would soon become altered because of the inevitable changes in human nature that follow the modifications in the nature of social relations." Thus, Marx's lack of interest in actually existing human beings, as distinct from abstract collectivities, is explained by his fixation on some imaginary, essential human nature that the future will bring forth after the rubble of inauthenticity and alienation is removed. Fatefully, the more one believes in such possibilities, the less important it becomes what people are like here and now and how these transient creatures are to be treated. Yakovlev also writes: "The very idea of taking the individual out of the aggregate of social relations, trying to reduce all contradictions of human existence to the contradictions of the economy . . . pushed aside the fact that the individual suffers not only from economic inequality but also from spiritual and bodily vulnerability, from fear of death, from the inherent solitude of human beings. The world and life create a multitude of problems that . . . cannot be fixed by achieving an equal relationship to the means of production."[159]

Yakovlev's critique of Marxian psychology was, not surprisingly, part of his critique of the overemphasis on matters economic: "Can a means of production determine to a decisive degree the views, ideas and beliefs, the life of the people in a society? . . . Can you deduce human essence from the way an individual makes a living? . . . The whole fullness of life disappears from such economic narrow-mindedness. The family disappears, as do love, power, . . . heroes, myths, the crimes of the Spanish Inquisition. The tragic disappears . . . Everything that is sublime disappears and everything that is amazing and astounding in history."[160]

These limitations led Marx to explain a wide range of human phenomena by alienation: "Marxist criticism of the so-called alienated forms of consciousness, in particular religious consciousness, meant a loss and even a destruction of many primal forms of consciousness necessary for life."[161] Here and elsewhere, Yakovlev takes note of Marx's dismissal of and hostility to tradition, including the moral values embedded in it. For Marx such values and traditions merely covered up different forms of exploitation or were reflections of false consciousness to be removed by liberating economic and political arrangements.

The simplified and unrealistic conceptions of human nature and psychology and the belief in their unproblematic transformation (rooted in Marxism) shed light on specific aspects of the Soviet system, including its manic drive to industrialize: "The harsh attitude toward the individual [in Marxism] was caused . . . by his optimism, his [Marx's] belief that human nature could be easily changed, that universal emancipation, universal release from the concerns and the passions of the selfish . . . person were not only necessary but possible." Marx was similarly and naively optimistic about industrialization, thinking it needed only to be dissociated from the profit motive, from capitalism. Yakovlev writes: "Marxism did not understand the tragedy of industrialism. Industrial civilization erodes and suppresses spiritual culture. A severe price must be paid for this . . . the loss of distinction between good and evil . . . a strictly technocratic treatment of the individual as an instrument of production—all of those collective farms, labor camps, slave labor. Everything is permitted that is economically useful."[162]

In Marxism, as in subsequent Soviet institutional practices, such long-term optimism coexisted with the short-term emphasis on social conflict, with "the obsession with class struggle," with the "revolutionary intolerance" that Yakovlev is also critical of. Marx saw little room in the world (here and now) for "conscience, solidarity and charity"; everything boiled down to the clash of economic interests. Yakovlev finds the root of political violence in the Marxian rejection of universal moral norms and in the attendant advocacy of a moral relativism tied to the presumed interests of the proletariat and the revolutionary struggle. But it was precisely "this special 'class' morality, which flouts universal human norms, [that] leads to indulgence of any action . . . Moral criteria are simply not appropriate under the conditions of a revolutionary coup d'état; they are 'revoked' by the brutality and directness of class warfare." Yakovlev also observes that "the idea that one should not fear creating victims in the course of serving the cause of progress, that the revolutionary spirit of the proletarian masses must be preserved at any cost, is very characteristic of Marx."[163]

The belief in a glorious and historically determined future was a major source of Marx's untroubled acceptance of political violence: "Belief in the inevitability of the coming communist world served to justify the numerous and senseless victims of the class struggle" ; "terror is the way of remaking human material in the name of the future."[164]

Yakovlev notes further confirmation of the authoritarian potentials of Marxism: "The tragedy of Marxist teaching is that it is alien to any dialogue. Marxism only conducted a monologue and never listened. It was always right . . . always claiming to know everything and to be able to do everything, thus proving its totalitarian essence."[165]

Indifference to human psychology also led to such strange contradictions as arguing on the one hand that the proletariat was the most abused, degraded, and even degenerate stratum of the population, a "social stratum lacking all traditional forms of social life, the family, tender feelings between parents and children . . . stripped of property, of hearth, and home and hope for the future," *and* on the other that it was to be the savior of humanity. True enough, the proletariat of Marx's day had nothing to lose, but, as

Yakovlev points out, "people who have nothing to lose are very easily pro-voked to senseless enterprises, are very easily manipulated and are carried away by ideas of violence and destruction. A hungry, angry, humiliated person who has nothing to lose is not bothered by his conscience."[166] Here Yakovlev strikes at the heart of the romantic Western veneration of some idealized victim group. In recent times the peasants of the Third World or the deprived ethnic minorities of Western urban centers have become the substitutes for the proletariat. And the substitution occurred precisely be-cause of the (correct) perception of Marxist intellectuals in the West that the Western proletariat was no longer the underprivileged underclass; hence, there was a need to discover new outlaw groups who have nothing to lose.

Yakovlev's rejection of the Soviet system was unconditional because it entailed the rejection of its ideological inspiration, theoretical foundations, and unrealizable ideals.

NATIONALISM IN THE BELIEFS OF THE LEADERS

Little was said in this chapter about the part played by Soviet-Russian na-tionalism in the beliefs of Soviet leaders and of the extent to which their beliefs merged with, or possibly replaced, ideological convictions based on Marxism-Leninism. The encroachment of such nationalism on ideology goes back to the 1920s and Stalin's insistence that socialism can be built in one country and the attendant fortress imagery of the Soviet Union. In the process of consolidating his power during the 1930s Stalin increasingly evoked symbols and traditions of Russian nationalism, and this trend cli-maxed during World War II, when traditional nationalistic themes were even more blatantly used to bolster national solidarity against the invaders. In-creasingly, Soviet and Russian nationalism came to be treated by the author-ities as interchangeable. The Soviet state became the quasi-sacred repository and embodiment of Marxist-Leninist ideals and heir to Russian nationalism and its putative spiritual superiority over the decadent, capitalist West.

A further factor contributing to the ascendance of nationalistic sentiment and legitimation was the post–World War II emergence of the Soviet Union as the second superpower of the world. Under both Khrushchev and Brezh-nev territorial-political expansion was consolidated in Eastern Europe (with brutal force when necessary) and continued globally in the Third World. As a superpower, as well as a contender with China for the leading role in the worldwide communist movement, the Soviet Union supported—militarily, politically, and economically—a considerable number of "national libera-tion movements" and self-styled Marxist-Leninist regimes. With numerous client states in various parts of the world and a military establishment equal to that of the United States, the other superpower, the Soviet Union became an imperial power and, in doing so, once more reached back to pre-Soviet Russian imperial aspirations and designs. The determination to reach mil-itary parity with the United States was also given impetus by the humiliation suffered in the Cuban missile crisis in 1962, after which Soviet efforts to build up its forces, especially its naval power, redoubled.

Because of these developments, it became difficult to separate, in the motivation of Soviet leaders, the strands of national pride, traditional Russ-ian imperialism, and a residual commitment to Marxist-Leninist values. There was a plausible connection, in their eyes, between the military-political strength and aspirations of the Soviet Union and its original ideological mis-sion. The expanding power and influence of the Soviet Union was a source of pride and legitimacy for its ruling elite, especially since in many corners of the world political movements and systems claimed to share the Marxist-Leninist legacy and sought to legitimate themselves by some blend of nation-alism and Marxism-Leninism.

The decline of Soviet global power beginning in the mid-1980s contributed to undermining the sense of legitimacy and confidence of the Soviet rulers; superpower nationalism and residual Marxist-Leninist zeal no longer found confirmation in what Brezhnev called the "correlation of forces" abroad. The future orientation of the system, so essential to its earlier dynamism, suffered serious setbacks. Now, for a change, there were national liberation movements in countries allied with the Soviet Union and depending on its support, such as Afghanistan, Angola, Ethiopia, Mozambique, and Nicaragua.

Arguably, the last generation of Soviet leaders were less strongly sus-tained by nationalistic motivation than their predecessors were; withdrawal from Afghanistan and Eastern Europe reflected a loss of self-assurance rooted primarily in domestic difficulties. The Soviet empire was in the end sustained by neither a robust nationalism nor a profound belief in the orig-inal ideals and their theoretical foundations.

CHAPTER 4

The Ambivalence
of High-Level Functionaries

"The declining elite becomes softer, milder, more humane and less apt to defend its own power." VILFREDO PARETO

In the previous chapter I discussed Soviet leaders indisputably and unambiguously associated with reform and social change. In this chapter I will be looking at individuals whose contributions to the transformation of the Soviet political system were more questionable and ambiguous but who, in any event, exemplify those in high positions during and after the Brezhnev era. Among them, Arbatov and Dobrynin were relatively enlightened and flexible functionaries (or Party intellectuals), exposed, because of their jobs, to Western political systems and their representatives. They were neither in a position nor of a disposition to initiate political change, but they were not unsympathetic toward it, within certain limits. By contrast, Gromyko and Ligachev can be seen as old, crusty fixtures with a provenance in the Stalinist past (Gromyko far more than Ligachev), but even they evince some recognition of the need for reform (Ligachev more than Gromyko); neither appears to have possessed the ruthlessness and single-minded determination needed to fend off the growing challenges to the nomenklatura's monopoly of power. All four may be viewed as transitional figures (Gromyko less so because of his age and his association with Soviet power that goes back to Stalin) between the truly old guard and the generation of reformers discussed in the previous chapter.

GEORGI ARBATOV (B. 1923)

Georgi Arbatov is among the former insiders and upholders of the system who in the postcommunist era considered it important to present his political life for public inspection and to restore or bolster his credibility abroad as well as at home. "Political disillusionment" is hardly an appropriate concept to apply to him, for it is unclear if he had any "illusions" about the system to begin with; it is doubtful that he ever possessed the mindset of the true believer.

Arbatov personifies the Party intellectual. Less charitably but not inaccurately, Vassily Aksyonov, the Soviet émigré writer, calls him a "professional agent of disinformation."[1] He was not a holder of power or high-level Party functionary but an adviser and expert on the West assisting the Soviet leaders in the exercise of power and especially in the making of foreign policy. He advised six successive leaders: Khrushchev, Brezhnev, Chernenko, Andropov, Gorbachev, and Yeltsin.[2] In this capacity he played an important part in the maintenance of the system; if, indeed, Arbatov was seeking through much of his career to move the system in a more liberal direction (as he repeatedly claims in his memoirs), his attempts must have escaped the attention of his numerous illiberal superiors.

He was among the handful of high-ranking officials who had a good grasp of Western and especially American domestic political affairs. His positions included membership in the Central Committee of the Communist Party, the Supreme Soviet, and the Academy of Sciences. The last, apparently, was a reward for his political services, because, as Richard Pipes observes, "Arbatov is not known to have produced any work that would qualify him for a doctorate in history, or to have made a contribution in any field of learning that would entitle him to a seat on the prestigious Academy of Sciences." Still, as Arbatov himself describes the system, honors such as membership in the Academy "could be earned only by abject servility," notes Pipes.[3] Arkady Shevchenko writes of him: "Pleasant and easygoing with superiors and friends, and more so with Americans and foreigners generally, Arbatov was arrogant and often rude with his subordinates. I have rarely known a more vigorous drummer for the Soviet system . . . Intelligent, ambitious and unencumbered by principle or scruple, Arbatov was ready . . . to serve anyone without the slightest hesitation if it served his own interest . . . As a director of an academic institution, he could pretend to be an independent spokesman, as those of the Western academic world often are . . . [His] institute is in fact a front used by the Central Committee and the KGB."[4]

Further light is shed on Arbatov's character in the recollections of Gorbachev's interpreter, Pavel Palazchenko, who mentioned that on the occasion of Gorbachev's 1988 visit to New York (when the police warned the public about traffic jams and against coming to Manhattan), "Arbatov, who was hovering near Gorbachev, even suggested that the whole thing might have been arranged in order to set New Yorkers against Gorbachev."[5]

Arbatov's background, is in one crucial respect, similar to those of the other Soviet figures discussed earlier. He, too, had personal experiences of political persecution as he was growing up. In 1938 his father was removed from his position in the Ministry of Trade, "accused of counterrevolutionary sabotage," and jailed for one year.[6] Arbatov senior was a member of the Party from 1918, having joined at age seventeen. He fought in the Civil War and showed every indication of being a loyal supporter of the system; he was even sent to Germany (with his family) in 1930 to work at the Soviet trade mission. Reading between the lines of his earlier autobiography covering 1953–1985, published in Russian, an American student of Soviet elite behavior, Charles Fairbanks, suggested that Arbatov's father was in fact "a high KGB operative in Germany and Japan."[7]

Georgi Arbatov was a recipient of the Order of Lenin, the Order of the October Revolution, the Red Star, two Orders of the Red Banners of Labor, and the Badge of Honor. It was characteristic of his servility that at a time when it was already clear that the Soviet economy was severely retarded in part because of the lack of computerization, he suggested, in a 1975 article, that the importance of computers in managerial efficiency was vastly overrated. This was a view calculated to please those satisfied with the traditional command management methods. "The claim that the United States was making a serious mistake in getting carried away with the 'electronic boom' set the minds of our leaders at ease," writes Ligachev in his memoirs, where he is highly critical of Arbatov's position on this matter.[8]

Arbatov may best be described as a sophisticated high-level propagandist whose task was to influence Western elites, policymakers, and public opinion. His fluent English and access to the Western media greatly helped him to perform this role, as did his excellent grasp of the susceptibilities of American elites and public opinion, especially their fear of a nuclear conflagration. It was among his tasks to convince these elites and publics about the peaceful intentions of the Soviet Union during a period (from the late 1960s till the rise of Gorbachev in 1985) when the Soviet Union still pursued vigorous expansionist policies in the Third World and embraced the interventionist Brezhnev Doctrine in Eastern Europe.[9] Arbatov was especially adept at the polemical use of the moral equivalence thesis.[10]

Richard Pipes, who was acquainted with him personally, points out that in Arbatov's book "virtually nothing remains of his earlier views . . . he now appears in a new guise: a secret dissident in the corridors of power, a kind of liberal mole who all along struggled to bring democracy and reform to the Soviet Union."[11] Arbatov favored certain reforms, a mild humanization of the system, in order to make it more presentable in the West and more efficient at home. Neither his memoirs nor his public record offers any evidence that he was engaged in any moral questioning of the inequities of the system and consequently desirous of its fundamental alteration. He was critical of Soviet human rights violations not on moral but on pragmatic grounds: "We behaved in a very stupid way by putting human rights in quotation marks or speaking of them as so-called human rights."[12]

Arbatov came from a poor Jewish family. Given that background, his social mobility was impressive, for the higher reaches of the Party were not noted for the presence of Jews. His Jewish background probably provided an additional source of caution and fear, and his successful advancement in a political career—despite such a background—must have been a source of a quiet pride. What Arbatov apparently learned from his father were "inner psychological barriers erected throughout a lifetime of caution." He writes: "To a great extent, intuition saved us both. He [his father] did not speak about certain subjects and . . . I did not ask any awkward or dangerous questions. You developed a sort of political sixth sense . . . Even by the age of fourteen or fifteen I understood perfectly well that the authorities arrested and destroyed completely innocent people . . . These were my parents' comrades and my father's friends. Each night in 1937 and 1938 I went to bed anxious. I even muttered a kind of secular prayer to myself: 'Just don't let them arrest my father!'"

During these years, he informs the reader, "people got out of the habit not only of speaking about forbidden subjects but even of thinking about them . . . there were many subjects that my father categorically did not wish to discuss with me . . . Only after the death of Stalin and after Lavrenti Beria's arrest [he was head of state security] did we start our heart-to-heart talks."[13]

It is difficult to determine what mixture of belief, loyalty, fear, and opportunism defined Arbatov's political career. Quite possibly it was the experience of Stalinist totalitarianism and the abiding fear it had inculcated that was the formative and determining political and psychological experience, in combination with his Jewish background. (There is next to nothing in his memoir about what it meant to be Jewish in the high echelons of he Party.)

Arbatov's political education continued as he "lived through the postwar ideological pogroms and new outbreaks of political repression." By this time, "I understood much of what was going on: the lies, stupidities, and perversions of the state system ostensibly working for our benefit." Moreover, "bit by bit I started to discover the extent of hypocrisy and political cruelty." But evidently he also discovered that it was possible to live with these discoveries, as an impressive understatement suggests: "Looking back, I try to assess how it has affected me. No doubt I have become more cautious and had to adjust by adopting appropriate patterns of behavior and political instinct."[14]

Despite all these experiences young Arbatov was ready to embark on a political career, applying, as he did after the war, to the Department of International Relations at Moscow University—hardly a place for people willing to display an independent mind or entertain, let alone express, doubts about the rectitude of the system. As Arbatov later describes rather matter-of-factly, numerous perks and advantages went with his job and with his rise in the hierarchy. In these reminiscences he does not betray any sense of unease or indignation about these privileges (such as one can find in corresponding accounts by Yeltsin, Dubcek, and Hegedus, among others); this strengthens in the reader the impression of gratified opportunism.

What precisely were his critiques of the system that he came to know as an insider and which he served during all his adult life? Whether to impress

Western readers or to find a new use for the moral equivalence perspective, he blames the Soviet "military-industrial complex" for the expansionist policies of the 1970s. His objections to Soviet intervention in Afghanistan seemed to rest, once more, on pragmatic rather than moral grounds. He reveals that he told Brezhnev at the time that "our intervention . . . was ruining détente and was helping the American extreme right in the forthcoming election." To be sure, it could also be argued that moral arguments would not have made much of an impact on Brezhnev.

Arbatov's concern with the nature and health of the Soviet system (not unlike Gorbachev's) was rooted in its declining economic performance, in its inefficiencies rather than its ethical failings. He criticized the growth of the Party apparatus, the selection and advancement of people "who were not very talented" and who were unencumbered by "notions of conscience and morality." Party resolutions were issued and forgotten: "Not once in my memory was anyone called to account for a wrong decision." Further," positions of responsibility were transformed into lifelong appointments." "Totally incompetent" officials were shielded from responsibility. During the years of "stagnation" (the Brezhnev era) members of the nomenklatura "were finally separated into a special caste." Even the people at the top were "absolute mediocrities," a trend that began under Khrushchev, according to Arbatov.[15] Brezhnev himself "was a typical product of the political elite of the times. He had a university diploma but was poorly educated and not really very literate. His abilities were meager, his cultural level was low. On those occasions when he did read something for his own pleasure, it was usually a magazine like *Circus* [an obscure magazine that detailed the lives of circus performers and listed programs]." Brezhnev preferred "gray, mediocre people and those with extremely questionable morals." Arbatov nonetheless managed to keep his positions and advised Brezhnev.

There was also corruption and nepotism. In the "administrative-command economy . . . everything (supposedly) belongs to the people, who turn out to be the same as nobody. From top to bottom the temptation arises to appropriate something for oneself."

The book ends with the author's avowal of his belief in the socialist ideal: "A religious person may remain loyal to his church despite disappointments in the clergy. The same applies to Marxism . . . I keep my faith in socialism

. . . associating it not with my country's current reality or with its propaganda, but with the ideals of social justice that had existed for centuries, since early Christianity . . . I for one have not lost my faith in the core of the socialist ideal, which is much closer to the social-democratic, rather than Bolshevik variety . . . Marxism cannot be held responsible for the political follies perpetrated in its name or for the fact that it was turned into an official state ideology and even state religion."[16]

Like any public affirmation of idealistic belief, the quoted passage is obviously self-serving. It is not surprising that after decades of faithful service of the powers that be, Arbatov had no desire to see himself (or for others to see him) as a mere opportunist or careerist. Indeed, his avowals are remarkably similar to the statements and attitudes of many representatives of the Western left who sought to salvage long-held beliefs and to come to terms with the collapse of communist systems. Arbatov knew that he could count on a measure of sympathy among Western readers similarly disposed though lacking in his occupational experience and proximity to power. This concluding statement suggests continuity with his past when he "learned brilliantly to mimic American liberals, to ingratiate himself by saying what his American partners wanted to hear."[17]

At last Arbatov raises the question, "How did I and people in positions like mine react to this general deterioration . . . ? Did we feel then, and do feel now, any responsibility for what was going on?" The question is good and important, but the answer is evasive. He admits having been "troubled" by the negative developments that he described. On the other hand, he did not know all there was to know about the true state of affairs. In any event, "like many others," he "tried to the best of my abilities to resist deterioration."[18]

Arbatov is likely to have been one among many in the political elite whose identification with the system (and concern for personal safety) was strong enough to allow them to work for it despite awareness of its defects. Such an awareness was not strong enough to prompt Arbatov to seek radical reform, nor strong enough to make him to yearn for the reestablishment of a more rigidly doctrinaire regime, nor to strong enough to induce him to oppose the reforms that led to the disintegration of the Soviet Union. People like him did not believe that the system was in mortal danger and thought that modest reforms would prolong its life indefinitely. Arbatov was far from a true believer (although he took for granted the social order he lived under) and was certainly not among those—their numbers rapidly dwindling—who would have taken drastic measures, including the ruthless use of force, to eliminate challenges to the system. Arbatov's attitudes were symptomatic of the decay of the Soviet system, which he neither hastened nor was able to retard.

ANATOLY DOBRYNIN (B. 1919)

There are numerous similarities between the personalities and political roles played by Arbatov and Anatoly Dobrynin. The latter was Soviet ambassador to the United States for a quarter-century and in 1986 became secretary of international affairs for the Central Committee of the Communist Party of the Soviet Union. (This committee, according to a former KGB officer, was the Party department "responsible for all the Soviet Active Measures," undertaken to influence foreign countries.)[19] Both Arbatov and Dobrynin advised the rulers in the Kremlin, both were important members of the Soviet political establishment, both were specialists in Soviet-American relations, and both acquired a certain Western veneer (along with a good knowledge of English) that made them effective spokesmen for the Soviet Union in the West. Both had an excellent understanding of how to manipulate and occasionally deceive members of American elite groups, or, as a former American ambassador to the USSR, Jack Matlock, says, "it was his [Dobrynin's] American interlocutors who mistook his charm and bonhomie for sympathy and understanding," even for a shared political outlook![20] Arbatov and Dobrynin were both proud of their American connections and insider status; both undertook to refurbish their images in lengthy autobiographical volumes for the benefit of Western readers and sought to distance themselves retroactively from the political agenda of their masters, although earlier they had sought to implement it to the best of their abilities.

This being said, their memoirs (if not their authors) greatly differ in substance and coverage. Whereas Arbatov ranges widely and covers much of his life, Dobrynin restricts himself to an extremely detailed, seemingly factual recounting of his diplomatic activities, sprinkling in a few "human interest" stories (e.g., lending his fur hat to President Ford; Kissinger's response to being taken on a fast automobile ride by Brezhnev; Dobrynin's three-year-old granddaughter at the desk in the Oval Office), but he manages to say very little about himself. His account is also remarkably free of expressions of spontaneous sentiment, an absence that is presumably a by-product of a life spent in the diplomatic service on behalf of a political system in which the line between the public and the private was sharply drawn and spontaneity was not considered a virtue to strive for.

It is difficult to reach a conclusion on the basis of these memoirs alone as to what degree Dobrynin was a clever opportunist, a closet reformer, or one of the more enlightened members of the elite who unwittingly contributed to, or reflected, the decay of the system and the corrosion of its animating beliefs. Although he is at great pains to record his occasional disagreements with hardliners in the Soviet leadership on specific issues, there is no joy or relief expressed upon the demise of a system he himself calls totalitarian. On the contrary, there is much bitterness toward Gorbachev for his contributions to the unraveling of the Soviet empire and toward Alexander Yakovlev, who "became Gorbachev's evil mastermind in inducing him to destroy the very structures of the party that upheld Gorbachev's power."[21]

Whatever Dobrynin's reservations about the system and its particular policies, he deeply regretted the passing of Soviet power; he was far too committed to his role in the service of the Soviet empire to question any of its fundamental attributes. As Ambassador Jack Matlock has observed, "He was comfortable with the basic direction of Soviet policy and the way it was implemented . . . As he saw it his job was to keep his superiors from blundering into suicidal conflict and to extract the maximum advantage from each transitory deal, not to end the antagonism which had led to an arms race."[22] Though favoring a less confrontational (or more selectively confrontational) policy with the United States, Dobrynin took for granted the persistence of a global equilibrium between the United States and the Soviet Union, an equilibrium compatible with the gradual expansion of Soviet power and influence. There is no suggestion in his memoirs that he was interested in altering any basic Soviet institution or structure in a significant way; nor does he indicate which, if any, Soviet domestic policies he would have wished to change.

Only in the brief introduction does he comment on the relationship between his commitments to the system and his pragmatic and more independent judgments and seemingly pro-Western inclinations: "My American interlocutors still wonder whether I was a true believer in the Soviet system, and indeed Ronald Reagan was not quite sure whether I really was a communist (I was). The fact is that I served my country to the best of my ability as citizen, patriot and diplomat. I tried to serve what I saw as its practical and historic interests and not any abstract, philosophical notion of communism. I accepted the Soviet system . . . as a historic step in the long history of my country, in whose great destiny I still believe. If I had any grand purpose in life, it was the integration of my country into the family of nations as a respected and equal partner."[23]

Such remarks illuminate the confluence of patriotic and ideologically based motives discussed at the end of the previous chapter. They suggest that Dobrynin's loyalty had stronger nationalistic than ideological roots and that he felt comfortable in a world characterized by the kind of superpower rivalry that allowed his country's global influence to expand without serious conflict with the West. He writes: "I wanted to avoid unnecessary confrontation . . . especially over ideology, in order to promote better personal relations and by extension create a better climate to work in." Presumably "necessary confrontation" was another matter. He thinks that his early technical training in engineering contributed to the "pragmatic, nonideological bent that characterized my approach to diplomacy." By contrast, "our foreign policy was unreasonably dominated by ideology, and this produced continued confrontation, especially through our involvement in regional conflicts 'to perform our international duty to other peoples.'"[24]

Those in the West, especially specialists in Soviet studies, who were always skeptical of the ideological commitments of the Soviet leadership (increasingly so after the death of Stalin) may note that, according to Dobrynin, Soviet leaders, even during the golden years of detente, were in fact beholden to ideology. Dobrynin had no illusions about the part played by ideology in foreign policy: "Soviet foreign policy was always closely connected to the philosophy and ideology of the Communist Party." Moreover, "members of the Soviet political leadership often spoke in the language of ideology even when conversing between themselves, falling into the language of the official newspapers . . . The way and form in which they expressed their thoughts inevitably affected its content."[25]

Dobrynin repeatedly and matter-of-factly characterizes the Soviet system in his time as totalitarian, being either unaware of the Western academic disputes about the applicability of this concept to the Soviet Union after Stalin or in disagreement with those who rejected it. Given his unhesitating use of the concept, it is all the more curious that he remains reticent about engaging in any serious criticism of the system and that his prime response to its unraveling is unmitigated regret.

Dobrynin's loyalty was probably based above all on his own spectacular social mobility, on the gratification that comes to a self-made man from achieving high status. He came from what he calls "a plain working-class family." In 1944, when he was twenty-five, the authorities decided that he should study at the Higher Diplomatic School, a decision that surprised him. As Dobrynin tells the story, Stalin decided that competent young engineers would make good diplomats.[26] It is likely that candidates selected for such training had displayed politically appealing qualities as well.

He took his career very seriously; he notes, for instance, that "the party congress [of 1971] marked a step in my career. With the increasing importance of our relations with the United States I had to conduct talks regularly with the highest officials in Washington; I was therefore advanced from alternate to full membership of the Central Committee." He also reports that he was awarded (toward the end of the Brezhnev era) the title Hero of Socialist Labor and the Hammer and Sickle gold medal , "the highest civil decoration in the Soviet Union. I was and remain the only ambassador to be honored in this way throughout the long history of Soviet diplomatic service." He does not hesitate to inform the reader of the details of the many honors and compliments he received both from his own government and from American political figures, including Presidents Reagan, Nixon, and Carter and leading members of the Congress, all listed by name. We also learn that after becoming the secretary of the International Division of the Party he "was allocated four personal bodyguards, a large ZiL limousine with radio telephone and a state-owned country house . . . [which] had its own staff: three cooks, four waitresses, two gardeners and a guard." There was also a tennis court, sauna, greenhouse, and fruit garden.[27] Like Arbatov, Dobrynin did not have a troubled conscience about such privileges.

He advanced rapidly after completing the school for diplomats. In 1947 Andrei Vyshinsky, then minister of foreign affairs, offered him the position of head of the Education Department in the ministry, but he did not accept. Instead he worked for five years under Valerian Zorin, deputy foreign minister, becoming his first assistant. In 1952 he became a counselor at the Washington embassy, where he remained until the end of his diplomatic career, in 1986. His stay in Washington was interrupted for one year when he was appointed to be one of Molotov's assistants in 1953. Before his appointment in 1962 as ambassador to the United States he also worked for Gromyko and the United Nations.

When he arrived in Washington in 1952, he was "a true believer in Marxism-Leninism. I believed in the ultimate victory of socialism over capitalism. My mind was clogged by the long years of Stalinism, by our own ideological blunders, by our deep-seated beliefs and perceptions, which led to our misconstruing all American intentions as inherently aggressive."[28] The lengthy narrative of his decades in Washington does not shed much light on how, when, and to what extent his mind became "unclogged," on how he moderated his ideological convictions. He does not reveal whether these changes in his outlook occurred because of better understanding the nature of American society and Western values or because of the gradual changes in the political climate in his own country. The reader may presume that both played a part, but because he spent so little time during these years in the Soviet Union, the Western experiences might have been more powerful, leading him to harbor views somewhat critical of the Soviet system, or at any rate its rigid ideological presuppositions and aging leaders. More likely, he became more of a political relativist without allowing the new insights to interfere with his public positions and career. A remark that he made to an American audience—"I didn't come here to say we are all right and you are all wrong"—might have been a rhetorical ploy. He reassured his audience that "no one in the Soviet leadership, including the most zealous supporters of communism, ever talked seriously about any concrete prospects for communism in the United States. Needless to say, I did not believe in any such prospect either, the more so because I had been living in the United

States for so long. In my boldest thoughts I never looked beyond the idea of our two systems peacefully converging somehow in the distant future."[29]

Which features of these two systems were to converge and in what manner he does not say. It is nonetheless plausible that his quarter-century in the United States had a somewhat subversive impact, if not on his conscious thinking, on his feelings: "I had spent many years in the United States and could see fairly clearly the pluses and minuses of both nations and their social systems. I tried to explain to my government the foreign and domestic policies of the United States . . . without much ideology." Nonetheless, he continues, "I too was strongly influenced by the philosophy of my country and the policies of my government which I represented abroad . . . But I always tried to be objective and was guided by the desire to improve relations between our two greatest nations."[30] What is not clear in such and other similar remarks is where the boundaries of such philosophical influences lay and in what ways they did or did not shape his behavior.

Though always loyal to his superiors in Moscow, Dobrynin differed from his predecessors in freely exposing himself to the temptations and social-cultural influences of the United States and took pride in being popular among American policymakers, even in being found likable by President Reagan, who wondered in his diary how a person like Dobrynin could represent the evil empire.[31] He was proud of his access to the political elites in the United States, including some of the wealthiest capitalists.

Probably Dobrynin was well aware that as an ambassador posted to Washington, he had the best of all possible worlds: a high-powered position in the Soviet hierarchy but one physically removed from it with more autonomy than he could have had at home, allowing him to live with all the comforts and personal freedoms of the West. He was not pleased when he was recalled to Moscow in 1986, though to take a high position.[32]

Dobrynin vigorously cultivated, partly for the benefit of American policymakers, the "two superpowers" scenario in which the Soviet Union was not noticeably different from the United States in pursuing its global interests, except for its irrepressible love of peace. His disagreements with official Soviet policy, such as they were, had little moral foundation; for example, he disapproved of the 1968 Soviet invasion of Czechoslovakia only because "it would certainly destroy the summit with the United States and spoil our relations with the West in general." In further commenting on the 1968 intervention he also took the opportunity to take a swipe at Alexander Yakovlev, who "then headed the Propaganda Department of the Central Committee, which provided rhetorical and ideological support for the whole Soviet operation." Curiously enough, Dobrynin denies that there has ever been such a thing as the Brezhnev Doctrine while freely admitting that "the determination never to permit a socialist country to slip back into the orbit of the West was in essence a true reflection of the sentiments of those who ran the Soviet Union."[33]

A similarly instrumental view is reflected in his comments on the refusal to allow Jews to leave the Soviet Union: "I never understood why we did not allow Jews to emigrate. What harm could it have brought to our country? . . . by solving this question we could have rid ourselves of a serious and permanent source of irritation between us and the West, particularly the United States." In fact, Dobrynin understood the reason for these prohibitions: "The Kremlin was afraid of emigration in general . . . lest an escape hatch from the happy land of socialism seem to offer a degree of liberalization that might destabilize the domestic situation"; elsewhere he writes that it was a mistake of the Soviet leadership not to differentiate between apolitical Soviet Jews who merely wanted to go to Israel and dissidents such as Sakharov and Solzhenitsyn: "All were lumped together as enemies of the Soviet state." Letting the Jews go "would have cost us little and gained us much."[34]

In a similar spirit, he writes, regarding the Soviet support of Cuban involvement in Angola, that "we played right into the hands of our opponents in the United States." As to Somalia and Ethiopia, "our supply of military equipment, the activities there of Cuban troops, and especially our airlift to get them there persuaded Americans that Moscow had undertaken a broad offensive against them for the control of Africa."[35] Once more we learn nothing about Dobrynin's view on the substantive merits of such Soviet policies.

He criticized the massive Soviet intervention in Afghanistan on the ground that it "had a disastrous effect on international relations" and because it "provided the American right with a . . . pretext for another spiral of the arms race" and not because of the enormity of destruction and killings it entailed. He was deeply and genuinely puzzled, it seems, by Carter's moral indignation about such Soviet actions and relegated it the realm of 'personal obsession.' American protests about Soviet actions in Afghanistan were no more than 'anti-Soviet hysteria.'"[36]

Likewise, human rights issues (i.e., their violations in the Soviet Union) are almost invariably mentioned as "irritants" or "major irritants" in Soviet-American relations rather than matters of substantive moral significance; he regarded their discussion by American officials as "direct interference in our domestic affairs." His attitude toward such violations, and the repressiveness of the Soviet system as a whole, may best be deduced from a remark he made about Khrushchev, who "was unable to imagine that anything else could exist in his country apart from the system based on the Communist Party's domination. He too, was a product of his time."[37] And so, presumably, were the repressions. Being a "product of one's time" becomes a convenient formula providing retroactive absolution for abhorrent policies of the past, and it was used in the recollections of other powerful figures as well (Ligachev and Sudoplatov, among others, discussed below). It is not clear what exactly Dobrynin and his colleagues had in mind by reference to "the times": Stalin's way of governing, public opinion, mass hysteria, economic underdevelopment, or possibly the myth of "capitalist encirclement"?

Given Dobrynin's reluctance to discuss his worldview and past beliefs in any detail, his remarks about important contemporaries offer help in assessing his views. It is especially noteworthy that he says little about Stalin, and whatever is said is not evaluative. Generally speaking, he was unimpressed by the leadership, in part because of its ignorance of the outside world: "Except for the handful involved in foreign affairs—Brezhnev, Gromyko, Kosygin, Andropov and the representatives of the military—very few members of the Politburo knew much about America. Their views were limited mainly to what they read in *Pravda* and *Izvestia*" He was critical of Khrushchev on account of his impulsiveness and risk taking. In turn, "Suslov was a very dull, highly dogmatic and ideologically narrow-minded person." He seems more tolerant of Brezhnev, under whom he flourished as ambassador, who was always interested in his views on Soviet-American relations, and who was committed to stability in international relations, as Dobrynin saw it. Nonetheless, he describes Brezhnev as inordinately vain, coarse, and unsophisticated in his tastes. His pride was an important element in his search for superpower status for Russia equal to that of the United States. When Brezhnev visited the United States, he "instructed the Soviet security service to organize his trip in such a way that he would in no way appear to the Americans inferior to the president of the United States."[38]

Dobrynin favored some of the changes in Soviet foreign policy proposed by Gorbachev, especially the "shifting from the idea of class warfare as the basis of the relationship between capitalist and communist states to the concept of security shared by East and West." He welcomed such changes, "which were long overdue, and some of which I have quietly long advocated." On the other hand, Dobrynin complains repeatedly about what he regards as Gorbachev's and Shevardnadze's undue willingness to compromise with the West and their failure to negotiate better deals ("with an inexplicable rush they actually gave away vital geopolitical and military positions"). He faults Shevardnadze for signing agreements without relying on the "expertise provided by professional diplomats"—it is not hard to guess whom he had in mind. Gorbachev and Shevardnadze "were often outwitted and outplayed by their Western partners."[39] The two monopolized decision-making in foreign policy, Dobrynin complains, and evidently paid much less attention to his advice than he was used to from their predecessors. In all these policies, Shevardnadze's Georgian nationalism played a part, Dobrynin believes, contributing to his indifference to the preservation of the Soviet Union and its empire.

Dobrynin further points out that high-level "discussions in the Kremlin were chaotic and dominated by Gorbachev's empty rhetoric. He accused the Communist leaders of Eastern Europe of failing to reform . . . Sometimes on the spur of the moment he hurried to visit those leaders and lectured them, but this only expedited the disintegration of local regimes, especially in the German Democratic Republic."[40] None of this pleased Dobrynin.

He was also critical of Gorbachev on more personal grounds: "Gorbachev . . . never remained too close or too long with any of his associates. He could easily abandon a former colleague, leaving him bitter and disappointed. It was not by accident that after his fall, not a single one of the Politburo members later defended the former general secretary." Moreover, as time went by, his "manner of handling the work of the Politburo was gradually changing. His style became more authoritarian."[41]

Dobrynin is right in noting that Gorbachev "unleashed forces he was unable to control," and he holds him responsible for the dissolution of the Soviet empire. Gorbachev, he says, "never foresaw that the whole of Eastern Europe would fly out of the Soviet orbit within months, or that the Warsaw Pact would crumble so soon." Dobrynin also holds Gorbachev responsible for "a bold unilateral reduction of our armed forces" and the associated decline of morale in the military."[42]

Nowhere in this volume is there the slightest display of moral indignation or regret regarding the profound flaws and misdeeds of the Soviet system, at home or abroad.[43] Even the Stalin era is treated with detachment; memories of the times of Stalin did not burden him or his family: "Like me, most of the new people [in the Higher Diplomatic School] were technicians who were in no way affected by the old ways of thinking. We did not feel particularly vulnerable to Stalin's excesses, about which we knew only vaguely at the time. All of my family were ordinary people . . . We felt as secure in Stalin's time as anyone could feel."[44] The choice of the word "excesses" is a good measure of this detachment, as is the ambiguous statement about the security that his family enjoyed under Stalin. Did he mean that they were as insecure as everyone else or that they enjoyed the maximum security anybody could? Also quite remarkable in a volume of such length is the lack of any reference to one of the most important historical events of his life and his country in this century: the Twentieth Party Congress and Khrushchev's revelations about Stalin; the reader has no idea how he reacted to these disclosures.

The only occasion on which he shows indignation over his government's policies was when he was not informed about the placement of missiles in Cuba, because "without knowing the facts we could better defend the government's false version of its strategy in Cuba. This deliberate use of an ambassador by his own government to mislead an American administration remained a moral shock to me for years to come ."[45]

It is hard to know what domestic and foreign policies Dobrynin would have advocated had he been more involved with high-level decisionmaking inside the Soviet Union. There is little doubt that he would have preserved Soviet domination over Eastern Europe, especially East Germany. He would certainly have kept a larger military establishment than Gorbachev did. It also seems that as long as the Soviet Union remained a first-class global power, Dobrynin was not too concerned about domestic matters; there is little in these memoirs to suggest that he nourished any interest in redressing the social and political injustices that the system institutionalized and perpetuated. Yet his long immersion in Western ways of thinking and acting might have eroded the harder edges of his political commitments and beliefs. Richard Pipes, for one, thought that "the decades in Washington . . . imperceptibly eroded his communist convictions . . . [and] at bottom he seems to have more in common with American liberals than with Soviet communists."[46] Although being compared by Pipes to American liberals is not a form of approbation, I think his view of Dobrynin's Americanization is somewhat overstated. Former Ambassador Matlock's concluding assessment of Dobrynin seems more persuasive: "For all his criticism of dogmatism and ideological blindness on the part of Soviet leaders . . . Dobrynin reveals in his assessment of Gorbachev his fundamental allegiance to that system . . . [he] was able to satisfy his superiors in Moscow throughout his long tenure in Washington because his attitude basically coincided with theirs."[47]

YEGOR LIGACHEV (B. 1920)

The case of Yegor Ligachev suggests that even among the leaders generally regarded as diehard supporters of the old order and opponents of serious reform, attitudes were changing in a way incompatible with the determination and ruthlessness required for preserving unconditional power and keeping the communist system intact. Although Ligachev became a bitter critic and adversary of Gorbachev, he "had no wish" to turn the clock back to 1985, only to 1987.[48] He, too, felt that the system needed reform, but wished to preserve its fundamentals. Contrasting him to Gorbachev, Stephen Cohen writes: "Both Gorbachev and Ligachev had spent their entire political lives rising through a ruling Communist Party apparatus created under Lenin, transformed into a vast castelike system by Stalin, and largely preserved by Khrushchev and Brezhnev. Gorbachev . . . somehow broke with that world and its characteristic ideology. Like the great majority of Party officials Ligachev . . . did not."[49]

A far less charitable view of Ligachev was put forward by Anatoly Sobchak, an uncompromising critic of the Soviet system and, as mayor of St. Petersburg (formerly Leningrad), member of the new generation of Russian politicians: "Long before the First Congress Ligachev was already a notorious figure in Moscow. Since the days of the ill-timed anti-alcohol decree which did so much damage to the country . . . Ligachev had carried the banner of a fighter for socialist principles. Cloaked in the garb of an orthodox Marxist, he led the crusade to unseat Yeltsin as Moscow party boss."[50]

The limitations of Ligachev's acceptance of change were also apparent to David Remnick: "He made little secret of his disdain for truly radical change . . . He would not countenance the creation of a multi-party system, the rise of competing ideologies."[51] Another source described him as a man who "very quickly reached the limit of what he was prepared to change. Private property, open criticism of Soviet history, political pluralism were all anathema to him."[52] A Hungarian reform communist, Gyula Horn also notes Ligachev's resistance to change in connection with reforming the kolkhoz system. According to Horn, Ligachev was invited at the initiative of Gorbachev on a study tour of the far less regimented and far more successful Hungarian farms. "He was taken on a highly informative tour, but those who are incorrigible can't be helped. After his return to the Soviet Union, he related his Hungarian experiences to the Party leaders, concluding, 'That, of course, is a small country where such policies are feasible. The Soviet Union as a great power cannot follow such policies.'"[53] On the other hand, in 1987 Ligachev favored independence for the East European countries under various degrees of Soviet control.[54]

Ligachev, originally a regional leader, took pride (as Yeltsin did) in being far removed, geographically speaking, from the corrupt political center, being close to the people and their problems in the provinces, in touch with life as ordinary people lived it. While this appeared to be an important factor in Yeltsin's disillusionment, similar circumstances did not undermine Ligachev's loyalty to the fundamentals of the system. Even in 1990 he declared, "To me Lenin is sacred," whatever precisely he meant by that, presumably loyalty to the revolutionary origins and perceived purity of the system and its founder.[55] Not only did Ligachev revere Lenin, but he was also capable of fawning on Brezhnev (but so were the liberal reformers). In 1981, at a speech to the Soviet Writers Union, he said: "You can't imagine, comrades, what a joy it is for all of us to be able to get on with our work quietly and how well everything is going under the leadership of dear Leonid Ilyich. What a marvelous moral-political climate has been established in the Party and country with his coming to power! It is as if wings have sprouted on our backs."[56] Whatever Ligachev's true estimate of Brezhnev's abilities, the quotation is a useful reminder of the nature of Soviet political culture, which demanded such tributes to the leader, regardless of his abilities and regardless of the beliefs of those who paid the tribute.

Age is another important variable in seeking to understand the differences in the attitudes toward reform of leaders who occupied similar positions in the hierarchy. Ligachev is a decade older than either Gorbachev or Yeltsin and therefore apt to be more rigid and less capable of entertaining the notion of radical change; he had more deeply internalized over a longer period of time the mindset of the high-level functionary. His *Memoirs* contain several unintended revelations of this mindset, even in the context of an eagerness to demonstrate an openness to what he regarded as reasonable reform. For example, he recalls the high-level deliberations concerning the wording of the obituary of Nekrasov, the writer who was in effect a defector, who had lived in Paris for several years prior to his death. At the time, the Politburo was distressed by a politically incorrect obituary published in *Moscow News*. Ligachev writes: "One must recall that back then [in 1987], new views about our compatriots who had moved abroad for various reasons had not yet been established . . . Gorbachev, Alexander Yakovlev and I took a united position on the publication of the obituary. We never touched on the artistic side of the writer's work, and dealt only with his political position as an émigré. At that time we had a completely different opinion of compatriots who had emigrated; all of us, top political leaders along with the rest of society, have rethought many things since then. As is only normal."[57] What Ligachev intended to convey was that until 1987 such "compatriots" who "had moved abroad" had been denounced in the media as traitors and scoundrels as a matter of course, and he himself and his colleagues considered denunciation the normal procedure at the time. What "the rest of society" thought of such policies is by no means clear, for it had no way to convey its opinions. Ligachev does not delve into the questions of why and how "top political leaders rethought" the matter since then or why they had held their earlier opinions.

On another occasion Ligachev complains that Yakovlev allowed the media too much criticism of the system. He writes: "How could Yakovlev, who had been in charge of ideology at the Central Committee for many years, speak of 'mirroring' as the main function of the media? Everyone . . . knew very well that the press and television were the mightiest levers of forming public opinion." Evidently Ligachev had no conception and little appreciation of the idea of independent public opinion free of political manipulation by the Party and took for granted the legitimacy of such manipulation even in the late 1980s.

Discussing the Kolpashevo incident (the inadvertent discovery and attempted concealment of mass graves of people executed by the state security organs in Siberia in the 1930s), he comments matter-of-factly on the different procedures for ascertaining truth and the different standards of truth in the old days and in more recent times: "It is clear that the outcome of the Kolpashevo incident would have been completely different, under conditions of glasnost and a new appraisal of certain periods in the past. Those KGB men, along with the population of Kolpashevo, would be organizing the reburial of those who had perished, regardless of which side of the political barricades they were on. But the decision back then corresponded to the mood of the society at the time."[58]

He was referring to the attempted cover-up of the massacre, which he regarded as natural and acceptable as long it was relegated to past political practices. More remarkable is the idea that such past practices "corresponded to the mood of the society." Ligachev would not or could not bring himself to recognize that these and other policies had nothing whatsoever to do with the mood of society (a highly imprecise concept, in any event) and everything with the policies of the Party leadership, which had little interest in gauging such moods, let alone allowing its policies to be influenced by them.

The remains of the old-line functionary outlook appear most clearly in Ligachev's attack on the radical reformers' critiques of the past, which he calls the "slander [of] our history": "The radicals' goal was to break down society, undermine patriotism, and deprive people of a feeling of pride in their Motherland . . . They acted like beasts of prey tearing our society to shreds, destroying the historical memory of the nation, spitting upon such sacred concepts as patriotism, and discrediting the feeling of pride in our Motherland." "Spitting upon something sacred" was among the favorite phrases of Soviet propagandists, their use going back to the Stalin era.

Ligachev's faith in planning is also among the "survivals" of the pre-perestroika worldview: "There is no dearth of achievements in the history of our country testifying brilliantly to the advantages of state planning. So it was in the period of industrialization in the 1930s, the conquering of space in the 1950s and 1960s, and the creation of the world-class western Siberian oil and gas complex in the 1960s and 1970s. No reasonable person can deny the economic advantages gained from planning; attempts to discredit the planning system have been perfidious . . . the planned economy, adopted for the first time on a large scale in the USSR, is an achievement of universal human significance."[59]

Ligachev's memoirs prompt one more digression on the truth-value of memoirs and autobiographies. Ligachev, despite his reputation as a hard-liner, comes across at times as a man neither entirely humorless nor without integrity. (The reviewer in the *New York Times* calls him "this honest Bolshevik.")[60] How did Ligachev succeed in making a relatively favorable impression on far from uncritical readers? Certainly not by listing his accomplishments and appealing traits of character. Although Ligachev does not hesitate to inform the reader of his accomplishments and positive traits, he does so in a restrained and reputable way. Above all, he stresses his moderation: "I am a staunch opponent of 'great leaps,' including those in the area of economic reform . . . As the saying goes, 'Haste makes waste.' I am sure that if we had moved ahead gradually . . . we would have progressed much farther along the road of reform. And we would not have neglected . . . social services."

Elsewhere he writes: "Many of us came from villages. Let us recall how a peasant gathers his resources and his strength and plans a new spacious house. He continues living in the old house as he proceeds with this complex task. Only later, when everything is ready, does he tear down the old building. We behaved differently: without having created anything new, we hastened to destroy the old."[61] Who could quarrel with such a reasonable argument?

Ligachev makes sure to inform the reader of his devotion to the environment, his love of Siberian cedar trees (some of which he planted in Moscow), his interest in the preservation of old buildings, his support for the performing arts and artists, his interest in museums, and the trust that he had earned from the "artistic intelligentsia." Ligachev devotes several pages in his memoirs to denials of the cover-up of the mass grave discovered in Kolpashevo (in Tomsk Province, of which he was the Party boss). He complains that "of all the accusations that people have unsuccessfully tried to hang on me in recent years, reproaches for concealing the Kolpashevo burial have inflicted the deepest spiritual wound."[62] But an American source asserted that "the provincial Communist Party chief who presided over that 1979 cover-up went on to become one of the country's most powerful man. He was Yegor Ligachev."[63] Presumably, information from the appropriate archives could settle these conflicting accounts.

Ligachev's politics and personality, like those of other figures discussed so far, must also be assessed against the background of his own knowledge and experience of the inhumanities perpetrated by the system that he served with dedication. Remarkably enough, it turns out that, like Shevardnadze, he married a woman whose father was killed under Stalin. Ligachev writes: "I knew what the year 1937 meant and not from hearsay . . . [I] learned it from the bitter experience of my own life. My father, the Siberian peasant . . . who had left his village to work in Novosibirsk, was expelled from the Party in 1937 (true, he was later readmitted). And my wife's father . . . perished during those years—he was arrested on false charges and executed . . . I felt very clearly what it meant to be married to the daughter of a persecuted general."

Ligachev's father-in-law, a Red Army soldier during the civil war, had by the middle of the 1930s risen to the rank of lieutenant general and become a staff commander in the Siberian Military District. Arrested in 1936, tried in 1937, charged with espionage as a "Anglo-Japanese-German" spy (in a trial lasting ten minutes), he was executed by firing squad. He never confessed. Ligachev learned the details of his death in 1989. In his recollection of such disasters, Ligachev seems to view the horrors of the Stalin era as if they were caused by destructive and uncontrollable forces of nature ("the times") ; sometimes he emulates Khrushchev in assigning all blame to the pathological personality of one human being who somehow managed to amass immense power only to abuse it.

Undoubtedly Ligachev also learned something about the political intolerance and institutionalized suspiciousness of the system when in 1949, while first secretary of the Novosibirsk Province Komsomol Committee, he "was accused of trying to wrest young people away from the Party and given the menacing label of 'Trotskyite.'"[64] Although there were no serious consequences, except the loss of his job (for a period of seven months), this was a memorable reminder of the arbitrary exercise of power.

The story raises once more the fundamental and intriguing question, How did Ligachev and others in similar positions and circumstances manage to regard the system as legitimate? Or else, how did they separate its improved post-Stalin legitimacy from what took place during the 1930s and 1940s?

The curious fact of the matter is that Ligachev, like others with similar experiences, retained loyalty to the system because he evidently did not see that its legitimacy had been fatally ruptured by the decades of Stalinism. For him, the enormity of the bloodshed did not vitiate what he saw as the great achievements of nation building, industrialization, and modernization. We do not learn from his *Memoirs* what tilted the scales toward the belief that despite all the horrors and arbitrariness, the accomplishments of the system outweighed its costs. Perhaps the very facts of his own survival and eventual high position and the associated accumulation of his own acts and gestures of commitment over time made the difference.

It is also noteworthy that the critiques of the system voiced by Ligachev (and by others) tend to lack the moral element and to focus largely on matters of efficiency. The following is a reasonably good summary of Ligachev's objections to the state of the Soviet system during and after the late Brezhnev era: "In later years the Brezhnev administration noticeably reduced the rate of economic growth. Abuse of power spread, discipline faltered, and entire regions of the country were immune from criticism. I would sum it up this way: The stagnation was not in the workplace but in the leading political body of the country—and in Marxist-Leninist theory as well. As a result the country remained poised at the threshold of the next stage of scientific and technological revolution." The concept of "stagnation" appears to have been designed to blunt moral indignation regarding the evils referred to. Ligachev remains reticent on the nature of stagnation in Marxist-Leninist theory while quite willing to attack such corruptions as the institutionalized gift giving by lower to higher functionaries, "the practice of making offerings to the leaders and arranging banquets for them during business trips."[65]

Even in such critiques there is little evidence of an awareness that the questionable means were employed in the pursuit of dubious or unattainable ends, that corruption was systemic and endemic and the unintended result of particular institutional arrangements, and that Stalin's rise to and long stay in power had something to do with the nature of the system that allowed individuals of his type to rise to the top. And when the inhumanities of the past are touched upon, Ligachev (like his colleagues) writes of them as obscurely tragic events without specific explanation or a locus of responsibility ("the times").

Ligachev's commitment to reform was qualified in exact proportion to his faith in the basic legitimacy of the system. Although he was not among those seriously disaffected, his qualified admissions of the deficiencies of the system provide some insight into the difficult process of political attitude change on the part of those in power who went much further than he did down the road to disaffection.

ANDREI GROMYKO (1909–1989)

Andrei Gromyko's memoirs illuminate the mentality and disposition of the powerholders who for a long time guaranteed the survival of Soviet communism. Among them, Gromyko—unintentionally, no doubt—contributed to the eventual demise of the system by championing Gorbachev's rise to power. His reflections illustrate the inner struggle, limited as it was, that many at the top were engaged in as they sought to preserve their lifelong commitments in the face of new political currents. More than most, Gromyko was successful in keeping the faith. According to his former assistant, Arkady Shevchenko, his "devotion to the Soviet system is complete and unreserved. He is now [in the early 1980s] himself a fundamental element of the system . . . at once its product and one of its supreme masters."[66] George Kennan has observed that the Soviet-Nazi nonaggression pact, the Soviet annexation of the Baltic republics, the deportations from eastern Poland, the Katyn massacre, and other morally troubling matters go unmentioned in his memoirs: "If he did know of these things, they made insufficient impression upon him to warrant mention in his memoirs."[67]

Gromyko resembles Ligachev in some ways, especially in retaining many old beliefs alongside certain cautious reassessments of the Soviet past and the Stalin era. But unlike Ligachev, Gromyko had little interest in any kind of reform. As his recollections unfold chronologically it seems that the injustices and irrationalities of his Party and government did not trouble him *when they occurred*. It is only in retrospect that he musters a moderately critical attitude about the system and Stalin, , mostly at the end of the book. Throughout the narrative the reader is expected to take for granted (as the author appears to) that Gromyko was uninvolved in the injustices perpetrated by the system.

Gromyko separates himself from those in positions of power, whom he holds fully responsible for the sins of the system and for not restraining Stalin. To his credit, unlike Khrushchev in his famous speech, Gromyko is not entirely satisfied by blaming everything on Stalin and his "diabolical cunning," though there is reference to that, too. It was his firm belief, according to the *Memoirs*, "that *everyone at the highest level of authority did know* about the criminal orgy of blood-letting . . . and knew that utterly innocent people were dying on the 'Leader's' instructions." He rises to high levels of indignation on account of the refusal "of these characters [to] express sincere repentance for the past."[68]

Gromyko made an important contribution to perestroika (and the events it set into motion) by nominating Gorbachev, on behalf of the Politburo in March 1985, to the post of general secretary of the Party. Having served the system for half a century, he was not one to initiate sweeping change or call its fundamentals into question; presumably he merely wished it to be rejuvenated. On the other hand, when change was on hand—originating in forces he had no control over (and probably no understanding of)—he was capable of acknowledging, at least in retrospect, certain failings of the system.

His retrospective posture resembles that of high-ranking KGB officials engaged in intelligence and counterintelligence (one of them, Oleg Kalugin, is discussed in the Chapter 5) who rationalized their activities as basically defensive and oriented to gaining advantage over dangerous foreign adversaries. In his roles as ambassador, foreign minister, and U.N. representative Gromyko could similarly distance himself from the policies and results of domestic repression. Nonetheless, even in retrospect he thought of himself "as a communist to the marrow of my bones" who respected "the profound learning of Marx, Engels and Lenin, and the great spirit of our people as they build the communist society." His confidence in the future was based, first, on "the fact that we have a wonderful people who are capable of solving the most difficult problems. Secondly, we have a wise and perceptive party, closely bound to the people. Thirdly, we have a leadership worthy of the great tasks it has set before society at this crucial stage."[69] Since the *Memoirs* were written (between 1979 and 1989), we may presume that the confident assertions quoted reflect Gromyko's feelings at the beginnings of perestroika.

Many old and seemingly frozen beliefs and attitudes are displayed in these *Memoirs*. It is still the United States and its "aggressiveness" that remains responsible for the Korean War. He also writes with a straight face that "we strictly observed the principle of non-interference in the affairs of other countries"; that in the West "the humanities are taught in strict conformity with the needs of the ruling elite" (unlike in the Soviet Union!); that as he assured the Pope, complete religious freedom prevailed in the Soviet Union. He believed at the time of writing these recollections that Soviet intervention in Hungary in 1956 "was absolutely justified": "In evaluating the events of 1956, the Soviet Union and the people of Hungary have a clear conscience." He recalls without any second thoughts his irritation with President Carter for raising the question of imprisoned Soviet dissidents, whom he generally regarded as troublesome, ordinary criminals. The Korean airliner downed by Soviet fighters remains, in his eyes, a spy plane "simply carrying a South Korean label.[70]

At the end of his *Memoirs* he asserts that "under socialism . . . the surplus product goes to the whole of society, which owns and disposes of the material resources . . . in accordance with the proper proportions and priorities. By its nature socialist society creates the possibilities of limitless expansion."[71] Given his lifelong commitment to and hard work for the system, the preservation of such beliefs is not altogether startling, and it would be unreasonable to expect sweeping reassessments. Nonetheless, late in life Gromyko publicly retrieved some painful experiences of the distant past (which did not interfere with the performance of his duties at the time). Thus at the end of his Memoirs he expresses disapproval of the collectivization campaign, sentiments that in all probability he had kept to himself in earlier decades. To be sure, his objections had more to do with the speed and methods of collectivization rather than its basic objectives: "As a student I made many trips to various villages at the time of collectivisation . . . [the peasants] simply could not understand why their land was taken away from them and turned into public property in such haste. And why was it necessary to take their last cow, to say nothing of their horses, and then force them to join the collective?"[72] He also describes a conversation with tearful, starving peasants awaiting deportation and later observes their deportation: "I spent a night in a hotel [in Vitebsk] and the next morning went out and encountered a column of men moving along the street . . . They were walking in ragged ranks under NKVD guards . . . they had refused to join collective farms . . . a heart-rending scene of inhuman treatment. More than fifty years have passed since those days, and yet I still retain a vivid image of the scene . . . We students watched with aching hearts as thousands of horses and carts carrying men, women and children rumbled through the environs of Minsk, Borisov and Vitebsk on their way to the north."[73]

There is another interesting recollection: In 1948, when he was on his way to visit his ailing mother in the countryside, he was suddenly summoned back to Moscow by Stalin. His wife was "terrified. After all, that was a time when people were arrested constantly." He also remembered "the oppressive circumstances in Moscow between 1934 and 1939. People would walk along the street with tense expression on their faces." He recalls that "the scientific secretary of our institute was arrested and I was appointed in his place." He admits to not feeling good about that,[74] but none of these experiences planted the seeds of doubt or profound moral revulsion.

At the end of the *Memoirs* Gromyko raises far-reaching questions that he apparently did not raise earlier in his life, when they might have interfered with his ironclad loyalty to the system. For example:

> Was it possible after the revolution of 1917 to avoid the development of a socialist state in which one man was enabled to concentrate unlimited power in his hands . . . ?

... The question properly arises: where was the party in all
this, and its committees, including the Central Committee? ...

... why was it that the cohort of Lenin's comrade-in-arms,
supposedly all hardened fighters for the workers' cause ... proved
incapable of recognising in good time the danger he posed ...

Why, after Lenin died, was the ruling nucleus incapable of following his admonition to remove Stalin as General Secretary? ...
Did Stalin manage to hoodwink everyone? One could say that
this is precisely what he did. But only because others wanted it.
Their own political ambitions played an important part.[75]

So what went wrong? When did it go wrong, and why? Here, Gromyko
shares some ground with Khrushchev, who stressed how intimidated members of the Politburo were by Stalin. Gromyko noted that "two or more
members of the Politburo never rode in the same car" for fear of being
suspected of conspiratorial intentions." Thus it is hardly surprising that
Stalin was not yet buried when "gales of loud laughter could be heard from
inside Khrushchev's office." Nonetheless, Gromyko maintains that "these
people, who were at one time respected and who exercised considerable authority, managed to turn themselves into uncomplaining executors of the
will of one man who has vowed to rule the state by illegal means ... why
did such figures as Molotov, Kaganovich, Voroshilov, G. M. Malenkov and
later A. A. Zhdanov and many others, not raise their voices against the
lawlessness?"[76]

The question also lingers: How did Gromyko and others in a similar positions and with similar awareness manage to continue working steadfastly
for the system and keep their belief in its moral superiority intact? It is likely
that at the time of these "dissonant" experiences Gromyko was not nearly
as disturbed by them as he thought, decades later, he had been. Likewise,
the way of thinking that he attributes retroactively to "the people" was his,
not theirs: "In both city and village throughout the period of Stalinism the
atmosphere was poisoned with tension. But on the whole, the population
lived with the thought that the Soviet Union was a great country, that it had
carried out a great revolution ... And was not the party, which he had created, in itself a guarantee that a future development of the socialist state

would follow the Leninist course? That was how people—in towns and villages—reasoned in those days."[77]

This serene belief in the Party—an abstraction that forever eludes the errors and crimes committed on its behalf and the corruption of particular human beings who led it—is the cornerstone of Gromyko's commitments and beliefs. As Kennan writes of him, "The Party became . . . his mother, his father, his teacher, his conscience and his master. He was never to question its ideals, its authority, its moral purity."[78]

SHARED ATTITUDES

Although to various degrees isolated from the suffering and deprivation experienced by ordinary citizens, most of the leaders, high-ranking functionaries, and Party intellectuals were not unaware of the shortcomings of the system (and the divergence between ideals and realities), but they succeeded in regarding them as necessary and unavoidable costs or as imperfections compatible with their fundamental beliefs.[79]

From the cases so far, it may seem that terms such as *political disillusionment, disaffection,* and *loss of ideological commitment* do not capture adequately the phenomena we are seeking to grasp. Evidently the disaffection was highly qualified, except perhaps in Yeltsin's case. It would be more fitting to call the process revealed by these autobiographical writings as a substantial decrease of political-moral certitude; earlier beliefs were not discarded wholesale but were somewhat shaken and occasionally reexamined, no longer totally taken for granted and no longer sufficient to provide motivation for the unhesitating ruthlessness that the successful defense of the system would have required.

Behind these recollections and reflections there still looms the old Bolshevik device used for dealing with internal conflict, the notion that the moral meaning of what one does in the short run is completely different from the moral meaning an action will have in the long run—the notion that a triumphant future will vindicate a problematic present and past. As Nathan Leites writes: "Bolsheviks do not consider the chance of attaining certain goals to be lessened by the . . . use of means which are at extreme variance with them . . . the Party must accept as a matter of course any expedient degree of discrepancy between means and ends . . . [it] must be prepared to inflict any amount of deprivation on any number of human beings if this appears 'necessary' . . . the refusal to use necessary bad means appears to the Bolshevik as an expression of stupidity; or as imperfect dedication to the great goal; or as self-centeredness which keeps one more concerned with not touching dirt and not feeling guilt than with transforming the world."[80]

Gorbachev's attitude, like the attitudes of some of his fellow leaders supporting reform, combined past and future orientation. These leaders believed that a good and noble start had been made under Lenin, but their certainty that the future would cleanse the system of whatever evil had transpired earlier was no longer unshaken. It is nonetheless possible, as one commentator has put it, that Gorbachev also believed deep in his heart (up to a point) that "the USSR was . . . the country that had been founded as the homeland of the promised communist future, and for that reason was to be preserved as *the* pioneer state of that new world. All the dislocations, all the crimes, the failures and pains had to be (and were!) conjured away by the logic of faith."[81]

Besides maintaining a flickering faith in ultimate vindication by the future, those in high position—who were to various degrees responsible for the flaws of the system—characteristically deflected radical reassessment of their beliefs by reference to the weakness and fallibility of (other) human beings, the raw material they had to work with. It was those other people's shortcomings and corruptibility which frustrated the realization of well-meaning policies and grand schemes. This allocation of responsibility was not so much the old, historically specific notion of Trotsky—who cautioned that, given the backwardness of pre-revolutionary Russia, the requisite "human raw material" was not available for building the new society—but a more general doubt about human beings and human nature. It represented a tacit rejection of the optimism of Marx and a renewed embrace of Lenin's pronounced ambivalence about human nature. These individuals did not readily confront the realization that the ideas and ideals of communism were themselves problematic and would have resisted implementation even under more benign historical circumstances, or the insight that the costs of a grand social experiment may outweigh its benefits.

CHAPTER 5

The Political Transformation
of East European Leaders

"We were carried away by what is often called the spell of power . . . we were in the thrall of history, intoxicated by our ability to ride it, to feel that we were controlling it . . . we ended up with nothing but the need for power." MILAN KUNDERA AS QUOTED BY ANDRAS HEGEDUS

"My idealism was not wholly pure; there was the temptation of . . . suddenly becoming one of the main movers and actors on the stage of history—all the more seductive since one feels one is acting for what is good while combining it with a personal career." EUGENE LOEBL

The evolution of the political attitudes of leaders in Eastern Europe illuminates the drawn-out process of the decay, delegitimation, and unraveling of Soviet communism. Their critiques of the system dating back to the 1950s and 1960s are hardly different from the critiques which gained prominence in the second half of the 1980s and culminated in the disintegration of the Soviet empire. The lives and changing beliefs of Andras Hegedus, Imre Nagy, Alexander Dubcek, and Zdenek Mlynar, two Hungarians and two Czechs, mirror and help us understand the characteristics of the Soviet empire in Eastern Europe and why it was doomed once the will to preserve it was gone in Moscow.

ANDRAS HEGEDUS (B. 1922)
The political disillusionment of Andras Hegedus (a sometime "great admirer of Rakosi," the Hungarian communist leader)[1] was a longer, better-

documented, and more self-reflective process than the corresponding dis-illusionment of the Soviet figures discussed so far; it was also far more complete. Hegedus was forced to give up his political career much earlier than the Soviet leaders were. In the fourth decade of his life he abandoned politics altogether and became a full-time intellectual and sociologist. I had the opportunity to converse with him in Budapest in the summer of 1992.

Since the political systems established in Eastern Europe after World War II were, by design, quite similar to that of the Soviet Union, the sources of questioning and disaffection were likewise similar, with one important exception. In Eastern Europe not even the most committed and idealistic supporters of the communist governments could claim that those systems would have come into existence and survived without the arrival and continued presence of the Soviet armed forces. In the Soviet Union the system was homegrown, whatever the degree of its reliance on the agencies of coercion. It was the imported character of the system that helped East Europeans to rapidly reach the conclusion that "socialism did not mean social justice, the end of exploitation and more freedom. What they understood by socialism from their experience was occupation by a foreign power and an alien leadership, diminished freedoms of every variety, the abuse of human ideals, an accelerated rhythm of work, and a wretched standard of living."[2]

Many leaders of the East European communist parties spent substantial, often formative periods of their life in the Soviet Union between the 1920s and the early 1940s. They returned to their countries in the company of the Soviet troops in 1945. Impressed by its power, they led lives dominated by "fear and loyalty" toward the Soviet Union (as in the case of General Jaruzelski).[3] Initially, dependence on Soviet power was welcomed by the native communist functionaries and did not lead them to question the legitimacy of their system of government. These communist leaders (especially in Hungary and Poland) did not expect to govern on the basis of popular support or legitimation; they were well aware that a great deal of "consciousness-raising" had to be done among the masses to gain their support. The Hungarian communist leader Mathias Rakosi said, "We must reeducate the whole population. Only a small part of it can be imprisoned."[4] In the meantime, reliance on the "fraternal assistance" of the Soviet Union was acceptable and unproblematic. Jakub Berman, a top leader of the Polish regime after

World War II with special responsibility for ideology and propaganda, allowed that the communists were a minority supported by the Red Army: "And so what? Nothing! That doesn't mean anything! Because what does the development of mankind teach us? . . . that it was always the minority, the avant-garde, that rescued the majority, often against the will of the majority . . . That's simply the way history is made."[5]

It was during the first shockwaves which followed the death of Stalin that the externally imposed character of these regimes became a serious liability even in the eyes of some of their leaders and supporters. In discussing the antecedents of the Revolution in Hungary in 1956, Andras Hegedus wrote with the wisdom of hindsight that "we copied mechanically the Soviet-type social institutions, and we strove to turn the traditional, thousand-year-old Western European orientation of the country completely toward Eastern Europe, that is to say, toward the Soviet Union. This aroused widespread popular resistance because these policies offended national sentiment."[6]

Matters symbolic generated as much discontent as those material and economic. For example, Hungarians resented the introduction of Soviet-style army uniforms and the Soviet-style flag as much as they did the scarcities that communist economic policies created and the one-party system that copied the Soviet model. The Revolution of 1956 was an eruption of protest against the defects of a political system all the more unacceptable since it was imposed from abroad.

Hegedus was among those initially unconcerned about the unpopularity of the regime and its dependence on Soviet power: "We thought that we were confronted by the forces of reaction while it was in fact a growing part of the whole nation that opposed our design. We felt that we had a historic mission and saw ourselves as the vanguard in the struggle for a world far superior to anything that had existed before."[7] Although such an attitude was more natural among the Party functionaries who had returned from Moscow (most of them fluent in Russian, some with Soviet wives), and were far removed from the attitudes and experiences of the vast majority of the native population, Hegedus was one of the small number of homegrown communists and an even smaller number among those of peasant origin. His social background in all probability helped him to recognize the harm that the system brought to the country.[8]

The reemergence of inequalities under communist systems supposedly dedicated to sweeping policies of redistribution invariably contributed to the erosion of political beliefs and certitudes. The attitude of Hegedus toward the politically earned and distributed privileges seems to fall between the attitudes of Yeltsin and Gorbachev. Hegedus was keenly aware of the privileges of the Party elite, although it appears from his account that they were not decisive in his gradual disillusionment—an attitude he shared with other figures discussed earlier. He mentions the black limousines with curtained windows (for those at the highest level, armor-plated Soviet-made ZiL), equipped with color-coded lights and special horns; the special phones and phone lines in the office; and villas in the hills of Buda, traditionally an upper-class residential district, many with swimming pools. Hegedus notes that as he advanced in the hierarchy, his and his family's living space expanded. There was also free access to the special stores with home delivery offering such otherwise unavailable luxuries as lemons, hard salami, and veal. The Party elite also had special resorts and medical facilities, even a tailoring service. According to his account, he and his family were uneasy about these amenities and privileges and declined some. All of them, he writes, "were supposed to serve the purpose of making it possible for us to concentrate on our work without petty distractions; in fact, they [the privileges] removed us from the daily experience of the population, from the world of low living standards . . . waiting lines and low incomes. These privileges made us blind and deaf, though perhaps not completely, to the cares of ordinary people."[9]

He recalls that when he was first served a luxurious meal in the Party Secretariat, he protested the privilege to one of his superiors. The latter explained that "my skills were of great value for the Party. I was ashamed, but from then on I did not reject the special meals."[10] As will be recalled, Wolfgang Leonhard as a young functionary experienced similar embarrassment upon finding that not merely were the meals in the Party headquarters dining rooms greatly superior to what was available elsewhere, but the dining rooms were segregated according to position in the hierarchy. Despite his ruminations and doubts, Hegedus had no discernible problem accepting these perks as long as his basic commitment to the system was intact.

Material privileges were not the only means of rewarding and separating the political elite from the rest of the population. While a great deal of Party rhetoric (in Hungary, as in other communist states, was devoted to the importance of being at one with the masses (to be sure, without relinquishing the "vanguard" role), the Party created various institutions which separated the political elite from ordinary people. Most important were the Party schools. They were boarding schools, "total institutions" (exactly in Goffman's sense) in which the pupils spent a few months or a year. The students came from all walks of life and included industrial managers, collective farm chairmen, army officers, writers, artists, administrators, and outstanding factory workers. Being chosen was a great honor and a stepping stone to a higher position. The main, ostensible purpose of these schools was to impart greater ideological-political enlightenment to the most promising supporters of the system and to deepen loyalties and convictions already demonstrated. These schools also enhanced an elite consciousness and helped to insulate the Party loyalists and functionaries from their society.

Hegedus attended a Party school for six months in 1946; at the time, he writes, he still had to struggle against his peasant background, which fostered "individualistic tendencies" and deprived him of the superior experiences and insights inherent in working-class collectivism. The spirit of collectivism at the Party school was fostered, among other things, by cutting off the participants from their family and friends and by introducing them to sessions of criticism and self-criticism. These were a vehicle for inculcating the proper virtues in the future (or current) members of the Party elite as well as a major device in the struggle against individualism and were dedicated to the obliteration of the distinction between one's private and public selves.[11] Hegedus compares the cloistered atmosphere at the Party school to that of a medieval monastery:" In this enclosed atmosphere peculiar rituals developed that combined elements of life in medieval nunneries and the barracks of the Austro-Hungarian monarchy. Faith and militaristic discipline were melded into a compound with which to fight the hated individualism and assorted 'ideological deviations.'"

The Party schools sought to shape not merely the political attitudes but the total personality of the pupils. Hegedus concluded later in life that the model personality to be developed had three principal characteristics. First was "the glorification of the Party. The Party, like some hidden divinity, appeared to be the repository of ultimate truths and was, as such, infallible. At the same time, it was also the ultimate judge of morality and unerring critic of matters cultural; as such, it could demand any sacrifice." Second was a sense of mission. including belief in the global liberation of the proletariat and the building of a harmonious social order free of exploitation and contradictions. Third was "the faith in Marxism-Leninism, the only true science." The main goal was to have faith replace thought and critical reflection. Hegedus recalled that when on one occasion an ideological functionary held forth on the wonders of the highest stage of socialism (communism), someone in the audience asked: "'Comrade Rudas, is it fair to assume that in communist society there will be no scoundrels?' Rudas got red in the face and dismissed the question as a provocation."[12]

Personal predisposition combined with such schooling shaped the dedicated Party functionary, who, like Hegedus remained incapable of shedding his beliefs for decades. The persistence of his faith is illustrated by his responses to the major Hungarian show trial, that of Laszlo Rajk, a former high-ranking (non-Moscovite) communist, and his associates. As Hegedus describes it, these proceedings were rationalized in stages: "First, we acknowledge the necessity of the Party purge on the basis of biographical factors; at that point, suspicion suffices to expel someone from the Party. [Next] we accept the necessity of the campaigns of vigilance under conflictual historical conditions, even at the expense of ourselves becoming innocent victims." My interviews in Hungary provided further illustrations of the willingness of committed Party functionaries and intellectuals to believe, at the time, that the charges were true.[13]

General Wojciech Jaruzelski of Poland also accepted such trials at face value: "In 1951 I and some colleagues were invited to attend a trial . . . the trial could not have seemed more credible. The prosecutor read the accusations. There was proof, witnesses . . . The accused . . . confessed. They expressed their regrets. How could we have doubted it? . . . Let's not forget the climate: the Cold War. NATO's formation . . . The Korean War . . . We lived in an atmosphere of permanent menace. Our mission was to defend our country and here people told us the enemy had agents in our ranks."[14]

Hegedus recalled that during his years in power several of his former friends were sent to the notorious Hungarian concentration camp Recsk under conditions often far worse than those experienced by communist political prisoners during the anticommunist Horthy era: "We comforted ourselves with the belief that we were fighting 'evil,' the forces of reaction, 'the enemies of people.' "

Another painful collision between the impulses of apolitical personal decency and political considerations occurred when, after the arrest of an old friend and political associate, he ran into the man's wife sitting by herself in a coffee bar. He hesitated about approaching her and finally turned around and left. He calls this one of the "most shameful memories" of his life."[15]

It is important to note that it was not ignorance or illusions about the existing political realities that allowed Hegedus to go about his tasks with a largely untroubled conscience—in fact his conscience was not completely untroubled. Rather, he marshaled arguments to silence his conscience, to quiet his doubts. As he puts it: "Poorly understood political considerations helped to repress ethical scruples and the horror over these crimes." In addition, there was concern over "the uncertainty of my personal fate"; that is to say, it was more prudent to go along than to question policies openly or admit doubts to colleagues and superiors.

Years later his response to the execution of Imre Nagy and his associates in 1958 reveals the persistence of similar attitudes: "Although there was much discussion [among the émigrés in Moscow, that is, former Hungarian communist leaders, after the Revolution of 1956] of the treachery of Imre Nagy . . . we were nonetheless stunned by the news of his execution. To which I must add . . . that while I was deeply shocked by the human tragedy involved, I felt no moral revulsion against those who made the decision. I well knew that all of us in Moscow . . . due to the logic of the situation could not have avoided rendering a similar harsh judgment, even if our inner feelings had protested against it."[16]

In the late 1950s the ends still justified the means. To subordinate means to ends is a common enough human disposition, but under ordinary circumstances this creates no great moral dilemmas. It is those in positions of power who are acutely confronted with this problem because they can employ more questionable and consequential means. The key issues for the powerholders like Hegedus were how profoundly the means conflicted with the ends, how far the means went in undermining, soiling, the desirable goals, and, for that matter, whether ends and means were necessarily linked. For instance, did people have to put up with mendacious propaganda in order to have better childcare facilities? Had the show trials and the associated torture of innocent defendants helped to reduce infant mortality or raise the living standards of industrial workers? Did the cult of personality improve the sense of community in urban areas? Had the stifling of free expression reduced crime rates, and so on?

It usually turns out that the laudable objectives had little to do with the questionable means used to achieve them. In fact, the relation was inverse: Because the leaders were convinced that they pursued great, historically unprecedented objectives, they felt free to use questionable means not only to achieve benign objectives but, above all, to stay in power and enhance their power. The possession of power at virtually any cost was posited as the precondition for attaining such more specific and indisputably laudable goals as full employment, better childcare, and lower crime rates.

One key question of this study is, At what point and under what circumstances does the sense of entitlement to use questionable means begin to waver? From Hegedus's account several factors emerge, shedding light on this process. First, it is important to bear in mind that the acquisition of beliefs and values was itself a lengthy and gradual process—in the case of Hegedus, beginning in his late teens. He became a communist at a time when such beliefs and activities brought danger, hardship, and punishment, for the Party was illegal under the previous anticommunist political system. (This sets him apart from the Soviet figures discussed earlier, for whom joining the Party and embarking on a political career was a secure choice encouraged and rewarded by the authorities.)

For most people, suffering experienced for their beliefs and principles becomes self-evident and durable proof that these beliefs are correct and deserving of unconditional loyalty and defense. In 1944, Hegedus, who belonged to the small communist underground in Hungary, was arrested and mistreated by his captors; he escaped from a moving train that was to take him to Germany. To be sure, the period in his life when being a communist was associated with danger and sacrifice was short compared to the period when the same affiliation meant power and privilege. Even so, the experience of risk taking and suffering created durable commitments and a readiness to subordinate means to ends. Ruthlessness often originates in such a personal history.

Hegedus offers the key to his life and political choices in the title of his book *Under the Spell of History and Power:* "It was the combination of a sense of historical mission with the need for power that made it possible [to persist in these attitudes] . . . But sense of the duty of the Party functionary also played a part . . . My generation was born into a historical transformation; many of us became active participants in major social changes. We got used to power and its privileges quickly, and its possession became one of our most basic needs."

Already in his youth Hegedus became convinced of the necessity of changing the social system he was born into and came to hate because of his experiences as a child of struggling, if not entirely impoverished, peasants. Moreover, he writes: "We [the communists] were beholden to a fetishistic belief in [historical] laws. We thought that Engels was right when he declared that the evolution of society is just as much subordinated to laws as evolution in nature and we were merely assisting the realization of these laws . . . all of us were equipped with defense mechanisms which enabled us to avert, or at least delay, a personal catharsis."

The catharsis of Hegedus took place under undramatic circumstances during his post-1956 Moscow exile. Presumably it was the opportunity for reflection and the freedom from high-pressure political work that made it possible to embark on what he called the second, more autonomous and independent phase of his life. More than another decade was required for him to rid himself completely of the lingering wish to return to power.[17]

However candid his account appears to be, it is not easy to discern the most compelling reasons for his disaffection and for the lengthy and halting nature of the process leading to it. It is equally difficult to know what was more important, the possession and exercise of power or the ideals justifying its possession. By 1956, he wrote later, "We [the leaders] were no longer orthodox Marxist-Leninists in the true sense of the word; most of us were guided by the practical considerations of retaining power. And yet our belief in the truth of our ideology played a great part in our thinking—at the time, less as a guide to our practice and policy than as a justification of our past deeds (including crimes) and rigidity."

Throughout his career as a committed high-level functionary there were incidents and short-lived moral conflicts which made him uneasy, but not uneasy enough to seek release from his political roles and activities. When he became minister of agriculture at age twenty-nine, he contributed to what he called the "militarization of agriculture." During his tours of inspection (on which he was transported in a black, curtained limousine) he was ambivalent about his role as he listened to the reports of the directors of state farms: "In the beginning I enjoyed these occasions, as they provided ritualistic gratification of the need for power; at the same time, there was a lurking unease. I learned a lot during this year and a half [while minister of agriculture], perhaps even to hate this grotesque, militaristic routine of exercising power; but these feelings remained concealed for years."[18]

In 1953 there is a troubled awareness, behind the mask of the self-confident and loyal Party man, of the damage done to agriculture and the peasant way of life by forced collectivization, the compulsory delivery of produce, and the campaigns against the kulaks. He also felt threatened by the show trials, knowing that he too could share the fate of many of the older generation of functionaries: "At the beginning of 1953 the gulf between my apparent self-assurance and an inner confusion was perhaps the deepest." He understood in early 1956 why one of the judges (Jonas) in the Hungarian show trials committed suicide—an act that Hungarian State Security sought to explain in terms of drugs and sexual perversions.

Khrushchev's revelations in 1956 was a key event in his political life, as it was for his Hungarian contemporaries and the generation of Party leaders and functionaries in the Soviet Union. He reports "reading the charges [against Stalin] with astonishment." The speech made him realize "how many innocent people were murdered in the Soviet Union under the despotism of Stalin."

Another moral-political milestone was the posthumous rehabilitation and reburial of Laszlo Rajk and his associates in 1956. Hegedus "shuddered" when reading a confidential report about the discovery of the hidden burial site in the woods near Budapest. It made him realize that "those who made this decision [about the place of burial] must have known that it was not a lawful execution but judicial murder. Victims of such murders were always buried in secret." At the ceremonial reburial "we the leaders of the Party and the state stood in the front of the mourners. There was intense hatred in the eyes of the crowd and especially the relatives [of the victims] directed at us."[19]

Such feelings and incidents notwithstanding, a break with the system was far from easy. It was not a simple matter to translate doubt and disillusionment into some sort of political action or gesture, especially for one of the leaders. No one resigned as a matter of personal conviction; resignations were ordered and were often followed by arrests. A somewhat similar situation occurs with the hypothetical decision to "resign" from the Mafia or some other organized criminal enterprise.

As the political disenchantment of Hegedus grew in the 1960s and 1970s, after he returned to Hungary, "objective conditions" made it easier for him to distance himself from the system and its official doctrines. Under Janos Kadar, the postrevolutionary leader of the country, withdrawal from political activity ceased to be life-threatening or otherwise punished. On the other hand, after Hegedus was allowed to return to Hungary from Moscow he knew that he could not reenter political life, discredited as he was by his association with the pre-revolutionary, Stalinist regime—in particular, by his summoning of Soviet troops in October 1956. During the 1960s and 1970s Hegedus was still on record as a supporter of one-party systems in Eastern Europe, and he kept his distance from the organized dissent of Hungarian intellectuals after 1975.[20]

Apparently two processes combined to release Hegedus gradually from his previous political beliefs and roles: his own reawakening and his being rejected by the system itself after 1956. Other circumstances made it easier to distance himself from the system and its ideology. He noted in a conversation with me that after the Revolution of 1956 he was still only in his mid-thirties. He had far more time left for a new departure than many other people in similar positions who were already in their fifties or sixties. By becoming a sociologist and working in a sociological research institute Hegedus found a new, supportive environment, which helped him put the past behind him.[21] His social origin and rural roots were important in this process, providing resources in the form of traditional values as well as experiences disconfirming the policies of the Party and the government.[22]

Hegedus, though disillusioned with "actually existing socialism," remained a democratic socialist or social-democrat and a critic of the right-of-center, nationalistic government that ran the country until its electoral defeat in 1994.

IMRE NAGY (1896–1958)

The case of Imre Nagy has obvious parallels with those of Hegedus and Dubcek (discussed below): all three were prime ministers at some point in their careers, and each had a lifelong commitment to the communist movement and system. Like Hegedus, Nagy had roots in the countryside[23] and a scholarly orientation. Like Dubcek, he spent many years in the Soviet Union and was also widely recognized for his personal decency. With Gorbachev he shared a misguided hope in the possibility of reconciling serious reform with the preservation of the fundamentals of the communist system.[24] But Imre Nagy was the only one who paid with his life for his rejection of actually existing socialism.

Imre Nagy did not engage in autobiographical writing except while in prison before his death;[25] we learn about his political evolution from his political writings and his actions.

Nagy was a loyal and committed communist and functionary most of his life. It was only in his last few years that he became a revisionist or reformist, a moderate who was shunted away from power.[26] In the penultimate period of his life, during the Revolution of 1956, he was briefly thrust into power by the forces of the Revolution he did not unleash. He took over the revolutionary government hesitantly and hoped almost till the very end for some rapprochement with the Soviet Union. Although he did not use the expression, he sought, like Dubcek, to create a "socialism with a human face" and a more autonomous Hungary within the Socialist Commonwealth. He was also a product of the political culture of the Party. According to a Hungarian source, "There is nothing to indicate that even during his Romanian exile [from late 1956, after he was abducted from the Yugoslav embassy in Budapest, to early 1958, when he was returned to Hungary] his theoretical thinking had undergone any fundamental change. It must be said: the legendary strength of his character for a long time also entailed the obligatory Party discipline of the Bolshevik."[27]

Unlike many supporters of the communist cause within or outside the socialist commonwealth, Nagy had his faith revitalized by the revelations of Khrushchev at the Twentieth Party Congress, which seemed to confirm his own beliefs and hopes for reform.[28] For many others the revelations showed the unimagined depths of the abuse of power, but for Nagy they were proof of the system's capacity to regenerate itself.

Imre Nagy was born into a peasant family, though his father became a railroad worker and his mother was a domestic servant before marrying. As a young man, Nagy moved to Budapest and worked in a large metallurgical plant. He was drafted into the army during World War I and taken prisoner in Russia. In 1918 he joined the Soviet Communist Party, as did many other prisoners of war and fought in the Russian Civil War. After his return to Hungary he worked in the illegal communist movement and was jailed for three years for his activities. In 1928 he chose emigration, first to Vienna, then to Moscow. After fifteen years in the Soviet Union he returned to Hungary, in 1945 with other Hungarian communists, in the wake of the Soviet troops. He became minister of agriculture and presided over the land reform. He was briefly minister of interior and, in 1947, presiding officer of the parliament. He opposed the rapid, forced collectivization of agriculture in 1948 and consequently was removed from political position and appointed dean of an agricultural college. In the summer of 1953, after Stalin's death, he became prime minister and set off on a more moderate course in an attempt to remedy the excesses of the previous Stalinist regime. In early 1955 he was once more shunted aside owing to the successful intraparty intrigues of Mathias Rakosi, the leading Hungarian Stalinist. Nagy was expelled not only from the Politburo and the Central Committee but from the Party as well, after being a member for forty years. Reportedly he was in tears when this last humiliation befell him.[29] He was out of power until the Revolution, when he was called upon to become prime minister. After the Soviet troops crushed the Revolution he was taken into custody, tried in secret, and executed in 1958 for being the leader of the "counterrevolution."

Imre Nagy was no Milovan Djilas, there is no evidence that he rejected the fundamentals of the system or questioned the postulates of Marxism-Leninism or the character of the Soviet Union. A sympathetic biographer writes that "he was a *believing* communist: he was fully convinced of his own and the Party's historical role . . . He was without any cynicism . . . He believed that the Party expected him to tell the truth." The same biographer observes that "in all probability he was also marked by the self-deception of honest party functionaries: by the conviction that beyond the difficulties, anguish, and torment—these unavoidable concomitants of the building of socialism—they did battle for the people and a better future." Nagy believed that Marxism-Leninism, if properly applied, could do wonders. His tragedy stemmed from his attempt to graft basic human decency onto the methods and policies of a ruthless, power-oriented political movement. Consequently a series of contradictions marked his career and character: "He wished to be humane amidst inhumanities . . . A good communist and patriot. It was impossible. He wanted to be a good Hungarian and a friend of the Soviet Union. He was prevented in this . . . by the leaders in Moscow whom he trusted and whom . . . he had served for some time, and whom, despite all, he would never betray. He was run over by those whose interests . . . he always held more important than his own."[30]

Like Dubcek, Nagy was a reformist and a moderate nationalist. Almost until his arrest in late 1956 he hoped that the post-Stalin leadership in the Soviet Union could be trusted and would allow a more independent and democratic Hungary to come into existence. The Soviet leaders on several occasions duped him into believing this. His final words in his trial sum up his convictions: "Twice during my life I tried to save the honor of socialism in the Danube Valley: in 1953 and 1956. Rakosi and the Russians prevented me from accomplishing this."[31]

Though Nagy was a loyal servant of the communist cause from his youth until the Revolution of 1956, there were early instances of mild insubordination and alleged right-wing tendencies during his exile in the Soviet Union when (in 1930) he was forced to engage in public self-criticism. His crime included the remark "I refuse to fawn on the [Communist] International."[32] In 1949 he had to engage in self-criticism because of his reservations about the policies of the Hungarian Communist Party in the immediate postwar period—specifically, rapid, forced industrialization and collectivization. There was another small deviation: he attended the Protestant church wedding of his daughter in 1946—"a gesture on the part of a prominent communist leader that was unusual and bizarre even at the time."[33]

Despite his oft-proclaimed attachment to and respect for Marxism-

Leninism, his concern with morality and decency led him to ideas that had little to do with Marxism. During the period when he was barred from any political activity he wrote: "We cannot become a socialist country until we ourselves have become new socialist beings who have been elevated to a higher plane of humanity, not only by our material welfare, knowledge and culture but also our superior moral point of view and pure ethical principles."[34] The failure to create such human beings was the most resounding of the failures of all existing socialist systems. "Pure ethical principles" was not the kind of idea that communist movements and regimes embraced.

The critiques of Nagy were never—as far as one can tell—directed at Marxism-Leninism or the Soviet Union, but at the Stalinist leadership and its policies in Hungary. Nagy spent almost half of his adult life in the Soviet Union and developed a deep loyalty to the Soviet leadership. We do not know what feelings he had as he weathered the Purges and show trials of the 1930s. An English author writes: "Nagy lived this quiet life [in the Soviet Union] right through the destruction of the kulaks, the famine in the Ukraine and the great terror. Bukharin, whose views on agriculture had shaped Nagy's own, much of the Hungarian émigré leadership, half of the intelligentsia in Moscow, went to their death. Nagy was untouched. In Moscow in the thirties as later in Budapest in the early fifties, he led a charmed life."[35]

Nagy shared with Dubcek the capacity to transcend the Soviet experience. Evidently the horrors witnessed during the 1930s did not lead to soul-searching, to questioning the regime or the cause. Dubcek had a better excuse: he was in his early teens at the time. Nagy was an adult. Perhaps he was able to overlook the Soviet experiences in the hope that an improved version of the system would be created in Hungary. The English author concludes: "In Moscow he closed his eyes to Stalin's terror . . . He kept his doubts to himself, cherishing the illusion that in Hungary things would be different."[36]

No matter what he saw in the Soviet Union it was impossible for him to back out of the movement voluntarily. Not only had he invested too much but the practical consequences of breaking with the Party in a communist state, especially during the lifetime of Stalin, were severe. He would have had to defect to start a new life.

When Stalin died in 1953, Nagy, speaking in the Hungarian Parliament, was "deeply shaken" and "crushed by grief" as he remembered the "leader of humanity."[37]

As in other cases of highly placed communist functionaries, Nagy's estrangement from the system coincided with his rejection by the system and his mistreatment by fellow leaders, the Rakosi clique, and later the Soviet leaders. Nonetheless, his personal grievances—the loss of membership in the Hungarian Academy of Sciences and the Party and the loss of his teaching position—were not the source of his critiques of the policies of the Hungarian Party but rather the result of his dissent from official policies. Nagy had no difficulty in reconciling his efforts to steer the system in a more moderate and humane direction with a basic and deep loyalty toward it. A far greater blow to his loyalty was his abandonment by the post-Stalin Soviet leadership in January 1955 during an official visit to Moscow. On that occasion "everybody turned on him, including his principal protector, Malenkov." Worse followed during and after the Revolution. Thus, while fresh Soviet troops were pouring into Hungary in early November 1956, Yuri Andropov, then Soviet ambassador to Hungary, repeatedly assured Nagy "without batting an eye that these were 'normal troop movements,' that there was no cause for alarm, that the agreements remained valid. These troops were to ensure the peaceful and expeditious withdrawal of the others."[38]

It was after the death of Stalin (in March 1953) that opportunities arose for Nagy to publicly express his apprehensions about the building of socialism in Hungary between 1948 and 1953. He focused on economic matters, though he was far from indifferent to the abuse of political power: "The road toward the building of socialism must not lead through the decline of the living standards of the working people, not through price increases and wage reductions . . . What kind of socialism would that be . . . which does not ensure bread . . . ? Who would be enthusiastic about a socialism that cannot provide meat, milk, or bacon? . . . The old economic policy . . . failed to take into account the human being and society; it narrowed the idea of socialism to increasing the production of iron and steel, to overindustrialization."[39]

Elsewhere he has written: "The degeneration of power is seriously endangering the fate of socialism . . . The People's Democracy . . . is obviously being replaced by Party dictatorship . . . Its aims are not determined by

Marxism, the teachings of scientific socialism, but by autocratic views that are maintained at any cost and by any means."[40]

He was also moved to express strong indignation about the loss of idealism and the erosion of public and political morality and in doing so offered a widely applicable critique of communist systems:

> The lofty ideals and principles of socialism . . . are increasingly losing their true significance in public consciousness due to the people's experiences in their everyday life . . . The violent contrasts between words and deeds, between principles and their realization is rocking the foundations of our . . . society and our Party. This contrast, of which people are becoming more and more aware . . . is leading to the loss of faith among the masses . . . The degeneration of power . . . [is] also evidenced by the fact that at present the number of persons imprisoned is greater than ever before . . .
>
> Public morality is an indispensable requirement of socialist society . . . individuals whose actions went counter to the morals of socialist society and to existing laws acquired positions in important fields of public life . . .
>
> There is a type of material dependence that forces men to relinquish their individualities and their convictions, which is not compatible with morality in public life . . . What sort of political morality is there in public life where contrary opinions are not only suppressed but punished with actual deprivation of livelihood . . . where those who are opposed in principle to the ruling political trend are barred from their professions . . . where a man is not only dismissed from his political office but from membership in the Hungarian Academy of Sciences and from his university teaching position as well . . .
>
> This all-powerful material dependence . . . is killing the most noble human virtues that should be especially developed in a socialist society: courage, resolution, sincerity . . . consistency of principle and strength. In their place, the leaders have made virtues of self-abasement, cowardice, hypocrisy, lack of principle and lies . . .

> ... On what sort of Communist morality do they base my
> expulsion from the party ranks because of my theoretical differ-
> ences with the policies of the Party leadership, while at the same
> time the accomplices in the mass executions of our comrades
> hold high office in the Party?[41]

Imre Nagy grasped what the moral collapse of communism meant. Repeatedly his indignation was provoked by the moral failings of the system,
especially by the gulf between theory and practice, ideals and realities.

Nagy remarked on another occasion: "If only we had eight to ten honest
people in the country who have some spine, all would be well!" Thus, in the
end and in a peculiarly un-Marxist fashion, Nagy fell back on old-fashioned
notions of honesty and dishonesty, betrayal and character.[42] (In the same
spirit Khrushchev reportedly remarked that if people stopped stealing from
the state for only one day communism could be built.)

Through much of his life, Nagy shared with others similarly committed
the belief that "Communism could rise above the crimes committed in its
name."[43] At the very end of his life he probably reached the bitter conclusion
that this was not the case.

ALEXANDER DUBCEK (1921–1992)

Alexander Dubcek's attitudes and political evolution were comparable to
those of Andras Hegedus. Both were leaders of an East European country
under Soviet control; both became disaffected after long service to the Party;
both were excluded from political power and participation later in life, though
Hegedus was treated better than Dubcek during that long period.

The differences between their careers, erosion of faith, and loss of power
may be more significant than the similarities. Dubcek was removed from
power by the Soviet intervention in Czechoslovakia in 1968 because he attempted to steer his country away from the Soviet model; Hegedus lost his
power as a result of the collapse of the communist government, of which
he was prime minister, during the Revolution of 1956. At the time, Hegedus was identified with the hardliners, not the reformers. Dubcek was a reformer in 1968 *before* the Soviet intervention, which was intended to halt the

reforms, whereas Hegedus was a loyal functionary at the time of the Soviet intervention in Hungary in 1956.

Dubcek's political career was much longer than Hegedus's; he served the Party in various capacities for three decades, from 1939 until 1969. Hegedus was a functionary for just over a decade, from 1945 to 1956. Unlike Hegedus, Dubcek made a brief political comeback between 1989 and 1992 after the fall of the communist regime, becoming the president of the new Czech parliament. He died in a car accident in 1992.

In their social background there are further important differences. Hegedus, as will be recalled, came from a largely traditional peasant family. Dubcek came from a working-class family which had a tradition of strong socialist and pro-Soviet beliefs going back to the 1920s. He was conceived, in his words, "by a pair of Slovak socialist dreamers."[44] His father, a carpentry worker, emigrated in the United States in 1912; there he met Alexander's future mother. The couple joined "one of the two newly established Communist parties . . . It was my mother, I was told, that brought my dad to the study of Marxism, which he soon accepted as his own creed." His father "was not just a revolutionary but a romantic."[45]

Dubcek's parents returned to Slovakia in 1921. Alexander was born there that year. Subsequently his family was among a group of Czech and Slovak communist workers who, intent on aiding the new socialist state, moved to the Soviet Union in 1925. They took equipment and machinery purchased with their own savings. In doing so, they "like most other members, sacrificed everything they had."[46] The young Dubcek stayed in the Soviet Union until 1938, mostly in Kirgizia and Gorky, and attended Soviet schools. Ironically, he enjoyed the confidence of the Soviet leaders early in his career because he had been brought up and completed his education in the Soviet Union and spoke good Russian.[47]

During World War II Dubcek participated in the Slovak resistance movement, and after the war he embarked on the career of a Party functionary. Unlike Hegedus, who transformed himself into a professional sociologist after his fall from power, Dubcek never became an intellectual. After he was removed from power in 1969 he went from being a high-ranking Party official back to being a manual worker. His memoirs are more concerned with events than with self- reflection and political soul-searching. He had little interest in theory. Just as his involvement with Party politics was more gradual and more natural than Hegedus's—representing no break with his family background—so, too, his distancing himself from the cause was more gradual and less dramatic. Perhaps Dubcek was temperamentally more of a moderate than Hegedus, both as a communist functionary and as an ex-communist.

It was, at least in part, a certain apolitical decency and moderation that apparently pushed Dubcek toward the path of reform during the 1960s. As Jan Sejna recalls, "Dubcek stood out as an honest man who sincerely believed Novotny [a hardliner, head of the Party, 1953–1968, and president of the republic, 1957–1968] . . . He was a thoroughly decent fellow . . . a man of total integrity, with no personal ambition; but he was unbelievably naive, and his naivete was to cost him his position and nearly his life."[48]

While Dubcek was growing up in the Soviet Union, there was no shortage of experiences that could have planted the seeds of doubt and disillusionment. His recollections from Kirgizia are of particular importance and potential relevance for the future rethinking of his views of the Soviet system:

> Collectivization announced itself by the arrival of peasants deported from their homes in the Ukraine and Russia and dispatched in freight cars to Siberia and Central Asia. I remember dreadful scenes at the Frunze railroad station. Some died en route, and those who survived, including children, looked like living corpses. They were so hungry that they ate fodder for pigs and poultry that was teeming with maggots. I can never forget the sight of a dead man with his belly blown out. I asked my mother what the man had died from, and she said, "From hunger." . . .
>
> I don't remember anyone who understood what was causing this misery. It was very disturbing for all of us, children as well as adults. At the same time, of course, we continued to live our normal lives. The grown-ups worked hard . . . We children went to school and did our homework . . . But life was not quite the same as before.[49]

Nonetheless, in an important sense, life was the same as before: these experiences evidently failed to undermine his parents' faith in the cause and the Soviet system. Dubcek does not tell the reader how they managed to avoid drawing unsettling conclusions from these experiences, or how they rationalized them, or what moral calculus enabled them to persevere in their political roles and commitments, if indeed they found these events disturbing. One can only guess that the enormity of their commitment (moving to the Soviet Union, having a long association with the Party, living with others similarly committed) and the lack of alternatives overpowered the moral confusion and revulsion that such experiences must have created.

It is possible, even probable, that true believers like Dubcek's family took refuge in ideas and attitudes that religious believers fall back on when confronted with horrible and meaningless occurrences which conflict with their beliefs. The believers will tell themselves that one cannot presume to understand divine justice or intentions, the hidden meaning of certain acts or events, the injustices and deprivations that innocent, good people often suffer. Similarly, the secular believer may seek and find reassurance in professing a limited understanding of the complex motives, designs, or long-range policies of the higher secular authorities in the possibility that there is some crucial, yet hidden, explanation of or scheme behind seemingly inexplicable and horrendous events, some higher wisdom at work, usually embodied in the Party and its leadership at any given time.

Dubcek also recalls the resistance to collectivization and its violent repression. One result of the collectivization campaign was the disappearance of fruit from the market as the local farmers destroyed their orchards rather than have them collectivized.

Unsettling and potentially disillusioning experiences continued after the family moved to Gorky during the 1930s.

> Good times were overshadowed by the strange and disturbing
> things happening around us from mid-1936 on . . . Revolutionary
> heroes whom we had been taught to admire were suddenly de-
> clared villains, put on trial and executed. In school we were in-
> structed to cut whole pages from our textbooks as truths changed,
> often overnight . . .

> Parents of some of my schoolmates suddenly disappeared, and
> when I asked their sons or daughters what had happened, they
> were never able to explain . . . It did not take long to learn that
> behind the "disappearances" were the secret police . . .
>
> The whole picture could not be put together for many years.
> For many of us it was Khrushchev's historical revelations in 1956
> that finally made it all clear. But that was twenty years later. Dur-
> ing the years 1936 to 1938 all political news in the Soviet Union
> . . . came from Soviet media . . . Soviet methods of socialization
> were very thorough, and even gossip seemed to disappear as
> people feared informers.

Even if "the whole picture" could only "be put together" twenty years later,
Dubcek still fails to explain how he and his parents handled these experiences at the time. Nor does he explain exactly what he meant by saying that
"Soviet methods of socialization were thorough"? Does it mean that he and
his parents were persuaded to accept the official justification of the terror?
Or that they stopped thinking about these matters because it was unpleasant and pointless to do so? Did they think that bad as these events were, the
survival of the system required and justified them? We do not know.

He does say that his father "chose not to talk about these affairs with me"
and that "whatever confusion I felt had little chance of rising to serious
doubts. The idea that the executed could all be innocent . . . was simply too
ghastly to think about . . . in 1938 even that skeptical humanist Lion Feuchtwanger . . . who had attended the trials of Radek and Bukharin, believed
the accused were guilty."[50] But Feuchtwanger was far from "a skeptical humanist" as far as the Soviet system was concerned; he was a gullible fellow
traveler predisposed to venerate it.[51] His agreement with the official interpretation is hardly proof of their authenticity; his gullibility does not help
to explain that of Dubcek and his family, if indeed they accepted the official
version of the events, as Dubcek implies, though he cannot quite bring himself to say so.

Dubcek also recalls that in 1938 his family, forced to decide about staying
in the Soviet Union or losing their Czechoslovakian citizenship, chose to
return to Czechoslovakia: "My father hardly hesitated despite his resolute

belief in socialism. He was not blind to what was happening around him, and he could not avoid critical thoughts and doubts." If so, such critical thoughts and doubts remained in tightly separated compartments—as in many similar cases when the basic commitment was at odds with the problematic experience. Although his father "could not avoid critical thoughts," this apparently had little effect on his behavior or his devotion to the cause.

After the return to Slovakia and during World War II the young Dubcek's loyalty was cemented by the conviction that the Slovak Communist Party "was the only organized body in clear and unambiguous opposition to fascism." While the Nazi-Soviet pact made him uneasy, "we never thought that Russia took this collusion seriously."[52]

It appears that up to this point and for years to follow, Dubcek at times realized that Soviet or Party policies were morally problematic (just as Hegedus did after World War II) but managed to maintain his loyalty: his basic values outweighed the doubts; the discrepancies between theory and practice, although dimly perceived, did not undermine his beliefs or affect his behavior. We do not get much information about what precisely these fundamental beliefs consisted of, perhaps because they were so deeply internalized that they were taken for granted.

After World War II a new component was added to his political loyalty: the feeling that Soviet strength and performance in the war legitimated the system. "In 1945 this spectacle of overwhelming Soviet power was my generation's primary impression of the war . . . This perception easily translated into illusions about the whole Soviet system, political as well as economic . . . I had not forgotten my early Soviet experience, but the memory of its dark side tended to recede in the face of the war. Moreover, I was not immune to the propaganda to which I had been exposed in high school, in Gorky, at the time of the purges when their victims . . . were presented as Nazi . . . agents . . . Thus the war strengthened in me the socialist convictions of freedom and social justice instilled by my parents."

While in the anti-Nazi resistance movement in Slovakia, Dubcek was treated by a doctor whose parents were White Russian exiles who had come to Czechoslovakia in 1917. After the war Dubcek wanted to look him up but learned "that the Russians [had] arrested him and deported him to the Soviet Union. 'Why would they do that?' I asked. 'They were picking up all

Russian exiles,' I was told. 'They had them all on a list.'" Dubcek was "appalled" and helpless but once more managed to digest another morally disturbing experience. Subsequently he sought the release of the doctor from the Gulag, which occurred in 1957. He writes: "The fate of this brave and good man never ceased to fill me with sorrow." But "I was still young, and I was disposed, by my upbringing, to great expectations: in the new, socialist order, economic growth would be planned, production . . . evenly distributed and everybody would get a fair deal . . . I had only vague ideas how such a new world would be built and function. But the Party, which I had joined at the age of seventeen, claimed to know it all; it claimed to have a scientific system for accomplishing its historic mission. All it asked for was patience, discipline and hard work. My belief in socialism was complete."

Until 1949 Dubcek worked in a yeast factory and, though a member of the Party, was "hardly more than a spectator of the dramatic developments of the early postwar years."[53] He saw the old injustices, unemployment, and inequality redressed by measures such as land reform, general health insurance and nationalization of industries. In 1949 he was summoned by the district Party Secretariat and offered a full-time Party job, which he accepted. From then on he rose in the Party apparatus from first secretary of the district Party organization in Trencin to a position on the Central Committee in Bratislava (1951), to regional secretary in Banska Bystrica (1953).

He notes that repression continued in his country well after the death of Stalin. In this dark period he was "confused and frightened." The experience left him with what he regarded as an important insight: "We learned one significant lesson . . . : that socialism is no safer than any other system from abuse by bad, unscrupulous, dishonest people. In my eyes at least, the idea itself did not thereby lose any of its purity and greatness. What was needed, I felt, was to bring the political system of socialism into harmony with its philosophical values." These somewhat naive reflections (reminiscent of Nagy's laments about dishonest people and low public morality) failed to address the question of why it was so difficult to reconcile the philosophical values (theory) with the workings of the political system (practice).

In 1955 Dubcek was sent to Moscow to study at the Higher Political School of the Soviet Communist Party Central Committee. This period in his life could have contributed to the evolution or rethinking of his political ideas.

While at the school he was impressed by Marx's ideas. "The question of the applicability of some of his ideas to the second half of the twentieth century did cross my mind, but I wasn't sure I had any firm answers." He was also troubled by the contradiction between Marx's idea of the dictatorship of the proletariat (associated with majority rule) and Lenin's (which was not). "I was disturbed by these questions but I never dared come out with them." While writing the memoirs, he asked himself whether the failure of socialism "was truly inherent in his [Marx's] ideas" but did not reach a definite conclusion.

Khrushchev's rapprochement with Tito took place while Dubcek was in Moscow. The event made a deep impression on him, for it "legitimized a socialist country's independence from the Soviet Union for the first time."[54] There was also "a flood of depressing news" from those released from the Gulag documenting Stalin's murderous policies—the type of information that he was not yet quite ready to absorb, he points out. He remained cautious and did not share with his fellow Czech students what he learned from Soviet students. But evidently the slow and cautious process of ideological rethinking began in Moscow.

In 1958, after his return home, he was appointed regional Party secretary for Western Slovakia; in 1960 was transferred to Prague as Czechoslovak Central Committee secretary for industry. In Prague he visited "the secluded recreational compound" that Antonin Novotny, the head of the Party, had built for himself, and reacted to it negatively: "I detested the whole idea of it—the isolated luxury enjoyed by the leadership under police protection." Dubcek did not wish to live in a big house; in the spring of 1968 he moved with his family into "a modest home" in a suburb of Prague. (But according to his translator and editor Jiri Hochman, "'the modest house' was . . . a spacious government villa in the most bourgeois pre–World War II quarter of Bratislava.")[55]

Ever since Milovan Djilas's exposure and analysis of the privileges of the Party elite, unease over such privileges has been a recurring theme in the writings of the disaffected. What we cannot tell is how important these sentiments were in the process of becoming disaffected: Were they part of a strongly felt moral indignation which undermined the commitment, or was the inability to rationalize the privileges the reflection of a commitment already weakened for other reasons? Dubcek mentions feelings and experiences which made him uneasy (including politically earned privileges), but he managed for many years to carry on with his work in the Party in spite of them, as did so many others.

In 1962 Dubcek became a member of the Central Committee of the Czechoslovak Communist Party and a candidate member of the presidium, as well as a member of the Kolder commission (named after its chair, Drahomir Kolder), which investigated the repressions of the early 1950s. The information gained in this capacity presumably hastened his reassessment of the system, or, as he puts it, "strengthened my reformist views and my determination to change things. As a member of the commission Dubcek learned about the *specifics* of suffering inflicted on the victims of the regime. They had been "subject to both physical and psychological torture . . . deprived of sleep . . . of water, of decent food, of civilized medical treatment . . . kept in cold cells, forced to sleep on concrete floors (even in the winter), threatened with cruel measures against their wives and children if they refused to sign fabricated confessions. I learned also that the personal involvement of the top Czechoslovak leaders reached almost savage proportions: top Party officials . . . had divided among themselves the property . . . of their former friends and colleagues whom they sent to the gallows. The memory is sickening." (The grabbing of the personal property "by former friends and colleagues" of the condemned was also a galling discovery for another high-ranking Czech functionary, Zdenek Mlynar; see below.)

Dubcek was "dumbfounded by the revelations." It was then that he assumed the office of Slovak Communist Party Central Committee first secretary, an appointment followed by full membership in the Czechoslovak Party presidium. By the end of 1963 he felt satisfied with the reforms that he had promoted while in his new office.[56]

Khrushchev's visit to Czechoslovakia in 1964 provided an occasion for reflecting on the Hungarian Revolution of 1956, which Dubcek had not viewed with much sympathy earlier. He writes: "I was in Moscow at the time . . . not the best place for an objective view. The whole dimension of the revolt was not entirely clear to me then. As a Slovak I was still inclined to see Hungarian events through the lens of my nation's experience, right up through World War II, when Hungary fought on Hitler's side . . . I was not disposed to disbelieve Moscow's interpretation of the rebellion."

It may be noted here that Dubcek was not altogether well informed about Hungarian affairs. For example, he believed that eleven of the thirteen defendants in the Rajk trial were Jewish, which was not the case, and that Rajk himself was Jewish, which was not true either.[57]

During 1963–1967, Dubcek continued the infighting with the hardliners in the Party over reform. What he and other reformers of similar disposition (including Gorbachev) did not seem to realize was that reforms carried forward beyond a certain point would undermine the very foundations of the political order that they sought to preserve. This problem was reflected in a conversation between Dubcek and Gomulka, the Polish leader, in 1968. Dubcek told Gomulka that "horrible injustices had been committed and never redressed," and he was "determined to redress all the old crimes and injustices." Gomulka's response was: "I understand in a moral and human sense. But I am afraid all this would bring about uncontrollable political consequences. It could undermine the position of the Party." Dubcek insisted that he wished to place "the Party's position on new, democratic foundations." Apparently unlike Gomulka at the time, he believed "that the Communist Party could enjoy public support and confidence." Dubcek also favored "a principled program of departure for the Party from the theory and practice of Leninism-Stalinism."[58]

The "discovery" of American-made submachine guns under a highway overpass in western Bohemia planted by Soviet agents revealed to Dubcek the duplicity of the Soviet authorities. Soviet and East German media "launched a campaign of alarm even before the [Czech] police located the hiding place." But by that time it was unlikely that Dubcek had many illusions left about his Soviet allies.

Brezhnev and his entourage, whom Dubcek met several times during the negotiations which preceded and followed the Soviet invasion in 1968, also made a highly negative impression. Dubcek was disheartened by the bullying coarseness, arrogance, and deceitfulness of the Soviet leaders. On one occasion, when he mentioned the support he received from his people in opposing the Soviet invasion, "Brezhnev retorted with his own theory of spontaneity: 'If I gave instructions, I too could have a ton of letters here in no time.'" But Dubcek's naivete and good faith ran deep: "Until the last moment, I did not believe the Soviet leaders would launch a military attack on us . . . It ran contrary my deepest idea of the value system I thought governed the relationships between socialist countries. It took the drastic, practical experience of the coming days and months for me to understand that I was in fact dealing with gangsters . . . until just before midnight August 21, I still believed that relations within the 'socialist camp' were essentially civilized. Surely the last thing I expected was that a meeting of the Presidium would end in a hunting down and kidnapping of half of its members, myself included." Shortly before his arrest he still expected a call that would clear up everything and convey that "this was all just a big misunderstanding."[59]

The 1968 invasion and the personal mistreatment he suffered in its wake terminated Dubcek's remaining attachment to "existing socialism." Another factor of great importance was that the Soviet Union was trampling upon the freedom and autonomy of another socialist nation—in short, his national pride was profoundly violated. Dubcek ended up viewing the Soviet leadership (the Politburo) as a "bunch of cynical, arrogant bureaucrats with a feudal outlook who had long ceased to serve anything but themselves."

Following the August 1968 invasion and after a brief period of grace during which he was appointed ambassador to Turkey (in 1969), Dubcek was expelled from the Party and made a nonperson. He was given a job as mechanic in the forest administration near Bratislava. He was also expelled from the Hunters' Association and the Union of Anti-Fascist Fighters. Between 1970 and 1989 he was under police surveillance.

In the last chapter of his book he writes: "By now, I had for many years believed that the kind of social order practiced in the Soviet Union and in Eastern Europe was a dead-end enterprise. Socialism, or any other modern social system, could not exist without democracy. That was the essential course correction that I was trying to carry out in 1968." He also came to the conclusion that the rise of Solidarity in Poland and the invasion of Afghanistan were key events in the decline of the Soviet system. More originally, he notes the death of Suslov, in 1982, as another milestone in the decay of the Soviet system, for "he was the last living link to Stalin in the Politburo."

Dubcek's views of the political system he served were doubtless also shaped by the experience that the system did not work, as distinct from its violation of Marxian ideals and his own strongly felt moral principles. He notes that "by the mid 1980s everything in Czechoslovakia was deteriorating, most notably environmental conditions and health."[60] Yet by comparison with much of Eastern Europe and especially the Soviet Union, Czechoslovakia was an exemplar of prosperity and efficiency.

Jiri Hochman's afterword to Dubcek's memoirs sheds further light on Dubcek's character but does not fully resolve the puzzle of how he managed to support the system for so long. He writes: "Dubcek was completely without cynicism. He tried to see the good side of everything . . . he always assumed that everyone had good intentions . . . He was often let down, but that never changed his basic nature . . . Dubcek was a moral man with the deeply ingrained Lutheran tradition and family rules of his ancestors. He loved one woman all his life and was a kind, patient, and gentle husband and father. The devious morals of Leninist 'dialectics' never seem to have affected his honesty, personal attitudes and behavior."

The author of these observations himself raises the question of "how Dubcek could have become a high Communist official with these characteristics." This is his answer: "Like most Slovak and Czech Communists during wartime and the early postwar era, he was no Bolshevik. He was a socialist, whose beliefs were easily compatible with his Lutheran family principles . . . he believed in social equality and justice . . . The Party he joined did not advertise that it was a criminal organization. The goals it claimed to strive for made him, like his parents before him, believe that he was becoming part of a movement to realize a centuries-old dream of a fair deal for all . . . In his last years Dubcek identified entirely with the ideas of European Social Democracy . . . in early 1992 he assumed the leadership of the Social Democratic party of Slovakia . . . By then he believed that the whole Leninist and Soviet phenomenon was a tragic miscarriage of history."[61]

Hochman also points out (in a personal communication) that Dubcek's knowledge of Russian and Russian ways was important in promoting his rise in the hierarchy.

The naivete of Dubcek, unexpected in a seasoned Communist Party functionary, is highlighted in a remark that Zdenek Mlynar reports from a conversation between Dubcek and Janos Kadar, the Hungarian communist leader. Kadar asked Dubcek: "'Do you *really* not know the kind of people you are dealing with?' He thought it unbelievable that Dubcek did not know. We were really fools, but our folly was the ideology of reform communism."[62] The people referred to were the Soviet leaders, Brezhnev and company.

It remains to be discovered and explained what mechanisms or techniques enabled such unscrupulous, flawed human beings to rise to the top so regularly in communist systems and what the nature of the affinity was between their personal characteristics and those of the system they created or perpetuated.

It is noteworthy that neither Dubcek nor Hegedus, nor, indeed, most of the Soviet leaders discussed earlier, voluntarily relinquished power as evidence of their disillusionment with the system they served. Most of them were pushed out of power by forces and circumstances over which they had no control. Even those disenchanted with the system entertained for long periods of time the illusion that they could reform or change it from within, that there was something left that could be reformed and was worth reforming.

ZDENEK MLYNAR (1931–1997)

Zdenek Mlynar, another high-ranking Czech communist, far less known than Dubcek, was more self-reflective and more anxious to understand the origins and unraveling of his political beliefs. His thoughts about his break with the Party are particularly illuminating of the process of disillusionment and its protracted nature. His account also sheds light, by implication, on how disenchantment with communist systems and ideologies differed in the East and the West. Those without power, , that is, Western sympathizers, often experienced far greater anguish and a deeper sense of guilt (or betrayal) than those who held power or assisted in its exercise in the communist states. A recent case in point is Eugene Genovese, the distinguished American social historian and former supporter of the Communist Party of the United States, who believed that American supporters of the Soviet Union were no less morally culpable for the crimes of the Soviet system under Stalin than Stalin and his henchmen were.[63] Rarely do we encounter similarly sweeping self-reproach on the part of those who actually exercised power, even after their loss of faith.

Generally speaking, three time-honored, retroactive explanations and excuses were offered by the chastened former powerholders in communist regimes for their actions (or inaction). One was unfamiliarity with the specifics of morally repugnant policies and their consequences. Another was the shifting of responsibility to those higher up. The third was a less clearly articulated belief that ends justify means, vindicating the questionable policies. The last boiled down to the key conviction that the whole was more important than the parts. This attitude allowed the faithful to divorce the Party (an instrument of higher purpose) from the specific mistakes made on its behalf by its leaders and to continue to perceive it as an infallible historical entity.

Mlynar studied law in the Soviet Union and was a trainee in the Soviet public prosecutor's office in Moscow in the early 1950s. He was often present at the interrogation of nonpolitical criminals in Moscow jails, including the notorious Lefortovo prison. He writes: "At the time I never dreamed that in another wing of the very same prison things were taking place that Solzhenitsyn afterwards wrote about . . . One could come into very close contact with this part of the Soviet police and judicial apparatus and not have any notion of the reality, or the extent of the neighboring kingdom of the Gulag." He observes that he was "embarrassingly sheltered" from the realities of the terror, insulated not merely from the experiences of the victims but from those of the "huge majority" of the nation.

Mlynar joined the Party in 1946 at the age of sixteen. He sees himself as belonging to a generation with a "black and white vision of the world" that believed "that the chief political virtues were consistency and radicalism."[64] The Soviet Union was "a land of hope for those who desired a radical departure from the past." But he also avers that his generation "knew nothing of the real conditions in the Soviet Union."[65] But information about such morally problematic matters was not decisive, as numerous examples have already shown. What mattered was the capacity to redefine the situation and whatever was morally problematic. Molotov was perfectly capable of insisting that those mistreated during the Great Purge were not innocent, though perhaps their treatment was a bit harsh; in light of their guilt, their treatment became excusable.

Besides the attractions of the Soviet Union magnified by its wartime role, ideology also played a part in Mlynar's attachment to the cause. "The keystones of [his] Marxist education" included essays by Stalin as well as *The*

Communist Manifesto and Lenin's *State and Revolution*. In retrospect, Mlynar wonders how he could have embraced such works "as a political bible" and concludes that it happened because of the "self-assurance" they provided by conveying "the very laws that govern the development of mankind and the world." These ideas helped him to establish without the shadow of a doubt what was progressive or reactionary, scientific or unscientific, good or bad, for the future of mankind. He recognized later in life that his beliefs were the source of arrogance and paternalism, of the believer's sense of superiority over the nonbeliever. He compares the self-assurance of his generation to the arrogance of Western European Maoists and other New Leftists of the 1960s.

His beliefs and the sense of privileged access to truth that ideology entails enabled him and his generation to support the repressive policies of the Party; to purge people and, at the same time, to consider it "natural, moral and just to be protected and given preferential treatment." These beliefs, forming "a closed system," explain his loyalty to the regime: "It was faith that kept me from drawing normal, logical conclusions from all those occasions in everyday practice and experience. After all, we committed young communists were living the same reality as everybody else, but that *reality spoke to us in a different language*" (my emphasis).

Here Mlynar refers to what has since become designated the phenomenon of selective perception. It was not so much an avoidance of reality, or insulation from it, but its reinterpretation that enabled him and others to persist in their beliefs. Mlynar writes: "Ideologically committed Stalinists, of course, also noticed aspects of reality that called their faith in doubt. But no particular conflict between reality and our faith could ever have been a strong enough argument against the faith *as a whole*" (my emphasis).

Mlynar's case further illustrates the length of time that the committed often needed to alter their worldview. He observes that of his twenty-five years in the Party he spent "twenty years undergoing this slow and painful process" of reassessment. Even after his expulsion from the Party in 1970, it took several more years to complete the process.

It is worth stressing again the combination of cognitive and emotional factors—the fixation on the whole, on some notion of the basic worthiness of the cause—as the key to the capacity to relegate the dissonant parts to relative unimportance for long periods of time. This was the paradigmatic feature of maintaining the fundamentals of political conviction in the face of dissonant realities; more simply, it was the triumph of focusing single-mindedly on ends and intentions over means and consequences.

A major source of the slow, almost imperceptible erosion of faith in Mlynar's case was the years spent in the Soviet Union: "Our experience of everyday life in the Soviet Union mercilessly shattered all our precon-ceptions about the 'Soviet Man.'"[66] Nonetheless, these experiences were not decisive. Even during the Slansky trial (the major Czechoslovakian show trial) Mlynar's belief remained essentially unshaken. The flaws of the system to which he had dedicated his life were redefined as "misunderstandings" or innocent errors; for a long time he succeeded, as had other believers, in shielding his core values and commitments from the encroachment of bad practices.

Thus he "could not believe that the same [Antonin] Zapotocky, [one of the Party leaders] who intervened so positively on my behalf [when Mlynar was under criticism in the Party for expressing reservations about Soviet policies] could ever have consented to the execution of his longtime col-leagues and friends were he not convinced of their irrefutable guilt." Years later he learned not only that Zapotocky was well aware that the charges were fabrications but that he " had "invited Slansky to his home for a party knowing that on his way home Slansky would be arrested. When Slansky was getting into his overcoat after the Party, Zapotocky telephoned the police officer responsible for making the arrest, and according to a prearranged agreement told him: 'He is on the way.'"[67]

In retrospect, this incident was an obvious invitation to moral revulsion. The interesting question is, Would familiarity with the particulars of deceit have caused serious moral revulsion at the time, when Mlynar's belief system was still largely intact?

Later in life Mlynar came to the conclusion that it was his five years in Moscow "that gave rise to my first serious ideological doubts," although he still had plenty of defenses against the onslaught of doubt. For example, it was not too difficult in the early 1950s to explain away the shortages and poverty in the Soviet Union as a result of World War II. He had no expec-tations that he would find the Soviet Union to be "a consumer's paradise."

What had been more bothersome was the "absence of values" or any sort of discernible idealism in the attitudes and behavior of Soviet people, who instead "tried to keep politics utterly separate from their personal lives . . . While we took it for granted that what we said in public we also thought in private, this was not so in the life of the Soviet people." He was also somewhat disturbed by "the significance vodka ha[d] in the life of Soviet people." In the student dormitory in a room that he shared with six other students (all World War II veterans), "when vodka appeared on the table [Stalin's] poster was turned face to the wall and the room then was dominated by a . . . portrait of a courtesan from czarist Petrograd painted on the other side." It was under these conditions that his Soviet interlocutors allowed some of their feelings about the system to emerge: "'I am a swine . . .' a drunken functionary of the Bolshevik party cried on my breast after he had voted at a meeting to expel a friend from the university . . . But the penitent Bolshevik slept it off, having ventilated his self-contempt; and, as far as I can recall, he went on behaving in more or less the same way . . . It is quite likely that to this very day after many a trial [he became a military prosecutor] he still gets drunk."[68]

Another experience which eroded his confidence in the Soviet system and the "new Soviet man" was witnessing a dispute among Soviet students who argued about whether Czechoslovak villages were really full of stone and brick rather than wood or clay houses with tile-covered roofs and not straw thatching. Most of the students could not believe that such opulence could have existed.

Learning about the extent to which bureaucracy controlled the lives of Soviet people and nurtured their fatalistic attitudes also filled him with unease. Besides a general impression of insolence, coarseness, and incompetence on the part of Soviet officials, there was the particular experience of seeing ordinary people as humble supplicants confronting officialdom: "The 'new Soviet people,' these 'creators of history,' stood before him [an official] cap in hand, and with timid deference, stammered out their feeling of injustice and injury, while the prosecutor, who was usually doing some other paperwork at the same time, sat behind his massive desk listening with only half an ear. Invariably he would dismiss 99% of the complaints as groundless. These elderly workers and wasted peasant women seemed like figures straight out of a film I had seen on the October Revolution . . . the verdict of this potentate, who again reminded me of the bureaucrat from Gogol's play, was awaited timidly."[69]

There was also the spectacle of a peasant delegation from a collective farm complaining about the loss of electricity on account of new university buildings which siphoned off the limited supply from villages outside Moscow. Their complaint was dismissed by an official who told them that they had "no legal right to electricity" and advised them to turn once more to the primitive forms of lighting (including "rush lights") that they had used before 1938. "After that I could not turn on the lights in my luxurious room in Lenin Heights [the university residence] without thinking of that scene," Mlynar writes. This was a classic instance of the clash between theory and practice: this was not the way ordinary Soviet people were supposed to act toward "their" officials nor the way the officials were supposed to act toward the people whose welfare and dignity they supposedly guarded. The highly visible disparity of power relations made a deep impression. Similar experiences led Mlynar and his Czech comrades in Moscow to resort to the hope that they would do things better at home. "Most of the young communists who studied in Soviet universities in the first half of the 1950s returned home with their ideological faith shaken . . . yet our communist faith still refused to yield to our experience."

The undermining of belief began, however imperceptibly, as these young Czech communists came to entertain doubts about "one of the party's most powerful incantations: the mandatory authority of the 'Soviet model.'" But their faith was rooted not merely in the excellence and inspirational qualities of the Soviet model but also in a belief in the evils of capitalism, which was beyond the limits of their experience to verify. "Whatever faults the Soviet Union may have had, there was no private capitalistic exploitation . . . and—so we thought at the time—there was no government policy of aggression, no power faction set on instigating a new war."

Also of importance were the lingering memories of Nazism, which the official propaganda sought to link to the Cold War. Mlynar writes: "It was impossible for us at the time to test these ideas against reality: trips to the West were impossible . . . We quite simply accepted the atmosphere and propaganda of the cold war as a truthful picture of the world . . . [C]onflicts like the Korean War completely justified . . . the evident militarism in the USSR . . . It genuinely seemed to us that nazism was on the increase in West Germany and that the foreign policy of the U.S. was an entirely unwarranted policy of imperialistic aggression."

This combination of defensive beliefs, limited information, a rigidly conformist political subculture, and, above all, the huge investment in a belief system kept Mlynar within the fold for a long time despite the negative experiences of his years in the Soviet Union. After five years in the Soviet Union and despite his fluency in the Russian language, upon his return to his country he "still had no idea whatsoever of the extent and forms of Stalinist political terror."[70]

Khrushchev's famous speech in January 1956 was another blow to the edifice of belief, although "our stay in Moscow had, at least in part, prepared us . . . and therefore it did not strike me like a bolt out of the blue." Perhaps more troubling was that while reforms were under way in Moscow, the earlier Soviet political model remained basically unchanged and unchallenged in Czechoslovakia; the Czechoslovak Communist Party struck Mlynar as an "organization that united people on the basis of their involvement with power."

In the mid-1950s Mlynar still managed to evade questions about his share of responsibility for the misdeeds of the system by shifting responsibility to the Party and the working class. To do so he still had to accept a metaphysical conception of the Party as profoundly different from its constituent members and even leaders, a view of it as an entity capable of transcending and dissociating itself from all the errors committed in its name or on its behalf. He recalls that "in discussions both in and outside party meetings, I gradually received a very concrete view of a terrifying reality. Yes, these and other people either knew or could deduce that they were sending doubtfully guilty, and even quite obviously innocent, people to prison or to their deaths. Nevertheless, their attitude was unequivocal. Are *we* responsible? We were just acting on orders from above, on party resolutions, on oral instructions from party dignitaries. So either the 'party' is guilty—or no one is . . . It was precisely the same logic on which Nazi war criminals usually based their defense: they were merely carrying out the Leader's orders." There was also the "fear for one's own life" argument, although the author admits that it should have carried little moral weight.[71]

As a department head in the Office of the Public Prosecutor in Prague from 1955, he was a part of the administrative machinery actively involved in repression, including confiscating the property of people convicted of political crimes and assisting in the forced collectivization of agriculture. Under such circumstances, the divergencies between ideals and realities once more assaulted him. For example, it became clear that "not a single apartment confiscated 'in the interests of the working class' had actually been allotted to workers in need of a place to live.'"

The next stage in his thinking was what he calls "reform communism," The attempted reconstruction of his worldview was stimulated in part by reading and rereading the classics of Marxism and other works on social philosophy. He felt that the Party leaders "abandoned Marx's scientific methodology and his commitment to truth" while he was still searching for a purified, revitalized theory. In the late 1950s and early 1960s he could derive some reassurance from the belief that "some of the essential ideas of our communist faith had genuinely been realized . . . There were no longer . . . capitalists, nor the old class and social divisions based on private property relations . . . People going about in rags, beggars in the streets, slums . . . had disappeared."

In retrospect he recognized that his view of these matters was "considerably oversimplified." He mistook the resignation of the masses for genuine acceptance of the system.

Another episode raises more fundamental issues of personal morality and the connection between the political system and the human beings in charge of it. Antonin Novotny was the head of the Party during much of the 1950s and 1960s. His

> ascent to the secretariat of the Central Committee was connected with his activity in 'uncovering the enemies within the party' and his zeal in the preparations for the trial against the secretary-general of the Communist Party of Czechoslovakia, Rudolf Slansky, in 1951–52.
>
> Novotny may well have been born without some basic human qualities . . . I saw some official documents that indicated an incredible thing: after the execution of the defendants in the Slansky

trial, their property was sold off cheap to surviving high-level functionaries, and on this occasion the Novotny family (Mrs. Bozena Novotna personally) bought the bedclothes and china tea service belonging to Vlada Clementis! [widow of the former minister of foreign affairs].

The thought that the first secretary of the ruling party and head of the state slept between the sheets belonging to a man whom he had helped send to the gallows is something incredible . . . And it was not as if the Novotnys did not know what they were doing. I talked about this matter to Lida Clementis in 1956 and I learned that Bozena Novotna had admired the Clementis's china tea service when she and her husband had been for a visit back in the days when Clementis was foreign minister.[72]

Here, Mlynar's indignation rests on an instinctive, apolitical sense of morality: there may be reasons to send one's political enemies to the gallows, but taking their property afterward cannot be rationalized; this was no longer a matter of the disjunction between theory and practice but a general, deeply felt moral violation.

Like other disillusioned communist functionaries and intellectuals, Mlynar came to be disturbed by the privileges of the Party elite, among them vacation homes, clinics, special shops, and a "recreational center" "surrounded by fences and guarded by police." There was also the matter of income inequalities—the salary of the secretary of the Central Committee (of the Party) was ten times the average monthly income in the country as a whole.

Again, the interesting question is, *At what point* did moral qualms about these privileges replace the previously untroubled acceptance of them as morally and practically justified? Mlynar notes how quickly he became "used to some of those privileges to the point where I no longer questioned them." Presumably at the time he got used to them he was far from his later realization that privileges "always spoil people, particularly when they are associated with power."

It is possible that he might have lived indefinitely with these conflicts had the Soviet Union not crushed the Prague Spring of 1968. The intervention represented "the ultimate debacle of my life as a Communist . . . this was the irrevocable ruin of everything I had devoted my life to over the past years, and in particular of reform communism." While he could rationalize the 1956 Soviet intervention in Hungary, he could not do the same in regard to his own country.

Mlynar felt a sense of unreality as he watched the Soviet soldiers in Prague from the window of Dubcek's office: "I remember saying to myself . . . yes, these are the same soldiers you welcomed and embraced joyfully on May 9, 1945, with whom you drank vodka and were friends for five years in Moscow . . . very soon their automatic rifles will be pointed, not at the czarist cadets in the Winter Palace . . . but at you, personally."

Initially he thought that the intervention resulted from "some kind of misunderstanding," not unlike that of the Soviet functionaries trying to understand their own imprisonment during the Great Purges of the 1930s. Subsequently he was among those taken to Moscow, "half hostage, half government guest," to be pressured to formally acquiesce in the Soviet intervention. Even in these final, cataclysmic moments the issue of ordinary human decency loomed large: "We were caught off guard by the Soviet Politburo's gangster tactics. But this too was part of our mistake. Kadar was right to ask Dubcek: 'Do you *really* know the kind of people you are dealing with?'"

After the Soviet intervention Mlynar was expelled from the Central Committee, then from the Party, twenty-four years after he had joined it. He stayed in his country for seven more years as a member of "the ghetto of outcasts."[73] Presumably many of his autobiographical reflections crystallized during those years.

Mlynar's account reaffirms that it was possible for Party leaders, high-level functionaries, and Party intellectuals to suppress, accommodate, or rationalize doubts and conflicts for long periods and that a seamless, unconditional approval of all the policies of the system was not an essential psychological requirement for staying in positions of power; even moral reservations about specific policies did not undermine an ultimate (or residual) commitment as long as the commitment could somehow be dissociated from the problematic means and outcomes. In particular, "the recognition of the ugly truth about the Soviet Union and its export of a police and military socialism was . . . a relatively slow process retarded by many layers of illusions. Even after the defeat in 1968 many Czech and Slovak communists would have liked to keep their hopes about the temporary character of Soviet imperialism . . . They refused to realize . . . that these features had existed in Soviet domestic and external policies since Lenin's and Trotsky's times and that, equally, internal forms of Russian communism have never been 'deformed' by Stalin or Brezhnev but [were] formed by Lenin and kept ever since."[74]

It was this nonrational core at the center (or bottom) of the commitment, a blend of hope and belief that somehow in the final analysis good would prevail over evil, that retarded and prolonged the process of disillusionment.[75]

THE INFLUENCE OF NATIONALISM

In each of these four cases (as well as in those of lesser-known East European functionaries interviewed for this project),[76] an injured national pride made a significant contribution to disillusionment. It is, however, also important to remember that these feelings and an apprehension about Soviet political, economic, or cultural domination remained suppressed as long as the basics of the commitment were in place.

In one unusual instance not examined in detail in this book, it was nationalism that nurtured loyalty to the Soviet Union, perceived as it was by the former Polish general Jaruzelski as the protector of Poland's borders. (Other Polish communists shared this attitude, according to the conversation reported by Teresa Toranska.)[77] Jaruzelski's faith in Soviet protection shaded into a diffuse admiration of and awe for Soviet power. As an American journalist has observed: "Jaruzelski had constructed his lifetime's ideology on the basis of his experience in the gulag: an experience of absolute, unlimited Soviet power." The last Communist prime minister of Poland, Mieczyslaw Rakovski, said: "Jaruzelski and the other generals came out of Siberia with the belief that this is such a force, such a power, that we have to accept this fact and all the consequences that spring from it . . . It is a generation limited by the tremendous experience of that power."[78]

Unique historical-generational factors played an important part in the political evolution of Hungary. The postrevolutionary Kadar leadership sought to dissociate itself from Stalinism, and although it imposed a reign of terror in the years immediately following the Revolution of 1956, much of the Kadar period reflected lessons learned from the Revolution. Several of the Hungarian respondents interviewed were convinced that the peaceful transfer of power in 1989 reflected a widely shared generational abhorrence of political violence that was the most important lesson of the trauma of the Revolution and its repression.

The other noteworthy aspect of the Hungarian case is its implication for the reformability of communist systems. As a number of those interviewed in Hungary argued (notably Mihaly Bihari, social scientist and former socialist member of parliament), Hungary under Kadar went as far as any communist system could in undertaking reforms, but in the end none of them were sufficient to assure its survival.

Each of the people discussed in this chapter spent substantial periods of his life in the Soviet Union and acquired experiences which made it difficult to idealize the Soviet system. For all of them, for much of their lives these experiences were locked up, as it were, and not allowed to intrude on their thinking and political careers (Hegedus is an exception since his extended stay in the Soviet Union occurred at the end of his political career). But it is also true that each of them hoped to construct a political system in his own country which would in some ways be unlike the Soviet system and more in tune with the needs and characteristics of their country and people. Although their lives and careers followed different trajectories, they all shared, at different stages in their lives, the realization that the political system they served needed either fundamental overhauling or replacement.

CHAPTER 6

Leading Specialists in "State Security" (Political Police)

"Hitler's more patent inhumanity provided an almost ideal diversion, drawing the limelight, which allowed the Soviet mass purges and MVD concentration camps to go almost unnoticed by the world at large." HENRY V. DICKS

"As a young man of twenty-four, I was confident we were not far from the 'shining future' that our leaders . . . promised us. That blind faith carried me forward for years, helping me to overlook the 1956 Soviet invasion of Hungary, the 1968 occupation of Czechoslovakia, the growing isolation and senility of our leaders. I myself spread a string of lies and disinformation to further our cause in the Cold War . . . I thought our system could be fixed. And then I collided with the KGB itself, and realized that what we had built was rotten beyond salvation." OLEG KALUGIN

"Stalin [introducing Beria to Roosevelt in Yalta]: ' . . . that's our Himmler! That's Beria.'" ANDREI GROMYKO

The dilemma of ends and means is most sharply revealed in the activities and reflections of those in power who were compelled by their position to resort to the most problematic means: routinely sending others to their death or to lengthy imprisonment. Among the individuals making life and death decisions were the leaders of the coercive apparatus, the organizers of show trials, Purges, deportations, assassinations abroad, and the Gulag system— the policymakers and supervisors, as distinct from those on the lower rungs who dirtied their hands, figuratively and literally, who could more persuasively silence their misgivings (if any) by their subordinate position. These specialists in high positions—like almost all those occupying positions of power in communist systems—believed that "politics isn't something you do for pleasure, and it's not something you do in order to be loved and understood."[1]

Ideally the specialists discussed below should include high-level decision-makers and planners—for example, Lavrenti Beria and Pavel Sudoplatov—as well as those who executed these programs and policies, such as KGB officers, guards, informers, interrogators, and torturers. Unhappily this ideal can only be approximated given the inevitable dependence on available sources. Former KGB operatives involved with foreign intelligence gathering have been more eager to come forward with their memoirs than those in other branches of the organization with less glamorous and far more distasteful jobs.[2] It is easier to regard intelligence or counterintelligence work as defensive than it is to so regard the domestic surveillance, coercion, and intimidation that these specialists were expected to perform within their own country.

We have limited knowledge of how the attitudes of the people in the coercive apparatus differed from the attitudes of those in other positions of power. Did they fall back on different rationalizations for their activities? Did they succeed in convincing themselves that the very unpleasantness of the tasks they undertook was proof of their dedication and moral rectitude, and, if so, for how long? It is hard to know what proportion of them were idealists and what proportion were attracted primarily by the elite status and the perks of these positions. With the passage of time the number of corruptible careerists presumably rose at the expense of the stern idealists.

The attitudes of those who worked for the KGB and corresponding organizations modeled after it in the other communist states are of special interest in this study because the collapse of communist systems could also be explained by the decline in their readiness to suppress dissent or opposition. If there was an erosion of political will at the top of the political hierarchy, as is argued here, it presumably extended to the specialists in coercion who were most directly responsible for maintaining the status quo (the feebleness of the effort to unseat Gorbachev in August 1991 suggests precisely such an erosion of will).

Markus Wolf, the former head of intelligence of the East German Stasi (political police or state security) has suggested that "people didn't fight to keep it [the system] alive" because it "didn't correspond to our ideals."[3] If a perceived discrepancy between ideals and realities translated into declining morale among the state security forces, we would have a dramatic illustration of the impact of political disillusionment on the survival of the system.

ATTRIBUTES OF POLITICAL VIOLENCE IN COMMUNIST STATES

The discussion that follows is also intended to narrow the gap between what we know about the two most repressive political systems in this century: Nazi Germany and the Soviet Union under Stalin.[4] There is no comparison between the Western and especially American moral awareness of the repressions perpetrated by Nazi Germany and the corresponding repressions perpetrated by the Soviet Union and other communist states. In this respect, the difference between the size of the political police of one communist state, East Germany (officially called the German Democratic Republic) and former Nazi Germany is revealing: The East German Ministry of State Security had 90,000 full-time employees as well as 110,000 regular informers; the full-time staff of the Gestapo in 1941 for the "vastly larger territory of Greater Germany . . . was fewer than 15,000. Even adding . . . other possibly comparable units one still cannot reach anything like the Stasi."[5] Only an East European witness of Stalinism such as Vladimir Farkas, a former high-ranking officer in the Hungarian political police, would argue that Soviet communism was more profoundly repellent than Nazism because, unlike the latter, it appropriated some of the "noblest ideals of mankind."[6] David Pryce-Jones locates the distinctiveness of Soviet political violence in the fact that "no other nation has ever done such damage to itself, killing so many of its own people while also laying waste to so many other countries."[7]

While Holocaust revisionism has been given much public attention and has been properly rebutted, the mitigations and benign reinterpretations of Soviet-communist mass murders have been more widespread and far more respectable, originating as they do with well-established American scholars who have not been dismissed as cranks or fanatics.[8] Robert Thurston, for one, never seemed to encounter an estimate of the victims of Stalin that did not strike him as too high, and although he allows that the inmates of the Gulag were not treated fairly by "Western standards of justice," he has found comfort in the fact that in 1937 they had the opportunity to buy Soviet state bonds—"an indication that they were still regarded as participants in society to some degree." A reviewer of his book noted that "by this curious standard, sheep being led to slaughter are participants in agriculture."[9] Buying these bonds (inside or outside the Gulag) was one more device to reduce the already meager incomes of Soviet citizens; their purchase was as "voluntary" as many other activities that the regime exhorted its citizens to undertake, such as work on weekends, marches on official holidays, attendance at political meetings, and voting in no-choice elections. No one has suggested that the victims of Nazism were treated unfairly according to Western standards of justice—as if according to some other standards (such as the Nazi one), their treatment might have been fair.

Not only have the moral responses to the two sets of mass murders been different, but far more is known about the Nazi planners and organizers of political violence and coercion than of their communist counterparts. There are numerous studies in English of the major figures of Nazi political violence (such as Eichman, Himmler, and Rudolf Hoess, the commander of Auschwitz), of the elite troops assigned to these tasks (the SS and the Gestapo), and of other Nazi elites and activists. Concepts have been devised to better understand Nazi murderousness and repression, such as "the banality of evil," "desk murderers," "authoritarian personality," and "obedience to authority."[10] Only those with personal experience of communist repression have suggested that the leaders and activists in these systems—which a Czech author has aptly called "police socialism"—had authoritarian inclinations, that is, that the system attracted "people of a dogmatic, autocratic character."[11]

Even more striking, and providing further evidence of the contrast here noted, Western visitors to communist societies have reported favorable impressions of "leading specialists," misperceiving them just as grotesquely as they misperceived the political system as a whole that these specialists helped to keep in power. Romain Rolland referred to Genrikh Yagoda, head of the Soviet political police and in charge of Soviet repressions in the 1930s, as "fine-featured, distinguished . . . he speaks with sweetness; he is impregnated with sweetness."[12] Maxim Gorky, the famous Soviet writer, too, was sufficiently shielded from political realities and impressed by the "successes of reeducation" to call Yagoda by an affectionate name, Yagodka (Little Berry), after he was taken by Yagoda on a tour of GPU camps displaying rehabilitated prostitutes and criminals.[13] Henry Wallace and his entourage on a conducted tour of Soviet concentration camps in Kolyma (Siberia) were favorably impressed by Ivan Nikishov, commander of these camps.[14] S. N. Kruglov, one of the directors of the Gulag administration, "made a favorable impression on President Truman" in Potsdam in his capacity as the official responsible for security and was "enrolled in the American Legion."[15] More recently, Tomas Borge, head of the Nicaraguan state security, charmed Günter Grass the famous German writer, as well as numerous American political tourists, among them a professor of philosophy who thought Borge was a good poet and "ran a prison system known as one of the most progressive in the world."[16] This misjudgment of a communist prison system is by no means exceptional.[17]

There seem to be four types of these specialists implicit in the existing literature, including that which deals with the Nazism. In the first group are the ideologically driven, putatively incorruptible, puritanical executioners (metaphorically speaking), exemplified in the Soviet case by Felix Dzerzhinsky and in the Nazi case by Heinrich Himmler. In part because of the influence of Hannah Arendt, this first type has been increasingly eclipsed in popular as well as scholarly thinking by "ordinary" individuals, the second type, exemplified by Adolf Eichman, supposedly personifying the banality of evil. These were people who found themselves in situations which imposed unappealing roles or duties on them; they followed orders without being driven by strong convictions.[18] Arendt is not alone in upholding images of wrongdoing unmotivated by principle. A former veteran of the Japanese imperial army who participated in the atrocities committed in China and "saw lots of torture scenes" observed that "the torturers themselves . . . were 'regular people' who simply did their job. Yet he acknowledged that some torturers were worse than others, and he drew a distinction between those who were 'cold' and others who were more 'humane.'"[19]

The third type emerges from more recent references to some of the personnel of the KGB. These were well-educated, often suave careerists who found satisfactory employment and mobility opportunities within this organization. According to Andrei Sakharov, they "traveled and read widely, and they knew far better than anyone else the true picture of desperation within Soviet borders and the realities beyond them." This was also the case in Eastern Europe, especially, East Germany, where "the Stasi men were always an elite, a group that benefited from opportunities for training and education of which many Easterners could only dream."[20] A former Czech dissident, Milos Calda, who had several encounters with the Czech political police, found the police "intelligent and cynical."[21] Oleg Kalugin, discussed below, belongs to this group to some degree.

Money motivated the otherwise uncommitted, as in communist Czechoslovakia, where even within the state security system domestic or internal surveillance was considered distasteful. According to a former employee "No one wanted to do this work—arresting and interrogating political people. So it paid well. I got eight hundred crowns a month more than in the old job." As time went by, the morale of the Czech state security declined: "By the end of the 1980s the StB didn't believe its own propaganda."[22] Eugen Loebl, a former high-ranking Czech official and one of the defendants in the Slansky trial, reported that "by increasing their output of confessions and arrest, my interrogators . . . were getting a higher bonus and . . . by discovering ever bigger spies and traitors, they were assuring themselves promotions and raises in pay."[23]

Material and "moral" incentives were not always easy to separate. Reportedly the Hungarian political police (AVO, later AVH) officers "were trained . . . for devotion, blind discipline, and were at the same time filled with a consciousness of mission and professional pride . . . Their self-confidence was further inflated by the fact hat they could fill their pockets with various allowances, bonuses and benefits."[24]

While the elite of the political police were well provided, the personal risks were also high: many erstwhile leaders and officers were devoured by the system, brought down by their successors. People imprisoned during the Great Purge sometimes met in prison those who had interrogated them earlier (this also happened in Eastern Europe). Hardly any head of the political police in the Soviet Union or elsewhere in the Socialist Commonwealth ended his life peacefully and with an untarnished reputation.

The fourth group consists of the least attractive human beings: amoral or unmistakably malevolent individuals, those at the higher level motivated by the lust for power and those at the lower one by sadism. The latter include the anonymous guards, torturers, and interrogators who enjoyed the suffering they inflicted on their victims,[25] often also believing in their guilt or human inferiority.[26] Sketches of such individuals can often be drawn from the memoirs of their former victims. A Hungarian defendant in the Rajk trial[27] writes: "The detectives . . . all fell upon me, threw me on the floor . . . kicked me all over my body. They . . . acted like a party of drunks intoxicated with rage. Nor for a moment did their fury appear simulated."[28]

It is this fourth group—seemingly composed of the kind of individuals who gravitate toward organizations of violence and coercion for undeclared personal motives—that has attracted the least social scientific interest. The same group conjures up associations with the concept of the "authoritarian personality," which used to be reserved for supporters of Nazism and other radical right-wing movements. Fred Greenstein writes: "Such an individual abases himself before those who stand above him hierarchically or whom he perceives as powerful and lords it over whoever seems to be weak, subordinate or inferior . . . such individuals . . . *think* in power terms . . . acutely sensitive to questions of who dominates whom . . . These authoritarian traits . . . hang together . . . : dominance of subordinates; deference to superiors; sensitivity to power relationships; need to perceive the world in a highly structured fashion; excessive use of stereotypes."[29] It did not even occur to the originators of the concept that these attitudes could be encountered elsewhere on the political spectrum.[30]

Victor Serge observed during the early years of the Soviet state that the apparatus of coercion attracted two contrasting types of individuals—the amoral and power-hungry, on the one hand, and the principled, on the other: "The Party endeavoured to head it [the Cheka, the first embodiment of the KGB] with incorruptible men like . . . Dzerzhinsky, a sincere idealist, ruthless but chivalrous, with the emaciated profile of an Inquisitor . . . But the Party had few men of this stamp and many Chekas: these gradually came to select their personnel by virtue of their psychological inclinations. The only temperaments that devoted themselves willingly and tenaciously to this task of 'internal defense' were those characterized by suspicion, embitterment, harshness and sadism. Long-standing social inferiority-complexes and memories of humiliations and suffering in the Tsars' jails rendered them intractable . . . the Chekas inevitably consisted of perverted men tending to see conspiracy everywhere."[31]

These observations are echoed in another characterization of those recruited into the Cheka: "Work in the Cheka . . . attracts corrupt and outright criminal elements . . . However honest a man is, however crystal-clear in his heart, work in the Cheka . . . begins to tell." Dzerzhinsky himself notes that "only saints or scoundrels can serve in the GPU, but now the saints are running away from me and I am left with the scoundrels."[32] In the estimation of Volkogonov only two types of investigative officers could be found in the NKVD by the mid-1930s: "unfeeling cynics and sadists bereft of the notion of human conscience."[33]

Further light is shed on the criteria for recruitment to these services from the recollections of a former Soviet agent, Nikolai Khoklov. He was instructed by his superior, Pavel Sudoplatov to "go search for people who are hurt by fate or nature—the ugly, those suffering from an inferiority complex, craving power and influence but defeated by unfavorable circumstances. Or people who have suffered not so much from hunger and cold, but from the humiliation connected with poverty . . . The sense of belonging to an influential and powerful organization will give them a feeling of superiority . . . For the first time in their lives they will experience a sense of importance, a close connection with power."[34]

Similar criteria were applied by the Hungarian political police. According to a former victim, the writer George Paloczi-Horvath, "The SP [security police] was constantly purged by General Peter [Gabor Peter, head of the SP]. Many former SP officers were with us in jail. They were arrested for the slightest sign of elementary decency. With this method General Peter succeeded in finding in a few years that criminal and potentially sadistic five per cent which is there in any given population."[35] Mehmet Shehu, head of the Albanian political police under Enver Hoxha, must also have belonged to that 5 percent, given his predilection to take revenge on pregnant mothers (of whom there were many because of the official pressure to increase the population) for the political misbehavior of members of their family.[36]

The idea that in every society there are groups of people who possess or develop a personality congenial to service in a repressive police force has been expressed by many authors. Antonio Candido, the Brazilian man of letters, observes that for these tasks "society needs thousands of individuals with appropriately deformed souls . . . society draws from these people the brutality, the need, the frustration, the depravity, the defect—and gives them the repressive function."[37] Josef Skvorecky, the Czech émigré writer, perceives the hardcore supporters of both Nazi and Communist systems as "people scarred by private hatreds, grounded in deeply negative personal experience . . . [people] with physical or psychological malformations . . . haunted by a feeling of insecurity . . . exploit[ing] ideas and movements to achieve a feeling of self-worth."[38] A Czech student of communist affairs, Peter Hruby, writes: "Every nation has a small percentage of potential criminals in its population. In totalitarian dictatorships these people . . . get their best chance and can really enjoy themselves, at the same time feeling proud that they are serving the great cause."[39]

Pryce-Jones goes so far as to suggest that even Western intellectuals supportive of various communist systems—such as Althusser, Foucault, Ernst Bloch, Lukacs, Marcuse—and "thousands more men of letters, academics and opinion-makers had a brutal and manic streak in their characters." For others, like Brecht, Neruda, Sartre, and Graham Greene, "it was a question of being on the side of the winners."[40]

Lavrenti Beria is aptly characterized by "the seeming absence of a human dimension in his personality." But Amy Knight also believes that "to portray him as an exception . . . is to misrepresent the very nature of the Soviet system during the Stalinist period."[41] According to Volkogonov, Beria's "predatory character and lust for power" made a deep (and favorable) impression on Stalin.[42] After Stalin's death in 1953, Beria, with exceptional hypocrisy, rebuked the Hungarian Stalinist leader Rakosi for ordering the use of physical force during interrogations and for the possibility that "innocent people could have been sent to jail."[43]

Beria's deputy and intimate friend Viktor Abakumov "tortured prisoners himself and followed Beria's practice of snatching attractive girls off the street, taking them home, and raping them."[44] Molotov—himself described as a man of "cold-blooded ruthlessness"—referred to Yagoda (Beria's predecessor) as "a filthy nobody who wormed his way into the party . . . We had to work with reptiles like that."[45] Reportedly, "Yagoda, who prized historical souvenirs, collected the bullets with which famous revolutionaries had been shot. When Yagoda was shot, his executioner, Yezhov, appropriated the historic bullets. When Yezhov himself was shot later, the bullets were preserved in his case record. The inventory attached to his file lists 'revolver bullets, blunted, wrapped in paper, inscribed Zinoviev, Kamenev.'"[46]

There was an affinity between certain personal traits and the political system: "Stalin and his lieutenants made their decisions with little or no regard for the Soviet people. Indeed, what bound them together was their contempt for human individuality and their ability to inflict terrible cruelty on their people with no remorse." A connection between official policies and less than creditable human traits is also noted by Luba Brezhneva, the niece of Leonid Brezhnev: "Continual official calls [in the 1930s] for crackdowns on the 'enemies of the people' had awakened the basest instincts . . . Informers were praised and held up as role models for the youths; they were also given financial rewards and promotions."[47]

Even if one agrees with the idea that every society has a certain proportion of human beings with a deformed psyche who can become promising recruits for a brutal police force, it does not follow that these individuals always find opportunities to indulge their propensities. Intolerant, vindictive, resentful, and authoritarian human beings have to be brought together in an appropriate organization and given a sense of entitlement by some ideology or "great leader" to act out their impulses. Erich Mielke, head of the Stasi, may qualify as such a prototype, for in him a variety of unappealing personality traits and ideological convictions came together in a mutually supportive way: "He had risen from rigging show trials to run the Stasi in 1957, staying in power ever since. Thuggish and greedy, he was also vain. The list which he drew up of his 250 medals and orders covered eighteen pages . . . in an echo of Herman Goering . . . [In his office] is a portrait of Felix Dzerzhinsky . . . and a death mask of Lenin."[48] Markus Wolf, who worked with him for decades, considers "Mielke . . . a warped personality even by the peculiar standards of morality that apply in the espionage world."[49]

The points made above contrast with the beliefs popularized by Hannah Arendt and taken up with seeming relish by many Western intellectuals and the educated public in the past few decades. Central to those beliefs is the idea that virtually anybody can become a mass murderer under the appropriate circumstances.[50] But there is a difference between those who relish and volunteer for such activities (or those who design and organize them for some "higher purpose") and those who find themselves under situational pressures to perform murderous activities.[51]

If the Nazi organizers of the extermination of the Jews could shift responsibility to higher authority and ultimately to Hitler, their communist counterparts had an even more helpful device at their disposal: the myth of the infallibility of the Party and belief in being on the winning side of a predetermined historical process. It was an article of faith among them that the Party was a unique, chosen instrument of history and social justice. A Czech communist intellectual says: "The Party was prepared to provide the certainty and assurance we lacked. While the democrats asked us to trust in ourselves, the Party offered the chance to put our trust in something we did not have to doubt."[52]

Georgi Piatakov, one of the early Bolshevik revolutionaries, reportedly said: "If the Party demands it . . . I will see black where I thought I saw white . . . because for me there is no life outside the Party."[53] George Kennan's observation about Andrei Gromyko captures this mindset: "The Party became . . . his mother, his father, his teacher, his conscience, and his master . . . And if it turned out that what the Party required to be done . . . involved apparent injustice or cruelty—well, one might regret that it was found necessary . . . But it was not one's own responsibility."[54]

Molotov was able to justify the bloodlettings of the 1930s even from the vantage point of the 1970s and 1980s. He "boasted that he personally designated the areas from which tens of thousands of . . . kulak families were selected for expropriation and deportation." He observed that "in collectivization . . . [your] hands must not tremble, you must not quake in your boots . . . and if anyone begins to shiver—beware!" Of the forced resettlements of various ethnic minorities he said: "It was a matter of life and death; there was no time to investigate the details. Of course innocents suffered. But . . . given the circumstances, we acted correctly." As far as the Purges were concerned, "of course there were excesses but all that was permissible, to my mind, for the sake of the main objective—keeping state power! . . . The terror cost us dearly, but without it things would have been worse."[55]

Jakub Berman took a similar, if somewhat more nuanced, view in retrospect: "I assumed that the terror of the Great Purge was a side effect of the search for a solution to the Soviet Union's extremely difficult international situation, and possibly also a result of Stalin's own internal struggles and contradictions . . . I accepted that it was a tragic web of circumstance which drew an enormous number of victims into it. Naturally, I tried desperately to cling to the thought that you can't make omelettes without breaking eggs."[56]

More recently, the persistence of the mentality illustrated by these quotations was demonstrated by Pol Pot of Cambodia. Shortly before his death he told an interviewer: "I do not reject responsibility—our movement made mistakes, like every other movement in the world. But . . . [w]e had no other choice . . . we had to defend ourselves . . . my conscience is clear. Everything I have done . . . is first for the nation and the people of Cambodia."[57] The familiar themes of self-exculpation are all present: relativizing the crimes by comparing them to those (allegedly) committed by others; defining mass murder as self-defense; alluding to a greater evil (the enemy) that left no choice but to take drastic measures.

Some loyalists preserved their commitments even while imprisoned and awaiting trial on false charges, Eugen Loebl among them. Even when pressed to make an absurd, self-incriminating confession,

> I told myself that I had to put aside all subjective feelings, my feelings of injustice, because the party was fighting for the future of the world. Because indeed there was a danger of enemy penetration . . . When I joined the party, and during all those years that I was a member, I felt that any subjective element, any sacrifice, was to be borne for the party's sake . . .
>
> I could not be shaken in my faith just because I had the misfortune to become the victim of something I could not understand, just because a bunch of opportunists and gangsters had got to the helm of the party and the state . . .
>
> I had always been able to persuade myself that throughout history, progress . . . had been accompanied by the suffering of innocents. I had also thought that it was not Marxism, not the system itself, but some unworthy people in it who were responsible for the evil that I witnessed.[58]

It was an integral part of communist political culture to believe that "the Party must be prepared to inflict any amount of deprivation on any number of human beings if this appears 'necessary' . . . The refusal to use necessary bad means appears to the Bolshevik as an expression of stupidity . . . or as imperfect dedication to the great goal; or as self-centeredness which keeps one more concerned with not touching dirt and not feeling guilt than with transforming the world . . . In politics one is not only permitted but required to violate the older code to which one remains attached in private life."[59]

George Lukacs, himself not involved in the dirty business of keeping the system in power, fully internalized this principle and expressed it with great precision: "The highest duty for communist ethics is to accept the necessity of acting immorally. This is the greatest sacrifice that the revolution demands of us. The conviction of the true communist is that evil transforms itself into bliss through the dialectics of historical evolution."[60] In the words of the former Polish communist Stefan Staszewski, the party "is always right; it is our honour, our happiness, our life's goal. And if you ask a communist about its infallibility, and if you also prove to him that for the past thirty-eight years of its existence in Poland all it has done is commit mistakes, he will say . . . : the party didn't commit mistakes; people committed mistakes."[61]

Sometimes the ultimate source of legitimation and vindication was Lenin. Edward Ochab, the Polish communist leader, said: "To me Lenin was a genius. In difficult moments especially, I reach for his works."[62] Lenin himself had no difficulty in legitimating political violence by both idealistic long-term goals and the short-term necessity of staying in power. Although eclipsed by Stalin in such matters, Lenin might be seen as a role model for generations of politically motivated executioners.[63] Dmitri Volkogonov says: "It is difficult to fathom how a man who loved Beethoven and Spinoza, who read Kant . . . could reconcile himself to a system permeated with police rule. How could Lenin, who claimed to be the leader of a new world, personally write the orders to hang, to shoot, to take hostages, to imprison in concentration camps, knowing that these would not remain mere words?"[64]

Especially helpful for Lenin and other communist revolutionaries and their successors in power was the idea that there can be a radical discontinuity between the present and the future and that the latter will not be contaminated by the practices of the present: "The use of means at sharp variance with the state of affairs under communism itself will not interfere with its ultimate realization. The Party must accept as a matter of course any expedient degree of discrepancy between means and ends."[65] It was an important insight of Alexander Yakovlev's that "by making the illusory future more important than humanity, Marxism gave people carte blanche to use any means when it came to power . . . Positive values—kindness, conscience, love, cooperation, solidarity, justice, freedom, the rule of law—were unfit, useless. They weakened the class struggle."[66]

Yakovlev, unlike those who absolve Marx of any responsibility for the outrages committed in his name, notes that Marxism grew into "the conviction that everything that corresponded to the interests of revolution and communism was moral. That is the morality with which hostages were executed, the peasantry was destroyed, concentration camps were built and entire peoples were forcibly relocated."[67] Dedication to the best interests of abstractions such as "mankind," "the masses," the "working classes," or the "toilers" at the expense of actual human beings played a similar role. Again, Yakovlev was well aware of this fateful dichotomy: "Dostoyevsky's Grand Inquisitor speaks of love for humanity. But complete contempt for an actual individual flows from this love."[68] Lenin embodied these attitudes, and his personality became fused with Soviet-communist political culture. According to Molotov, "In some cases he was harsher than Stalin."[69]

The myth of the infallibility of the Party might have been more helpful in silencing doubt over morally questionable policies than devotion to a single leader was. The Party was an institution that could be divorced from the errors of particular human beings who led it and who were mortal; it transcended the lifespan of the individual. George Kennan writes: "For anything undertaken in response to the will of the collectivity (in this instance the Party), no matter how distasteful, no matter how unattractive from the standpoint of individual morality, there could be no guilt, no questioning, no remorse."[70]

Generations of Soviet Party functionaries and, before them, revolutionaries internalized the myth of the Party, which allowed them to divest it of all responsibility for the errors and horrors committed on its behalf. This even included the early generation of highly educated idealists, the original revolutionaries: "Kamenev, Zinoviev, and Trotsky all extolled the Terror in

public. Even the humane Bukharin reportedly stated that 'proletarian coercion in all forms, beginning with execution, is the method by which communist man is fashioned from the human material of the capitalist epoch.'"[71]
Lev Kamenev "shared the near mystical belief that the Party was the sole
embodiment of correct thinking. And . . . [he shared] the desire to root out
any thinking held to be incorrect."[72]

Many of the early generation of idealistic and highly educated revolutionaries succumbed to similar beliefs and justifications. It was indeed "one
of the great psychological puzzles . . . why so many intelligent, educated
Communist Party members . . . looked into the abyss, saw the arrests, the
midnight executions, the suppression of all dissent . . . recalled the reign of
the guillotine that had followed the French revolution, vainly spoke out in
protest—and then came back loyally to the Party fold."[73]

Ideological convictions (or some primitive variant of them) were also helpful in postrevolutionary times, as the remarks of Dmitri Tokaryev, commander
of the murder squad in the Katyn Forest (where over fifteen thousand Polish
officers were killed on Stalin's orders), indicate: "These Poles were class enemies . . . I am proud of the work that I did in defense of our revolution."
Apparently not all of those carrying out the "work" were entirely untroubled,
as is suggested by the regular supply of vodka each execution team was given
every night.[74]

Several decades later, displaying a similar sense of political duty had milder
requirements, but the mentality remained the same: "Judge Zubiets . . . had
sentenced the dissident Irena Ratushinskaya to prison for her poetry and
religious faith. 'Times were different then . . . [he said.] I did my duty.'"[75]
He, too, felt vindicated. So was Stalin in the eyes of Jakub Berman, since
he committed his crimes "convinced that they were serving the cause of the
revolution, and thus [were] guided by ideological principles." Berman also
believed that history will be kind to him for his victory over Hitler "despite
all the foolish acts he committed."[76]

Pavel Sudoplatov writes in a similar spirit: "We must recall . . . the mentality of idealistic Communists in the later forties and early fifties. The worst
crime that Anna [his wife] and I could conceive of for a high-ranking party
or government official was high treason . . . Party business was sacred."[77]

Vladimir Farkas recalls the part played by the idea of the Party (or "the sacredness of Party business") in personal betrayals: "I first observed in the case of my father [minister of defense and member of the group of four running the country] and Janos Kadar the capability of abandoning former comrades-in-arms, their mistreatment, and the hideous point of view—which may be compared to that prevailing during the Spanish Inquisition—that whatever they said was the word of the Party and the truth of the Party, because the Party is never mistaken."[78]

The prevailing anti-individualistic, collectivistic ethos also made it easier to commit atrocities or mistreat others on political grounds. The Soviet system, no less than Nazi Germany, fostered "obedience to authority." As Igor Kon, the Russian social scientist writes: "By placing social (state, party, group) loyalties above individual rights Marxist collectivism tends to nourish moral irresponsibility and expedient conformity."[79]

Loyalty to the Party is less helpful for understanding the motives of the generation of post-Stalin and post-Khrushchev leaders and functionaries who were neither participants in a revolution, nor the highly idealistic vanguard of radical social change following one. For them, legitimation by idealistic belief was replaced by a way of habitual thinking (or nonthinking) as regards the Party's power to legitimate expedient but amoral policies. Each generation of leaders (and their underlings) took it for granted that their goals were sublime enough to sanitize—from the long-range historical perspective—the means used to attain them; each subscribed to Lenin's belief that "our morality is completely subordinated to the interests of the class struggle of the proletariat" and that "everything that is done in the proletarian cause is honest."[80] There was great latitude in deciding what the interests of the proletariat were, but there was no doubt that the Party and its leaders were the ultimate arbiters of these decisions.

Not surprisingly, those in the lower echelons of the apparatus blamed those above them for their actions. A former colonel in the KGB argued that "the system made us develop hostility to each other, the system itself! . . . Hostility, revenge, denunciations, spy mania, all that was encouraged—all stemming from the man himself, the man with the mustache. From top to bottom these base instincts were encouraged!"[81] These attitudes were indeed encouraged, but not everybody responded in the same way.

Not only former KGB officials but even those who assisted the regime in the regimentation of the arts resorted to these time-honored excuses and rationalizations. One of them was Tikhon Khrennikov, a mediocre official composer and a favorite of Stalin's. He was infamous for the denunciation of Prokofiev and Shostakovich in 1948 "which set the tone for Soviet censure and oppression [in the arts] for decades to come." More recently, he has asserted that in doing so he merely obeyed the order of the Central Committee, that "he didn't write the speech that was thrust into his hands a few hours before he was due to speak." Moreover, "nobody could say no to Stalin . . . My conscience is clear . . . You had to live in that atmosphere to understand what was going on."[82] Ilya Ehrenburg, a lifelong political survivor, evinced this mentality in writing about the reign of Stalin in his autobiography: "I knew about many crimes but it was not in my power to stop them. Yet why make the point? Far more influential and better-informed people than I were unable to stop them." Given Stalin's great authority, any opposition would have been pointless, and its absence "was not at all a matter of lack of personal courage."[83]

The conscience of Vladimir Kryuchkov, the last head of the KGB (and leader of the 1991 putsch against Gorbachev), was also clear. In a conversation with David Remnick he said: "If there has to be repentance [for KGB activities], then let everyone repent. You should repent for what you've done to the Indians . . . If you repent, we will too. My attitude toward Stalin is clear: I condemn the repressions. I condemn the totalitarian forms of rule that Stalin developed . . . He became the head of the Soviet state when there was only a plow, and left it when the state had an atomic bomb . . . Believe me in twenty or thirty years Stalin will be referred to as a kind of genius."[84]

Kryuchkov also averred that he had "nothing to do with the struggle against dissent," which led his interlocutor to observe that he "seemed perfectly capable of lying with a serene sense of self-possession and righteousness," another apparent qualification for the position he had filled.[85] His memoirs demonstrate further that he was not among those who harbored doubts about the political system he served. On the contrary, he believed that up to 1985 all was well: "As of 1985 nobody could doubt the power of the Soviet Union . . . In all major indices of development we held second place in the world after the United States . . . The country possessed a powerful industrial base . . . agriculture generally satisfied the needs for food

and raw materials; science was considered well advanced worldwide . . .
In the accessibility of education, medical care, and culture . . . in the scope
of housing construction we were peerless. The people were well fed, clothed
. . . although there was . . . a great shortage in the assortment, quality, and
availability of certain consumer goods."[86]

He had fond memories even of the old days (under Stalin after World
War II) when he worked at a prosecutor's office, times when even "the strictest
measures . . . [were] justified and received popular support."[87] Kryuchkov
cut his teeth, so to speak, under the tutelage of Andropov in Hungary in
1956, who, as may be recalled, assured the Hungarian revolutionary government about the speedy departure of Soviet troops while they were in fact
pouring in.

Kryuchkov had reservations about the disclosures of Khrushchev at the
Twentieth Party Congress, since "the masses were not ready for such a step."[88]
If he had any qualms about the system, they had to do with "the period of
stagnation" during the Brezhnev era, when "a virus of apathy and passive
expectancy" spread through society.[89] He had nothing but admiration for
the founding fathers (Marx, Engels, and Lenin) and no question in his
mind that "actually existing socialism" of the Soviet variety was far superior
to anything capitalism could offer. There was also great pride in the superpower status of the Soviet Union. None of these beliefs and motives translated into the ruthlessness necessary to assure the success of the 1991 coup, of
which he was a major organizer. In his biography he intimates that the conspirators wished to avoid bloodshed.[90] He had little doubt that the policies
and errors of Gorbachev, Shevardnadze, and Yakovlev were responsible for
the collapse of the Soviet Union.

Kryuchkov's reminiscences (like some of the others discussed before) are
pertinent to George Kennan's observation regarding the self-conception of
Soviet leaders: "Many foreigners would be amazed . . . to learn with what
self-satisfaction and complacency . . . a great many senior Soviet statesmen
have come to look back upon their own part in the dramatic, and so often
terrible, events of their own time."[91] These attitudes—including the capacity
to "li[e] with a serene self-possession"—were not peculiar to Soviet leaders.
Chinese General Chi Haotian, minister of defense at the time of this writing, who was the official in charge of the massacre on Tiananmen Square

in June 1989, averred on his visit to the United States in December 1996 "that no one was killed during student demonstrations six years ago."[92]

In the final analysis, two approaches might be the most useful to understand the political attitudes and beliefs of the people whom I call the leading specialists. The first emphasizes idealistic commitment (at least as a starting point), the second its seeming opposite: the love of power and other flaws of character, even human depravity. Often it is difficult to separate these two sets of attitudes, since lofty ideals tend to be the most compelling justification for holding onto or maximizing power by any means available and for crushing mercilessly those who would challenge its possession

Let us look once more at the first approach. I argued that high-ranking officials in charge of the political police were directly confronted with the potential dilemma of ends and means. They had to use the most distasteful means; therefore, they needed particularly strong convictions and defenses to assure themselves that what they did was essential and justified by some higher authority, purpose, or morality. Even the Nazis were aware of this need and occasionally faced up to the task of explicitly justifying the mass murder of civilians, as in the notorious speech that Himmler gave to SS leaders.[93]

The most satisfactory way to assuage incipient guilt or disgust was, for the "specialists" and their superiors, to remind themselves of the long range goals and benefits they were striving for and of the ideals enshrined in the theory which guided them. Jakub Berman a Polish leader in charge of ideological matters said " . . . I am . . . convinced that the sum of our actions . . . will finally produce results and create a new Polish consciousness . . . there will finally be a breakthrough in mentality which will give it an entirely new content and quality. And then, we, the communists, will be able to apply all the democratic principles we would like to apply but cant apply now, because they would end in our defeat and humiliation.[94]

Those who felt that higher purposes demanded that they act ruthlessly often claimed that such measures were temporary necessities. Jakub Berman did not deny "the adverse consequences of the pressure of the Stalinist apparatus [political police] on our [Polish] apparatus . . . But even then I felt this was something temporary, flowing not from the nature of the Soviet state but from the situation of the time . . . an accidental consequence of a tangled web of historical factors and of Stalin's attitude."[95] Thus, even Marxists fell back on accident and human nature when seeking excuses for wrongheaded policies.

There was also the time-honored recourse to the notion of collective self-defense, as in the remarks of Molotov quoted earlier. Throughout much of its existence the Soviet Union, together with its allies, justified the various campaigns of coercion and violence as strictly defensive measures essential for the survival of the system under attack by enemies of exceptional cunning and evil. A high-ranking Soviet political police officer illustrated the cunning of "the enemy"[96] (an almost mythical entity, the counterpart of the Party, and its literary incarnation, the positive hero) by the story of a group of captured anticommunist spies awaiting execution. In front of the firing squad they cheered Stalin and the Soviet Union: "They did so . . . in order to sow confusion even at the last moment of their lives, in the minds and hearts of the soldiers executing them, by suggesting that they were going to shoot loyal communists."[97]

The conviction that those arrested represented the mythic figure of the enemy was also helpful in fusing the professional justifications with a more personal rage. A Hungarian victim recalls: "It was obvious that these primitive men [those administering the beatings], beside themselves with rage, were not shamming . . . they were firmly convinced that they were dealing with a dangerous, stubborn spy, a determined enemy of the State, who refused to confess." A Czech political prisoner had a similar experience with his interrogator: "He was trying so hard to hurt me that his breathing grew heavy and labored . . . Never before or since have I seen someone so passionately involved in his work. It was incredible to me that I had done anything to make someone that angry with me."[98]

The struggle for a new world required painful sacrifices. Lenin warned that "there are no . . . serious battles without field hospitals near the battlefields. It is altogether unforgivable to permit oneself to be frightened or unnerved by 'field hospital' scenes. If you are afraid of the wolves, don't go into the forest."[99] This took care of ends and means.

More recently, vague references to "the times" served a similar purpose. During prolonged emergencies a "temporary" suspension of ethical standards was acceptable. Major General Karbainov, de facto spokesman of the KGB, found comfort in the spirit of the times as he discussed the activities of his organization: "What can one say about the trials of the 1960s and 1970s concerning dissidents?" he said in 1989. "These were criminal processes conducted in accordance with legislation in force at the time . . . some of these processes were marked by subjectivism. Such were the times."[100]

Sudoplatov, too, believes that the historical context provided absolution: "I do not intend to justify what I did as a member of the foreign intelligence service from the 1920s to the early 1950s. That was a different time, a different historical period." This was also the view of Ramon Mercader, the assassin of Trotsky who wielded the pickax, whom Sudoplatov employed in this task. Mercader thought of himself as " a professional revolutionary, proud of his role . . . He told me [Sudoplatov]: 'If I were to relive the 1940s I would do the same thing, but not in the present-day world [of 1969].' He did not repent his murder of Trotsky. He quoted the Russian saying 'One does not choose the time to live and die' and said, 'I would add to that. One does not choose the time to live, die or kill.'" Sudoplatov comments: "It is clear to me now that present morals are incompatible with the cruelty of the revolution, civil war and power struggles that follow them . . . There was no way for Stalin to treat Trotsky in exile as merely a writer of philosophical books; Trotsky was an active enemy who had to be destroyed."[101] Volkogonov writes that Mercader was persuaded by Naum Eitington—another high-level NKVD operative organizing the assassination—that "he would be merely 'carrying out a just sentence' issued in Moscow and that this enormous honor would make him a hero forever."[102]

Those involved in the planning and execution of the most notorious show trial in communist Hungary, that of Laszlo Rajk and his associates, offered similar rationalizations. Mihaly Farkas, father of Vladimir Farkas, minister of defense, and one of those intimately involved in the Rajk case, said in 1957: "We acted in the best conviction that we fought the enemy." Mathias Rakosi, head of the Hungarian Communist Party, who used to be called, with good reason, "the most outstanding Hungarian disciple of Comrade Stalin," had this to say in retrospect: "In the Rajk affair the Hungarian leadership too must bear responsibility. Nonetheless, it must be taken into account that all that happened in 1949. The international situation must be considered; these matters have to be examined, but not from the perspective of *abstract moral principles*."

When Rajk and his associates were arrested, Rakosi offered the Hungarian Politburo the following explanation: "'When there is trouble, it is always connected to the machinations of the enemy. *We are not worried about suspecting everybody alive.* The growth of suspiciousness that is going to occur, is all right. When you cut down trees, the chips will fly.' Rakosi also related that when he was in jail there was a man who had tuberculosis of the bone; his whole foot had to be amputated. He implored the doctors to cut off only a small part. 'He was operated on four times, and four times the tuberculosis remained in the bones. His whole leg had to be amputated [in the end], but he died. Had he allowed his whole foot to be amputated early on, his life could have been saved.'"[103] It may be noted here that those advising, encouraging, or ordering political violence often thrive on organic or surgical metaphors; the body politic is thus equated with the human body.[104]

Even when the fraudulence of the Soviet show trials was no longer in dispute, they were still justified as expedient by the remaining true believers, such as Jakub Berman: "He [Stalin] got the idea . . . because at some point he . . . came to the conclusion that accusing his enemies, who were hindering him and spoiling his plans, on political grounds alone would not be convincing, and that in order to get rid of them . . . he would have to destroy them morally as well . . . You also have to remember that all this was happening when . . . the Soviet Union faced a very real danger from Germany, so that unity of action and the closing of ranks were also essential." Similar judicial proceedings in Poland after World War II were justified in the same spirit: "Sometimes the interest of the individual has to be subordinated to the interests of the state, and when the state is threatened, suspicions are magnified in order to render them more plausible."[105]

The second approach to understanding the actions and attitudes of the specialists relies more heavily on the lure of power than on ideologically inspired certainties and rationalizations. The likes of Beria, Yagoda, Yezhov, Sudoplatov, and Gabor Peter were in all probability attracted to their positions and activities because of an overdeveloped need for power and a pleasure in its unconstrained exercise. People with such a disposition took advantage of the opportunities provided by the political system and its institutions of coercion, but they did not create these institutions. This disposition is different from pure sadism, from the pleasure of inflicting pain.

Nonetheless, there is a continuity between the sense of power that comes from planning and ordering the imprisonment or extermination of large groups of people and the sense of power that the torturer-interrogator possesses who can do whatever he wishes to his victim (short of killing him prematurely).

It is likely that inflicting pain and death, even from a distance, was not impelled but only rationalized by ideological justifications, that nonideological motives were also at work. Evidently some of the high-level specialists had traits of character that were helpful in their work. Reportedly Beria had "a special predilection" for "old-fashioned instruments of torture."[106] Lazar Kaganovich, a close associate of Stalin's, wrote "'Hooray!' on the margin of the NKVD lists of names of those to be executed as 'enemies of the people,'" Andrei Gromyko recalled.[107] (We do not know whether his enthusiasm was genuine or simulated to impress Stalin.)

Stalin, according to Khrushchev, issued instructions to beat the accused in the Purge Trials to extract confessions. Rakosi offered this rationale for beating the defendants in the Rajk case: "The Horthy police [of the pre-communist system] began the interrogation of communists by beating them up thoroughly, and we are treating the enemy with great consideration; that is wrong. Beating is a necessary method of the AVH, and it needs to be used." Gyula Princz, one of the Hungarian officers administering the beatings, said: "'We beat them as long as they refused to confess.' They were beaten because 'even during the investigation they continued their hostile activities,' that is, they denied the charges. Some had to eat salt, others had to lick the toilet bowl, or had water dripped on their head." Farkas senior instructed Princz to beat Rajk until he admitted being an agent of the imperialist powers. Gabor Peter, head of the AVH, demanded that the interrogators show "unwavering hatred" of "the enemies of the Party."[108] Eugen Loebl, a defendant in the Slansky trial in Czechoslovakia, recalls the beliefs of his chief interrogator: "Sentimentality was out of place in these times of stepped-up class war, when capitalism and Socialism were locked in a deadly struggle."[109]

The official encouragement of hostility and vindictiveness toward such enemies and the institutionalized verbal aggression probably also helped to legitimate the impulses of some ordinary people which under different circumstances would not have found outlet in acts of political hatred and violence. Eyewitness reports of Soviet criticism and self-criticism meetings, where a certain amount of spontaneous audience participation was encouraged, and of similar sessions in Cambodia and during the Cultural Revolution in China, suggest that these regimes often succeeded in tapping into the aggression and the scapegoating impulses of people not professionally involved in political violence and coercion.

The reflections of a former Red Guard illuminate the pull of violence and the blend of motives (including sadism, group pressure, and solidarity) which played a part in the commission of brutalities during the Cultural Revolution in China: "Beating is addictive. The dark side of human nature, whenever it is given a chance to surface, will explode . . . I remember one day when the students at our school couldn't find anybody to beat . . . [they] went to a nearby commune. The commune leadership pointed out to them a landlord who was also labelled as a bad element, who was . . . 'dragged to our schoolyard. He was beaten to death . . . Beating was the only way to show one's hatred [toward the enemy, that is] as well as one's love to the great leader . . . Beating someone to death involved . . . a whole group. No one dared to show weakness. Non-participation was a sign of a weak revolutionary . . . 'sympathy' [toward the victim] was an unheard of term.'"[110] The well-established human capacity for dehumanizing and demonizing other human beings makes it possible to order, witness, or participate in their mistreatment without compunction.

Finally, we must remember that the bulk of the political violence under communist systems (as under Nazism)—unlike many outbursts of ethnic violence—was premeditated and calculated.[111] It would be hard to argue that the specialists in the KGB and similar organizations were carried away either by their own impulses or by spontaneous group encouragement. This still leaves us with the possibility, indeed probability, that many of those most intimately involved with ordering or inflicting violence found it a congenial rather than a painful exercise of duty.

PAVEL SUDOPLATOV (1907–1996)

Pavel Sudoplatov, the high-ranking Soviet political police officer who organized the assassination of Trotsky, among others, "pursued his grisly career in the sincere belief that he was carrying out the higher will of the proletariat," according to Volkogonov (who interviewed him in connection with his biography of Trotsky).[112] He was also among the few such officials who unburdened themselves of their past in writing. His interviewers write: "The intelligence career of Pavel Anatolievich Sudoplatov coincided almost exactly with Stalin's thirty-year reign . . . Sudoplatov worked in the Administration for Special Tasks, an elite unit of the Soviet intelligence service, becoming its wartime director. He defined the meaning of the word 'special' with blood, poison, and terrorism . . . He remains a believer in the dream of communism and attributes its fall to the lesser men who followed Stalin . . . He saw himself as 'a soldier at war' in justifiable combat." Sudoplatov himself writes: "My Administration for Special Tasks was responsible for sabotage, kidnapping, and assassinations of our enemies beyond the country's borders . . . After the war I continued to run illegal networks abroad whose purpose was to sabotage American and NATO installations in the event [of] hostilities."[113]

Despite the lack of contrition there is a recurring attempt throughout Sudoplatov's book to confront in some manner the moral aspects of his life's work. For example: "It is strange to look back fifty years and re-create the mentality that led us to take vengeance on our enemies with cold self-assurance. We did not believe that there was any moral question involved in killing Trotsky or any other former comrades who had turned against us. We believed that we were in a life-and-death struggle for the salvation of our grand experiment, the creation of a new social system that would protect and provide dignity for all workers and eliminate the greed and oppression of capitalist profit."

In addition to these contextual defenses ("the times"), there were more specific justifications. "Active operations" (involving violence) were "logical actions taken to prevent damage to our agent networks or to our interests." Here, again, violence is redefined as defensive and therefore acceptable.[114]

These and similar comments suggest that the key to understanding the political murders and mass murders of our times is their transformation, in the minds of the perpetrators, from acts of aggression into acts of self-defense. Unarmed, unorganized Jewish civilians of all ages could be perceived as genuinely threatening by the Nazis, and their extermination became a measure of necessary self-defense. Soviet leaders and their high-level subordinates, having defined a wide variety of groups and individuals as mortally dangerous, found it unproblematic to justify the lethal measures they took against them.

Defining and redefining more and more broadly and generously what constitutes a threat to a political system appears to be a relatively recent trend; both modern warfare and political conflict rely heavily on such defensive justifications. In earlier times strong and undisguised beliefs and passions, or cold calculation of advantage provided sufficient entitlement to massacre or dispossess groups which were different or whose possessions were coveted. The conquerors, crusaders, colonizers, tribal chiefs, and assorted aggressors of the past did not claim self-defense as they overran their neighbors, or others in distant lands, or brutalized outgroups within their society; they conquered and killed without recourse to elaborate rationalizations. In the twentieth century the reliance on self-defense as a vindication of aggression and repression has become increasingly popular, especially on the part of the most intolerant and ruthless political systems.

Sudoplatov, like many former Western supporters of the Soviet Union under Stalin, also found vindication for his beliefs and behavior in the anti-Nazi policies of the Soviet Union and its victory in World War II: "The end of the war is still vivid in my memory as a glorious event that washed away all my doubts about the wisdom of Stalin's leadership. All heroic and tragic events, losses and even purges, seemed to be justified by the triumph over Hitler." As the implicit argument goes, given the overwhelming, exceptional moral evil that the Nazi regime embodied, the Soviet system deserved credit, even in its Stalinist incarnation; the Soviet regime redeemed itself for the privations it inflicted on its people by defeating the Nazis.

The ends and means argument was recast into a tabulation of costs and benefits: admittedly bad things happened in the Soviet Union, but they were the price paid for great achievements. It is tempting to question Sudoplatov's notions of what constitutes an achievement. He writes: "Despite their crimes, Beria, Stalin, Molotov and Pervukhin succeeded in transforming the Soviet Union from a backward agrarian hinterland into a superpower armed with sophisticated nuclear weapons."[115] For him the survival and superpower status of the Soviet Union were self-evident accomplishments, the cornerstone of his belief system and his professional work. His thinking in this regard is very similar to that of Kryuchkov, who also gave credit to Stalin for making the Soviet Union a nuclear power.

In the course of examining the attitudes and beliefs of Sudoplatov (and, by implication, others in similar positions) a question arises: Would his attitudes have been different if he had ever witnessed an execution, assassination, or torture-interrogation? Did he ever see the corpses of people killed on his orders and by his organization? If indeed he was insulated from the visual experience of his policies, it would probably have been easier for him to support them. On the other hand, we know that he did not shy away from lively discussions with subordinates about the most expedient methods of assassination to employ.

Not only were the high-level specialists removed from the tangible human consequences of their policies; they inhabited a rarefied sphere of privilege insulated from sordid realities of other kinds as well. Vladimir Farkas recalls: "I did not see or experience at the time that I lived in an intimidated country whose people hated its illegitimate rulers and the AVH. The simple explanation is that my work at the AVH precluded all such opportunities while my nonwork time was spent in the narrow family circle."[116]

Sudoplatov lived under similar circumstances, yet he, at least in retrospect, developed some reservations about the system he served. The rise of his critical reflections coincided with his personal loss of power (as was the case with Andras Hegedus and other high-ranking officials discussed earlier). After Stalin's death in 1953 and Beria's subsequent fall from power (and execution), Sudoplatov, as an associate of Beria's, was imprisoned for fifteen years. His American interviewers write: "After nearly all his friends were executed or imprisoned he began to question the efficacy of Stalin's socialist morality. In Stalin's final years . . . [he] saw his position . . . erode and his privileged life threatened. He thought at first that it was the result of bureaucratic inefficiency and mistakes. Only when he was arrested and interrogated did he realize that the regime's real purpose was not a noble social experiment." This realization was apparently the sharpest in the moments of his arrest when his guard took away his "Swiss chronometer wristwatch bought fifteen years earlier in Belgium . . . This petty theft ended what was left of my Chekist idealism. How such an act could occur in the security service occupied my thoughts." The incident conveys the impact of experiencing humiliation and powerlessness as a source of new insights and attitude change.

Sudoplatov expresses at least one pragmatic reservation about the misdeeds of the system: "History shows that no top-secret decisions, no secret crimes or terrorist plans can be concealed forever. This is one of the great lessons of the breakdown of the Soviet Union and Communist party rule. Once the dam is broken the flood of secret information is uncontrollable."[117] This, then, is another lesson: you will be found out.

Further light is shed on Sudoplatov's character and activities from the account of a post–World War II defector and former officer of the political police, Nikolai Khoklov, who was directly under his command. Khoklov's job was to eliminate some of the enemies of the Soviet Union abroad, such as a Russian émigré in Paris who, as Sudoplatov put it, "bothers us very much . . . [and] must be put away." Khoklov's fellow assassin did not survive the operation. Sudoplatov reportedly said, "I am afraid there will be no time left for saving the agent. It is best to get rid of him also . . . Take along one more fountain pen, and that's all." (The pens in question were miniature, noiseless firearms.) When Khoklov expressed misgivings about his mission, Sudplatov was perplexed: "'What is this with you again? Is it possible that you cannot control yourself?' . . . There was no anger in his voice, rather an unconcealed exasperation."[118] These recollections present the matter-of-fact disposition regarding ends and means that was an essential qualification for Sudoplatov's position.

Sudoplatov apparently managed to avoid a final and decisive break with the system that he had loyally served, although at one point he says that "we must feel repentant for the innocent, because knowingly or unknowingly they were involved in the operation of a monumental, oppressive machine in a backward country; the magnitude of the repression still shocks me."[119]

OLEG KALUGIN (B. 1932)

I first learned of Oleg Kalugin from the evening television news in the late 1980s. Identified as a former KGB general, he was interviewed on the ongoing changes in the Soviet Union; he struck me as an impressively articulate and intelligent man, even a man of integrity, if the latter attribute could be reconciled with long and distinguished service in an organization such as the KGB and a "father-son relationship" with its head, Andropov.[120] He spoke excellent American English, for reasons which became clear later. I thought that he would be an ideal source of information for this study: a man in the belly of the beast who turned against it, a pillar of the system who withdrew his support.

Although not "a specialist in coercion," narrowly defined, Kalugin was a member of the highest political-repressive elite, a major general and the counterintelligence chief of the KGB, and, as such, he was prepared to use whatever methods were required in the pursuit of his professional objectives.

For Kalugin, as for others of his (and earlier) generations, Soviet victory in World War II constituted a cornerstone of the legitimacy of the system— proof not merely of the patriotism of Soviet people and their ability to endure hardships and deprivations but of the superiority of the Soviet political system—"the ultimate proof that our Communist system was the best in the world." At age fourteen he joined the Young Communist League and became head of its school organization. At seventeen he resolved to make spying for the motherland his vocation. It is not difficult to reconstruct the mindset of the bright and personable young man with a talent for languages seeking a career that combined privilege, excitement, and civic virtue. He decided "to join the secret police and become an intelligence agent. The KGB . . . seemed like the logical place for a person with my academic abilities, language skills and fervent desire to fight class enemies, capitalist parasites, and social injustice."[121] His father, a former (low-ranking) member of the NKVD (predecessor of the KGB) "strongly objected" to his choice.

When Kalugin joined, the KGB "was looking for a new generation of bright young officers, untainted by the crimes of the Stalin era. I was to be one of the new guard." The KGB sought to attract people of high intelligence whose loyalty rested more on the guaranteed privileges than on ideological convictions, though it was never easy to separate these two motivations. The politically virtuous were convinced that their privileges were well deserved, and enjoyment of privileges strengthened this conviction.

Kalugin entered the KGB training schools with a set of taken-for-granted

beliefs in the Soviet system and its official values. At the beginning of his career, "when I headed to New York as a young man of twenty-four, I was
confident we were not far from the 'shining future' that our leaders from
Lenin to Khrushchev had promised us. That blind faith carried me forward
for years, helping me to overlook the 1956 Soviet invasion of Hungary, the
1968 occupation of Czechoslovakia, the growing isolation and senility of our
leaders. I myself spread a string of lies and disinformation to further our cause
in the Cold War."[122] Such feelings resembled those expressed by Kalugin's
role model later in life, Kim Philby (the notorious spy), who, upon being recruited to the Soviet intelligence service, said: "I did not hesitate. One does
not look twice at an offer of enrollment in an elite force."[123]

Kalugin was sent to the United States to start his spying career under
the cover of graduate work in journalism at Columbia University. He was
"greeted by a smiling Immigration officer. 'Welcome to the United States'
he said, as our group of spies, Intelligence officers and Communist Party
bureaucrats happily arrived in the land of the free."[124] Following his year
at Columbia (1958–1959), he was sent back to the United States, first as a
correspondent for Radio Moscow, later as press attaché at the Soviet embassy in Washington; under both covers he spent much of his time seeking
to recruit spies. He stayed until 1970. Reassigned to KGB Headquarters in
Moscow, he was deputy head and then head of the Foreign Counterintelligence Directorate between 1970 and 1980; he was promoted to general in
1973. Between 1980 and 1987 he was deputy chief of the Leningrad KGB;
in 1987–1990 he was assigned to the Academy of Sciences and the Ministry
of Electronics in Moscow. In 1990 he broke with the KGB.

Kalugin's tasks over the years included intelligence gathering, disinformation, and, later, counterintelligence. Sometimes these activities involved
violent methods, as, for instance, when defectors abroad were to be tracked
down, then kidnapped or liquidated. While the head of the Foreign Counterintelligence Directorate he asked Andropov's permission "to order assassination of the two traitors," that is, two KGB defectors from the 1950s.[125]
He was involved to a much-debated degree in the notorious Markov case
and, according to John le Carré, had no remorse about it.[126] Kalugin also
organized the planting of a bomb in the Munich headquarters of Radio

Liberty, though his aim was "not to hurt anyone but rather to move the rabble-rousing station out of Munich and Germany."[127]

His views of instrumental political violence and deception were wholly pragmatic. He deplored the execution "of leading Muslim clergymen and their families" in Afghanistan because these actions would "set off a never-ending cycle of revenge and violence" rather than because these executions were wrong in themselves. He was nonjudgmental about Andropov's "total lie" to Imre Nagy during the 1956 Hungarian Revolution.[128]

The strength of Kalugin's commitments was reflected in his untroubled acceptance of the archetypical relation between ends and means. He "lost no sleep" over "dirty tricks," organizing, for example, a "rabid anti-black letter-writing campaign" directed at African U.N. missions and purportedly perpetrated by American racists (the intention was to show the depth of racism in the United States) and another campaign, designed to prove anti-Semitism in the United States, which involved hiring people to desecrate Jewish cemeteries and paint swastikas on synagogues.[129]

In the spring of 1993, I met Kalugin at the Hoover Institution in Palo Alto, California, where he had come to give a talk. I had a lengthy one-on-one conversation with him in which I asked him about the roots as well as the more immediate sources of his political disillusionment. He gave three sources, each of which is also discussed in his memoirs.

One was the official duplicity and make-believe associated with political participation. An example was an exceptionally articulate "ordinary worker" who spoke at a Party meeting and turned out to be a Party activist; it was a stage-managed affair. He also described the incident in his book:

> As a member of the regional [Leningrad] Communist Party
> Committee . . . I remember . . . how impressed I was as a seem-
> ingly simple worker stood up and delivered an eloquent speech
> on the region's social problems. After the meeting, I told the local
> Party boss how intelligent this common man had seemed, and
> how our educational standards appeared to be improving. The
> boss enlightened me, however. The worker hadn't just stood up
> and made an extemporaneous address. Party officials had chosen

him a month in advance, had written his speech for him and had drilled him . . . to deliver it. It was all scripted in advance, as was every meeting of the regional Soviet and Communist Party Committee. It was a charade.[130]

This, then, was an encounter with the proverbial appearance-reality gap which he discovered late in his career after being transferred from the glamorous world of espionage and counterespionage to the mundane tasks of domestic KGB officialdom. The spurious spontaneity that Kalugin found so repellent was an inherent part of the system, of its endemic, recurring misrepresentation of the truth; it was a form of socialist realism[131] applied to political life.

During his Leningrad "exile" Kalugin accompanied Grigory Romanov, the first secretary of the Party of the Leningrad area, on his tours of inspection. This description, too, is from his memoirs:

These trips were invariably scripted, enabling Comrade Romanov to see the best that our rural regions had to offer. Most collective farms were, in fact, a mess . . . Many of our villages looked straight out of the 19th century, with people living in ramshackle wooden cottages that lacked running water and indoor toilets. But Romanov and other exalted guests never saw that reality. They invariably were squired around the handful of model collective farms . . . Potemkin village[s] . . . Smiling collective farm workers would tell the dignitary how great everything was and then all the top local officials . . . would repair to a private dining room attached to the collective farm's cafeteria. There the group would sit down at tables groaning with food and drink and the marathon toasting and vodka guzzling would begin.

Among the memorable incidents which disturbed Kalugin in this period was a reprimand that he received for passing (in his car) the mayor of Leningrad, who was generally "driven to distraction by people who dared to pass his long black Chaika limousine."[132] Passing him was a symbolic offense against the leading role of the Party in Soviet life.

Another, more specific reason for disaffection was the discovery that the local (Leningrad) KGB was unwilling to crack down on corrupt Party officials. His report of the corruption to superiors in Moscow was of no avail, evidence of even more far-reaching corruption and the impossibility of remedying it. Once Kalyugin began to question what he saw around him, especially the corruption of the nomenklatura, he found support for his experiences in the writings of Milovan Djilas, especially *The New Class*, which "mirrored" his own views.[133]

These incidents left him with the feeling that, in the words of the poet Akhmatova, "everything is stolen, betrayed, soiled."[134] He was repelled by the ossified, stagnant character of the Brezhnev regime and by Brezhnev himself, whom he considered unfit to lead the country and incapable of bringing about reform.

Kalugin dated his sharp break with the system to 1990, but the disillusionment had been growing for years. For example, in the spring of 1979, when crossing the border from Finland to the USSR, "for no apparent reason I was overcome by feelings of sadness and foreboding. I looked at the neat Finnish cottages and my heart sank when I thought of crossing into Soviet territory at Vyborg, a gray and gloomy town. The prospect of returning to Moscow, where the media would be prattling on about the Five-Year Plans and the triumph of socialism, made me ill . . . I had the disquieting feeling that I was returning not so much to my homeland, but to prison."

On another occasion in the 1970s Kalugin was at the Czechoslovakian-Austrian border with a Soviet delegation and the symbolic visual juxtaposition of the two systems yielded similar feelings: "Not far from Bratislava, we disembarked [from a patrol boat on the Danube] and inspected the barbed-wire barrier separating Czechoslovakia from Austria, 150 yards away. On the other side of the river, Austrian families picnicked . . . Children flew kites as parents unpacked food and made campfires. It was a picture of idyllic contentment . . . Silently we stood on our side of the barbed wire, surrounded by watch towers and dour Czech border guards with carbines. The contrast between the two scenes could not have been sharper, and I sensed that everyone in the Soviet delegation was thinking the same thing: They are the ones who are free and we are the ones in a prison camp."[135]

While the seeds of disenchantment were planted decades earlier (though without interfering with the energetic performance of his duties), what accelerated the growth of disillusionment was not merely a disinterested realization of the grave flaws of the system. Personal conflicts and loss of standing within the organization played a part. ("In 1980 I was sent into high-level bureaucratic exile in Leningrad, where for seven years I saw at close range the rot of the Brezhnev era.")[136] Disillusionment coincided with and was accelerated both by what he regarded as an unjust demotion and by the opportunities the new (Leningrad) position provided for a closer look at Soviet realities. Kalugin writes: "After more than two decades in the rarified world of espionage . . . I was brought back to earth in Leningrad. Returning to my hometown as a domestic KGB general was a depressing and sordid revelation . . . I had a perfect vantage point from which to see the absurdity and advanced decay of Soviet Communism. At close range I watched the top men in the KGB and the Communist Party . . . and . . . how out of touch with reality they became. They inhabited their own Byzantine world of privilege and power . . . in my seven years in Leningrad I came to see we had created not only the most extensive totalitarian state apparatus in history but also the most arcane . . . this terrifying centralized machine, this *religion* that sought to control all aspects of life . . . I was forced to stick my nose in the reality of Soviet life, and it was an enormous comedown."

The nature of the domestic KGB work was disillusioning: "Our leaders were busy issuing reports about the rosy situation in the country and applauding one another at countless congresses and conferences. The security people were busy with nonsense . . . I became less and less interested in my work."

Matters became worse when he came under suspicion of working for the CIA: "It took my own personal collision with the KGB hierarchy—and the subsequent derailing of my career—to make me see the light. Before, all the suffering and injustice of our system had been an abstract thing to me. I didn't really *understand* until I, too, had suffered at the hands of the Soviet system. That may not be admirable, but in my case it was the truth."[137]

It is to Kalugin's credit that he admits that without his personal conflict with the KGB his doubts about the system might have had little impact on his behavior. Though the seeds of disaffection reached far back into the past, the attractions of his career compensated for them. It was the personal injustice that made it possible to grasp the capacity of the system to be unjust to others as well. Without his personal troubles he might have continued to cling to his belief that the system could be salvaged.

Even after the intensification of doubts and reservations, until his resignation from the KGB in 1990 he believed that the system could be reformed. Kalugin writes: "Khrushchev's speech and his ensuing efforts to reform Soviet society indelibly marked my generation, which included men like Gorbachev and Yeltsin . . . my contemporaries and I balanced a strong belief in Communism with the painful realization of the enormous blunders and cruelty that had characterized our state. Our faith in Communism was so strong that Gorbachev, even after being ousted in the failed coup . . . would return to Moscow still proclaiming his belief in the 'Socialist choice.'"

His beliefs stood the test of his prolonged (ten-year) stay in the United States, although the stay contributed to their slow erosion. While he was shocked by the contrast between the lively and colorful quality of American life as opposed to the "gray, monochrome world" of the Soviet Union, he managed to balance such impressions against the belief that Soviet achievements in science and the space program proved the vitality of the Soviet system and its capacity to overcome poverty and backwardness; he believed that his country would overtake the United States, as Khrushchev had promised in an unguarded moment. At the same time, the impressions gained during his travels in America and the freedom to talk to people in every walk of life "contrasted sharply with the mood of my country, where such a friendly, open attitude often was met with a stiff rebuke or a door slammed in one's face."[138]

Still, the "twinges of doubt" were overcome or brushed aside without serious harm to the fundamentals of his beliefs and commitments. Life in the United States was interesting and far more comfortable than life in the Soviet Union, even for a member of the nomenklatura. Yet even in the privileged (American) setting Kalugin could see himself (as did Dobrynin) fighting for the good of the cause. He came to resemble Western sympathizers with communist systems: for him, too, it was easier to be a fighter for communism in Washington, D.C., than in the USSR ("returning to the Soviet capital made me realize that worshipping Communism from afar was one thing. Living in it was another thing altogether"). Back in Moscow he often dreamed of "the bustle of Broadway . . . Greenwich Village . . . the emerald lawns of Riverside and of Fort Tyron Park . . . [and] longed to return to America."[139]

Kalugin's beliefs were further undermined by observing the decline of ideological commitment on the part of Westerners volunteering to spy for the Soviet Union: "Rising to head the directorate [of Foreign Counterintelligence] in 1973 it became increasingly clear why we were lagging behind America in the field of espionage: Virtually no one believed anymore in the Soviet Union . . . [whereas] the great spies of the early Soviet days, the Philbys or the Rosenbergs, came to us because of what they saw as our noble Communist experiment . . . All that began to change in 1956, when Khrushchev . . . showed that our 'Socialist achievements' had been built on the bones of our people. True communist believers, such as Philby, began to dry up and disappear."

The death of Andropov, his mentor, was another blow to his hopes and beliefs: "Andropov's passing left me profoundly depressed. Indeed, I date my utter disillusionment with the KGB to early 1984, when Andropov's demise and . . . other events forced me to see that there was no hope of reviving my career, or of redeeming the old Soviet system."[140] As in other cases discussed, the process of disillusionment was prolonged, and its various stages were compatible with the retention of a diffuse, basic belief in the system despite specific, disillusioning events. One of these was the invasion of Czechoslovakia in 1968. Realistically enough, Kalugin concludes that "had I been bolder, had I been more of a dissident I might have resigned . . . after the Soviet tanks rolled into Prague. But I was no dissident, no Sakharov or Solzhenitsyn. I was a product of the system, a patriot, and defection was . . . out of the question. I suppose I was also a slave to my ambition and to the illusion that the system . . . could be reformed."

Kalugin was further discouraged by what he regarded as the organizational-professional degeneration of the KGB that went hand in hand with the degeneration of the system as a whole. By 1990 there were more KBG employees in Moscow alone (47,000) than people working for the FBI and CIA combined. He writes: "The KGB, the Party apparatus and the gargantuan military-industrial complex . . . were draining the country dry . . . The average Soviet, meanwhile, was living virtually a Third World existence."[141]

Kalugin, as others in high position who came to question the system, was mostly concerned with the spread of corruption, rather than other important systemic flaws, such as the concentration of power, the lack of accountability of the leaders, or the institutionalized intolerance and repression. He recalls that "during my years in Foreign Counterintelligence, I was constantly running up against nepotism, cronyism and corruption . . . By 1980, only the most dottering Party bosses still believed the rubbish about the Soviet Union building a true, egalitarian system. Our Communism had degenerated . . . into a . . . system in which the party elite divided up the spoils . . . while the masses were left with cheap vodka, fatty sausage . . . I was frequently forced to hire inferior officers because they were relatives or friends of Party big shots . . . I encountered . . . blatant corruption and misconduct on the part of well-connected diplomats and ambassadors . . . The last years of the Soviet Union validated the old saying: A fish rots from its head."[142]

For a long time, deploring corruption was also compatible with retaining faith in the idealized view of the system and with evading a fundamental reassessment of its defining and problematic characteristics. He did not ask, What disposed people to corruption? Why did the New Soviet Man or New Socialist Man fail to emerge or fail to survive and resist corruption? Why were there so few of them, if any?

Kalugin's perception of himself as a professional battling the external enemy contrasted with the corruption of the leaders back home, isolated from reality behind their walls. He made a sharp distinction between involvement in the activities of foreign counterintelligence and those performed by the KGB on the domestic front: "It was difficult for me to imagine how my domestic counterparts could carry on, year after year, harassing our own citizens . . . when I was assigned to the KGB's Leningrad office in 1980, I found myself increasingly depressed over the often meaningless tasks I was given. In Foreign Counterintelligence, our enemies were external and our national security was indisputably involved. We also fought on a roughly equal footing with the CIA and other agencies . . . It was a war of wits and skill and nerve."

Elsewhere he has written: "We in the KGB's foreign operations were . . . proud that we trained our sights on foreign enemies . . . not on our own people . . . most of us in Intelligence viewed the domestic KGB as an unsavory, cruel and totalitarian organization, and we were glad to have as little to do with it as possible." His occupational role required little supporting ideological reflection: "In the later 1970s, running one of the KGB's most important directorates, I can honestly say that I loved my work. My job was always challenging, placing me at the heart of the Cold War competition . . . I traveled the world, overseeing Counterintelligence operations . . . I was not so blind that I didn't see how far we were falling behind the West, how corrupt the upper reaches of the Communist Party [were], and what a senile fool Brezhnev had become. But I had not given up on my country, nor on the idea that it could be reformed. The great illusions which had determined my worldview since birth still stayed with me, tattered as they might have been."[143]

Professional pride and a sense of adventure also help to explain why Kalugin admired Kim Philby, the British master spy. Kalugin's fascination with Philby, I believe, was largely apolitical: here was a man in the same profession, pursuing the same objectives with success and bravado. Philby was something of a Renaissance man, a connoisseur of good food, wine, and women, a world traveler, a widely read, well-educated bon vivant and raconteur. Apparently for Kalugin, Philby was in a curious way a symbol of the West, of Western ways and their attractions; he represented the best of all possible worlds: he was a sophisticated Westerner who supported what Kalugin regarded as the untarnished ideals of his profession, a Westerner imbued with, but not deformed by, solid communist values and virtues. Even in retrospect he considered his relationship to Philby "one of the most rewarding and fascinating in all my years in the KGB." This relationship flourished during Philby's long Moscow exile, when Kalugin looked for ways to rescue him from obscurity and personal decay. When Philby died in 1988, Kalugin was deeply moved: "I was overcome with a sense of grief and loss. Philby had become a true friend . . . But my melancholy went deeper than that. Philby had been a symbol of that generation that believed in Communism. He had been a romantic who embraced the Soviet Union . . . Now in 1988, Philby was stretched out before me, and the dream we had both believed in was as dead as my good friend. We had both been betrayed."[144]

Kalugin's case once more shows that unwavering ideological conviction was not a necessary requirement for working devotedly for the system. It was *after* his mistreatment and personal grievances that he gave up on the idea that the system could be reformed. This is not to say that his loyalty was derived entirely from his privileged and powerful position. He was a product of the system, but his intellect and his experiences in the West gradually subverted his belief in it, though he managed to hold disillusionment at bay almost until the demise of the Soviet Union.

When Trotsky discussed the difficulty of building socialism in one country, he omitted one important factor. It was the presence of the Western, non-socialist world, a standing rebuke to and refutation of everything the Soviet system claimed and stood for. Kalugin is an example of the effects of exposure to this world.

Beginning in June 1990, Kalugin became a vocal public critic of the KGB, and two weeks later he was stripped of his rank, awards, and pension. In the same year he ran on an anti-KGB platform for a vacant seat in the USSR Congress of People's Deputies and was elected. At the time of this writing he ran a consulting business in Moscow.

VLADIMIR FARKAS (B. 1925)

Vladimir Farkas served in the Hungarian political police (AVO or AVH) between 1946 and 1955; his highest rank was lieutenant colonel. By birth a member of the ruling elite, he was the son of the minister of defense, Mihaly Farkas. Between the ages of fourteen and twenty he lived in the Soviet Union. He returned to Hungary in 1945 and joined the Hungarian political police. At one point in his career he headed the foreign intelligence gathering operations; he also participated in the preparation of some of the major Hungarian show trials. In October 1956 (before the Revolution) he was imprisoned in the course of the de-Stalinization campaign and spent three and a half years in prison. After his release the postrevolutionary Kadar regime continued to treat him with some hostility. He never reentered the nomenklatura but worked in modest administrative positions at various state enterprises. He retired in 1985.

Vladimir Farkas wrote a long, detailed, and seemingly sincere book about his experiences and feelings entitled *No Excuse—I Was a Lt. Colonel in the AVH* (available only in Hungarian). Unlike Sudoplatov and others in high positions, Farkas made a complete and unqualified break with the system and even its unrealized ideals. He writes: "The summer of 1949 was the time

when I should have called a halt on the road which led to my active participation in a reign of terror . . . I consciously undertook not merely to separate power from morality and law but also to accord unconditional primacy
to the interests of power . . . This attitude led predictably to my intoxica-
tion, conceit, and arrogance . . . I was proud at the time to be working with
the AVH."[145]

In 1991 and 1992 I met him in Budapest and interviewed him. At the time
he expressed support for Scandinavian socialism, or social-democracy. I
detected a lingering resentment toward the West, the United States in particular, for abandoning Eastern Europe to the Soviet Union after World
War II.

The story of Farkas resembles the others examined earlier. He, too, lived
with his doubts and reservations for a long time before his faith finally eroded.
His political self-presentation appears credible since a person intent on por-
traying himself in a more flattering light would have preferred to convey
that he was unaware of the flaws of the system and served it in the belief
that all was well until some shocking revelation jolted him.

Why did it take him (and his colleagues in disaffection) so long to draw
the appropriate conclusions from his experiences? Most obviously, the pressure of the social-political setting, especially the fear of punishment, made
it difficult to draw such conclusions and act on them. The expectations of
those around him also kept him in line, anxious as he was not to be cut off
from the community he was a part of, including a close family. There was
also a residual belief in the reformability of the system. According to Jan
Sejna, people stayed with the system despite their doubts because "when
you have power at too young an age [this applies to both Sejna and Farkas],
you tend to ignore questions of right and wrong, especially if you are blink-
ered by a sense of dedication, as I was. By the time you get round to won-
dering whether what you are doing is wrong, it is too late; you are already
enmeshed in the Party machine . . . You have only two choices: either to
go on as before; or to speak your mind, be expelled from the Party, and be
finished for life. In the latter event not only would you yourself be finished,
but so would your family."[146]

As in other cases (Dubcek, Hegedus, Nagy, Sudoplatov, and others), the
principled, or disinterested motives for rejecting the system are hard to

separate from the loss of official position and imprisonment—which, for Farkas, occurred during de-Stalinization. In other words, the system rejected him as much as he rejected the system. Only after being rejected by the system were his reservations converted into the wholesale renunciation of earlier beliefs, his own misfortunes being among the proofs of the degeneration of the system. This is not to say that the reservations and doubts were not genuine.

For a long period in his life Farkas, too, entertained the notion that noble ideals were sullied by individuals of questionable character. While he stops short of offering a theory about why former idealists and revolutionaries allowed the system to be deformed (and even participated in its deformation), the conclusion drawn from his recollections and reflections is by now familiar. It was the combination of power and privilege—and the attendant distance from ordinary people and ordinary morality—that corrupted the leaders.

A good portion of his memoirs consist of the meticulous reconstruction of his struggles with the communist hierarchy following the political changes after the death of Stalin. In 1955 he was dismissed from the AVH, and in early October 1956 (before the outbreak of the Revolution) he was arrested and accused of the mistreatment of political prisoners, among them Janos Kadar, who came to rule the country for over three decades after 1956. The young Farkas became a victim of de-Stalinization as well as the power struggles within the Hungarian Party following the death of Stalin. He insists to this day that he (and his father) were scapegoats for the crimes of the entire Rakosi regime.

The story of Vladimir Farkas is unusual not only because of the length of his soul searchings but also because of the connections between his political beliefs and his father, who was a major political figure. The struggle with the beliefs and commitments passed on to him by his father was part of a highly ambivalent personal relationship, as he makes quite clear. Less clear is whether his father's longer-held and far more doctrinaire commitments hastened or slowed the son's disaffection.

The political attitudes and beliefs of Vladimir Farkas were products of his childhood and upbringing. He was, in the American terminology, a "red diaper baby" of Jewish background. He was named Vladimir in honor of

Lenin. His father was a functionary in the Czechoslovak Communist Party as well as the Communist International, working in various European countries before World War II. His parents, both communists, got divorced early in his life, and he was raised by his grandmother until age fourteen. Much of his early life was spent in communist youth organizations. He got his first assignment from the Party while still in grade school (to take food to imprisoned communists). He writes: "I was born into the communist movement just as other children are born into loyal Catholic, Protestant, Jewish, or Muslim families."[147]

Between the ages of ten and thirteen he formed an image of the Soviet Union as an "earthly paradise." At age fourteen he was sent there to join his father. As the train crossed the Soviet border the Red Star on the cap of the border guard moved him to tears of joy. At age seventeen he was sent to a Party school in preparation for Party work in Hungary after the war. He spent six years in the Soviet Union and became fluent in Russian. As he recalls, "It was at this party school that I became a convinced communist. Up till then, my family environment was the only source of my faith in the reality and truth of communist ideals." He left for Hungary at age twenty (in 1945), taking it for granted that "the [communist] movement was led by a deity [Stalin] incarnate in human form who was omniscient, omnicompetent, and ready to solve all our problems."[148] One of his first assignments in Hungary after joining the political police in 1946 was the monitoring of phone conversations, a task he undertook without misgivings. During the first weeks of his work he realized that "I did not join a conventional police force protecting the state but an organ of repression the chief task of which was to promote, with all means possible, the seizure of power by the communist party." At the time he believed that he was fighting for the victory of a social revolution which was "fought under the banner of the noblest human ideals."[149]

Unwavering belief in the truthfulness of Party communications was an essential part of his attitude. At the beginning of the Hungarian show trials in 1949 he "did not hesitate for a moment" to believe his boss, Gabor Peter, chief of the Hungarian political police, when he disclosed that respected veterans of the communist movement were in fact hardened agents of the Western intelligence services. He found an excellent rationalization for these allegations: in the Soviet Union it was discovered twenty years after the October Revolution that trusted associates of Lenin were imperialist spies; if so, why could the same phenomenon not occur in Hungary? Belief in the authenticity of the Hungarian show trials presupposed belief in the Soviet ones, which defied common sense in exactly the same measure.

At this juncture another interpretation of the attitude of the young Farkas may be put forward. Not only was he a product of a seamless set of early political influences, but his sparse and difficult relations with his family predisposed him to throw himself into the political community and Party work. In Hungary he married the daughter of another nomenklatura couple; he himself was a junior member of the nomenklatura. The authorities supplied him with a fully furnished suburban home in one of the best districts of Budapest, which he considered wholly "natural." He was provided with a domestic servant selected and paid by the AVH; he and his family were entitled to shop in the special store established for important state and Party officials. Such insulation from the realities of Hungarian life in the late 1940s and early 1950s explains why he writes that "at the time I did not see or sense that I was living in an intimidated country . . . The simple explanation of this must have been that in the course of my work at the AVH I had no opportunities [to obtain such experiences] and my nonwork time was spent in the narrow family circle. On the other hand, my first theoretical doubts did emerge."[150]

At work he was initially impressed by his Soviet adviser-supervisor, who struck him as a humane and highly educated man. Doubt and disappointment followed when the adviser proposed matter-of-factly that a prisoner be beaten for failing to confess to various concocted absurdities. Farkas went along with the suggestion, and the prisoner was handed over to those who administered the beatings.

Another revealing event and a further test of his commitments was the execution by hanging of Laszlo Rajk and his alleged accomplices. As a high-ranking AVH officer, Farkas was expected to attend. The guests were to watch the executions of Rajk and his accomplices in a prison courtyard from upstairs windows in the company of various Party leaders. Refreshments were served. He recalls that most windows were closed on account of the cold weather, and he did not go near any of them, as he could not bear to witness the event. It was reported to him that one of those to be executed shouted "Long live the Communist Party and the Soviet Union," while another yelled "You deceived us."[151] (The accused had been promised that their lives would be spared if they confessed as was demanded.) The executions and hearing these last words were among his most traumatic experiences and sorely tested his faith. Nonetheless, he stayed with the AVH for another six years and then was fired.

Immediately after these executions (and the hard work that preceded them, preparing the accused to play their part in court), Gabor Peter organized a festive boat excursion on the Danube in honor of the Soviet adviser. (The celebration of such operations had precedents in Soviet history. It was recalled by one of the participants that "a big banquet" had been organized to celebrate the conclusion of the Katyn massacre of Polish army officers in 1940.)[152] To cheer up those in attendance, the Soviet adviser related the story of other enemies of the communist system who, when in front of the firing squad, also cheered Stalin and the Soviet Union. Farkas writes: "Apparently Belkin [the Soviet adviser] wanted to make sure that none of us would doubt that we had eliminated highly dangerous enemies of socialism."[153]

Whatever his emerging doubts were during the late 1940s and early 1950s, "unfortunately I felt that under the conditions of the global situation and given the internal problems of the international communist movement, any wavering on my part would have been tantamount to betrayal. When a worldwide clash between socialism and imperialism was imminent, I could not conceive of breaking rank. I accepted consciously that the universal moral and legal norms had to be subordinated temporarily to the interests of the victory of the socialist system."[154]

The crisis of conscience was averted by the conviction that the *fundamental objectives* of the system remained intact and unimpeachable. This was a position widely relied on by functionaries and leaders. The reflections of Edward Ochab, among the most highly placed leaders in communist Poland, illustrate the attitude: "During the years of struggle against the armed reactionary underground . . . the military courts passed numerous death sentences . . . It was a difficult period in the life of our nation, but *viewed as a whole*, it was the greatest turning point in our country's history" (my emphasis).[155]

Ochab repeatedly refers to "the international situation as a whole," say-ing that "we had no guarantees that they [the Western powers] wouldn't leap at our throats at any moment." He praises the Soviet Union as the defender of Poland but also calls it a "country of enormous deformities, yet one which represents a different road for the development of mankind, a road that *in its broad outline* is in accordance with the interests of the whole international proletariat" (my emphasis). He further argues, in mitigation of the domestic repression, that "even such bitter things . . . have to be viewed from a broader perspective. You have to see the long-term consequences." As for supporting the Soviet position against Tito in the late 1940s, "even if the Soviet Union had been wrong, . . . in this specific historical situation we had to go along with the Soviet Union . . . The fundamental interests of our state, our working class . . . required that this alliance, and the common march forward, be maintained."[156]

As these remarks indicate, functionaries in the countries under Soviet dominance could argue that overwhelming Soviet power could not be de-fied; more importantly, their axiomatic belief in the myth of the Soviet Union as the bulwark of all existing socialist systems and the best hope of mankind persisted.

Farkas (like others in similar positions) believed that the work he was engaged in was intended to protect his country from the enemy. He was persuaded by another Soviet adviser that the socialist countries were not engaged in "spying," that the word was applicable only to the imperialists: "While the imperialist intelligence services seek to destroy the socialist sys-tems, our goals are purely defensive."[157] The adviser maintained that this was a crucial and, at the time, believable distinction and rationalization that enabled not only the specialists but the leaders and political planners as well to support virtually any morally dubious policy. Feeling besieged was a venerable Bolshevik tradition that became an essential part of the political culture and provided sanction for the violent and inhumane poli-cies in every communist system.

By the middle of 1955 the inner conflicts intensified, although Farkas was still "captive to the Stalinist loyalty to the Party, in the light of which it was inappropriate to separate the interests of the Party from that of individual Party leaders." He elaborates: "On the one hand, I began to recognize that participating in the fabricated investigations [associated with the show trials], brought me into conflict with the socialist ideals that I had imbibed with my mother's milk. Unwittingly I betrayed them, since I was an active participant in an antisocialist and antinational dictatorship. It was unbearably difficult to recognize all this. What happened in my country I regarded for a long time merely as an outcome of erroneous political practices and inexperienced leaders."[158]

The lack of alternatives is another explanation of why he and others stayed the course. Bela Szasz, a former Hungarian Party intellectual and later a political prisoner recalls the remarks of a former victim of the Stalinist regime in Hungary: "What can I do? I have neither trade nor profession. I am a professional revolutionary, that's all I am good for."[159]

Farkas was arrested a few weeks before the outbreak of the Revolution of 1956 and learned of it while in jail. Even in jail he viewed the Revolution as a loyal communist was supposed to: "It was my belief that the Soviet Union could not remain idle in face of this [the Revolution] because that could lead to the unraveling of the entire socialist bloc." At the same time, he was still ready and willing "to separate the crimes and violations of legality from the communist movement and the socialist ideals." The lynching of AVH members on the streets of Budapest further restrained him from sympathizing with the Revolution. In January 1957, while still in prison, he believed in the possibilities of the renewal of socialism.[160] In the spring of 1959, after rereading some works of Lenin, he concluded that "the root of the problems is to be found in our failure to apply the Marxist-Leninist principles creatively . . . Let us return to Lenin."[161]

The list of experiences conducive to but not directly leading to his break with the system is long. It includes becoming aware of his privileged circumstances in the Soviet Union during the war while great suffering and shortages afflicted the masses. Despite his insulation from everyday reality he heard of the arrests and deprivations visited upon ordinary Soviet people and sensed the pervasive atmosphere of mistrust. He writes: "It may be asked why the many disappointments and unfulfilled hopes failed to distance me from the communist ideals . . . There were several reasons. As I recall . . . in the beginning of 1941 there was a visible improvement in living conditions in Moscow . . . On the streets there were more better-dressed and less gloomy people. The streets appeared cleaner."[162]

The outbreak of war between the USSR and Germany wiped the slate clean: "Amazingly enough, I was greatly relieved [by the announcement that the war had begun]. I knew all about the horrors of war; nonetheless, my first reaction was that, after all, I was in the right place. The fact that from now on, the Soviet Union was fighting fascism swept away all the accumulated reservations and confusion in a second."[163]

A more deeply troubling early experience took place after his return to newly liberated Hungary in 1945. On the streets of Budapest he was robbed of his watch by drunken Soviet soldiers.[164] When he indignantly reported the incident to his father, he was asked, "How did you know that they were really Soviet soldiers?" Farkas senior suggested that they were probably Ukrainian nationalists who had fought alongside the Nazis wearing Soviet uniforms.[165] Vladimir accepted the explanation.

Another early incident that made him wonder about political morality was the execution of the former (precommunist) Hungarian prime minister Laszlo Bardossy: "Until now I thought that only communists behaved with dignity in court . . . I had hoped that at the execution I would see a broken man . . . [Bardossy] stood in front of the firing squad with dignity . . . while, on the one hand, I was horrified by the execution, on the other, reluctantly I felt respect for him. I decided at the time that I was not going to witness any more executions."[166]

Soon after Farkas joined the AVO he came upon a troubling instance of the theory-practice gap. In 1946 the Communist Party proclaimed its commitment to building a democratic, multiparty system. At the same time, the AVO (already under communist control) was tapping the phones of politicians deemed right-wing in orientation and forwarding the recordings to Rakosi himself, head of the Party: "My first response was that all that the Party was saying in public—including denials of being interested in monopolizing power—was not true. This realization hit me hard, since up till now I had believed every word of the leaders of the Party . . . Thus I realized that we said one thing and did another, yet I failed to reach the conclusion that the policy of the Hungarian CP was immoral and dishonest."

He explains his attitude as follows. On the one hand, he believed that the Party had proved itself through land reform and through its energetic involvement in the rebuilding of the war-torn country and therefore deserved support. On the other hand, comparing the conditions in Hungary with those in communist Yugoslavia and Poland, which, unlike Hungary, had large antifascist resistance movements during the war, he concluded that the liquidation of the remnants of fascist political forces had to become the task of the political police in Hungary.[167] Once more, doubts about methods were silenced by the importance of the goals.

The methods used by the political police to extract confessions also bothered Farkas. Senior officers explained to him that the unfortunate "excesses" had to be understood in light of the desire for revenge by some members of the AVO who had suffered under the previous regime because they were either Jews or communist underground fighters. He also learned

> that the AVO physician [Dr. Istvan Balint] . . . who used to belong to the former illegal communist underground pointed out in his lectures on the psychology of investigatory practices that sometimes it was necessary to beat those detained, but it must be done without causing death.
>
> I was stunned by this. I did not expect that the tortures of the Gestapo . . . would be continued by the Communist Party, the leader of the struggle against fascism . . . In those days I spoke about these matters with several people who worked for the AVO. Many of them condemned these practices. At the same time everybody pointed out . . . that no great revolution was capable of preventing temporary outbursts of revenge . . . Unhappily, after two and a half years [of working at the AVO] I myself accepted the necessity of using physical pressure.[168]

Two other circumstances helped Farkas to acquiesce in the use of torture. One was that he himself did not engage in it, nor did he witness it (although this has been hotly debated).[169] More importantly, there was ample pressure on him to regard these practices as normal and unavoidable, if somewhat regrettable. It was not so much a matter of obedience to authority as conformity to the taken-for-granted beliefs of people around him whom he trusted and respected. Given his personal isolation and dependence on the nomenklatura subculture, it would have taken an unusually strong will and sense of autonomy to defy his superiors and peers by criticizing these methods and risking his own dismissal or worse.

Farkas succeeded in persuading himself for a long time that these methods were temporary and that the good of the cause justified using them. It is also likely that, given the high position of his father and his desire to be seen as independent of his father, he found it especially important to conform to the requirements of the organization he worked for.

He was troubled by various incidents nonetheless. For example, "it was most unexpected to learn what was done . . . to Istvan Ries [a social-democratic minister of justice in the coalition government that preceded the communist takeover in 1948]. He was tied to an armchair and above his head was a container from which water dripped. When I heard of this, I summoned Bauer [the interrogator in charge] and demanded an explanation. He noted my lack of historical knowledge and pointed out that this method had been used by the Chinese in antiquity to obtain confessions . . . He added that the method was very effective and, whenever used, led to insanity or breakdown. I became angry about this; he could not understand why and finally shrugged and said . . . he would stop. But it is a great pity, he added, since Ries was about to confess."[170]

Farkas also learned about a particularly brutal beating given to Noel Field, an American arrested in connection with one of the show trials. "I recall that my first response was, these cannot be our methods, since we ranked such methods among the crimes against the nation and humanity during the trials of the former members of the Hungarian Nazi political police after 1945."[171]

He was present when a report was made of an even more brutal beating, administered to Rajk in the presence of his father, Janos Kadar (before *his* arrest), and leaders of the AVH. Although he had no doubt that Rajk was an enemy who had managed to infiltrate the Party, he "shuddered" upon hearing of the beating and asked cautiously "whether it was indeed essential to use such methods in our system." His father responded by asking if he remembered the words of Gorky, who allegedly said, "If the enemy refuses to surrender, he has to be annihilated." Then Erno Szucs, a high-ranking

AVH operative, added: "When political crimes are committed, the enemy rarely leaves incriminating evidence. If he doesn't break down after being unmasked and obstructs the disclosure of his and his accomplices' activities, there is no other means left than merciless beating . . . we are now in the frontlines of the sharpened secret class struggle between the two world systems. Thus we must adapt to the circumstances. We are on the offensive, but time is of the essence because it is our responsibility to prevent the enemy who has infiltrated the Party from carrying out his subversive activities. Just as in a war the forces on the offensive prepare the way for the infantry with aerial and artillery bombardment, so we, too, must rely on merciless physical pressure to fulfill the same function as the air force and artillery during war."[172]

On another occasion Farkas was upset by the unintended death of two alleged conspirators who expired during a particularly brutal interrogation. In the course of the investigation of the mishap, he was summoned to Rakosi, who regretted the deaths because of the information that the victims took with them. Then "he gave a short lecture on the necessity of physical pressure in the investigation of political crimes. He said that this is done under every political system . . . As he saw it, physical pressure brought to bear on the enemy was a legitimate means of retaliation."[173]

These arguments were no different from other versions of the ends and means scheme except for the military metaphors; militarizing political conflict further justified the brutal methods.

In preparing for the Rajk trial Farkas also learned "how the leaders of the Party were capable of rejecting their former comrades-in-arms . . . they could take the terrible position (the only precedent for which might perhaps be found at the time of the Spanish Inquisition) that whatever they say is the word of the Party and the truth of the Party, because the Party never makes an error. It was from them that I first heard the argument that the defendants can help the Party only with their repentant confession."[174]

Another idea increasingly adopted by the AVH people and promoted by their Soviet advisers was that "the best measure of our success is the degree of the hatred we earn from the internal and external enemy."[175] This was apparently a variant of the theme introduced in the Soviet Union in the 1930s: that the viciousness of the cornered enemy justifies ceaseless "vigilance" and continued repression. Both themes sought to justify repression at a time when there was little obvious threat to the system, internal or external. By early 1950, Farkas recalls, he was used to identifying the enemy on the basis of the guidelines provided by the Party.

In the final analysis, his participation in the AVH work resulted from "a tight and perverted faith, blind obedience to authority, and the infection caused by being close to power. It also meant a lot to me that two of my coworkers were highly respected members of the former underground communist movement."[176]

The problems at work were not the only sources of his unease regarding the character of the political system ("unease" is a recurring word in many of these accounts; it captures a state of mind and moral sensibility that allowed people to work for the system but not without misgivings). The privileges of the nomenklatura, including his own father, also concerned him, though not nearly as much as the activities of the AVH. After Farkas senior moved into his new villa, "we were also invited by Father and his wife [his stepmother]. I was put off, to begin with, by the long stone wall and the iron gate we could not enter without being thoroughly checked by the guards. We then proceeded to a beautifully maintained huge park . . . There were three identical buildings of this type, each with a tennis court and a swimming pool . . . the mansion we now confronted, stunned. But apparently my father and his spouse enjoyed their new residence."[177]

The lies and betrayals that affected him were both official and personal. He concluded that "the Soviet leaders vilely betrayed him [Farkas senior] . . . and sacrificed him" during the de-Stalinization campaign. After expulsion from the Party his father collapsed in tears.[178] It was Farkas's abiding conviction that both his father and himself were scapegoats for the sins of the Hungarian communist regime under Rakosi. Despite his reservations about his father, he was "disgusted" with the way the Party and the Soviet leadership treated him. These were matters of ordinary decency that he could not dismiss on grounds of political necessity.

Another example of the subordination of basic human decency to a political agenda was evident in the part played by his mother-in-law, herself a Party functionary, in his arrest, which took place during a visit she paid him and his family at an unusual time. When the bell rang, she hastened to open the door to two AVH officers, who had come to arrest him. She had little interest in saying good-bye to him, and it dawned on him that "her visit was a party assignment. Apparently its object was to assure that my arrest take place smoothly, without fuss or resistance."[179] In a similar spirit, Rakosi had invited Rajk and his wife to his house for friendly socializing. In the course of the visit he asked for photos of the Rajk baby. "He carefully inspected them and praised his development; he promised to visit us next Thursday to see the baby." This happened the day before Rakosi had the baby's father arrested. "He was exceedingly jovial and affable," Mrs. Rajk recalls.[180] Gabor Peter, when his time came, was also arrested in the home of Rakosi, whom he visited to report a mining accident. Reportedly, Farkas senior was also present, hiding behind a curtain to come forth at the moment of the arrest shouting histrionically, "It is time to end the game!"[181]

Such deceptions were not limited to Hungary. In communist Czechoslovakia, when "the Party leadership feared that Clementis [the foreign minister, soon to be arrested for the Slansky show trial] might defect, President Gottwald invited Lida [his wife] to the Hradcin palace, assured her of his complete confidence in Clementis and suggested that she travel to New York and tell her husband that the President trusted him implicitly. So Lida flew to New York."[182] Clementis returned in her company, was arrested, tried, and executed.

Stalin, too was a master of such deceptions. According to a Polish communist, Roman Werfel, "There was an estate in the suburbs of Moscow where old Bolsheviks lived; each had his own little Finnish house. Stalin had one of them . . . and Vera Kostrzewa [an old Polish communist who emigrated to the USSR in 1924 and worked in the Comintern] lived next door to him. One day she was pruning roses in her garden. Stalin came up and said, 'What beautiful roses.' That same evening she was taken away and shot; Stalin knew about it. But in 1944 when our delegation came to see him, he suddenly asked, 'You used to have such nice people, Vera Kostrzewa, for instance—do you know what's become of her?'"[183]

Volkogonov reported that "when the wife of his [Stalin's] closest aide since 1928, A. N. Poskrebyshev, was arrested, to the pleas of his faithful arms-bearer Stalin replied: 'Don't panic. The NKVD will sort it out.'"[184]

Despite all the painful personal experiences, the final turning point in the political evolution of Vladimir Farkas came only after the invasion of

Czechoslovakia in August 1968. The invasion upset him, especially since Soviet aggression was aimed at another socialist country, one seeking to humanize itself. There were also his childhood connections with that country, which made its invasion more unacceptable. Farkas writes: "I came to the conclusion that I served mistaken and harmful policies which provoked the justifiable dissatisfaction, anger, and hatred of the masses . . . At the time [the years following the 1956 Revolution] I believed that this justified dissatisfaction was exploited by the political forces which sought the ultimate destruction of the system engaged in the building of socialism. I still thought at the time that we were engaged in the building of socialism. It took many more years to see things clearly. The turning point was August of 1968."[185] In fact, it took twelve years, from his arrest in October 1956 to the 1968 Soviet invasion of Czechoslovakia, for him to become fully aware of "having served a bad cause." He did not believe that perestroika would rectify the system.[186]

When he was tried under the postrevolutionary Kadar regime, he was asked if he felt guilty for his participation in the preparation of the show trials under Rakosi and the associated lawlessness. He did not feel guilty in the legal sense, he said, although he had participated unwittingly in the mistreatment of people who turned out to be innocent. He continued: "I know that I am morally responsible for what happened, a responsibility all the greater since I grew up in a family of professional revolutionaries and thus since my childhood have belonged to the most just, most honest, purest movement, the communist movement led by the Soviet Union. Therefore it is particularly shameful and burdensome that I let myself be used in these deplorable affairs, that I came into conflict repeatedly not only with socialist humanism but with the unwritten laws of general humaneness and universal moral standards."[187]

The root cause of his bitter disappointment in the system besides his own mistreatment was the magnitude of the gap between its ideals and practices. He repeatedly returns to this point, and it is for this reason that he finds the communist system more pernicious than the Nazi: in the Nazi case, the professed ideals of the system were not so far removed from its practices.

Until his imprisonment he succeeded in keeping a tenuous balance between the forces supporting his political commitments and those eroding it.

His early experiences, family loyalties, Soviet indoctrination, group pressures at work, and the privileged isolation from the social-political realities of life in Hungary combined to counteract the morally problematic experiences which created his "unease." There was also fear. He learned, for example, that the same Szucs, the high-ranking AVH officer who had earlier explained with such gusto and confidence the necessity of torture, himself had been arrested as a spy. "Perhaps we began to realize that any of us could meet his fate . . . It was then for the first time that it occurred to me that in the tense global situation, working for the AVH was no guarantee of personal safety."[188] That is to say, concern for personal safety and survival was among the factors which exerted a potent pressure to conform, to remain loyal to the system and its changing policies. It was the same fear that kept the population at large in line and forced everyone to wear the mask of conformity.

Most of Farkas's doubts and reservations stemmed from what he observed while working for AVH and from his own subsequent arrest. There is hardly any reference in his memoirs to the disastrous economic policies, the suppression of free speech, and other systemic failures. And, as noted above, while he found the privileges of the nomenklatura distasteful, there was little indignation about the general problem of the new social inequalities. Curiously, the revelations of Khrushchev's Twentieth Congress speech failed to stimulate soul searching, as it had in other committed supporters of the system. He recalls that it "did not have such a big impact. I had strong but mixed feelings about it. I said to myself, if indeed such crimes were committed . . . by Stalin, they had to be revealed . . . because the reputation of the Soviet Union must be restored . . . I also had reservations about the way in which Stalin was exposed. I thought this step should have been better prepared . . . I suspected that the speech served not so much to further the liquidation of Stalinism as to augment the personal power of Khrushchev."[189] He had reservations about Khrushchev himself, given his earlier contributions to the crimes of Stalin. These were the musings of a still-loyal functionary.

The case of Vladimir Farkas lends strength to the observation that specific experiences recognized as morally problematic can be tolerated and contained as long as a superior moral justification and social support remain available and convincing.

MARKUS WOLF (B. 1923)

Arguably, Markus Wolf's loyalty to the communist ideals and regimes was overdetermined. As a Jewish refugee from Nazi Germany, he owed his life to the Soviet Union; his loving parents raised him in communist beliefs and loyalties; he spent eleven of his formative years in the Soviet Union under concentrated indoctrination; and he was rewarded at an early age with the trust of the system and a high position in one of its most important agencies. All these influences combined throughout his life to prevent any serious cracks from developing in his loyalty. It was the collapse of Soviet communism itself and its immediate antecedents which led him to question the system at a time when its capacity to survive was already in doubt.

Markus Wolf, who was for three decades head of the foreign espionage department of the East German political police (Stasi), has much in common with two individuals already discussed on these pages. With Oleg Kalugin he shares the professional pride in the espionage game and the apparent conviction that his activities were largely defensive and necessitated by the Cold War. With Wolfgang Leonhard (whom he knew in his youth) he has in common the German communist family background, an upbringing in the Soviet Union (from age eleven), and being sent as a highly committed young functionary to build up the East German communist regime after World War II. There are also important differences: Leonhard was not Jewish, and his mother was sent to the Gulag despite being a communist refugee from Nazi Germany, whereas Wolf's parents suffered no similar fate. Leonhard defected in 1949, whereas Wolf spent his whole life working for East German state security. His autobiography suggests that he succeeded in suppressing whatever doubts he had about the cause with the momentum of lifelong beliefs and commitments and the Party discipline that he had absorbed. Only in the late 1980s were his "hopes of reforming the socialist state . . . shattered."[190]

After World War II, Wolf returned to East Germany from the Soviet Union and worked for the communist radio station in Berlin, in that capacity covering the Nuremberg Trials. Having learned the full dimensions of the Jewish persecution, he decided to dedicate his life "to ensur[ing] that this kind of inhumanity would never again happen . . . So it was natural that

I would want to become involved in anti-Nazi activity in Germany. And so I joined the intelligence work of the East German state. Many other Jews took a similar path, becoming active in the Stasi to hunt down former Nazis."[191]

Wolf repeatedly claimed that "the remilitarization of the West" and the alleged prominence of former Nazis in West German political and military institutions were the major reasons for working for Stasi. He construed his Stasi activities as purely defensive: "We also feared the possibility of a big atomic war. Our task in intelligence was to prevent any such surprises."[192] He claimed that he "didn't see the intelligence service as part of the repressive structure. And refusal [to work for it] would have been impossible, given my understanding of duty, party discipline, and the demands of the Cold War." If the grand ideals had to be compromised "with murky practices," it was because "the United States and its European allies were trying to destroy our attempts to bring socialism to German soil. And on it went, the rollcall of excuses, until we were awakened from the dream in 1989."[193] For him the dream was lifelong , culminating in a much delayed and qualified awakening.

On the first page of his memoirs the major themes (and apologies) are introduced: "We East German Socialists tried to create a new kind of society that would never repeat the German crimes of the past . . . Our sins and our mistakes were those of every other intelligence agency. If we had shortcomings . . . they were those of too much professionalism untempered by the raw edges of ordinary life . . . The integration of the foreign intelligence service into the Ministry of State Security meant that the service and I were charged with responsibility for both internal repression in the German Democratic Republic and cooperation with international terrorists . . . Our side fought against the revival of fascism . . . for a combination of socialism and freedom, a noble objective that failed utterly but which I still believe is possible . . . Crimes were committed by both sides in the global struggle."[194] Here we have the essential messages of the memoir: the original good intentions, the circumstances which shaped and mitigated the methods used, and a measure of qualified regret. He also quotes Bertolt Brecht on ends and means: "'What baseness would you not commit, / To stamp out baseness?' . . . We had all internalized such rationalizations in pursuit of a better, socialist world. Almost everything was permitted, we felt, as long as it served the Cause."[195]

Wolf makes much of his German-Jewish background and the decisive part that Soviet anti-Nazi policies played in the development of his political loyalties: "For us [Wolf's family] the Soviet Union seemed to be the only country that was really unequivocally opposed to Nazism. We knew little of the purges or of the anti-semitism surrounding Stalin."[196] More crucial was that, when they were fleeing Jewish persecution in Germany, "the only country that would take us in was the Soviet Union." (German Jews did not seek or gain refuge in the USSR unless they were closely associated with the German Communist Party.) His father, a politically active doctor, had been a member of the German Communist Party since 1928 and, according to another source, was "an important communist intellectual in the Weimar Republic."[197]

In an interview with *Tikkun*, a liberal American Jewish journal, Wolf steadfastly played the Jewish card, insisting, for instance, that East German intelligence "never operated against Israel or targeted Israeli intelligence"—a highly questionable claim given the well-documented East German assistance to Arab terrorist groups. *Tikkun*'s reporter asked him why the communists did not do more to educate people (in East Germany) about anti-semitism. He responded: "I pushed this question out of my mind. Inside the Communist Party, the intellectuals felt that this problem was something so far from our ideology that we thought it could not exist and if it existed we ought not to speak about it."[198] Thus did Wolf handle "dissonance": if the Communist Party should have done more about anti-Semitism but did not, dwelling on the matter would have been painful and problematic. He managed "to push the question out of his mind," presumably because his communist identity and work for the state security organization was more important than his residual Jewish identity.

Similar mechanisms were at work in his handling of early experiences in the Soviet Union, which included the disappearance of his teachers during the Purges of 1936–1938. ("We children noticed that adults never spoke of people who had 'disappeared' . . . and we automatically began to respect this bizarre courtesy.") These experiences and his responses to them were similar to those reported by Dubcek and Leonhard during their stay in the USSR.

Wolf, Dubcek, and their respective parents shared the capacity to assimilate, digest, and cast aside such experiences as irrelevant, in the final analysis, to their fundamental commitments and loyalties. Even the Soviet-Nazi Pact of 1939 went unquestioned by Wolf, for the official Soviet explanations were "convincing enough . . . at the time."[199]

Elsewhere he sheds further light on how he succeeded in ignoring facts of life which did not fit into his worldview: "Some people asked how someone who had experienced the Moscow trials of the 1930s could remain silent. I believe that one develops an ability to ignore, an ability that my brother and I developed. We believed that in our own areas of work—my brother in the arts, I in the intelligence service—we could achieve something. We simply ignored what was happening around us."[200]

As to his activities as a Stasi operative:

Wolf: I did the same work as any state intelligence operative did, like the CIA. The Stasi or German State Security had an internal security division, roughly equivalent to your FBI, to which I had no connection, and an external intelligence gathering division, roughly equivalent to your CIA, which I headed.

Tikkun: But the CIA, the KGB and other such operations are notoriously vicious organizations. You can't pretend that you don't have blood on your hands.

Wolf: I was not involved in any such things, nor were people who worked for me . . .

Tikkun: But you had knowledge of the repression in other branches of the Stasi.

Wolf: I began to recognize that there was something wrong in the Stasi only in the 1970s, when repression was directed against intellectuals, writers, actors, and dissidents . . .

Tikkun: Why did it take until the late 1970s for you to recognize that there was something wrong in the system?

Wolf: The first break in my consciousness occurred in 1956 [with] Khrushchev's revelations about the problem. I was concerned about the use of Soviet troops to put down rebellions in various countries but *I saw these problems as a result of the conflicts of the Cold War* [my emphasis].[201]

So here we have it. Stasi was no different from the CIA and the FBI (the moral-equivalence thesis), nor was his work from that of any other state intelligence operative. The last head of the Czechoslovak state security, Alojz Lorenc, made a similar point: "Every country has an StB [the Czech state security organization] . . . It is a Hobbesian world. Agents are to government leaders as the sun is to life."[202]

Wolf's attitudes conform to the pattern already identified: deep convictions coexisted with flickering ambivalence and an easily suppressed awareness that not all was as it should be—in terms of either communist ideals or certain basic, unspoken moral norms. Nonetheless, the goals sufficed to overcome unease over the means used to attain them.

For Wolf, there were also some special circumstances: "We German Communists had perhaps the most complete blind spot of all the foreigners in Moscow about Stalin's crimes, since we had been rescued from death or imprisonment in Germany by the Soviet Union . . . doubts about what was going on were overshadowed by . . . Hitler's brutal regime, and I was incapable of seeing our socialist system as a tyranny . . . There was perhaps a rough streak in its methods, but we always felt that it was *essentially a force for good.* This approach was to determine our thinking throughout the Cold War. It meant that whenever we heard any unflattering portrayal of our own side our first question . . . was not 'Is this true?' but 'What are they trying to hide about themselves by accusing us . . . ? Once this mental defense system had been perfected, few criticisms could hit home" (my emphasis).[203]

"Essentially a force for good" is the key to the attitudes examined here. The word "essentially" allows for the recognition of blemishes and imperfections but permits their subordination to distant but compelling objectives, thus preserving the fundamentals of commitment while the moral significance of matters (supposedly) less essential is substantially reduced. Wolf also writes: "People have asked me how it could be that I, a reasonably sophisticated young man from a cultured family, could block out of my mind so many of these uncomfortable events?" He did not have to "block them out," only relegate them to moral unimportance. "Ideological filters," the other concept he introduces, helped to legitimate the subordination of the present to the future, the means to ends. These filters also determined what he found believable or not. He recalls that when after the war a West Berlin Social

Democratic paper reported that people were tortured by the East German secret police in the cellar of the same building where he lived, he was convinced that the paper had invented the story (he learned later that it had not).

This was not an isolated incident: "Throughout my career I overlooked, minimized, or rationalized similar episodes and I can only remind the reader again how my character was formed in the struggle against fascism; we came to feel that against such tyrannical opponents, almost anything goes . . . for much of my life I had no doubt that we Communists stood on the side of social renewal and justice. This had helped excuse the Moscow show trials . . . and now the exigencies of the nascent Cold War would help us overlook . . . attacks on the German Social Democrats who had survived the Nazis . . . Perhaps I already felt exempt from some moral norms, a sense bolstered by the confidence that the Communist machine could never turn against me, one of its children . . . then and now I never put the crimes of the Communist regime in the same class as those of the Nazis."[204]

Even so, certain events and incidents were problematic. There was, for example, the 1953 uprising in East Germany crushed by the Soviet forces: "We were stunned by the violence and hatred that had welled up in our midst . . . it was a rude awakening as to just how unpopular our beloved system had become . . . it became clear to me that notions of 'fascist adventurism' and 'counterrevolutionary putsch' conjured up by our leadership were pure propaganda. But this did not shake my own commitment."[205]

Wolf had occasional qualms about the Soviet treatment of East Germany (in particular, using it as an enormous repository for Soviet troops and weapons, including nuclear missiles), but he had "grown accustomed to the Soviet [Union]'s behaving . . . like an occupying power who expended scant concern for our sensibilities." He envied Cuba for making its own revolution without the help of Soviet troops.[206]

Thus commitment and misgivings coexisted almost to the very end. It is not quite clear from the memoirs when the misgivings became more powerful, even though he writes that the famous Khrushchev speech in 1956 was "the catalyst": "The exact origin of my long and painful breaking with Stalinism is hard to ascertain; the slivers of doubt that penetrated my ideological defenses . . . in the early fifties were probably the beginning. But like many Communists of my generation, the event that shook my carefully nurtured worldview was Khrushchev's speech . . . it was the source of great pain . . . It was as if, at one stroke, our worst fears about the system . . . had come true."[207] But simultaneously he was relieved, he claims, and began to nurture hopes that a new beginning was possible.[208]

If one pillar of his commitment was future vindication by the lofty goals originally set, the other pillar was what he perceived as the alternative: "The foundation of all my thinking about the Cold War was that the West and its system did not present an acceptable alternative . . . It remained my unshakeable belief that the socialist system, for all its terrible failings, represented a better potential model for mankind than the West. When it came to the crunch, for all the growing doubts I had about Communist practice, I believed that we must never cede influence in Europe."[209]

The way of life of the high-ranking functionary also helped to maintain his commitment: "I was well insulated from the hardships afflicting ordinary people in my country." The privileges of the nomenklatura to which he belonged "made for a comfortable life. I was too weak to say no these privileges." Insulation from realities had another aspect: he had never seen the prisons of East Germany, although he knew that they were characterized by "total disregard of prisoners' dignity." Moreover, "I could not fail to be fully aware from the very beginning how rough the game had become. I do not claim ignorance of the brutalities of life within our own country."[210]

Work satisfaction, too, helped keep him going: "My work at the top of the intelligence service satisfied me. I was convinced of its necessity and I was deeply committed to it." He also derived satisfaction form "the special sense of being part of a family attached to the KGB"[211] and took pride in being the head of what was, according to him, the best intelligence service in the Soviet bloc.

The pervasiveness of thinking in terms of ends and means colored even the occasional disapproval of some means. Thus he considered "wet jobs" (assassination, physical violence) "primitive and unproductive solution[s]" or "signs of weakness" rather than simply wrong. The choice of vocabulary reveals his basic political attitude. Neither in the book nor in the *Tikkun* interview (despite the prodding of the interviewer) does Wolf show moral indignation or revulsion about the practices of his organization and regime.

At best he finds the repression distasteful and unnecessary, especially if directed at the intelligentsia. In any event, there was nothing he could do about it. Even rationalizing the Berlin Wall was easy: "I believed there was no other way to save our country at that time." Concerning the support for various terrorist groups provided by his organization "These unholy alliances were, on both sides, the tragic product of the Cold War."[212]

While at times he recognizes that "whatever we did that was wrong cannot be excused by what the West did," he cannot help making precisely that excuse throughout the book ("The Cold War was a brutal struggle and terrible things were done by both sides in the name of winning it"). Nor could he resist recourse to another well-worn rationalization: "But I still make a distinction between regimes in which human dignity and liberty are curtailed as the result of an overzealous policy of state security—which was the result of East Germany's internal repression—and [those in which there is] the systematic use of torture to punish political opponents . . . This is a moral distinction that I hope readers will accept in the interest of coming to terms with the *excesses* of the time" (my emphasis).[213]

By the early 1980s he started to think of retirement. There was apparently a long history of bad blood between him and his boss, the head of state security, Erich Mielke. He also came to feel that the system was "locked into a precipitous spiral of decline. All this sapped my professional morale and my energies, leaving me deflated and with increased misgivings." Honecker of East Germany "had become just another elderly leader clinging power." He felt that unless he became a member of the Central Committee or the Politburo, he "could have no influence on the Party's course under Honecker"; but he claimed that he did not wish to become a member. In any event, Mielke was "determined to block me" from becoming a member.[214]

Apparently the rise of the Solidarity movement in Poland also contributed to the decline of his convictions, not because it was a reflection of widespread discontent with the system but because "the Communist state . . . [in Poland] lacked the confidence to fight back." He does not tell us how he would have handled Solidarity. Another reason for his decline in faith was "the aging and unresponsive leadership in Moscow" before Gorbachev. In mild self-criticism he notes at the end of the book that he was "too slow in making . . . [his] desperation clear," and he wonders "whether I waited too long before saying loudly what I really thought and felt. It was not lack of courage but the futility of protest . . . that made me hold my peace."[215]

When asked if he still "agree[d] with some parts of communism," he had no difficulty separating theory from practice:

Wolf: Yes, I do. Communist ideas are not the same as the reality that existed in our countries. The realities had nothing to do with the ideas in which we believed. The ideas were the outcome of a long struggle of millions of people for freedom, social and economic rights . . . The capitalist system has no answers to the great problems. I still believe in these ideas and I am sure they will come back.

Tikkun: So why weren't you saying "this is not communism"?

Wolf: Eventually I came to recognize that it was a deformed system . . . It was only after I retired that I understood that the whole system couldn't work because it . . . didn't correspond to our ideals . . . people like me . . . gave our youth and much of our life to fight the Nazis. We wanted to change the world for the better. This is also a Jewish message. But unfortunately we used the wrong means for the right goals.[216]

Vindication by good intentions became the last resort: "We wanted to change the world for the better." It seemed to matter little that in the course of this attempt Wolf and his fellow idealists made the world quite a bit worse.

Throughout the memoirs, Wolf, perceiving himself as "a refugee from a fallen utopia," seems to fluctuate between admitting that the rationalizations and excuses were flimsy and morally disreputable and insisting that, on the whole, everything he did was understandable and not particularly reprehensible; above all, the failure of the system had no relevance to the attractiveness of the ideals pursued in morally dubious ways ("my life has been marked . . . by watching the abuse of power practiced in the name of the socialist ideal in which I still believe . . . I never knowingly betrayed my ideals and therefore cannot feel that my life was without purpose"). In the end, he admits that "our system was incomparably inferior to most of the pluralist democracies of the West."[217]

More recently, Wolfe still appeared unrepentant, even cocky. At a lecture delivered in Berlin he "confessed to no crimes or sins or even misjudgements

. . . he asserted [that service to Stasi] was 'a great honor, a duty, a chance to do something for our country' . . . He said that he spent his life serving 'humanism and anti-fascism' and felt 'no need to dress myself in sackcloth and ashes.'"[218]

It is doubtful that Wolf engaged in any genuine soul searching *before* the system collapsed, and his reassessment after 1989 is highly qualified.[219] He was a hardened and successful Stasi official who refrained throughout most of his career from asking serious questions about the system or reflecting about its animating values. If he ever needed moral reassurance, there was the memory of the anti-Nazi struggle and the Cold War and the alleged moral equivalence between his side and the other.

Wolf's attitudes and rationalizations were shared by his colleagues. One of them told Timothy Garton Ash: "I wanted to work for a better world . . . The system went wrong, because of human nature."[220] Another Stasi officer said in 1990: "'I was convinced that the goal . . . to build a socialist state and a socialist economy was feasible and good for everyone.' . . . In effect the Ministry of State Security defined its collective role not as cops but as social workers . . . at the end the agents became mystified that their clients so resented their paternalist supervision." And there was the Stasi officer for whom "the harmony of individual and social interests in socialism was an actual reality."[221]

Wolf exemplifies the attitudes that a Czech author attributed to the communist leaders in his country: "It is hard and sometimes impossible to give up the ideals of youth . . . the whole life of devoted service to the Party . . . It is almost impossible to accept the fact that instead of serving progress and happiness, a whole life was spent serving a murderous tyrant and a criminal organization. An attempt, therefore, has to be made again and again to prove that it was not all wrong, that the principles were good . . . and only some mistakes, some deformations have taken place against the will of the protagonists."[222]

Markus Wolf was one among many former high-level functionaries who refused to ask probing questions about the chronic divergence between ends and means. Why was it so compelling to pursue those lofty ends with dubious means? Was it conceivable that the nature of the ends had some bearing on the means used? What assurance was there that the ends were worthwhile and attainable? These were not questions that Markus and his colleagues were able or willing to raise.

These profiles highlight the similarity between the mindset and motivation of the specialists in charge of protecting communist systems and the leaders and leading functionaries, discussed in earlier chapters, in charge of setting policy. For the most part, a questioning of the system and, less frequently, its legitimating ideas began either when or after the individuals concerned came into personal conflict with the system (resulting in demotion, transfer, or the loss of power).[223] Disillusionment was also stimulated by growing indications of the inefficiencies of the system, particularly notable when comparisons with the West became possible.

The specialists shared with the leaders a long-range vision that allowed them to subordinate means to ends and the present to the future. They were people characterized by a "contradictory combination of cynicism and idealism [which] makes possible all the other contradictions demanded of the Communist. It is the reason why fine and devoted human beings can become conscious agents of organized evil; can with equal vigor and selflessness organize a movement of Asian coolies under circumstances of incredible terror and deprivation, or direct a system of slave camps which . . . destroys millions upon millions of helpless people."[224] In many instances these attitudes were also linked to the love of power and privilege and to assorted personal pathologies.

Another striking pattern among those discussed was that virtually none of them questioned—even after distancing themselves from the system and its policies—the basic values and goals and the theory in which they were embedded. While it became possible, slowly and painfully, to recognize the discrepancy between ends and means and the degradation of the former by the latter, there was little scrutiny of the ends that almost invariably came to be pursued by morally questionable means.

There is little evidence in the lives of the individuals discussed above (or in the source materials) that they were "ordinary" human beings in the sense in which Hannah Arendt popularized the related notion of the "banality of evil." Ordinary human beings do not reach the positions of power that these people reached; they do not excel in activities which require exceptional impersonality and ruthlessness, nor do they devote their lives to remote and unrealizable goals which provide the sense of entitlement to rise above the moral restraints which govern, however haltingly, the lives of ordinary human beings.

CHAPTER 7

Conclusions

The Unity of Theory and Practice

"Attempts at reform had . . . accomplished what famines, terror and military defeat had failed to effect—the destruction of the Communist state." ADAM ULAM

"Revolutions dissipate their energies as their elites age and die off. Like the rings of a tree, the younger the elites of a revolutionary regime are, the further they are from the original shoot." VLADIMIR ZUBOK AND CONSTANTIN PLESHAKOV

"A religion that reserves paradise for the next world is never put to an empirical test, but a secular religion like Marxism-Leninism, which promises paradise in this world, is forced to engage in ceaseless effort to remake reality in order to confirm its own legitimacy." DAVID SATTER

Nothing would be more gratifying at this point than to declare that this study has succeeded in unearthing and isolating a major factor, hitherto unknown or overlooked, that explains with a new clarity and finality why Soviet communism disintegrated between 1989 and 1991. I will have to settle, like other authors, for less sensational conclusions.

The growing awareness of the complexity of all things human and social has made it more difficult than ever to satisfy our desire for concise, causal explanations of great historical events and dramatic social changes. Two impulses struggle with one another as we strive to better understand the turning points of history and the puzzles of collective behavior. One is the old-fashioned desire to grasp fundamental causes, to be able to say that X caused

Y; the other is the fear of simplifying and oversimplifying. It is particularly difficult to explain and anticipate major historical events which seem to hinge on the unobserved decisions and choices of particular individuals at particular moments in time.

In this book I focused on twenty-two important political figures of different generations, ranging from the world-famous (Gorbachev, Yeltsin) to those largely unknown in the West (Vladimir Farkas, Zdenek Mlynar). They had in common either an important role in the running of communist systems or proximity to the center of power. They also shared a growing realization that the systems were seriously defective and failed to live up to their original ideals.

As I discussed in the first chapter, hardly anybody either in the West or within the Soviet bloc anticipated the rapid and decisive unraveling of Soviet communism when it actually occurred,[1] although many were cognizant of the decay of the system. Among the symptoms of decline I focused on the diminished sense of legitimacy of the rulers—their faltering will to power and shaken ideological certainties. As Daniel Chirot observes, "Among those who ruled Soviet-type systems, there was a corrosive loss of faith in what they were doing, and this destroyed their morale and ability to fight to save themselves."[2] This was, in brief, the idea animating this book, but it was only *after* the collapse that I came to this conclusion, along with a handful of other observers, including Chirot. Presumably the loss of faith of the political leaders was not in the forefront of scholarly interest because it is difficult to observe and prove, especially in comparison with more tangible, even measurable social facts such as declining productivity, the decay of public health, and lost or inconclusive wars. The intangibles of human belief, motivation, and will remain major and apparently unsurmountable obstacles to the accurate prediction of social-political change.

It has been a major proposition of the book that although enormous economic problems fatally undermined the Soviet Union, its collapse had more to do with the ways economic weakness was perceived and registered by the political elite and, less importantly, by the population at large. This is far from saying that the economic difficulties did not matter—they mattered because they were seen in a different light both by the elites and by the people. One important factor was the passage of time: things were not getting better; the difficulties, all could see, were not temporary.[3] John Lewis Gaddis reaches a similar conclusion: "The events of 1989–1991 make sense only in terms of ideas. There was no military defeat or economic crash; but there was a collapse of legitimacy. The people . . . suddenly realized that . . . [the] emperors had no clothes on." Also very important, as Eric Hobsbawm writes, is that "it became impossible to hide the fact from the local populations that other countries had made more material progress than the socialist ones [had]."[4]

Chernobyl was an especially vivid and symbolic reminder of the technological backwardness of the Soviet Union, a reflection of "a society in decline."[5] In Gorbachev's words, it was evidence "not only of how obsolete our technology was, but also of the failure of the old system."[6] Whereas in the past, the Soviet system could rely on legitimation by technological accomplishments—huge hydroelectric projects and steel mills in the 1930s, the harnessing of atomic energy for both military and peaceful purposes after World War II, Sputnik in 1957—by the 1980s no such achievements were available to bolster the self-confidence of the ruling elites and distract the attention of the masses from their daily frustrations and material deprivations.

Imperial expansion abroad used to be the another major source of legitimation. Cuba in particular represented a vindication of the pro-Soviet revolutionary tides sweeping the Third World and was a special source of pride for the Soviet leaders, "an ideological fountain of youth." Reportedly, "Anastas Mikoyan, on returning to Moscow from Cuba, was exuberantly rejuvenated . . . [the] Cuban revolution brought him back to the early days of the Russian Revolution."[7] Castro's durability notwithstanding, the pro-communist revolutionary tide crested and began to ebb: Soviet forces could not subdue the guerrillas in Afghanistan, nor could pro-Soviet regimes in the Third World defeat their own anticommunist insurgents—indeed, these regimes increasingly became economic burdens to the Soviet Union rather than political assets. By the 1980s Soviet leaders and elites had less and less, if any, reason to believe that history was on the side of Soviet communism, or, in Brezhnev's words, that the "correlation of forces" worldwide favored the Soviet bloc.

In retrospect, it is clear that Paul Kennedy's term "imperial overstretch" describes the Soviet Union far more accurately than it does the United States, to which he applied it. Soviet expansionism (or imperialism), unlike the American, was vital for the maintenance and legitimation of the economic-political system and played an important role in diverting attention from its brittleness.[8] For both the outside world and Soviet citizens it seemed inconceivable that a political system that had controlled the largest military forces in the world,[9] simultaneously supported several guerrilla wars and uprisings, had had effective control over numerous governments abroad, and was treated with the reverence the superpower status exacts—that such a super-power was so close to unraveling.

Let me also note here—and not merely as an example of the gulf between Marxist theory and Soviet practice—that the legitimacy and dynamism of the Soviet system, such as it was, rested in large measure on the stature of two powerful leaders: Lenin and Stalin. There were no leaders after Stalin who were capable of conferring legitimacy by the force of their personality or ideas, and their absence contributed to the decay of Soviet communism. Each long-lived communist regime resisting reform and preserving its coherence has been dominated by a supreme leader: Albania by Enver Hodza, Cuba by Castro, China by Mao, North Korea by Kim Il Sung, Romania by Ceausescu, and Vietnam by Ho Chi Minh. In each case, the demise of the leader has undermined stability and become a precondition of radical change.

I have argued that Soviet communism unraveled not so much because of massive popular discontent as because of the changed attitude of those who presided over it. The more doubts the political elite developed about their system and empire, the harder it became to protect it with determination and the unhesitant use of force against the challenges it faced, including domestic popular discontent, ethnic unrest, guerrilla uprisings (in Afghanistan, Angola, Ethiopia, Mozambique, and Nicaragua), and the subversive influences of the West, which earlier totalitarian controls had managed to fend off.

To the extent that the leaders articulated their loss of conviction it has taken three forms. First, they argued that it was the weakness or moral corruption of particular human beings (such as Stalin or Beria) that frustrated the grand design, that the wrong people grabbed power and were the source of the decay. Second, the retroactive questioning of the system began, and often ended with, an awareness of its economic malfunctioning or inefficiency—it did not deliver, it lagged behind the West. Third, and least frequent, they connected disillusionment and questioning to the recognition of some basic flaw in Marxist-Leninist theory or the communist ideals, which resisted implementation (Yakovlev made this argument). Sometimes their questioning was connected to specific, personal experiences. However, disillusioning experiences were neutralized as long as the overall structure of belief, routinized commitment, and the associated acceptance of privilege were in place.

Both the beginning and the end of Soviet Communism provide support for a belief in the power of ideas, including those of a Marxist-Leninist derivation. It was a blend of idealism and revolutionary power hunger—against a background of suitable economic and historical conditions—that brought the Soviet system into existence.[10] Following Stalin's death, the part played by ideology in shaping the Soviet system and its policies came to be much debated among Western scholars. More indisputably, Stalin's formative influence and the structures he built survived his death despite his successors' "fitful and half-hearted efforts at 'de-Stalinization'"; they "continued to work within the framework he created because they knew no other method of governing."[11]

As the end approached, the guardians of the system could rely neither on the sense of legitimacy provided earlier by unchallenged power, surface unanimity, and public rituals nor on the certainties they used to find in the official belief system or military might and territorial expansion. An allegedly modern social system which could not adequately feed its population and could not prevent a sharp rise in infant and adult mortality in times of peace had obviously failed its people, and those failures eroded the self-assurance of its leaders. There were also specific unfulfilled promises, such as Khrushchev's to catch up with and overtake the United States in productivity and material living standards. Yet these failed promises were not necessarily fatally delegitimizing moral failures from the rulers' point of view; evasions and excuses could be found, up to a point, to deny or explain away such matters, as had been the case before the 1980s.

The system failed even more profoundly with regard to its original commitment to social justice, the creation of a sense of community, establishment of trust between the citizens and their leaders, and treatment of the masses as responsible adults capable of making certain choices. Above all, it failed by institutionalizing a pervasive and distinctive mendaciousness.

The rulers' final loss of conviction was rooted both in their experiences of the malfunctioning and inefficiency of the system and, to a lesser degree, in their grudging recognition that there were some basic moral flaws which caused great human suffering that were integral to its institutions. It is important to remember, however, that the loss of conviction both among the leaders and the led occurred not merely because of the institutional failings but because those failings took place against the background of the theory-practice gap, which underscored the moral aspect of the failings. As Alexander Wat, a disillusioned Polish communist intellectual, says, "The loss of freedom, tyranny, abuse, hunger would all have been easier to bear if not for the compulsion to call them freedom, justice, the good of the people."[12]

This study thus reinforces the proposition that ideas can make a significant difference to political realities, to the political behavior of people and the functioning of institutions. In the light of new archival materials John Lewis Gaddis has concluded that "the new sources suggest . . . that ideology often *determined* the behavior of Marxist-Leninist regimes; it was not simply a justification for actions already decided upon."[13] Henry Kissinger proposes another interesting source of the convictions of the Soviet leaders who followed Stalin: "'Apprenticeship to Stalin guaranteed psychological malformation' so that his heirs 'made their nightmarish existence . . . tolerable [only] by a passionate belief in the system to which they owed their careers.'"[14]

It was the disenchantment with the failed ideals and applications of Marxist-Leninist socialism in the last generation of the political elite—together with widespread popular cynicism caused by the gulf between theory and practice—which brought the Soviet system down, against the background of endemic economic difficulties and the political institutions which suppressed innovation and rewarded conformity.

These developments can be traced to a speech and its revelations. What was revealed by Khrushchev at the Twentieth Party Congress in 1956 had a lingering subversive effect on the attitude and behavior of generations of Soviet and East European people, especially the Soviet Party intellectuals who came of age in the 1960s. Quite possibly the single major determinant of the disposition of this elite was Khrushchev's unexpected demystification of Stalin and much of Soviet history ("it was like being hit over the head with the hammer . . . a sudden blow").[15] These revelations were followed by a lengthy and not instantly discernible process of decay, delegitimation, and stagnation.

Khrushchev and his successors could not restore the legitimacy of a political system that allowed an individual like Stalin to come to power and abuse power on a vast scale for decades. Mathias Rakosi of Hungary was among those who recognized the shattering long-term impact of Khrushchev's revelations. In the aftermath of the speech he warned Andropov: "You can't act in this way. You shouldn't have hurried. What you have done at your congress is a disaster. And I don't know what will come out of it, either in your country or in mine."[16]

The second powerful illustration of the impact of ideas is glasnost. Like Khrushchev's speech, glasnost entailed a flood of new information and revelations that showed how unjust, wasteful, inefficient, and mendacious the system was. The revelations resonated with the experiences of ordinary citizens. Glasnost, contrary to official hopes, did not lead to ideological rejuvenation.[17] A Hungarian journalist I interviewed told this joke about glasnost: "A relative asks the forensic doctor: What was the cause of death of the deceased? The doctor's answer: It was the dissection itself."

Glasnost was not the safety valve it was intended to be. On the contrary, it validated the widespread, if unexpressed, awareness of the discrepancy between theory and practice, propaganda and daily life—a discrepancy which was more radical and more vividly experienced than in pluralistic societies, which expend far less energy on promoting idealized versions of their political ideologies and institutions. Under the communist systems here discussed (as in others which still survive) " lying was . . . a way of life. Parents did not talk openly in front of their children. At meetings, or in the presence of strangers, people expressed one view, and among friends . . . another, usually the opposite . . . [an] incredible amount of corruption . . . permeated every facet of society."[18] It bears repeating that corruption as such need not be destabilizing or profoundly delegitimating if the powers-that-be do not insist that the opposite is the case. As the prominent Hungarian reform communist Imre Pozsgay put it in an interview with me. "After the revelations of glasnost, nobody in the apparat could continue working with an untroubled conscience."

A Czech informant, Pavel Bratnik, recent member of the parliament and former dissident, told me that to be a successful functionary one had "to close one's eyes to reality." During glasnost this became difficult; in the end, impossible. Glasnost allowed ordinary people to learn about virtually everything that was wrong with the system and at the same time to realize that their dissatisfactions were widely shared. Not only those in the elite but ordinary people too were now in a position to compare their way of life with that in the West and with what their officials had earlier told them about the West. The comments of a Russian cabdriver about his visit to West Germany are probably typical: "There were dozens of different types of bread. I never in my life saw such abundance and I felt pain for my country. I began to think that only fools live in Russia. My father and mother never saw such abundance and my relatives never saw it and never will see it."[19] One of the Soviet respondents interviewed for this study (a former manager of a big state-owned company in Voronezh) recalled his trip to Italy in 1991: "This experience came as a shock . . . there was an abundance of goods and no crowds in the shops . . . I talked to an Italian and asked him what his major problems were. He said that they were finding parking space and selling his products . . . These are not our problems; we have plenty of parking space."[20]

The crisis of authority prompted by the revelations of glasnost became especially destabilizing due to the failed attempts of Gorbachev to reorganize and reinvigorate the Party: "In the end the party's bureaucratic structure failed to adjust to the changes initiated by its own leadership. Gorbachev was unable to turn the party into a tool of reform . . . The old hierarchical mechanism of authority . . . collapsed as a result of Gorbachev's reforms, which undermined the capacity of the party bureaucracy to control change," writes Sergei Grigoriev, a former assistant press secretary of Gorbachev.[21] Given the centrality of the Party in Soviet political life, its disarray made a major contribution to the unraveling of the system.[22]

The collapse of Soviet communism left few citizens with sentiments such as those voiced by the widow of Bukharin, Anna Larina: "Despite my sufferings and the camps I always thought we would live through this, that this terrible business was just something on the surface and the real thing, socialism, would prevail in the end. I always felt that Bolshevism had been liquidated by one person, Stalin."[23] Not many in the Soviet bloc countries shared the belief that "this terrible business was just something on the surface".

The leaders of the Soviet Union during the 1970s and 1980s were revolutionaries neither in spirit nor in practice. Even the remaining believers among them were incapable of entertaining the expectations and the ruthlessness that were part of the revolutionary attitude. The ruling class was, as Zhores Medvedev observes, "sterile, inefficient and conservative" and had "degenerated into a gerontocracy . . . The final symbol of this degeneration has been the death of three General Secretaries in office within less than three years."[24] Vladimir Kryuchkov's impressions of the aging Brezhnev bear this out: "What I saw exceeded all my apprehensions. At the table was seated a seriously ill man who rose with great difficulty to greet me and after that could not take a breath for a long time, having literally collapsed back into the armchair." Less frequently noted is that even under Gorbachev the political elite was not rejuvenated. Mikhail Heller writes: "A notable feature of the Gorbachev 'revolution' is the total absence from it of young people. There are no young people among the officials surrounding the general secretary."[25]

It was not only the age and infirmity but also the mediocrity of these leaders, especially those around (and including) Brezhnev, that undermined the system.[26] These people were incapable of reinvigorating Soviet communism. Alexander Dubcek writes: "I often reflect on the causes of the collapse of the Soviet Union. How could this giant power crumble so quickly and so completely? There . . . is one elementary explanation: the system inhibited change. It fed on dead doctrine and prevented a natural replacement of leaders. When they finally tried to do something about it, it was too late."[27]

By 1996 Gorbachev himself—who, despite his unintended dismantling of the system, remained a believer in some improved version of socialism—

reached the conclusion that things had been wrong from the beginning. He no longer venerated Lenin and the October Revolution: "Had the Russians continued along the path of the February revolution, had they continued on the path of political pluralism, it would have been a different situation . . . it would have been much better . . . The main mistake of the Bolsheviks was that their violent emergency measures and methods were not temporary at all . . . The rather artificial model created by Marx, which was made even more utopian by what the Bolsheviks added to it—that model was imposed by force and that model did violence to the human being . . . We have the record of other countries who industrialized themselves too, but with ground rules and democracy. In Russia it was all bloody experiments."[28] These were remarkable admissions: that the October Revolution was a mistake, that Marxist ideals violated human nature and had to be imposed by force, and that the use of such force was not a temporary expedient.

By contrast, a surviving communist dictator such as Castro retained his political will and sense of legitimacy; he had no second thoughts. In 1995 he said: "I am profoundly convinced that what we have been doing is the fair thing to do. It is the noblest thing to do and the most humane, and we will never be repentant for that . . . I have no choice but to continue being a communist, like the early Christians remained Christian. I feel like the early Christians . . . Our main objective is to preserve the revolution . . . and the achievements of socialism."[29]

The last generation of Soviet leaders also differed from the generation of professional revolutionaries who took over in Eastern Europe after World War II. An example is Edward Ochab. In his words: "I became . . . a professional revolutionary. I read Lenin's *What is to be done* when I was still in high school . . . where Lenin maintains that the socialist revolution needs 'professional revolutionary' cadres . . . who would be prepared . . . to spend months crawling along sewers and would be in charge . . . of organizing the masses. That was when I said to myself: that's me. And I don't regret it."[30]

The generation of Soviet and East European leaders who allowed power slip from their hands were, unlike Jakub Berman, another Polish communist leader, no longer capable of "consolation in the thought that some day . . . people would arrive at the truth, and the injuries that had been done would be made good"; the last generation of Soviet leaders no longer had the kind of "endurance and dedication to the cause . . . to accept what was happening despite all the distortions, injuries and torments."[31] The increasingly aged rulers of the USSR were isolated from the social-political realities that the majority of the people experienced in their daily lives. This isolation in the rarefied reaches of the nomenklatura, which endured well into the 1980s, also contributed to the decay. Even if the leaders eventually came to the halting realization that all was not well, the enormity and depth of the problems were not evident to them for a long time.[32]

Although the political police prepared reports of the public mood, these reports were softened as they made their way up through the bureaucracy.[33] Reportedly Gorbachev said at the Central Committee plenum of April 1989 that "none of us had good knowledge of the country we live in."[34] Yuri Afanasyev notes that "no country and no people had a history as falsified as ours."[35] As I pointed out in the first chapter, in a system in which everybody was forced to pretend to be loyal and committed, it was difficult to distinguish the genuine supporters (even among the elite) from the opportunists who would desert the system when conditions allowed them to do so without risk. These are among the unanticipated costs of enforced political conformity.

Among the political elite were those who in their youth had learned of Khrushchev's speech and later formed a moderately cohesive and congenial group—they were sometimes called "children of the 20th Party Congress"[36]—who had also worked together in Prague in the 1960s on the journal *Problems of Peace and Socialism*. Some twenty years later several of them became advisers and supporters of Gorbachev.[37] As Yuri Afanasyev recalls of this group, they had felt "elation and hope . . . at the time of the 20th Party Congress in 1956 . . . [and] great disappointment . . . when all the anti-Stalinist policies begun under Khrushchev collapsed."[38] What they also had in common—"the key to this generation, aside from the whiff of freedom during the Khrushchev years"—was that they "had largely escaped the great unifying events of their grandparents' and parents' generation, the 1917 revolution and Stalin's Great Patriotic War [World War II]."[39]

These people knew a fair amount about the world outside, especially the West, and not only about the abundance of cars and supermarkets; many of them actually set foot on the soil of countries supposedly inferior to the Soviet Union morally as well as materially. Such experiences renewed and deepened the conflicts between theory and practice and played an important part in the discreditation of Soviet communism; the new information also made clear that their own system assiduously lied about the West. Gorbachev writes of his trips abroad: "We were amazed by the open and relaxed attitude of the people we met and marveled at their unrestrained judgment of everything, including the activity of their governments . . . my previous belief in the superiority of socialist democracy over the bourgeois system was shaken . . . Finally, the most significant conclusion drawn from the journeys abroad: people . . . were better off than in our country. The question haunted me: why was the standard of living in our country lower than in other developed countries?"[40]

Learning about the West weakened their capacity to dismiss as unimportant the failures of their own system, supposedly made on account of the great vision it sought to realize. The men of the sixties had reason to doubt that the direction and basic blueprint of their system was sound, and they could no longer dismiss specific failures as irrelevant to the fundamentals of their beliefs and worldview. It was no longer clear what was "typical" or systemic and what was incidental or transient. The sixties generation of Soviet leaders and Party intellectuals, those who came to (or near) power in the 1980s, differed from their predecessors in that they were no longer capable of ignoring or repressing politically and morally problematic evidence or disregarding information; their skill in handling cognitive dissonance was greatly diminished.[41]

The various political actors discussed in this book shared the ability to work for communist systems for long periods of time while aware of the moral and practical defects. They entertained "over a considerable period of time a continuing series of doubts and questions, quickly repressed, but not fully dealt with and intellectually overcome, so that they . . . sapped and weakened the foundations of Marxist belief."[42] In most instances they allowed themselves to publicly recognize the flaws of the system only when its decay was well advanced and unmistakable. Unlike for some Western communists who had no power, the process of disillusionment or disengagement among those who held power in communist states was lengthy and incremental, sometimes lifelong, without searing flashes of illumination or seemingly abrupt conversions. At the same time, as the historian Orlando Figes points out, "by the late 1980s and early 1990s the hardliners had lost their nerve." He suggests that their avoidance of "another Tiananmen Square" could be explained by two facts: they had parents who were not strangers to Stalin's bloodshed, and they were inhibited by their higher education. But he believes that "perhaps above all, yet hardest to weigh, was the leadership's own loss of faith in the Communist system."[43]

This book provides a substantial sampling of the discontents and doubts of people in power under the political system they served. While a good deal has been known about popular dissatisfaction with communist systems, the political disenchantment, or at the least the significant decline of commitment on the part of those in power, had not been examined before as it has been in this book. It was my intention to show that the line between doubt and discontent, on one side, and the erosion of political will, on the other, was repeatedly crossed in both the Soviet Union and countries of Eastern Europe. Not only did the leaders lose the political will required to keep their regimes in power in the face of growing popular discontent, but they were also incapable of solving the severe economic problems their societies faced. The domestic weaknesses, belatedly recognized by the men in power, also undermined their will to project and exercise power abroad, and once it came to be widely perceived that the authorities no longer had the determination to keep the empire intact, domestic delegitimation and discontent dramatically increased.

A surprising and cheering conclusion that we may draw from the scrutiny of the characters and careers of several of the individuals discussed above is that human beings are sometimes capable of changing their beliefs and behavior for the better in unexpected ways. The younger generation in particular provides excellent illustrations of this. For example, Yegor Gaidar (born in 1956), acting prime minister under Yeltsin, "grew up as one of the most golden of the 'golden youth,' the children of the elite, and heir to one of the most revered names in the Soviet Union. His grandfather . . . was one of the youngest commanders in the Russian civil war. Later . . . [Gaidar] became one of the most honored children's writers of the Soviet period, spinning patriotic and officially sanctioned tales of brave revolutionary boys and girls . . . [As of 1992] Gaidar is a committed capitalist. It is an extraordinary transformation, typical of the best of Gaidar's generation."[44]

An example of an even more striking transformation is provided by General Dmitri Volkogonov, a man of the older generation who went from being in charge of ideology and propaganda for the military forces to being a devastating critic of the system and its founding myths and came to question the legitimacy of its entire history.

Another example of such a fundamental political reorientation is provided by another former general, Ivan D. Yershov, who was second in command of the Warsaw Pact forces which invaded Czechoslovakia in 1968. Such was his loyalty to the regime that in 1976 he refused assistance to his daughter, who was attempting to join her émigré husband in the United States. Later he came "full circle in the agonizing journey that began on the Czechoslovak border . . . in 1968 when he locked away his disturbing initial conclusion that 'this glorious mission to save socialism was a lie.'" While the case of his daughter contributed to his disillusionment, its more distant roots lay in the proverbial gulf between the realities that he encountered in Czechoslovakia in 1968 and their propagandistic redefinitions by the authorities.[45] "We thought we were responding to a cry for help from the Czechoslovak people," he said. "As soon as we crossed the border, we saw it was not true. There were no people to greet us . . . Every road sign was destroyed, removed or turned in the wrong direction. Simple people, had covered the roads with three-pronged devices to puncture our tires. They were terrified of our arrival." Subsequently he lost his commission and the privileges that went with it; he was censured by the Party and forced into retirement.[46] His case is reminiscent of others discussed earlier, for the appearance-reality gulf began to matter *after* some personal problems and hardships gave him license, so to speak, to confront its full implications.

The extent of the attitude change among many of the better-known reformers has also been remarkable and is underscored by recalling how deeply involved they used to with the system. For example, "as both the police chief and later the Party leader of . . . Georgia, Shevardnadze was capable of brutal attacks on local dissidents . . . Yakovlev, for his part, was prepared to work in the Party ideological department of the Central Committee for the beastly . . . Mikhail Suslov. Yeltsin's best known act as the Party boss of Sverdlovsk . . . was to bulldoze the last residence of Nicholas II to prevent it from becoming a royalist shrine. All of them were prepared to compromise to make their way up the Party ladder."[47] Shevardnadze in particular underwent profound changes of outlook and arrived at insights remarkable for a former member of the Soviet political elite—for example: "Tanks and machine guns may only be employed as arguments within the appropriate ideological frame . . . the executioner has always been preceded by the inquisitor, the axe and block foreshadowed by the dogmas of faith."[48]

Unlike the collapse of the other major totalitarian system of the twentieth century, Nazi Germany, the fall of Soviet communism did not bring with it an unequivocal, worldwide delegitimation of the ideas which originally inspired the system and its founders. Among Western academic intellectuals in particular, Marxism continues to enjoy respect, and many remain preoccupied with its rehabilitation.[49] For some, the most important aspect of the collapse of Soviet communism is that it has provided a new opportunity to "recenter . . . the debate on our own society." Bruce Cumings, an American historian, means that new, hard-hitting critiques of American society may now be advanced, based on a purer version of Marxism no longer burdened by association with the likes of Erich Honecker.[50]

In the eyes of many Western beholders the collapse of the Soviet bloc did not resolve the question of the relation between Marxist theory and Soviet-communist practice. As Michael Radu points out, "Many of us, intellectuals . . . cannot seem to make peace with the truth that an idea so 'nobly motivated' could have produced such unmitigated disaster . . . there is a powerful reluctance to connect the horrors of Soviet reality to the errors of the socialist idea."[51]

Less nostalgia for the founding theory has been evident in the former Soviet empire. "Statues of Marx and Lenin were cleared away by the thousand. Squares all over the empire from Estonia to the Pamirs have nothing but holes and perhaps a few rivets and stanchions to show where heroic statues of the founders of Marxism-Leninism were once rising larger than life."[52] Such delegitimation of the founding fathers has been compatible with the emergence of a degree of popular nostalgia for the modest, non-competitive securities that the old system provided.

It was among the proud claims of Soviet communism that it succeeded in uniting theory and practice—an assertion some its critics vigorously denied, while others, perceiving the theory in darker colors, readily agreed with it. To this day there is no agreement regarding the relation between theory and practice or the role that theory played in the fall of the Soviet Union. It is, of course, difficult to evaluate the claims and counterclaims, given the often contradictory meanings and messages of the "theory"—the situation is reminiscent of the attempts to measure the correspondence or divergence between the Holy Scriptures of Christianity and its institutional practices. But Marxism was far more vulnerable to the problem of reconciling ideas and realities than Christianity, since the fulfillment of *its* ideals was to take place here and now. The promises of Christianity (and most major religions) are projected into another plane of existence; those of Marxism were to be realized in this world. There was no indication that this fulfillment was approaching.[53]

Nevertheless, it is hard to deny that an effort was made to realize some of the theory, and it resulted in a proliferation of unintended consequences. Martin Malia poses the issue with great clarity: "The problem is this: Since socialism set out to realize the 'noble dream' of human equality and fraternity, how could it have produced such palpably bad results in Soviet practice? One way to solve the problem . . . is to blame bad results on Russian backwardness, or on the failure of the Western revolution to come to Bolshevism's rescue, or on the heritage of Ivan the Terrible, and by these means to exonerate socialism itself . . . Another 'solution' is to say that Soviet Communism was not genuine socialism." Western intellectuals who remain attached to Marxism or some variant of it have adopted the arguments outlined by Malia. He is among the few Western authors who have argued that "the Soviet experiment turned totalitarian not *despite* its being socialist but *because* it was socialist" and who has also insisted that "all the basic institutions of the Soviet order, as they had emerged by 1935 . . . were the creations of ideology."[54] Milovan Djilas wrote: "The idea itself contained the seeds of its own inglorious, future collapse. They lay in wait within the very idea of communism . . . no one killed communism off. The idea was left to rot away by itself . . . it stood revealed as the purest banality, as a gross over-simplification . . . Such visions may encourage us to sacrifice and goad us into noble acts, but they are also opiates to the soul and can unseat the mind . . . the idea dried up in proportion as the reality legitimized by it grew stronger."[55] In short, theory and practice were congruent, not dissonant.

Unlike many Western intellectuals, the East European intellectuals whom I interviewed (see the Appendix) were also virtually unanimous in their conviction that there was a link between the theoretical inspiration and the practical results. The discrepancy which in so many cases eroded belief in the system existed between the promises and ideals entailed in the theory, on the one hand, and the results of implementing it, on the other, but not between the theory and the official policies and institutions built to implement the promises and ideals; the policies and institutions inspired by the theory failed to yield the results hoped for.

While it would require another volume to do justice to the topic, a few important aspects of the relation between Marxist theory and Soviet practice should be noted. The founders of the Soviet Union were unquestionably inspired by the central ideas of Marx, especially the ideal of maximizing socioeconomic equality and creating material abundance. The new and vastly improved social order was also expected to include harmonious relationships among all groups in society (with the exception of the enemies of the new society, who were to be removed swiftly and painlessly) and a new sense of community and trust among the citizens. All historically known forms of human misbehavior (crime, greed, selfishness, lack of compassion, envy, etc.) were expected to "wither away."

The key institutional measure to attain these goals was the abolition of the private ownership of the means of production; the key political measure was to be the dictatorship of the proletariat, who would exercise power through the Party. Leszek Kolakowski writes: "Marx seems to have imagined that once capitalists were done away with the whole world could become a kind of Athenian *agora:* one had only to forbid private ownership of machines or land and, as if by magic, human beings would cease to be selfish and their interests would coincide in perfect harmony."[56] Even Lenin believed (before he took power) that relatively little violence would be required to remake society and expunge exploitation and that all forms of human misbehavior would wither away after the workers seized power and established control over the economy.[57]

We cannot guess what Marx might have thought of Lenin's idea of substituting the Bolshevik Party for the dictatorship of the proletariat or of his attempt to pull off the socialist revolution in a largely peasant society. Still, what Lenin and his followers strove for was not so different from what Marx aspired to; just the setting was, and (arguably) the means used. There was no way to attempt to accomplish what the Russian revolutionaries set out to accomplish without huge concentrations of power and harsh applications of force.

In the debates about the relation between Marxist theory and Soviet-communist practice in the West, surprisingly little has been said about the doctrine of class struggle, an essential part of Marxism. As a Czech author notes, "The basic belief in a class struggle without mercy is surely one of the roots of the problem."[58] Informants interviewed in Eastern Europe also suggest that class struggle is a preeminent example of the connection between theory and practice and a major explanation of the coercive practices of communist systems and their untroubled resort to violence. Belief in the omnipresence and inexorability of class struggle desensitized practitioners and provided powerful legitimation for the generous use of violence to create a social system in which violence would no longer be needed.

Was there an affinity between certain features of the theory and the personality of its interpreters in power seeking to apply it? Yakovlev asked: "Why was it that the particular features and peculiarities of Marxism . . . became the basis for Party ideology? Why was this ideology in particular seized upon so passionately by the original fanatics?"[59] Both Lenin and Stalin—and, for that matter, Marx—were possessed of a sense of mission, inclining them to self-righteousness, intolerance, and contempt toward those who disagreed with them. There is a common denominator of intolerance and militancy in the attitudes of Marx, Lenin, and Stalin (and their followers); they perceived themselves as unique historical protagonists engaged in the effort to bring about a vast, unprecedented improvement in the way people lived and thought. Such aspirations were compellingly linked to a fierce intolerance of any obstacle in their path. The intensity of the vision was such that the actual beliefs and attitudes of the ordinary people who were to be up-lifted and transformed ceased to matter; their "false consciousness" was to be ignored or "cured" by any means available. Barrington Moore notes that like Lenin, "Marx in his more abusive moments . . . became a full-blown guttersnipe. These are not trivial matters. A good social and cultural history of polemical styles would reveal a great deal about politics."[60] There is a connection between verbal and physical violence in the great mass mur-ders of the twentieth century, as verbal dehumanization almost invariably preceded inhumane treatment.

The personal attributes of the founding communist fathers, leaders, and theoreticians were thus well matched to the gigantic and problematic tasks of social engineering they undertook. More skeptical, tolerant, or reflective leaders would not have been able to set about and continue the forcible re-modeling of a huge country and the reluctant beneficiaries of their policies. Without the certainties that their beliefs provided, the campaigns of political violence and coercion would have been far less ruthless. By the same token, as we reach the 1970s and 1980s, there is a decline of belief, and "without the prop of ideology, the Party's will to coerce eroded"—that is how Malia sums up the conditions leading to glasnost and the final unraveling of the Soviet system.[61]

One hopeful conclusion this study suggests is that—other things being equal—political systems which combine utopian aspirations with highly concentrated political power are less durable than those without these at-tributes. Further, the attempt to achieve goals which are inherently unreal-izable as well as unpopular implants fundamental weaknesses in a system which eventually lead to its demise. As Richard Pipes puts it, in the Soviet case these objectives amounted to "the aspiration to rationalize all aspects of life, to create a social milieu which would eliminate moral choices and the inequalities resulting from them by instituting complete harmony between the interests of the individual and those of society."[62] The unpopularity of communist governments was due not so much to their proclaimed goals—social justice, equality, a new sense of community, the rational distribution of resources, material progress—as to the methods the realization of these goals required. People dislike political systems which routinely interfere in their personal lives and invade what they regard as the private sphere.[63] The political attempt to create harmony between the private and public spheres tends to lead to the subordination of the private to the (questionably defined) public interest. It was on behalf of the ideals of Marxism-Leninism that such subordination came to be institutionalized under Soviet-style socialism.

This is not to suggest that unjust or inefficient political systems cannot persist for long periods of time. They can and do. But when they do, there are at least two important requirements. One is a determined and efficient police force ready to impress on the population the hopelessness of any dissent or criticism, let alone actual political resistance. Second, for corrupt, inefficient, and unjust systems to stay in power they must display a benign neglect of the private lives of citizens, allowing them to pursue their customary ways of life and familiar routines—as was the case in traditional autocracies. In short, it is easier for people to tolerate nontotalitarian than totalitarian repression.

In light of the above it is doubtful that Soviet communism was reformable, although at the end of the 1980s there was hope—more in the West than in the East—that it might be. For instance, according to Stephen F. Cohen, "the emergence of a Soviet leadership devoted to radical reform confounded most Western scholars . . . who had long believed that the Soviet Communist system lacked any capacity for real change."[64] Given what transpired, it could still be argued that the system was reformable in principle; the Soviet Union might still be with us if only the reforms had been applied earlier (or later), and more (or less) sweepingly, if only those in charge had pursued the course of reform more prudently. I agree with all those (and their number has grown over the years) who aver that the reforms, glasnost in particular, doomed the system, which was not reformable—if by that we mean that it could have retained its basic institutional framework, including one-party rule and the union of the fifteen republics.

Another finding that emerges from this study is that the political beliefs of committed communists had an unmistakably secular-religious quality. As Leszek Kolakowski observes, "Marxism has been the greatest fantasy of our century. It was a dream offering the prospect of a society of perfect unity, in which all human aspirations would be fulfilled and all values reconciled

. . . The influence that Marxism achieved, far from being the result of its scientific character, is almost entirely due to its prophetic, fantastic, and irrational elements."[65]

In almost every case discussed in this volume the commitment to the system seemed to rest on abstract, nonempirical beliefs and largely symbolic matters. I am referring here in particular to the recurring proposition of many of the protagonists that the "fundamentals" of the system, or "the system as a whole," or its "overall direction," were for long periods of time sufficient to silence their doubts in the face of disturbing empirical phenomena. These abstract beliefs allowed their upholders to remain unaffected by empirical realities. A convenient degree of insulation from ordinary life under state socialism was also helpful, but, above all, it was the capacity for compartmentalization, the ability to focus on a handful of abstract notions or deeply internalized values (usually acquired in their youth) which shaped their behavior. This explains the evident and highly functional dissociation of ends from means.

If one had been in a position to ask the communist leaders while they were in power what precisely they meant by the "fundamentals" of the system, or "the system as a whole" (by what Koestler calls "the doctrine of unshaken foundations")[66] they might have said that they meant that power was in the right hands, the hands of people who had a basic and historically tested commitment to advance social justice; that the system, whatever its flaws, was nonetheless self-evidently superior to capitalist ones, which rested on a foundation of private property, and better than any other that had ever existed. Even George Lukacs, the philosopher, was, as of 1967, prey to such axiomatic and unexamined beliefs, having remarked that "in my opinion even the worst socialism is better than the best capitalism."[67] To believe this, Lukacs had to entertain a quasi-religious notion of socialism that took for granted the essential, self-evident ethical superiority of its goals and overlooked all facts which might have called it into question. As a Hungarian commentator puts it, the case of Lukacs "illuminates with special clarity the self-deception, the stubborn clinging to illusions and lies" that characterized the hardened adherents of the system and "proves that in the maintenance of the Stalinist edifice intellectual supports played a secondary role compared to the psychological and moral ones."[68] In the end, it came down to matters of faith.

The kind of disposition sketched here is very similar to that of conventional religious believers who accommodate to and rationalize the horrors, injustices, and irrationalities of life here and now with the help of their deep belief that the world is ordered, just, and permeated by divine purpose (even if it is not perceived and fully understood by ordinary mortals) and that a divine dispensation will eventually right all wrongs, if not here than in some other world or plane of existence. The hopeful future is of the same importance for the religious believer as it is for the devotee of communist society (communist in the Marxist, utopian sense), a society in which all contradictions will be resolved and all conflicts and scarcities, material or affective, eliminated. This is how Eugene Loebl describes this attitude: "A person accepted certain fundamental assumptions and based a whole worldview upon them . . . As long as I believed in the historical mission of the proletariat, in the ultimate significance of the ownership of the means of production . . . as long as I felt that the result of our fight would be the creation of a humanistic world, I was able to condone any means of achieving this end . . . This scientific objectivity that left no room for subjective values, and the absolute emphasis on the end without any concern for the means to that end, were the factors I found to be responsible for the inherent dehumanization of Marxism."[69]

Another way to describe the tendency to overlook factual detail in favor of grand theoretical design is to think of it as extreme "contextual thinking." It was possible for a Hungarian communist to tell his interlocutor in a discussion of the Soviet show trials: "Do not look at the details . . . but consider them in their total political context."[70] Hannah Arendt draws attention to a similar disposition in the thinking of totalitarian leaders: their "extreme contempt for facts as such, for in their opinion a fact depends entirely on the power of the man who can fabricate it."[71] Such indifference to facts follows from the theoretical orientation of communist leaders, from their conviction that practice is subordinated to theory, and the latter can mold the former.

The secular-religious aspects of the system and its ultimate delegitimation are reflected in the Lenin cult and its demise. The final loss of legitimacy came about when public criticism of Lenin was allowed to surface during the late years of glasnost, climaxing in demands to close down his mausoleum in Red Square. Nothing was left to sacralize the Soviet system.

There is little doubt that in the end neither the communist political elites nor their subjects had many illusions left regarding the correspondence between the original theoretical intentions and the practical results of their attempted implementation. Ordinary people paid little attention to the theory to begin with (despite all attempts at indoctrination), and with the passage of time the leaders, too, paid less and less, preoccupied as they were with staying in power and keeping the structures of power intact. Isaiah Berlin illuminates these dynamics between theory and practice: "The corollary of this overreliance on theory . . . is that if the facts—that is, the behavior of living human beings—are recalcitrant to such experiment, the experimenter becomes annoyed, and tries to alter the facts to fit the theory, which in practice means a kind of vivisection of societies . . . The theory is 'saved' indeed but at too high cost in useless human suffering."[72]

It was tempting for the political elites to suggest, as many of them did, that it was the weaknesses and failings of human beings, not the substance of the theory and its ideals, that were responsible for the ultimate failure of the system. While as a general proposition it can hardly be debated that most human beings are not habitually idealistic and self-denying, some ideas and ideals are more difficult to implement than others; human weaknesses play different parts in the functioning of social and political institutions and systems, depending on the kind of theory which animates them. Marxism nurtured unrealistically high expectations of the perfectibility of human beings and, partly for that reason, neglected institutional safeguards against less-than-admirable human qualities and their political expression.[73]

In the end both the unity and the disunity of theory and practice contributed to the unraveling of Soviet communism, that "great and barbaric experiment," as one of the Russian informants called it. The disunity was far more apparent: the public ownership of the means of production did not end the exploitation of the workers or make the system more productive; the dictatorship of the proletariat was no more democratic than parliamentary systems under capitalism; the Communist Party was not composed of the most selfless representatives of the working classes; the leaders were not invulnerable to corruption; workers did not have reason to believe that they were masters of their lives and of the means of production; communist prisons were no more humane than those in capitalist countries, and so forth.

But there were also connections between Marxist theory and practice, including the Marxist belief which communist leaders shared and acted upon that private property and the desire for profit were the ultimate source of all evil. Likewise, Marx's contempt for peasants was embraced and institutionalized. A similar contempt for and hostility to traditional religious beliefs and practices also became official policy. The elitist-paternalistic streak in Marx (magnified in Lenin), too, found full expression in the character of the ruling party and its relationship to the masses. There was a clear connection between belief and economic policies and their failures (for instance, the establishment and perpetuation of collective farms), between the political will of the leaders and its ideological roots.[74]

It is also likely that specific miscalculations on the part of the Soviet leadership had theoretical inspiration, such as the belief that the "correlation of forces"—Brezhnev's phrase again—would favor the Soviet bloc, that Western capitalism would undergo a crisis, and that more of the Third World would rally around the Soviet Union.[75]

In the final analysis, it was the conception of human nature and condition embedded in Marxism that most clearly linked theory to practice. It is increasingly clear that "communism was based on a theoretical misdiagnosis of the human condition"[76] and, one may add, on a peculiarly contradictory conception of human nature. It was this misdiagnosis that blinded the leaders to the limits of their coercive social engineering. It was both theory and practice that fatally undermined communist systems and, in the end, eroded the convictions of those who attempted to implement the theory and its ideals.

Appendix

The Interviews

In pursuing a better understanding of the end of Soviet communism I sought verbal information from people who had lived under these systems and belonged to the social-political types which were central to this study. These conversations were not intended as major sources of information; they were supplementary to the printed sources. Particular personal experiences and incidents often illuminated larger generalizations about these systems, especially in regard to the springs of political disillusionment. The interviews were helpful as a background against which the written sources, as well as my own ideas, could be tested; they were carried out in 1991, 1992, 1994, and 1996. Those interviewed were found through personal contacts.

I sought out three types of people: (1) former Party functionaries; (2) former Party intellectuals; and (3) former dissidents, critics of the system. Almost all the interviews were taped; a few were transcribed. I had a total of fifty interviews, half of them in Hungary, a dozen in Czechoslovakia, and the remainder in Slovenia, Romania, and Russia. The handful of Soviet interviews were conducted by my research assistant, Alexei Koltakov, a native of Russia, using the questions I had put to my informants in the other countries. The Soviet interviews were taped, transcribed, and translated; all others were also taped.

Most of those interviewed were intellectuals of some variety; even the politicians and former functionaries among them have published widely (but, as a rule, only in their own country). They included academics in history, sociology, economics, philosophy, ethnography, physics, and other subjects; dissident writers (three among them distinguished and known outside their countries: Ivan Klima of the Czech Republic and Miklos Haraszti and

Gyorgy Konrad of Hungary); journalists; middle-level Party functionaries and some high-level ones (Andras Hegedus, Rezso Nyers, and Imre Pozsgay of Hungary); two former high-ranking political police officers (Vladimir Farkas and Oleg Kalugin); lesser-known Party intellectuals in charge of arts and the media; former dissidents, some of whom occupied political positions in the postcommunist governments (including members of the Czech and Hungarian parliaments).

There was no uniform set of questions, but certain basic issues were discussed, depending in part on the personal history of the informant. I was most interested in pursuing questions central to this study: Why did Soviet communism collapse, and why at that particular time? Did my informant expect it to happen? I wished to learn about the relation between Marxist theory and communist practice, the political will of the top leaders, the sources of political disillusionment, the major flaws of these systems, and the way my informants experienced them.

Many of those interviewed or members of their families had been harassed or imprisoned during the communist rule; the dissident writers were not allowed to publish. Unexpectedly, another shared experience was a visit to the West, including the United States, during the 1970s and 1980s. Several of the Hungarians completed their higher education in the Soviet Union, and many others visited the country. In virtually every instance the Soviet experience was disillusioning and required great efforts to be neutralized as long as those concerned were still loyal to the system.

Most of those interviewed did not anticipate the collapse of their respective communist regimes, at least not when it took place, although none regarded them as stable, successful, or legitimate. A Russian informant (former manager of a provincial state enterprise) blamed the collapse on the holders of power, Gorbachev in particular: "Having power . . . such as none of the existing states on this planet had, and allowing this exceptionally powerful state to disintegrate—was something truly extraordinary . . . if he [Gorbachev] had suppressed Baltic nationalism in a more decisive manner, we would not have had the problems of Karabakh, Tadjik, or Chechen nationalism later. These were all links in a chain. The weakness of one leading politician became a tragedy for the whole nation." This opinion was shared by the other Russian informants, whereas the East Europeans praised Gorbachev for contributing, intentionally or not, to the disintegration of the Soviet empire.

There was consensus on the unreformability of these systems and a recognition and vigorous affirmation that glasnost brought them down, or, more precisely, brought down the Soviet Union, which was the guardian of the other regimes in Eastern Europe. None of the respondents believed that the system could have been salvaged or reformed, not even the Czech respondents, who regarded "socialism with a human face" (associated with the reforms of 1968) as unrealizable. Hungarians were equally skeptical; in fact, several stressed that the example of Hungary showed that not even the most far-reaching reforms could have saved these systems, and several believed that the reforms weakened rather then reinvigorated the systems. Miklos Haraszti (former dissident, writer, and member of the postcommunist parliament) thought that once individual needs and personal consumption were deemed legitimate (as they were in Kadar's Hungary), the system undermined its own claim to legitimacy, which had earlier been based on collectivistic doctrine, and by doing so further weakened itself economically, since it became increasingly dependent on Western loans. A Russian informant (a historian at Voronezh University and a former Komsomol functionary) saw the decay as beginning in the 1960s and mainly rooted in the failure of the Soviet Union to keep up with the West in scientific and technological achievements; it lost the "historic competition."

The Hungarians considered the Kadar regime well ahead of the Soviet Union in its own version of glasnost; they believed that in Hungary the delegitimation of the system was not so much a result of glasnost—given the more permissive policies of Kadar—as a result of the economic failures of the regime, which by the mid-1980s was unable to meet the popular expectations it had created. It should be noted that Hungarian living standards during the 1970s and 1980s were much higher than those in the Soviet Union; Hungary was unique as a "colony," remarked one of my informants (Miklos Szinetar, former art director of state television and current director of the state opera), since it was the envy of the colonizers, who visited Hungary to shop and eat well.

An interesting finding was that most of those interviewed in Hungary and Czechoslovakia did not question the authenticity of the show trials of their youth (the Rajk and Slansky trials, respectively) *when they took place.* They were shocked, astonished, dismayed, and *eventually* dubious, but did not imagine at the time that they were staged. (Vladimir Farkas mentioned that his faith in the authenticity of the Soviet Purge Trials was greatly bolstered by the book of Joseph Davies, the American ambassador during the trials, who was innocent of any understanding the Soviet system, including its judicial procedures and political trials.)

Few of those I spoke to were inclined to separate theory from practice, and they generally held Marxism responsible in part or in full for what transpired on behalf of these ideas. Gyorgy Konrad said, "An ideal is worth only as much as it means in practice." A Slovenian writer pointed out that Marx was anxious to change the world, not merely to theorize about it—mere theorizing was an activity Marx held in some contempt. Nor did Marx make any bones about the necessity of violence (the midwife imagery) to bring about the cleansing revolution. A Czech informant (an academic-intellectual and an early critic of the regime) blamed Marxist theory—its militancy and its aspiration to build a classless society—for the evils of the system. Another Czech informant, Ivan Klima, blamed Marxism for its support of class hatred; he also noted the intolerance the theory fostered. Klima suggested that the promises of Marxism impressed intellectuals chronically dissatisfied with reality. A Slovenian writer located the responsibility of Marxist theory for the character of these systems in the pursuit of equality, a condition, he believed is alien to human nature, hence its pursuit was bound to lead to the use of force. Mihaly Bihari, author, academic, and prominent critic of the Kadar regime, as well as a recent socialist member of the Hungarian parliament, said that "only the most dogmatic true believers could argue that nothing was wrong with the theory," that it was only human nature or the practical problems which led to the well-known results; a major error of Marxism was the belief that history is the history of class struggles. He was also among several informants who emphasized the important differences between developments in Hungary and in the Soviet Union: in Hungary the Party itself was ripe for reform, a huge reform-oriented intelligentsia existed, at least half of them Party members; trends for reform were strong within the Party. In addition, as others also stressed, the Kadar regime was inhibited by its guilt over the repressions which followed the Revolution of 1956; the peaceful transfer of power to the opposition (in 1989) was strongly influenced by the fear of a recurrence of the bloodshed of 1956. Some put it even more strongly; a Soviet trained Hungarian journalist believed the Party committed virtual suicide: its internal debates sapped its energy.

My informants widely believed that economic failures and malfunctioning were major causes of the collapse, a Czech informant suggesting that such failures contributed to the decay mainly by undermining the self-confidence of the ruling elite: "Hardships are more acceptable if they are justified or backed up by conviction."

Hardly anyone I spoke to believed that Soviet leaders—at any rate, in the post-Khrushchev period—were motivated by ideological convictions. For the most part, they viewed the leaders as cynical, opportunistic, and interested only in preserving their power and privileges. Yet Klima emphasized that the system needed ideology to function. Rezso Nyers, a Hungarian moderate who used to be a high-ranking official in charge of economic affairs during the Kadar era, noted that many officials in Hungary, including Gyorgy Aczel, disagreed with policies they nonetheless implemented, though they sometimes complained about them in private. He perceived the root of these attitudes in their unexamined youthful commitments as well as the pressure of Party discipline.

Some among the Hungarian informants had no wish to repudiate the Kadar regime and its performance during the 1960s and 1970s—or their own participation in it—viewing the system as a worthwhile experiment, an attempt to meld some liberal freedoms with socialist controls and egalitarian policies.

Several informants noted (as have many Western historians during the past half-century and more) that, according to Marxist theory, revolutionary change was supposed to take place in highly developed Western Europe, not in backward Russia. Another recurring notion was that the Soviet Union was essentially an expansionist country, and once expansion came to a halt, the loss of momentum further undermined the shaky legitimacy of the system. As one respondent (a Soviet-trained historian and former dean at Budapest University) put it, "The system could not absorb its conquests."

As far as sources of disillusionment are concerned, aside from a wide range of personal experiences which do not lend themselves to easy classification and summation, the impact of Khrushchev's Twentieth Party Congress speech was cited the most often. A Soviet informant (historian and former Komsomol functionary) recalled how that speech confirmed some remarks that his Stalinist father (a commissar in the army) had made much earlier about repression in the army. Several Hungarian respondents also mentioned the Imre Nagy speech in Hungary in the summer of 1953, which, while not going nearly as far as Khrushchev's, included admissions of the serious shortcomings of the system. The Rajk and Slansky trials also planted seeds of doubt, even in those who initially treated them as authentic.

Increasing contacts with or exposure to the West through reading, travel, or study were especially important for the Hungarians during the 1970s and 1980s, although Czech as well as Slovenian informants also had such opportunities. Many thought that the "root cause" of the collapse of communist systems was the increasing number of people who knew how far behind the West the socialist countries of Eastern Europe were, especially in regard to access to consumer goods. The moral bankruptcy of the Brezhnev regime was also frequently mentioned, including the lack of conviction of the Soviet leaders. One informant (Miklos Szinetar) recalled the anecdote about Brezhnev telling a joke to Willy Brandt: "What would Marx say if he were still alive? Workers of the world, forgive me." That Brezhnev would tell such a joke was an unmistakable sign of moral corrosion at the highest level, and there were many other signs as well. In a similar spirit, Michael Radu (in *Collapse or Decay?*) writes that "as a citizen of Ceausescu's Romania during the 1970s this author heard the best political jokes not from the enemies of the regime but from Securitate [political police] agents, an experience common throughout most of Eastern Europe."

A shared observation of the four Slovenian writers was that Marxism was unable to deal with ethnic problems—a weakness former citizens of Yugoslavia found especially significant. Another important experience they shared—and one which provides another example of the failure of Marxism to anticipate the accumulation and abuse of power in the hands of a few— was that of the privileges of Tito. Every one of the Slovenians also mentioned critically the failed experiment of the workers' councils in Yugoslavia, held in great respect by many Western intellectuals as a pioneering method of transferring power and self-determination to the workers.

I asked all the informants about specific personal experiences or incidents which undermined their faith in the system. Here are a few. Gyorgy Konrad, as a teenager, saw a man, apparently just released from the headquarters of the Hungarian KGB (AVH) in Budapest, crying as he embraced a woman waiting for him on the street. A Czech academic intellectual, as a child, learned that a neighbor was put away for twenty-five years after confessing to imaginary crimes; someone he also knew at the time made a bonfire of Party newspapers and was sent to the uranium mines for doing so. A Hungarian journalist recalled his dismay at the solemn burial of a coal miner, a "shock worker" who was crushed by rocks while trying to overfulfill his production quota. A prominent former dissident and journalist (Janos Kenedi), when in his early teens, served as a courier during the 1956 Revolution and later learned that highly qualified engineers had been forced to work as laborers for supporting of the Revolution; in 1968 he was further radicalized by the Soviet intervention in Czechoslovakia. A Party intellectual prominent in the agitprop branch of the Kadar regime recalled witnessing the rape of Hungarian women by Soviet soldiers in 1945 and reporting it to the Soviet military authorities—an action illustrating his youthful belief in the Soviet authorities. For a former Soviet journalist and assistant press secretary of Gorbachev (Sergei Grigoriev), the political awakening came in the library of Singapore University on his first trip abroad, where as a student he came upon the forbidden fruit of Western historical and social scientific writings. Another Soviet informant, a former middle-level Party functionary, currently head of a furniture company in Russia, recalled how during an election campaign he was told quite matter-of-factly by his superiors to report a higher voter turnout in his district than was the actual case; everyone else was doing this. A Slovenian informant talked about the luxurious way of life of Tito and the fact that when Tito took over a palatial residence on the shore of Lake Bled, ordinary mortals were not allowed to walk anywhere near, whereas no such restrictions existed when the king of Yugoslavia had lived in the same palace.

In one way or another most informants alluded to the theory-practice gap in accounting both for their own disenchantment and for the general delegitimation of the system. A Russian historian at Voronezh University made numerous references to the privileges and hypocrisy of the nomenklatura, comparing them to "a priest who says one thing in the church and something totally different when he steps out of it." Alluding to Party officials with whom he was personally acquainted, he said, "I could not respect a person who had two truths, one for the common people and another for the privileged elite." He recalled a Party secretary "who told everybody that he hated red caviar but who ate it just because other people could not afford to buy it." Losing trust in the people who represented the Party and its official beliefs was followed by losing respect for Party ideology. A Hungarian informant recalled how a Party official he knew managed to avoid any punishment for running over somebody in his car.

Those interviewed shared political and social attitudes which had far more to do with their experience of living under a political system imposed by or modeled upon the former Soviet Union than with the peculiarities of their respective cultures and countries.

Notes

CHAPTER 1 The Human Factor in the Failure of Communism

1. By communist systems I mean those that (1) legitimated themselves with some version of Marxism-Leninism, (2) were ruled by a single party (usually called "communist"), (3) placed the economy under state control, and (4) were in effect police states. Most of them were initially modeled after and allied with the Soviet Union. Archie Brown offers similar defining features. [See Brown 1996: 310.] The precise contribution the Marxist ideological heritage made to the institutional arrangements of these states remains in some dispute.

2. For a study of the links between personality and politics see Greenstein 1969. Another little-known and valuable study that focuses on individuals in order to understand larger political issues is Hruby 1980, which examines the evolution of the attraction to and disenchantment with the communist system experienced by a group of Czech intellectuals.

3. Maier 1997: 38.

4. For a summary survey of popular dissatisfaction see "The Nature of Discontent with Communist Systems" [in Hollander, *Decline and Discontent*, 1992].

5. A recent study making use of newly accessible archival materials reaches the conclusion that "communist ideology not only mattered but actually determined the behavior of East bloc leaders." [Quoted in McMillan 1997: 20.]

6. Tsipko in Yakovlev 1993: xviii.

7. Possibly the only systematic study of defectors in English is Krasnov 1985.

8. Berlin 1969: 91, 45, 115.

9. Boldin 1994: 296.

10. For an American assertion of this position see Schweizer 1994.

11. Vladimir Pozner, who used to be a journalist-propagandist for the Soviet Union and who frequently appeared on American television during the 1980s (a child of American communist parents who moved to the USSR), writes of his own change of heart: "The more Soviet society changed . . . the more I changed with it." [Pozner 1992: 97.] Pozner means that the change in Soviet society made it easier for him (and others) to entertain critical sentiments repressed earlier, because public criticism became widespread and legitimate.

12. Brown 1996: 316–317. See also Kennan 1996: 316.

13. Zubok and Pleshakov 1996: 5, xii.

14. Gellner, "Introduction," in Glebov and Crowfoot 1989: xiv.

15. Kuran, "Inevitability," 1995: 1528.

16. Ulam 1992: 382.

17. Shevchenko 1985: 239.

18. Zubok and Pleshakov 1996: 77, 276.

19. Gellner in Glebov and Crowfoot 1989: xvii.

20. Szasz 1971: 223.

21. Csepeli and Orkeny 1992: 1. Walter Laqueur writes: "The sudden collapse [is] difficult to explain even in retrospect. Why did the huge edifice collapse without even having been seriously challenged?" [Laqueur 1994: 71.] It was subsequently claimed that the CIA predicted the Soviet collapse, largely on economic grounds. [See Berkowitz and Richelson 1995.]

22. Talbot, introduction to Arbatov 1992: 10; Dallin 1992: 282; see also Kirkpatrick 1990: 274.

23. Kapuscinski 1994: 314; see also Draper 1992: 7; and Chirot in Chirot 1991: 12.

24. Quoted in Powers 1996: 20.

25. Laqueur 1994: 57, 59, 99.

26. Quoted in *Freedom Review,* 1992 : 7.

27. Quoted in Laqueur 1994: 120, 211.

28. Lewin 1988: 131, 133.

29. "Cracked Crystal Ball," 1979: 136, 141; Pipes 1984: 50, 60.

30. David Pryce-Jones points out that "the facade was completely false. An unbroken history of dissent, strikes, uprisings and armed rebellions was ruthlessly suppressed from the rest of the world in order to pretend to communist unity and solidarity." [Pryce-Jones 1995: 36.]

31. Malia in Brinton and Rinzler 1990: 405.

32. Gaddis 1997: 292, 222.

33. Richard Pipes has suggested that "the fiasco of Sovietology . . . may well have had its root cause in the determination of political scientists to act like physicists or biologists . . . But . . . the study of mankind differs fundamentally from the study of nature . . . in part because unlike molecules and cells, human beings have values and objectives that preclude their being analyzed in a value-free, unteleological manner." [Pipes 1995: 160, 156.]

34. Lipset and Bence 1994: 202.

35. For a statement of Soviet successes in the Third World see Rubinstein 1988: 565.

36. For example, Bertell Ollman has written: "Paradoxically enough, the objective conditions for socialism in the USSR are now largely present, but because of the unhappy experience with a regime that called itself 'socialist' the subjective conditions are absent . . . On the other hand . . . the Soviet Union might be saved by a socialist revolution in the West as our capitalist economy goes into a tailspin." [Ollman 1991: 460.]

37. Heller and Nekrich 1986: 730; Djilas 1998: 315.

38. Shevchenko 1985: 487–488.

39. Sejna 1984: 100–103, 109–111.

40. Zubok and Pleshakov 1996: 181.

41. Quoted in Shipler 1983: 194; see also Sharansky 1988: 31.

42. Quoted in Pryce-Jones 1995: 24.

43. Aksyonov 1992: 612.

44. Cottrell 1998: 40; quoted in *Freedom Review,* 1992: 6.

45. Solnick 1998: 2, 5.

46. Kuran, *Private Truth,* 1995: 262, 275, 119.

47. Loebl 1976: 228.

48. Konrad 1991: 179; Kuran, "Inevitability," 1995: 1529.

49. Adam Ulam points out "how trivial in comparison with its past disorders were the ailments that afflicted it [the Soviet regime] in the beginning of the 1980s . . . a lowered rate of growth of the GNP . . . an elderly and somnolent ruling oligarchy; active dissent by just a tiny segment of the intelligentsia" [Ulam 1992: 389.] Chirot also emphasizes the relative unimportance of economic factors in the unraveling. [See Chirot in Chirot 1991: 4, 9.]

50. Somin 1994: 84. See also Jowitt 1997: 43; and Odom 1998: 393–394.

51. Lowenhardt 1995: 48.

52. Kennan 1996: 51.

53. Dallin 1992: 286–287, 298; quoted in Pryce-Jones 1995: 365.

54. Quoted in Kaiser 1991: 379.

55. Remnick, May 1996: 45.

56. J. Steele 1994: 78, 202, 209.

57. Vadim Bakatin's description of disorder and irresoluteness among the conspirators confirms these assessments. [Bakatin 1992: 9–22.]

58. "Conversation with Robert Conquest," 1993: 10.

59. Mikoyan, Gromyko, and Frol Koslov, respectively. This information was imparted in Moscow in 1959 during a meeting between those quoted and Averell Harriman. [Quoted in Gaddis 1997: 242.]

60. George Paloczi-Horvath, a Hungarian journalist who spent several years in communist prisons, has speculated on the mentality of his tormentors: "Utter degradation and unbearable pain leave curious traces on the subconscious mind. They lead to almost senseless moral perfectionism in some people and to a pent-up craving for revenge in others. This latter type feels that by his past suffering he is justified in doing anything." [Paloczi-Horvath 1959: 207.]

61. See Clark and Wildavski 1990: 322. Charles Maier was similarly puzzled in regard to East Germany, noting that "world history offers no recent parallel for such a peaceful ideological rout," pointing to the "quick demoralization of the rulers," and asking, "How do we explain the virtual abdication of authority?" [Maier 1997: 58, 56, 57.]

62. Malia 1993: 80.

63. Clark and Wildavsky 1990. Chirot also emphasizes the "moral bankruptcy" and "moral rot" of the system as a prime cause of its collapse. [Chirot 1991: 14, 20.]

64. Kennan 1996: 254.

65. Figes, September 1995: 7.

66. Stanley, December 1995. According to Robert Conquest, Volkogonov's learning

during the 1980s of Stalin's massacre of Soviet officers in the 1930s was the beginning of his disillusionment. [Conquest 1995: 8.]

67. Pipes, "Seeds," 1996: 9; quoted in Remnick, *Lenin's Tomb*, 1993: 408–409.

68. It is similarly puzzling, to take an American example, why it took approximately half a century for Herbert Aptheker (lifelong supporter and leading intellectual of the Communist Party of the United States) to reach the conclusion that the Soviet system was "authoritarian, brutal and guilty of colossal crimes" [Klehr and Haynes 1992: 12] while he used to denounce those among his colleagues who had reached similar conclusions much earlier.

69. Aksyonov 1994.

70. Aksyonov 1992: 613.

71. See, for example, Shane 1994.

72. Andrew and Gordievsky 1990: 624. See also Dallin 1992, esp. pp. 293, 295.

73. Boldin 1994: 35–36, 281–282, 284. See also Brezinski 1989, esp. pp. 30–40.

74. Brezhneva 1995: 218.

75. Ibid., 226, 232, 233, 242–243, 351.

76. Ibid., 148, 159, 184, 185, 184.

77. Ibid., 162.

78. Palazchenko 1997: 21. According to Archie Brown, there was a long-term trend in the decline of ideological conviction: "*The declared aim of building communism . . .* may have been already ritualistic for Communist leaders by the 1970s. (Khrushchev was perhaps the last believer in the withering away of the state . . .) Under Gorbachev . . . the character of Soviet discourse changed. Increasingly influential reformers spoke of a better and different 'socialism' rather than of 'communism' and by 1990 many of them had abandoned socialism as well." [Brown 1996: 313.]

79. Klima, "On Honesty," in Klima 1994: 95.

80. Quoted in Brinton and Rinzler 1990: 239–240.

81. For an extended examination of this phenomenon see also Kuran, *Private Truth*, 1995, chap. 16.

82. Quoted in Brinton and Rinzler: 401.

83. Dobrynin 1995: 611.

84. Ibid., 612, 615.

85. Fantel 1995.

86. Quoted in Koch 1994: 241.

87. Quoted in Larina 1993: 127. On the other hand, Andrei Sakharov, the nuclear scientist and later one of the most prominent and influential critics of the Soviet system, while engaged in secret research on the atomic bomb "lived for eighteen years . . . near a slave labor camp, and every morning he watched long lines of prisoners trudge to and from it, guard dogs at their heels." [Remnick, *Lenin's Tomb*, 1993: 166.] Apparently Sakharov managed to overlook this vista, morally speaking, until much later, when (presumably) it became one of the elements which ignited his doubts and moral indignation.

88. Quoted in Remnick, *Lenin's Tomb*, 1993: 114.

89. Hegedus 1988: 283.

90. Meray 1983: 282.

91. It has been written of the late Marshall Voroshilov, who was by no means exceptionally ruthless by Soviet standards, that "he had sent his comrades to the firing squad but loved animals; he had obtained bread for the starving children of Petrograd but kept his refrigerator locked and inaccessible to his own grandchildren." [Brezhneva 1995: 231.]

92. Volkogonov 1990: 238.

93. Stalin reportedly remarked that "to choose one's victims, to prepare one's plans minutely, to slake an implacable vengeance, and then go to bed . . . there is nothing sweeter in the world." [Quoted in Souvarine 1939: 485.]

94. For a discussion of such differences see Hollander 1994. See also Benoist 1998, esp. p. 186.

95. Adorno's famous study was the major source of these mistaken beliefs. For a critique see especially Edward Shils, "Authoritarianism, Right and Left," in Christie and Jahoda 1954.

96. A rare exception to this generalization is a largely forgotten book by Zevedei Barbu, an author of Romanian origin, who compared Nazi and Soviet totalitarianism and the types of people attracted to those ideologies. [See Barbu 1956.] Nathan Leites, in his similarly forgotten book [Leites 1953], also discusses certain aspects of the social psychology of the founders of the Soviet system.

97. Quoted in Resis 1993: 278.

98. Zubok and Pleshakov 1996: 82.

99. Kennan, October 1988: 4.

100. Quoted in Remnick, *Lenin's Tomb*, 1993: 442.

101. Tyler 1996.

102. Greenhouse 1991.

103. Quoted in "For the Record," 1993: 9.

104. Shenon 1991: 3.

105. Stanley 1991; "Communism Is Not Dead, " 1991.

106. "On with the Show," 1993: 24.

107. Kinzer 1993; Honecker quoted in Puddington 1993: 64.

108. Quoted in Rosenberg 1995: 331. A postcommunist publication in Hungary described Honecker as "one of the last among the generation of petty and predictable functionaries who had replaced the earlier generation of stylish mass murderers." According to a German psychoanalyst, Reimer Hinrichs, quoted in the article, "Having become a functionary at age 17 in the communist movement, Honecker became intellectually stunted, emotionally paralyzed and rigid, obsessed with power, narcissistic, with a streak of sadism." [*Magyar Narancs*, July 1994: 19.]

109. Quoted in "Gorbachev-Yeltsin Session," 1991: 6.

110. Quoted in "We Weren't Following Orders," 1996.

111. Sudetic 1990: 6.

112. Ibid.

113. The eruptions include the East German uprising in 1953, the uprisings in Hungary and Poland in 1956, the Czech attempt to transform the system in

1968, and the guerrilla wars in Afghanistan, Angola, Ethiopia, Mozambique, Nicaragua, and Tibet.

114. Crossman 1949.

115. See, for example, Konrad and Szelenyi 1976.

116. Joseph Revai was the prototypical Party intellectual, *the* leading Hungarian Party intellectual and a member of the top leadership in the postwar years. He personified both intolerance of free expression and elitism. While mercilessly criticizing and silencing writers unwilling to abide by the rules and regulations of socialist realism or insufficiently reverential of their Soviet literary role models, he regularly ordered for himself the latest works of Thomas Mann and other Western writers which he would not allow to be published in Hungary.

117. The ready acceptance in recent years on the part of so many American academics of the imposition of speech codes and other restrictions on the free exchange of ideas on American college campuses is another illustration of the weak attachment of many Western intellectuals to the values of free expression.

118. An early attempt to probe such matters is to be found in Leites 1953.

CHAPTER 2 Defectors and Exiles: Disillusionment Before the Fall

1. There are some exceptions to this proposition. Arguably, the writings of Solzhenitsyn did far more to discredit the system than did the expression of discontent by many critics who stayed.

2. The concept of cognitive dissonance was introduced by Leon Festinger (1957) and refers to situations which compel believers to explain away facts which contradict their beliefs.

3. Soviet soldiers captured by Germans during World War II were coercively repatriated en masse by American and British troops after the war in deference to the Yalta agreement. [See Bethell 1974; see also Epstein 1973; Tolstoy 1977.] The fear of being returned was poignantly rendered by an escaped Soviet pilot who resolved that if that happened, he would "hold [a] nail to his temple at the decisive moment and bang his head against the wall with all his strength." [Pirogov 1950:5.] Similar determination was shown by a Soviet woman defector who, after being recaptured by Soviet diplomats, jumped from the window of the Soviet consulate in New York. [Kasenkina 1949.] In a case not widely publicized but personally known to me, a Soviet exchange scholar at Harvard University repeatedly tried to commit suicide in 1964 owing to the conflicts that his defection created and the pressures put on him by the Soviet authorities. After recovering from a nervous breakdown he was returned to the Soviet Union under circumstances which left unclear what his own preference had been. A limited survey of Soviet kidnappings of defectors from abroad may be found in "Border Controls," in Hollander 1983.

4. An exception is Krasnov 1985. See also Tanenhaus 1990. For a Soviet émigré writer's view of defectors see Voinovich 1985: 54–60.

5. Schuman 1946: 667–668.

6. Laqueur 1994: 23.

7. A history of the "Iron Curtain"—that is, the measures taken to prevent unauthorized departures from communist states—remains to be written. A limited examination of these policies can be found in "Border Controls," in Hollander 1983.

8. See, for example, Pacepa 1987: 189 regarding Ceausescu's attitude toward defectors. The author was the head of Romanian intelligence services.

9. Serge 1963: 358.

10. Ibid., 372.

11. Ibid., 374, 262.

12. Ibid., 1.

13. Ibid., 374–375.

14. Ibid., 68.

15. Ibid., 89, 148–149.

16. Ibid., 99.

17. Kopelev 1980: 118–119.

18. Serge 1963: 131, 125, 128, 129.

19. Ibid., 233.

20. Ibid., 261.

21. On the other hand, a delegation of Soviet writers in Paris which included Ilya Ehrenburgh, Mikhail Koltsov, and Nikolai Tikhonov "fulfilled instructions and declared without a blink that they knew nothing of the writer Victor Serge— these, my good colleagues of the Soviet Writers' Union! All they knew of was . . . 'a confessed counter-revolutionary.'" [Serge 1963: 318.]

22. Ibid., 264, 273–274, 280, 322.

23. The difference between the ideological underpinnings and rhetoric of Nazism and Soviet communism may be the key to the very different responses of Western intellectuals toward Nazi Germany and the Soviet Union under Stalin—two dictatorships exacting immense human sacrifices in the pursuit of their objectives. Although the Nazi rhetoric was greatly inferior to the Soviet, there was little divergence between Nazi theory and practice. In the Soviet case, the corresponding divergence was substantial and was overlooked for several decades or rationalized in terms of the lofty goals pursued.

24. Serge 1963: 112–113.

25. Ibid., 266, 238.

26. Ibid., 188, 191–192.

27. Aron 1957: 35, 42–43.

28. The essay of the same title is in Enzensberger 1974.

29. Serge 1963: 313.

30. Ibid., 348.

31. Kravchenko 1946: 436.

32. Spiegel 1966: 1, 9.

33. Kravchenko 1946: 2 and, on how he arrived at the decision to defect, 452–453.

34. Books such Smith 1936, Souvarine 1939, Ciliga 1940, Krivitsky 1940, and Barmine 1945 had little impact and garnered little publicity.

35. Kravchenko 1946: 468.

36. Ibid., 3, 473.
37. Ibid. 36–37, 50–51, 55.
38. Ibid., 63.
39. Ibid., 86–87.
40. Ibid., 92.
41. Ibid., 91, 105, 107, 118, 105. For a major Western study of the famine see Conquest 1987.
42. Kravchenko 1946: 122, 132.
43. Ibid., 153, 172, 185.
44. Ibid., 215, 216–217, 446–447.
45. Ibid., 178.
46. Ibid., 278.
47. Ibid., 323, 412.
48. Ibid., 279, 284–285, 284.
49. Ibid., 296, 297, 415.
50. Ibid., 318.
51. Ibid., 396–397, 418–419.
52. Ibid., 393, 414.
53. Ibid., 189, 312.
54. Ibid., 305.
55. Ibid., 299, 422.
56. Ibid., 198.
57. Ibid., 327.
58. Ibid., 199, 201, 204.
59. Ibid., 452.
60. Shevchenko 1985: 5.
61. Ibid., 18.
62. Ibid., 469, 455, 466.
63. Ibid., 21, 231–232. For further discussion of elite privilege see also pp. 424–425.
64. Ibid., 24, 25, 115.
65. Ibid., 69–70, 71, 86, 88.
66. Ibid., 98, 113, 124.
67. Ibid., 485.
68. Barron 1987.
69. Grigorienko, 1982: x.
70. Ibid., 16, 17, 18.
71. Ibid., 36.
72. Ibid., 39.
73. Ibid., 40.
74. Ibid., 41, 42.
75. Ibid., 62, 63.
76. Ibid., 74, 95–96, 98.
77. Ibid., 103–104.
78. Ibid., 116, 139, 201.
79. Ibid., 215.

80. Ibid., 171.
81. Ibid., 144, 182, 183–184.
82. Ibid., 192.
83. Ibid., 200.
84. Ibid., 174.
85. Ibid., 207–208.
86. Ibid., 216.
87. Ibid., 222.
88. Ibid., 240, 231, 240.
89. Ibid., 265, 267, 270.
90. Ibid., 271, 274, 285, 288. Other dissidents also report the perplexity of inter-rogators unable to comprehend the motivation of those who became critics of the system. Valentyn Moroz writes: "The KGB officer[s] . . . were all 'reeducat-ing' me. 'Well, what did you want? You had a good job, an apartment . . .' They spent several hours trying to prove that a man has nothing more than a stomach and so many meters of intestines." [Moroz 1968: 86.]
91. Leonhard 1958: 516.
92. This is again the technique of reasoning that Arthur Koestler calls "the doc-trine of unshaken foundations." [Koestler 1945: 165.]
93. Leonhard 1958: 51–52, 53, 55.
94. Ibid., 89.
95. The same attitude was apparent among Western intellectuals who did not ben-efit from the training that Leonhard received. [Hollander 1981: e.g., 423–425.] Apparently human beings gravitate to such modes of thinking in defense of deeply held values or beliefs; often these attitudes are a response to cognitive dissonance.
96. Leonhard 1958: 20.
97. Ibid., 74.
98. Ibid., 44, 55–56.
99. Ibid., 116–117.
100. For a discussion of criticism–self-criticism see Hollander 1983: 115–126.
101. Leonhard 1958: 249–250, 251.
102. Koestler 1961: 123–124.
103. Leonhard 1958: 165, 181–182.
104. Ibid., 194, 186.
105. Ibid., 231.
106. Ibid., 370–371, 390–391, 393.
107. Ibid., 476–477, 477–478.
108. Ibid., 477–478.
109. Ibid., 202–203, 441.
110. Ibid., 502, 503–504, 504–505.
111. Ibid., 496, 498.
112. Sejna 1982: 13, 16, 17, 159, 18.
113. Ibid., 159.
114. Ibid., 21.

115. Ibid., 23, 24.
116. Ibid., 24, 36.
117. Ibid., 29, 32, 33, 70.
118. Ibid., 86, 164.
119. Ibid., 166–167, 165.
120. Ibid., 158.
121. Ibid., 159.
122. Ibid., 160, 160–161, 162.
123. Ibid., 163, 164.
124. Ibid., 34, 35, 162.
125. Ibid., 186.
126. Ibid., 186.
127. Ibid., 187, 190–191, 189.
128. A more negative portrait of Sejna emerges from the recollections of Jiri Hochman, translator and editor of Dubcek's autobiography. Hochman questions Sejna's idealism and recalls his involvement in black marketing and other shady deals. [Personal communication, July 1997.]
129. Sejna 1982: 16.
130. Ibid., 16.

CHAPTER 3 Soviet Leaders: The Reformers

1. Colburn 1994: 89, 90, 94.
2. Brown 1996: 308. Natan Sharansky, former Soviet dissident and political prisoner, was far more skeptical; see Sharansky 1997.
3. In Conquest, foreword to Sudoplatov and Sudoplatov 1994: x.
4. Quoted in Mary McCarthy, *Intellectual Memoirs: New York, 1936–1938* (New York: Harcourt Brace, 1992), 43. For further comments on the difficulty of the autobiographical enterprise see Wat 1988: 9.
5. The point needs qualification in light of the ascendance of confessional autobiographies in recent years in the United States. These volumes, redolent with experiences of victimization, include bouts of self-reproach; perhaps their authors hope to be accorded instant absolution in recompense for their candor. Politicians and celebrities in the world of entertainment are the most frequent producers of such writings.
6. M. Gorbachev 1987: 69.
7. Mlynar 1990: 25.
8. To what degree his behavior and policies after becoming president of the Russian Republic invalidate or discredit his earlier positions and beliefs is difficult to decide. I believe that his rejection of the communist system was genuine; his subsequent behavior may be ascribed to the familiar corruptions of power and undue attachment to it.
9. Keller 1996: 9.
10. Shlapentokh 1990: 102.
11. Orlov 1991: 315.

12. A member of his family, his grandfather, was executed in 1937. [See Bakatin 1992: 31.]

13. Even Gorbachev's interpreter's grandmother was arrested "as a former member of the 'Trotsky-Zinoviev opposition'" in 1949. [See Palazchenko 1997: 2.]

14. Volkogonov "had lost both his parents to Stalin's terror in the late 1930s when his father was shot and his mother deported to a concentration camp." [Pipes, "Seeds," 1996: 9.] These recollections, revived during glasnost, may well have fueled his fierce critiques of the system, conveyed in his biographies of the three founding fathers, Lenin, Stalin, and Trotsky.

15. Aczel was a provincial Party secretary in 1950 when a childhood friend and his wife were arrested: "As soon as he learned of their arrest he rushed to Budapest and went to the Central Party building . . . to vouch for the innocence of his friends; he was referred to the AVH (state security) headquarters, where a colonel listened with great interest . . . rang for the guard and had him escorted straight down to the cellar." [Hodos 1987: 89.] After 1956 Aczel was put in charge of Hungarian cultural affairs, which he controlled in a more permissive manner than his predecessors had. Janos Kadar, not discussed in this volume, was installed as the new head of the Party in Hungary by the Soviet Union after it had crushed the Revolution of 1956; in the early 1950s, under Rakosi, he had been jailed and tortured.

16. Jaruzelski of Poland, who sought to suppress the Solidarity movement, was in the Soviet Gulag as a teenager. During World War II his family was interned in Siberia and nearly starved to death. [See Rosenberg 1995: xxii, 129.] Rokossovsky too was Polish born but moved to the USSR with his family at an early age. "He was a veteran of . . . Lubyanka prison and the Siberian camps and had been tortured by the NKVD." Jaruzelski of all people wrote of him: "How can you explain that a man who was a victim of Stalinist terror gave his approval to the execution of men when the only proof of their guilt was a confession extracted under torture?" [Quoted in ibid., 136.]

17. When the Politburo voted on the fate of Molotov's wife, he did not dissent. [Zubok and Pleshakov 1996: 80.] His wife was arrested in 1949 and "charged with abuses of power in the cosmetics and textile trust that she directed and then with loss of secret documents," as well as with having had sexual relations with two officials in her ministry. It was also held against her that she met Golda Meir before the October Revolution or during the Civil War. [Sudoplatov and Sudoplatov 1994: 327.] Molotov's reminiscences do not suggest that this incident led him to reassess his loyalty to the system or to Stalin.

18. Gromyko 1990: 379.

19. Brezhneva 1995: 64–65.

20. Sudoplatov and Sudoplatov 1994: 62.

21. Gellner, "Introduction," in Glebov and Crowfoot 1989: xiii.

22. Medvedev 1986: vii.

23. Tatu 1991: 10.

24. Kaiser 1991: 23; see also Brown 1996: 25.

25. Ruge 1991: 16–17. Kaiser too believes that because "Gorbachev was six in 1937,

the worst year of Stalin's Great Terror . . . he was old enough to absorb the traumas that struck his own family during those terrifying times." [Kaiser 1991: 22.]

26. Medvedev 1986: 27.

27. M. Gorbachev 1996: 24.

28. Jurgens 1990: 18.

29. Quoted in Tatu 1991: 21. But according to Brown, her dissertation "was solid empirical research and by no means apologetics." [Brown 1996: 34.] Raisa Gorbachev's ideological zeal manifested itself in her meetings with Nancy Reagan, whom she repeatedly lectured on Marxist-Leninism. [Reagan with Novak 1989: 338–339.]

30. Boldin 1994: 85.

31. Remnick, *Lenin's Tomb*, 1993: 149.

32. Ibid., 194.

33. Ruge 1991: 241–242; see also M. Gorbachev 1996: 59.

34. Brown 1996: 31. In turn, Medvedev believes that sharing a room at Moscow University with Mlynar for five years must have been a "profound influence" on Gorbachev. [Medvedev 1986: 43.] On the other hand, Mlynar himself has undergone considerable political transformations over time (see Chapter 5). He was a loyal functionary in training when he went to the Soviet Union.

35. M. Gorbachev 1996: 66.

36. Ibid., 47.

37. Quoted in Tatu 1991: 77.

38. Brown 1996: 118–119.

39. Kaiser 1991: 18, 19.

40. Brown 1996: 121, 308.

41. Malia in Brinton and Rinzler 1990: 429.

42. Sobchak 1992: 128, 129.

43. M. Gorbachev 1987: 10.

44. Ibid.

45. Pipes 1987: 34.

46. M. Gorbachev 1996: 239–240, 329.

47. Shevchenko 1985: 489.

48. Simes 1995: 60; Bodzaban and Szalay 1994: 64, 66.

49. Kennan, January 1988: 6.

50. Brown 1996: 93.

51. M. Gorbachev 1987: 21–22.

52. Ibid., 10–11, 18–19, 21–22, 24, 25.

53. Brown 1996: 120, 155.

54. Quoted in Kissinger 1993.

55. Quoted in Mlynar 1990: 171.

56. Rush 1993: 22–23. More recently, Jack F. Matlock, Jr., has written that he was the kind of person the "nomenklatura's filtering apparatus . . . was designed to exclude." [Matlock, December 1996: 34.]

57. Brown 1996: 29.

58. Quoted in ibid., 316.

59. Leonhard 1986: 2.

60. Oates 1988: 19, 16.

61. *People*, December 1988: 33. In the same year a Gallup poll found him among the ten most admired men in the United States; it was the first time a Soviet leader appeared on this list. [See "Gorbachev and Hart,"1988.]

62. Boldin writes: "Had it not been for the support of Western leaders and part of Western public opinion . . . he [Gorbachev] would long ago have been fully isolated, living in fear of his own people's anger." [Boldin 1994: 295.] Archie Brown takes a highly negative view of Boldin ("a self-centered careerist") and questions his credibility. [Brown 1996: 103, 33, 103.]

63. Tatu 1991: 42; Boldin 1994: 32.

64. Brown 1996: 42–43; see also pp. 115, 225–226.

65. M. Gorbachev 1996: 100.

66. Tatu 1991: 5, 12, 26–27.

67. Quoted in Kaiser 1991: 29.

68. Solovyov and Klepikova 1992: 126–127.

69. Ruge 1991: 36–37.

70. Solovyov and Klepikova 1992: 126.

71. Ibid., 154. In a similar spirit Arkady Shevchenko writes: "His territory enjoyed special care and generous funding from Moscow because of the famous Caucasian mineral springs, around which developed resort towns favored by the elite. The mineral waters became . . . a foundation of Gorbachev's rising career . . . As the local party boss, Gorbachev had the opportunity to meet them, many times, and, as the Russians say . . . to show himself at his best." [Shevchenko 1985: 245–246.]

72. Quoted in Tatu 1991: 48–49.

73. M. Gorbachev 1996: 113.

74. Quoted in Ruge 1991: 9.

75. Quoted in Morrison 1991: 15.

76. Voslensky 1984: 213, 212.

77. Boldin 1994: 68.

78. Hollander 1981: 156–160.

79. Quoted in Moore 1989: 27.

80. S. Steele 1992: 52.

81. Orlov 1991: 315, 316.

82. D'Encausse 1993: 232.

83. Quoted in ibid., unnumbered front-matter page.

84. Keller 1987; see also "Separate but Equal Soviet Style" [editorial], *New York Times*, April 21, 1987.

85. Semprun 1980: 138–139.

86. Kapuscinski 1994: 94. Even before perestroika, television could not conceal the physical decrepitude of the last durable ruler, Brezhnev, in his final years.

87. Charles Fairbanks has pointed out that Beria, Malenkov, and Khrushchev also

occasionally practiced what might be called a limited glasnost in order to undermine their opponents in the Party, but neither went as far as Gorbachev. [Personal communication, March 1997.]

88. Sobchak 1992: 168.
89. Ibid., 169, 170.
90. Quoted in Stanley, March 1995: 10.
91. Tatu 1991: vii.
92. Boldin 1994: 298.
93. Ibid., 297.
94. Fairbanks 1993: 48, 50.
95. Ibid., 53, 52.
96. Quoted in Tatu 1991: 105.
97. Tatu 1991: 104.
98. Solovyov and Klepikova 1991: 44. Boldin recalls Gorbachev "changing suits almost daily and meticulously choosing shirts, fashionable ties, and elegant shoes. I was often astonished by how concerned he was with external considerations." [Ibid., 1994: 39.] For further details of Gorbachev's interest in material perks and comforts see Boldin 1994: 195–206. This source also provides a summary of the status privileges of the nomenklatura.
99. Ruge 1991: 77, 102, 103.
100. Jurgens 1990: 140.
101. R. Gorbachev 1991.
102. Yeltsin 1990: 70, 162–163, 157–158, 160; see also Morrison 1991: 48.
103. Remnick, *Lenin's Tomb*, 1993: 195, 515. Yakovlev said in a conversation with me (on September 7, 1998, in Washington, D.C.) that at the present time Yeltsin's privileges greatly exceed those of Gorbachev; he perceived this development as a major misfortune resulting from the corruption that power brings.
104. Yeltsin 1990: 157.
105. Kenneth Murphy writes: "The almost complete absence from the book of explicit moral argument, let alone moral outrage and condemnation . . . follow[s] from the concentration of Gorbachev's attention on the practical problems of action." [Murphy 1992: 338.] These attitudes also followed from Gorbachev's conviction that the fundamentals of the system were not morally problematic and did not have not be tampered with. [See also ibid., 328.]
106. Yeltsin 1990: 165–166.
107. Ibid., 168.
108. Solovyov and Klepikova 1992: 136.
109. Shevchenko 1985: 205; Gromyko 1990: 18; Sudoplatov and Sudoplatov 1994: 413.
110. The conversation took place at the Hoover Institution in Palo Alto, California, on May 4, 1993.
111. Yeltsin 1990: 119, 153–154, 157.
112. Solovyov and Klepikova 1992: 45.
113. Malia 1994: 472.
114. Solovyov and Klepikova 1992: 140, 127.

115. In February 1992 he averred that "the idea of socialism lives on and . . . the quest . . . to find a new form for putting the socialist idea into practice is ongoing." [M. Gorbachev 1992.]

116. Solovyov and Klepikova 1992: 24.

117. Yeltsin 1990: 24, 26, 27.

118. Ibid., 28, 29, 30–31, 33–34, 36, 44.

119. Ibid., 130, 82, 23, 25.

120. Solovyov and Klepikova 1992: 116–118.

121. Ekedahl and Goodman 1997: 29, ix, 30, 43, 65.

122. Quoted in Ligachev 1993: 168.

123. Ibid., 169.

124. Ulam 1992: 395.

125. Ekedahl and Goodman 1997: 7, 12, 133.

126. Ligachev charged him with losing Eastern Europe. [Ligachev 1993: 161.]

127. Shevardnadze 1991: ix.

128. Shevardnadze 1991: 14.

129. Quoted in Montefiore 1993: 18.

130. Shevardnadze 1991: 16.

131. Ibid., 18.

132. Ibid., 19.

133. Ibid., 11–12.

134. Ibid., 12.

135. Ibid., 3, 5.

136. Ibid., 9.

137. Ibid., 20.

138. Ibid., 22.

139. Ibid.

140. Ibid., 23, 24, 56.

141. Ibid., 27, 28.

142. Ibid., 37.

143. Ibid., 26, 54.

144. Horn 1994: 251.

145. Cohen and Heuvel 1989: 34–35.

146. Remington in Yakovlev 1993: vii.

147. Tsipko in Yakovlev 1993: xvi, xx.

148. Yakovlev 1993: 65, 7, 56–57, 8.

149. Cohen and Heuvel 1993: 73, 72. In a conversation with me on September 7, 1998 (in Washington, D.C.), Yakovlev confirmed the negative impact the American media had on him at the time of his stay at Columbia University in New York. He said that "unfortunately" that visit did little to deepen his understanding of Western ways or American society. During his much longer stay in Canada he was impressed by Canadian agriculture and the work ethic of Canadian farmers; he spent a few days living with farmers. For further comments on Yakovlev's earlier negative attitudes toward the United States see "Moscow's Anti-American Reformer" in Kirkpatrick 1990: 38–39.

150. Cohen and Heuvel 1993: 39, 69, 40.
151. Ibid., 37, 44, 45.
152. Ibid., 51, 57.
153. Ibid., 70, 71.
154. Ibid., 42.
155. Keller 1989: 33.
156. Steele 1994: 175. He also confirmed in the 1998 conversation that the visit to Prague in 1968 made a "terrible impression"; he asked Soviet tank drivers why they were there and they had no idea.
157. Yakovlev 1993: 2.
158. Ibid., 4.
159. Ibid., 59, 37.
160. Ibid., 44–45.
161. Ibid., 52.
162. Ibid., 58, 49.
163. Ibid., 9, 54, 15, 29, 17.
164. Ibid., 11, 38.
165. Ibid., 8.
166. Ibid., 60–61.

CHAPTER 4 The Ambivalence of High-Level Functionaries

1. Aksyonov 1992: 614.
2. Strobe Talbot, introduction to Arbatov 1992: x.
3. Pipes 1992: 40.
4. Shevchenko 1985: 279.
5. Palazchenko 1997: 104.
6. Arbatov 1992: 12.
7. Fairbanks 1993: 52.
8. Ligachev 1993: 45–46.
9. Brezhnev declared in 1968 at the time of the invasion of Czechoslovakia that military intervention to assist members of the Socialist Commonwealth threatened by Western "subversion" was legitimate.
10. As reflected in Cohen and Heuvel 1989.
11. Pipes 1992: 40.
12. Quoted in Cohen and Heuvel 1989: 320.
13. Arbatov 1992: 7, 14.
14. Ibid., 4, 22, 23.
15. Ibid., 244.
16. Ibid., 84–85, 200, 223, 224, 225, 244, 246, 251, 250, 347, 353.
17. Pipes 1992: 42.
18. Arbatov 1992: 241.
19. Levchenko 1988: 179. Levchenko defines active measures as "both covert and overt techniques for influencing . . . the behavior of foreign countries . . . [they]

may be used to undermine the confidence a citizenry has in its leaders, to destroy a leader's or a nation's credibility, or to disrupt relations between nations." [Ibid., 326.]

20. Matlock, February 1996: 12.
21. Dobrynin 1995: 618.
22. Matlock, February 1996: 12.
23. Dobrynin 1995: 4–5.
24. Ibid., 6, 15, 472.
25. Ibid., 191, 474, 473.
26. Ibid., 16.
27. Ibid., 220, 511, 605, 615.
28. Ibid., 26.
29. Ibid., 197.
30. Ibid., 546.
31. Ibid., 354, 504.
32. Ibid., 601.
33. Ibid., 170, 179, 183.
34. Ibid., 267, 268, 158, 159.
35. Ibid., 363, 407.
36. Ibid., 438, 444, 446.
37. Ibid., 380, 128.
38. Ibid., 218–219, 130, 276, 278.
39. Ibid., 600, 636, 576, 628.
40. Ibid., 632.
41. Ibid., 638.
42. Ibid., 632, 626–627.
43. A similar point was made in Schoenfield 1995: 69: "He [Dobrynin] does not reprove Soviet foreign policy because it was in any way wrong, because it enslaved whole countries . . . There is not a word of regret in these memoirs for the fate of his countrymen, who by daring to protest the policies of the Kremlin . . . ended up spending long years in prisons . . . [his] indictment of Soviet foreign policy does not rest on ethical grounds . . . morality is a category he does not appear to apprehend."
44. Dobrynin 1995: 16.
45. Ibid., 74–75.
46. Pipes 1995: 38.
47. Matlock, February 1996: 12.
48. Stephen Cohen, introduction to Ligachev 1993: xxxii.
49. Ibid., xxx. It may be noted here that Cohen's highly positive assessments of Gorbachev appear to be colored by a desire to cast him in a role similar to that of Bukharin, another Soviet leader greatly admired by Cohen.
50. Sobchak 1992: 46.
51. Remnick, "Counterrevolutionary," 1993: 38.
52. Schmemann 1993: 7.

53. Horn 1991: 181. Charles Fairbanks was told by Ligachev in 1993 that "'what amazes me in American agriculture is the distribution system.' He had no idea of the market." [Personal communication, March 1997.]

54. J. Steele 1994: 174, 176.

55. Ligachev 1993: 36.

56. Quoted in Remnick, *Lenin's Tomb*, 1993: 187–188.

57. Ligachev 1993: 98, 99.

58. Ibid., 103, 266.

59. Ibid., 286–287, 316.

60. Schmemann 1993: 7.

61. Ligachev 1993: 270, 275.

62. Ibid., 256.

63. Hochschild 1993: 30; see also Hochschild 1994, in which the massacres and their cover-up is further discussed.

64. Ligachev 1993: 255, 257, 258.

65. Ibid., 15, 207. For a further discussion of his attitude toward and experiences with bribes see ibid., 205–206.

66. Shevchenko 1985: 192.

67. Kennan, October 1988: 27. In point of fact, Gromyko, in the American edition of the memoirs, did make reference to the annexation of the Baltics, calling it their "unification with the USSR." [Gromyko 1990: 34.]

68. Gromyko 1990: 537, 316.

69. Ibid., 345.

70. Ibid., 164, 170, 173, 213, 231–232, 292, 297.

71. Ibid., 343.

72. Ibid., 369.

73. Ibid., 369–370, 374.

74. Ibid., 371, 365, 366.

75. Ibid., 353, 354, 363, 372–373.

76. Ibid., 356, 357, 357–358, 364.

77. Ibid., 371.

78. Kennan, October 1988: 5.

79. Even Ilya Ehrenburg, the writer, far more sophisticated than most Party intellectuals, could say that "'no matter what happened . . . however agonizing the doubts,' he kept faith with Stalinism." [Quoted in Ignatieff 1997: 32.]

80. Leites 1953: 105, 109, 114–115.

81. Murphy 1992: 372.

CHAPTER 5 The Political Transformation of East European Leaders

1. Szasz 1971: 221.

2. Meray 1983: 160.

3. Rosenberg 1995: 129.

4. Quoted in Punkosti, *Rakosi a Csucson*, 1996: 370.

5. Quoted in Toranska 1987: 257.

6. Hegedus 1988: 185.

7. Ibid., 187.

8. Hegedus writes: "My generation was not so cut off from Hungarian society as those who returned from Moscow. We had many ties of kinship and friendship to those who either directly experienced or had a feel for the grievances of various social strata or the nation as a whole." [Ibid., 187].

9. Ibid., 169.

10. Ibid., 166.

11. See "Criticism and Self-Criticism," in Hollander 1983: 115–126.

12. Hegedus 1988: 124, 126, 125, 126–127, 129, 128–129.

13. Of the twenty-five individuals interviewed in Hungary some were too young in 1949 to be aware of political events like the Rajk trial; those who were old enough readily acknowledged that, shocked as they had been, they could not imagine that the charges were fabrications. See also the Appendix.

14. Quoted in Rosenberg 1995: 174–175.

15. Hegedus 1988: 188, 149.

16. Ibid., 246, 324.

17. Hegedus 1988: 188, 58, 189, 321, 332, 326.

18. Ibid., 285, 225, 184.

19. Ibid., 246, 195, 220, 252, 272, 273.

20. Personal communication from Rudolf Tokes, a specialist in recent Hungarian politics.

21. Hegedus told me that he became a sociologist in part to better understand the Revolution of 1956.

22. Interview in Budapest in August 1992.

23. Nagy grew up in a small town rather than a village. He was born into a peasant family but his father became a railroad worker; his mother was a domestic servant before getting married.

24. Peter Unwin writes: "For all his human warmth, Nagy at the beginning of 1956 was out of touch with the forces that were beginning to stir men to action. In the Revolution it took him days to reach the understanding that he could not serve both Communism and man and to decide that he must give man priority." [Unwin 1991: 119.]

25. It is far from clear why these writings have not been published even in Hungary.

26. His Hungarian biographer suggests that his communist beliefs "differed in their pragmatic, liberal and national features from those of his times" and that within the communist movement he was seen primarily as a spokesman of the peasantry. [Rainer 1996: 541–542.]

27. Sukosd 1996.

28. Meray 1983: 129.

29. Ibid., 124.

30. Ibid., 38, 45, 55, 126, 328.

31. Quoted in ibid., 384.

32. Ibid., 24–25.

33. Rainer 1996: 351. "Even at the time" refers to 1946, when a coalition government

ruled and when the takeover of Hungary by the Communist Party was still two years away. In 1955 the incident was used by Rakosi to discredit Nagy inside the Party. [Ibid.]

34. Nagy 1957: 43.

35. Unwin 1991: 39–40.

36. Ibid., 230, 232.

37. Meray 1983: 46.

38. Ibid., 90, 273, 274.

39. Quoted in ibid., 70.

40. Nagy 1957: 50.

41. Ibid., 46, 55, 56, 58.

42. Meray 1983: 102, 111–112.

43. Unwin 1991: 118.

44. Dubcek 1993: 1.

45. Ibid., 6, 11.

46. Ibid., 12.

47. Sejna 1982: 181.

48. Ibid., 171–172.

49. Dubcek 1993: 22–23.

50. Dubcek 1993: 26–27, 27.

51. Abundant evidence of his political attitudes can be found Hollander 1981.

52. Dubcek 1993: 29, 33, 36.

53. Ibid., 48–49, 57, 58, 60.

54. Ibid., 64, 69, 70, 71.

55. Hochman, personal communication, July 1997.

56. Dubcek 1993: 83, 151, 84, 85, 84–85, 87, 95.

57. Ibid., 97, 77.

58. Ibid., 135, 136, 147.

59. Ibid., 166, 168, 178, 179, 182.

60. Ibid., 265, 266.

61. Ibid., 276–277, 277, 278.

62. Mlynar 1980: 232.

63. Genovese 1994.

64. Mlynar 1980: 16, 10, 1.

65. Ibid., 2. A contemporary of Mlynar, Otto Ulc, disagrees: "Mlynar was born the same year as I and unless I am mistaken he also entered the Prague law school the same year, 1949, as I did . . . I refuse to accept his self-serving assertion that his—i.e., also my—generation desired radical departure from the past, embraced the communist cause, and knew nothing of the real conditions in the Soviet Union. At least 90 percent of us did not fit this characterization." [Personal communication, March 1997.]

66. Mlynar 1980: 3, 4, 5, 6, 8.

67. Ibid., 9. As will be shown in the next chapter, using such deceptions was standard operating procedure at the time.

68. Ibid., 10, 11, 13.

69. Ibid., 14, 19–20.
70. Ibid., 21, 22, 22–23, 15.
71. Ibid., 27, 29, 33, 34, 35.
72. Ibid., 38, 45, 49, 50, 65–66.
73. Ibid., 67, 128, 131, 146–147, 177, 179, 232, 259.
74. Hruby 1980: 234.
75. A similar observation was made in an early discussion of political disenchant-ment among communist intellectuals: "So long as the basic idea is accepted and the Party's role in attaining it is regarded as indispensable, the believer can see no reason why any crime, even any seeming betrayal of the revolutionary ethos, cannot be justified by superior ends." [K. A. Jelenski, "Varieties of Disenchant-ment," in Urban 1964: 93.]
76. For a detailed discussion of the interviews see the Appendix.
77. Toranska 1987.
78. Quoted in Rosenberg 1995: 142.

CHAPTER 6 Leading Specialists in "State Security" (Political Police)

1. Quoted in Toranska 1987: 276.
2. Timothy Garton Ash came to the same conclusion in the course of researching the East German political police: "The officers most ready to meet me are mainly from the foreign intelligence service . . . they feel they have less, or even nothing to be ashamed of. Those whose business was spying on their own people are much less eager to talk." [Ash, "Rome File," 1997: 169.]
3. "Markus Wolf," 1994: 93.
4. Arguably, China under Mao was in the same league. However, since some of his spiritual heirs are still in power, documentation of the mass murders under his rule has been limited and incomplete.
5. Ash 1997: 84–85. For a more general discussion of these differences and similari-ties see Hollander 1994 and Fall 1995.
6. Interview in Budapest, summer 1992.
7. Pryce-Jones 1995: 10. The same could be said of Cambodia under Pol Pot.
8. For prime exhibits see J. Arch Getty, *Origins of the Great Purges* (New York: Cam-bridge University Press, 1985); J. Arch Getty and Robert T. Manning, eds., *Stal-inist Terror: New Perspectives* (Cambridge: Cambridge University Press, 1993); Sheila Fitzpatrick, *Education and Social Mobility in the Soviet Union* (Cambridge: Cambridge University Press, 1979); Robert Thurston, *Life and Terror in Stalin's Russia* (New Haven: Yale University Press, 1996).
9. Miner 1996: 14.
10. Hannah Arendt introduced the first two, Adorno the third, and Stanley Mil-gram the last. An indicator of the social scientific indifference toward political violence under communist systems is a recent symposium on the legacy of the Milgram experiments. Not one of the fourteen contributions raised the question of the applicability or relevance of Milgram's experiments to political violence in communist systems, past or present. [See "Perspectives," 1995.]

11. Hruby 1980: 222.
12. Quoted in Conquest 1996: 44.
13. Quoted in Radzinsky 1996: 260–261.
14. See Hollander 1981: 156–159.
15. Levitsky 1972: 229.
16. Hollander, *Anti-Americanism*, 1992: 277–280; see also Brentlinger 1995: 200–201.
17. For further examples see Hollander 1981: 140–160, 335–346; see also Hollander 1987.
18. Such individuals were encountered by a former Hungarian political prisoner: "The cruelty of our guards always abated as soon as they were safe from the supervision of their superiors . . . Any AVH-man [Hungarian political police] who did not swing his truncheon with requisite fierceness . . . was in danger of becoming suspect in the eyes of his superiors . . . in an intimate man-to-man setting, the AVH-man would indirectly dissociate himself from the brutality of his companions." [Szasz 1971: 202–203.] These lower-level "specialists" were apparently not driven by either strong convictions or personal pathologies.
19. Quoted in Kristof 1997: 8.
20. Sakharov quoted in Remnick, *Lenin's Tomb*, 1993: 354; Caryl 1996: 18.
21. Calda is a professor of American literature at Charles University in Prague; I interviewed him in Prague in 1992 and the spring of 1993 at the Hoover Institution in Stanford, California.
22. Quoted in Rosenberg 1995: 53, 55.
23. Loebl 1976: 155.
24. Szasz 1971: 70.
25. Visual evidence of such attitudes is available in the photos of SS soldiers displayed in the Holocaust Museum, in Washington, D.C. They are broadly smiling and appear cheerful while performing their grisly tasks; often they are purposefully photographed next to their victims. The photos were taken by their comrades or relatives, not some hostile outside observer.
26. For example, in communist Poland "many people in the security apparatus. acted the way they did . . . in the conviction that repression was the right thing." [Jakub Berman, quoted in Toranska 1987: 333.]
27. Laszlo Rajk, a veteran communist and minister of the interior (the police), was suddenly arrested and accused of wide-ranging conspiracies. After a show trial in 1949, in which he confessed to being a long-standing enemy of the communist system, he was hung. The trial followed the pattern of the Moscow trials of the 1930s. Shortly before the October 1956 revolution he was reburied in a public ceremony and rehabilitated.
28. Szasz 1971: 15, 21.
29. Greenstein 1969: 103–114.
30. The point was forcefully made by Edward Shils in Christie and Jahoda 1954.
31. Serge 1963: 80.
32. Quoted in Conquest 1968: 544.
33. Volkogonov 1990: 229.

34. Khoklov 1959: 165–166.
35. Paloczi-Horvath 1959: 233.
36. Horn 1991: 112.
37. Becker 1995: 75.
38. Skvorecky 1986: 37.
39. Hruby 1980: 223–224.
40. Pryce-Jones 1995: 72.
41. Knight 1993: 10, 229.
42. Volkogonov 1990: 236.
43. Rainer 1996: 513.
44. Wolf 1997: 208.
45. Resis 1993: xix, 257.
46. Radzinsky 1996: 345.
47. Knight 1993: 8; Brezhneva 1995: 54.
48. Pryce-Jones 1995: 233.
49. Wolf 1997: 66.
50. Receptivity to this thesis points to a strong social-critical disposition. If all of us are corruptible to the point of committing heinous acts when so ordered, it says something about the type of society that produced us. Collective responsibility, or "complicity," removes the moral distinctions between perpetrator and all those who were spared from being thrust into that role; thereby attention is diverted from the individual to the social circumstances and pressures.
51. But C. Browning found that members of police units had the opportunity to excuse themselves from executing Jews by shooting, but most did not avail themselves of it (*Ordinary Men* [1993]). If so, their moral indifference is quite extraordinary. Daniel Goldhagen makes the same point even more strongly in *Hitler's Willing Executioners* (1996).
52. Quoted in Hruby 1980: 38.
53. Quoted in Malia 1994: 268.
54. Kennan, October 1988.
55. Resis 1993: xvi, 243, 195, 265, 278.
56. Quoted in Toranska 1987: 206.
57. Thayer 1997: 14, 15, 16.
58. Loebl 1976: 54, 108, 115.
59. Leites 1953: 114, 115–116, 117.
60. Quoted in Bell 1981: 547.
61. Quoted in Toranska 1987: 135–136.
62. Ibid., 43.
63. Further light is shed on Lenin's attitudes toward and policies concerning political violence in Pipes, *Unknown Lenin*, 1996.
64. Quoted in Remnick, November 1996: 120–121.
65. Leites 1953: 141. See also pp. 109, 114, 115–116, 117, 105, 124.
66. Yakovlev 1993: 40.
67. Ibid., 39.

68. Ibid., 38.
69. Resis 1993: 107.
70. Kennan 1996: 236.
71. Radzinsky 1996: 153–154.
72. Hochschild 1994: 80.
73. Ibid., 79.
74. Quoted in Pryce-Jones 1995: 13.
75. Ibid.
76. Quoted in Toranska 1987: 345.
77. Sudoplatov and Sudoplatov 1994: 325.
78. Farkas 1990: 322.
79. Quoted in Shalin 1996: 188.
80. Quoted in Sudoplatov and Sudoplatov 1994: viii.
81. Quoted in Hochschild 1994: 66.
82. Quoted in Stanley 1996.
83. Ehrenburg 1967: 307.
84. Remnick, July 1996: 43. Gabor Peter, the head of the Hungarian political police between 1947 and 1953 who was subsequently jailed, reportedly also said, "I don't feel guilty and I am awaiting the new trial." [Punkosti, "Hoherkomedia," 1996: 98.]
85. Remnick, July 1996: 43, 42.
86. Kryuchkov 1996: vol. 2, p. 372.
87. Ibid., vol. 2, p. 22.
88. Ibid., vol. 2, p. 44.
89. Ibid., vol. 1, pp. 98–99.
90. Ibid., vol. 2, p. 356.
91. Kennan 1996: 234.
92. Quoted in "China's Defense Chief, " 1996. See also A. M. Rosenthal 1996.
93. Himmler said to the SS Group Leaders in October 1943: "I shall speak to you here with all frankness on a very serious subject. We shall now discuss it absolutely openly among ourselves; nevertheless, we shall never speak of it in public. I mean . . . the extermination of the Jewish people. It is one of those things [of] which it is easy to say . . . 'That's clear, it is part of our programme, elimination of the Jews . . . we'll do it.' And then they all come along, eighty million good Germans, and each has his decent Jew . . . Most of you know what it means to see a hundred corpses lying together, five hundred, or a thousand. To have gone through this and yet . . . to have remained decent, this has made us hard. This is a glorious page in our history that has never been written and never shall be written." [Quoted in Fest 1970: 115.]
94. Quoted in Toranska 1987: 354.
95. Ibid., 309.
96. "The enemy" was the politicized version of evil, both as a highly general and a very specific concept. On the one hand, there was in the Soviet-Communist mythology an entity called the "enemy" without further specification. On the other hand, the concept was often given political or sociological substance and

specificity, as, for example, when it referred to "capitalist ruling classes," "kulaks," "Trotskyites," "Titoists," and so forth.

97. Quoted in Farkas 1990: 241.

98. Szasz 1971: 21; Levy 1974: 84–85.

99. Quoted in Leites 1953: 105.

100. Quoted in Trimble 1997: 10.

101. Sudoplatov and Sudoplatov 1994: 5, 81. Mercader told the court in Mexico
that "he had been disillusioned by Trotsky when commissioned by him to go
to Russia, murder Stalin and make preparations for the assassination of other
communist leaders." He had the requisite attitude not merely to carry out an
assassination but also to lie shamelessly and inventively for the good of the
cause. [Levitsky 1972: 147.]

102. Volkogonov 1996: 459.

103. Quoted in Punkosti, *Rakosi*, 1996: 159–160, 169, 207.

104. The root of this attitudes may be located in Christian thought. Saint Jerome
wrote: "The tainted flesh must be cut away, and the infected sheep cast out
from the fold: lest the whole house burn, the mass be corrupted, the body become infected and the flock perish." [Quoted in Gunter Lewy, *Why America
Needs Religion* (Grand Rapids, Mich.: Eerdmans, 1996), p. 3.]

105. Quoted in Toranska 1987: 327, 331.

106. Levitsky 1972: 132.

107. Gromyko 1990: 378.

108. Punkosti, *Rakosi*, 1996: 182, 197, 196.

109. Loebl 1976: 55. Loebl further recalls that prior to his own imprisonment he too
subscribed to the belief that ends justify means: "Lenin had said: 'When trees
are felled, splinters fly.' And hadn't the church burned thousands . . . of innocent victims to save their souls in the name of heavenly love?" Loebl adds: "I
became acutely conscious of the problem only when I was on the other side,
in prison. It is so easy to talk about revolutionary theories, flying splinters and
necessary victims until you become a victim yourself. Suddenly you realize that
it is not an abstract enemy who is being persecuted; the victims of persecution
are human beings . . . crying out in real pain." [Ibid.]

110. For a former Red Guard's reflections see Gong 1995: 157.

111. One qualification should be introduced here: while the political violence in the
Soviet Union during the 1930s was certainly planned and initiated from the
top, it did get out of hand insofar as the waves of mutual denunciation were
spontaneous and motivated by fear and the instinct for self-preservation.

112. Volkogonov 1996: 387.

113. Sudoplatov and Sudoplatov 1994: xii, 3.

114. Ibid., 4, 389, 430.

115. Ibid., 170–171, 478.

116. Farkas 1990: 245.

117. Sudoplatov and Sudoplatov 1994: xvi, 127, 284. "Chekist" refers to members of
the Cheka, the first incarnation of the Soviet political police after the October
Revolution, which had more of an aura of revolutionary incorruptibility than

did its successor agencies, variously abbreviated as OGPU, NKVD, MVD, and, most recently, KGB.
118. Khoklov 1959: 135, 136, 140.
119. Sudoplatov and Sudoplatov 1994: 55.
120. Kalugin 1994: 253.
121. Ibid., 10, 12.
122. Ibid., 24, 6.
123. Quoted in Pryce-Jones 1995: 72.
124. Kalugin 1994: 28.
125. Ibid., 238.
126. Kalugin told John le Carré in Moscow: "Listen, all we did was carry out the sentence [of a Bulgarian court]. It was completely legal." [Le Carré 1995: 33.] For Kalugin's response to le Carré see his letter in the *New York Times Book Review*, April 2, 1995. Kalugin also wrote about the incident in the British tabloid newspaper *Mail on Sunday* under the headline "I Organized Markov's Execution." [See Bukovsky 1996: 40.]
127. Kalugin 1994: 196.
128. Kalugin 1994: 232, 255.
129. Ibid., 213, 224, 225.
130. Ibid., 312.
131. Socialist realism was the term officially given to politicized art and literature in the Soviet Union and other state socialist systems. It required presenting social and human realities not as they could actually be observed but as they were supposed to be according to ideological blueprints provided by Party officials specializing in such matters. [See Sinyavski 1960; Hollander, "Models of Behavior in Stalinist Literature," in Hollander 1983.
132. Kalugin 1994: 307-308, 309.
133. Ibid., 313.
134. Ibid., 319.
135. Ibid., 166, 247.
136. Ibid., 5.
137. Ibid., 287-288, 296, 284.
138. Ibid., 21, 27-28, 30, 32.
139. Ibid., 62, 63.
140. Ibid., 123, 305.
141. Ibid., 109, 108, 110.
142. Ibid., 215.
143. Ibid., 227, 148, 166.
144. Ibid., 131, 146.
145. Farkas 1990: 233, 244.
146. Sejna 1982: 21.
147. Farkas 1990: 16, 14.
148. Ibid., 19, 28, 53, 57, 79.
149. Ibid., 111.
150. Ibid., 209, 210, 245.

151. Ibid., 240.
152. See Remnick 1991: 74.
153. Farkas 1990: 241.
154. Ibid., 278.
155. Quoted in Toranska 1987: 39.
156. Ibid., 59, 45, 48.
157. Farkas 1990: 291.
158. Ibid., 401.
159. Szasz 1971: 218.
160. Farkas 1990: 449, 473.
161. Ibid., 530.
162. Ibid., 51, 52, 43.
163. Ibid., 44.
164. It was an experience that young Farkas shared with tens, if not hundreds, of thousands of Hungarians in 1945. The craving for watches on the part of Soviet soldiers inspired many jokes about the "liberators." The difference between the behavior of the Soviet troops (which included large-scale raping and looting as well) witnessed by millions of Hungarians and the official images of these troops was among the extreme divergences between reality and propaganda and among the challenges to the legitimacy of the system.
165. Farkas 1990: 88.
166. Ibid., 92–93.
167. Ibid., 109, 109–110.
168. Ibid., 118–119. The same physician referred to in the Farkas quotation subsequently became a teacher at the university in Budapest: "In the middle of the 1960s, we, students of psychology, were instructed by a huge man . . . about the bodily limits of resistance to external injury to the skin, muscles, joints, and nerves, about the burden that can be imposed upon them. His name was Dr. Istvan Balint, and he used to be the medical colonel in the AVH who distinguished himself as the founder of the scientific study of beating people." [Perczel 1998: 5.]
169. When I was an adolescent in Hungary, it was widely rumored that Vladimir Farkas had participated in the mistreatment of Janos Kadar in prison. When I met Farkas, he vehemently denied these allegations.
170. Farkas 1990: 274.
171. Ibid., 181.
172. Ibid., 202.
173. Ibid., 324, 326.
174. Ibid., 233–234.
175. Ibid., 255.
176. Ibid., 338.
177. Ibid., 363.
178. Ibid., 431, 430.
179. Ibid., 438.
180. Punkosti, *Rakosi*, 1996: 188.

181. Zinner 1996: 22.

182. Loebl 1976: 208.

183. Quoted in Toranska 1987: 104.

184. Volkogonov 1996: 356.

185. Farkas 1990: 459.

186. Ibid., 564, 582.

187. Ibid., 512.

188. Ibid., 316.

189. Ibid., 405–406.

190. Wolf 1997: 4.

191. "Who Is Markus Wolf?" 1994: 52.

192. Ibid.

193. Wolf 1997: 57, 58.

194. Ibid., xi–xii.

195. Ibid., 233.

196. "Markus Wolf," 1994: 52.

197. Ibid., 45.

198. Ibid., 52.

199. Wolf 1997: 28, 30.

200. "Tales of a Master Spy," 1991: 28.

201. "Markus Wolf," 1994: 92.

202. Quoted in Rosenberg 1995: 58.

203. Wolf 1997: 37–38.

204. Ibid., 40–41.

205. Ibid., 63.

206. Ibid., 224, 311.

207. Ibid., 83–84.

208. Ibid., 85–86.

209. Ibid., 87.

210. Ibid., 99–100, 211, 213.

211. Ibid., 102, 226.

212. Ibid., 196, 103, 249.

213. Ibid., 250, 340, 250–251.

214. Ibid., 317, 316.

215. Ibid., 316, 318, 320, 346.

216. "Markus Wolf," 1994: 93.

217. Wolf 1997: 325, 341, 345, 347.

218. Kinzer 1995.

219. A reviewer of his memoirs writes: "Wolf still cannot bring himself to believe that there was anything wrong with the theory itself. All that was wrong was the manner in which the theory was put into practice." [Buruma 1997: 43.]

220. Ash, "Rome File," 1997: 170.

221. Maier 1996: 152–153, 48.

222. Hruby 1980: 221–222.

223. This also applied to the disillusionment of numerous Czech communist intel-

lectuals: "When some of them became victims of these theories, in prison and in concentration camps, the comrades attempted to rethink the problems of socialist justice"—and much else, one might add. [Ibid., 4.]

224. Meyer 1961: 25.

CHAPTER 7 Conclusions: The Unity of Theory and Practice

1. In a recent study Rudolf L. Tokes correctly observes that "the general trends of systemic change in the 1980s in communist party-states showed unambiguous evidence of political entropy, economic stagnation and rising social discontent. However, none of these symptoms of decline had been a conclusive predictor of the East European regimes' collapse by the end of 1989." [Tokes 1996: 306.]

2. Chirot 1994: 233.

3. Chirot writes: "The moral base of communism had vanished. The elites had lost confidence in their legitimacy. The intellectuals . . . disseminated this sense of moral despair and corruption to the public . . . The cumulative effect of such a situation over decades cannot be underestimated. Those who had hope . . . were replaced by those who had never had hope and who had grown up knowing that everything was a lie." [Chirot 1991: 19.] As Charles Maier puts it, "Late socialism suffered from its own progressive and characteristic degenerative disease."[Maier 1996:58.]

4. Gaddis 1997: 283; Hobsbawm 1997: 4.

5. Taubman 1986.

6. M. Gorbachev 1996: 189. The following sheds further light on Soviet nuclear technology and the mentality of workers asociated with it: "Valerii Legasov, first deputy chairman of the Kurchatov Institute of nuclear physics in Moscow, worried when he found a worker on a nuclear power station failing to finish the seams on a water cooling pipe; he had, the man said, too many seams in his daily output target. A station director told Legasov to calm down, saying: 'What are you worried about? A nuclear reactor is only a samovar. It's much simpler than a thermal plant . . . Nothing will happen.'" [Cottrell 1998: 40.]

7. Gaddis 1997: 181.

8. Adam Ulam writes: "It had been the Soviet Union's role as a superpower . . . that obscured the internal weaknesses of the Soviet system." [Ulam 1992: 381.]

9. The USSR had more men under arms than the United States, had more nuclear weapons and missiles, more tanks and artillery pieces. To be sure, the quality of many of these weapons was inferior to those of the United States.

10. Conditions were different in Eastern Europe, where it was the arrival of the Red Army that created the prerequisites for setting up communist states. To be sure, their leaders—often escorted by the Soviet troops—were well equipped with the essential ideological baggage and motivated to create Marxist-Leninist societies modeled after the Soviet Union.

11. Gaddis 1997: 14, 293.

12. Wat 1990: 173. A somewhat similar argument was put forward more recently by Igor Kon, the Russian social scientist: "Among the causes contributing to the demise of the Soviet empire one has to count the psychological crisis that gripped Soviet society in the early 1970s and wore it down through the 1980s. Apathy, cynicism and alcoholism had as much to do with the collapse . . . as falling prices on world oil markets and corruption among Soviet officials . . . perestroika failed to deliver on its promise . . . because its architect . . . underestimated the depth of the anger that enveloped Soviet society after its cherished myths were exposed." [Shalin 1996: 121.]

13. Gaddis 1997: 290. Timothy Colton argues in the same spirit: "If . . . ideology is understood less restrictively as a somewhat elastic cultural system . . . then I for one am struck how ideological a good deal of Soviet conduct was and by how difficult it was for actors to break out of the mold." [Colton in Grigoriev 1995: 5.]

14. Quoted in Gaddis 1997: 208.

15. Ochab, quoted in Toranska 1987: 55.

16. Rakosi, quoted in M. Gorbachev 1996: 62.

17. As David Satter puts it, " A theocratic system . . . does not easily lend itself to doctrinal reconstruction. By trying to preserve the structure of an ideological state without an ideology, Gorbachev started a process that could end either with the end of reform or with the fall of the Soviet Union." [Satter 1996: 417–418.]

18. Eugene Loebel, on life in Czechoslovakia, in Loebl 1976: 225. Another Czech author writes: "The government, courts, public and almost all private life practiced the law of jungle. No one could feel safe and in order to survive everybody had to lie, cheat and steal." [Hruby 1980: 231.]

19. Quoted in Satter 1996: 193.

20. See the Appendix. Shevardnadze too asked: "Why don't we have consumer goods? Why can't we travel round the world when everybody else can?" [Quoted in Pryce-Jones 1995: 112.] It may be recalled that Yeltsin was overwhelmed on his first visit to the United States by what he saw in the supermarkets.

21. Grigoriev 1995: abstract and p. 162.

22. "When the CPSU was banned following the failure of the August 1991 coup, virtually no one rose to to defend it . . . Neither in Moscow nor anywhere else in the country were there any pro-party rallies or demonstrations although at the time the party could claim almost 16 million members, a large network of regional and local branches, and strong party organizations in the army, the KGB and the Ministry of Internal Affairs." [Grigoriev 1995: 1.] See also Solnick 1998 on the erosion of authority.

23. Quoted in Remnick, *Lenin's Tomb*, 1993: 68.

24. Medvedev 1986: viii.

25. Kryuchkov 1996: vol. 1, p. 98; Heller 1988: xvii.

26. "There had been a . . . visible decline in the calibre of party leaders from Lenin's to Khrushchev's generation, but in previous times it would have been impossible for men like Kirilenko, Grishin, Romanov, Shcherbitsky, Kunayev, Tikhonov and Chernenko to reach Politburo and Secretariat status." [Medvedev 1986: 122.]

27. Dubcek 1993: 165.
28. Quoted in Remnick, November 1996: 118.
29. Quoted in "Castro's Compromises," 1995: 58.
30. Quoted in Toranska 1987: 88.
31. Ibid., 208, 207. Berman was in charge of ideological and cultural matters in communist Poland after World War II until 1956.
32. As one of them, Len Karpinsky, said: "The nomenklatura is on another planet . . . It's not simply a matter of good cars or apartments. It's the continuous satisfaction of our own whims . . . Your every wish is fulfilled . . . It's a life in which everything flows easily . . . You are like a king: just point a finger and it is done." [Quoted in Remnick, *Lenin's Tomb*, 1993: 172–173.]
33. This point was made (among others) by one of my Hungarian informants who used to be a prominent journalist during the Kadar era. He had studied in the Soviet Union for several years and was in his youth an idealistic supporter of the system.
34. Quoted in Kaiser 1991: 402.
35. Quoted in Cohen and Heuvel 1989: 101.
36. Cohen, "Introduction," in Cohen and Heuvel 1989: 19.
37. On the influence of the "60s people" see, among others, J. Steele: 1994: 25. Charles Fairbanks also emphasizes the elite background of the major movers of glasnost. [Fairbanks 1993.] See also Burlatski in Cohen and Heuvel 1989: 177 confirming the coherence of this group.
38. Quoted in Cohen and Heuvel 1989: 99. Somewhat less charitably, David Remnick characterizes the "'men of the Sixties' . . . [as] half-brave, half-cynical careerists, living a life-in-waiting for the great reformer to come along and bring the Prague Spring to Moscow. While they took few of the risks of the dissidents, the best among them refused to live the lie, finding subtle ways of declaring at least a measure of independence from the regime . . . They kept something alive within themselves." [Remnick 1991: 77.]
39. Keller 1993: 36.
40. M. Gorbachev 1996: 102–103; see also pp. 149–150.
41. By contrast, under Brezhnev "incumbent Party leaders assumed that communism was forever; that challenges could always be suppressed by inquisition, imprisonment, and execution . . . No understanding of the protest, no recognition of their own unpopularity or vulnerability, disturbed the minds of Brezhnev and his cronies." [Murphy 1992: 252.]
42. Meyer 1961: 157.
43. Figes, March 1995.
44. Erlanger 1992: 73.
45. Quoted in Andrew Rosenthal 1989. A remarkable illustration of this gap can also be found in a painting the Soviet magazine *Ogonok* published after the 1968 invasion: a Soviet tank and its crew are surrounded by a group of smiling Czech civilians handing them flowers. I saw the painting in the washroom of a Hungarian friend, where it was placed as an example of black humor. The painting recalls another example of Soviet socialist-realist art that sought to leap over the

gulf between ideals and realities—a painting (a photo of which is still in my possession) of Khrushchev on his 1961 visit to the United States addressing American dockworkers, who are beaming at him. Such a scene never took place. American dockworkers and their unions expressed their sentiments by protesting at the Soviet warship where Khrushchev stayed (anchored in the East River), circling it in a tugboat carrying signs denouncing him.

46. Andrew Rosenthal 1989.

47. Remnick 1991: 76.

48. Shevardnadze 1991: 21.

49. For a discussion of such responses see Hollander, October 1995.

50. Cumings in Chirot 1991: 125. Cumings also argues that East European communists misunderstood Marx and "institutionalized this failed understanding"—another way to the conclusion that the theory had nothing to do with the practices it had inspired.

51. Radu 1995: 120. Such attitudes were powerfully illustrated by the fate of a resolution defeated with only one vote in its support that was proposed in 1990 at the annual meeting of the Organization of American Historians. The resolution expressed support for new initiatives within the Soviet Union "seeking to place history on a footing of respect for truth and avoiding deliberate falsehood" and offered regret that in the past "the Organization never protested the forced betrayal of the historians' responsibility to truth imposed upon Soviet and East European historians by their leaders." [Quoted in Washburn 1992: 2.]

52. Pryce-Jones 1995: 22.

53. Chirot writes: "The fundamental reason for the failure of communism was that the utopian model it proposed was obviously not going to come into being. Almost everything could have been tolerated if the essential promise was on its way to fulfillment." [Ibid., 21.]

54. Malia 1994: 498, 512. Petro Grigorienko, the Soviet dissident, says: "Some writings characterize Marxism-Leninism as a democratic and humane movement, but from the same Marxism-Leninism have come extreme totalitarian, dictatorial and antihuman theories and affirmations." [Grigorienko 1982: 208.]

55. Djilas 1998: 302, 305, 289; see also Kolakowski in Tucker 1977, esp. pp. 284, 291, 296.

56. Kolakowski 1978: 527.

57. These uncharacteristically unrealistic ideas were expressed at some length in his *State and Revolution*. It would be interesting to know how Lenin would have interpreted the discovery reported by Robert Conquest: "We now have the individual case files of some of the several hundred blind or legless or otherwise incapacitated people who were sentenced to imprisonment late in 1937 but were executed, after resentencing, early in 1938 on the grounds that they would be useless at forced labor." [Conquest 1997: 9.]

58. Hruby 1980: 17.

59. Ibid., 65.

60. Moore 1987: 131.

61. Malia 1994: 496.

62. Pipes 1994: 64.
63. For a discussion of the universality of such attitudes see Berger 1977.
64. Cohen in Cohen and Heuvel 1989: 14. In contrast to Cohen, the Hungarian sociologist Rudolf Andorka observes: "The socialist system was capable of change, even if the changes eventually led to its total collapse. The direction of these changes was, however, not toward a model 'midway' between the Western capitalist and the Eastern socialist systems." [Andorka 1993: 319.]
65. Kolakowski 1978: 523, 525.
66. Koestler 1945: 123–124.
67. Quoted in Tokes 1996: 469.
68. Litvan 1988: 157. The deception Lukacs engaged in was not confined to himself. Upon his return to Hungary from Moscow after World War II he failed "to enlighten his friends and disciples at home about the degeneration of the revolution that was to redeem the world." In a postwar letter sent to a friend in the United States he described the years of fear and humiliations in Moscow "as a 'good period' spent with good works and growth." [Ibid.]
69. Loebl 1976: 118–119.
70. Hodos 1987: 55.
71. Quoted in Murphy 1993: 337. This disposition is also shared by postmodernist academics.
72. Berlin 1996: 30.
73. In the same vein, a former officer of the Stasi (East German political police) said: "'The system went wrong . . . because it was bound to go wrong, because of human nature. People can't be transformed, turned into something other than they are.' Communism failed to allow for what he calls 'the inner Schweinhund' [swinishness]." [Ash 1997: 193–194.]
74. "Political will was ultimately the primary determinant of economic action, and this will was based on a very coherent world view developed by Lenin, Stalin and other Bolshevik leaders." [Chirot 1991: 5.]
75. See also Ekedahl and Goodman 1996: 49.
76. Wisse 1997: 41.

Bibliography

Aczel, Thomas, and Tibor Meray. *Tisztito Vihar* (Cleansing Storm). Munich: Griff, 1978.

Aksyonov, Vassily. "Intellectuals and Social Change in Central and Eastern Europe." *Partisan Review,* no. 4, 1992.

———. "My Search for Russia's Revolution." *New York Times,* op-ed, November 22, 1994.

Andorka, Rudolf. "The Socialist System and Its Collapse in Hungary," *International Sociology,* September 1993.

Andrew, Christopher, and Oleg Gordievky. *KGB: The Inside Story.* New York: Harper-Collins, 1990.

Arbatov, Georgi. *The System: An Insider's Life in Soviet Politics.* New York: New York Times Books, 1992.

Aron, Raymond. *The Opium of Intellectuals.* London: Secker and Warburg, 1957.

Ash, Timothy Garton. *The File: A Personal History.* New York: Random House, 1997.

———. "The Rome File." *New Yorker,* April 27–May 5, 1997.

Bakatin, Vadim V. *Izbevlenie ot KGB.* (Deliverance from the KGB). Moscow: Novosti, 1992.

Barbu, Zevedei. *Democracy and Dictatorship.* New York: Grove Press, 1956.

Barmine, Alexander. *One Who Survived.* New York: Putnam, 1945.

Barron, James. "Petro Grigorienko Dies in Exile in U.S." *New York Times,* February 23, 1987.

Becker, Howard S. *Antonio Candido on Literature and Society.* Princeton: Princeton University Press, 1995.

Bell, Daniel. "First Love and Early Sorrows." *Partisan Review,* November 4, 1981.

Benoist, Alain de. "Nazism and Communism: Evil Twins?" *Telos,* Summer 1998.

Berger, Peter L. "Are Human Rights Universal?" *Commentary,* September 1977.

Berkowitz, Bruce D., and Jeffrey T. Richelson. "The CIA Vindicated—The Soviet Collapse *Was* Predicted." *National Interest,* Fall 1995.

Berlin, Isaiah. *Four Essays on Liberty.* New York: Oxford University Press, 1969.

———. "On Political Judgment." *New York Review of Books,* October 3, 1996.

Bethell, Nicholas. *The Last Secret: Forcible Repatriation to Russia, 1944–1947.* London: Deutsch, 1974.

Bodzaban, Istvan, and Antal Szalay, eds. *A Puha Diktaturatol a Kemeny Demokraciaig* (From Soft Dictatorship to Firm Democracy). Budapest: Pelikan, 1994.

Boldin, Valery. *Ten Years That Shook the World: The Gorbachev Era as Witnessed by His Chief of Staff.* New York: Basic, 1994.

Brentlinger, John. *The Best of What We Have: Reflections on the Nicaraguan Revolution.* Amherst: University of Massachusetts Press, 1995.

Brezhneva, Luba. *The World I Left Behind.* New York: Random House, 1995.

Brzezinski, Zbigniew. *The Grand Failure.* New York: Scribner, 1989.

Brinton, William M., and Alan Rinzler, eds. *Without Force or Lies.* San Francisco: Mercury House, 1990.

Brown, Archie. *The Gorbachev Factor.* New York: Oxford University Press, 1996.

Bukovsky, Vladimir. "Secrets of the Central Committee." *Commentary*, October 1996.

Buruma, Ian. "Wolf in Wolf's Clothing." *New Republic*, July 14 and 21, 1997.

Caryl, Christian. "The Undead." *New Republic*, December 16, 1996.

"Castro's Compromises." *Time*, February 20, 1995.

"China's Defense Chief Minimizes Tianeanmen Toll" [AP]. *Daily Hampshire Gazette*, December 11, 1996.

Chirot, Daniel, ed. *The Crisis of Leninism and the Decline of the Left: The Revolutions of 1989.* Seattle: Washington University Press, 1991.

———. *Modern Tyrants.* New York: Free Press, 1994.

Christie, Richard, and Marie Jahoda, eds. *Studies in the Scope and Method of the "Authoritarian Personality."* Glencoe, Ill.: Free Press, 1954.

Ciliga, Anton. *The Russian Enigma.* London: Routledge, 1940.

Clark, John, and Aaron Wildavsky. *The Moral Collapse of Communism.* San Francisco: Institute for Contemporary Studies, 1990.

Cohen, Stephen F., and Katrina Vanden Heuvel, eds. *Voices of Glasnost: Interviews with Gorbachev's Reformers.* New York: Norton, 1989.

Colburn, Forrest D. *The Vogue of Revolution in Poor Countries.* Princeton: Princeton University Press, 1994.

"Communism Is Not Dead, U.S. Party Leader Says." *Boston Globe*, August 31, 1991.

Conquest, Robert. *The Great Terror.* London: Macmillan, 1968.

———. *The Harvest of Sorrow: Soviet Collectivization and the Terror-Famine.* New York: Oxford Press, 1987.

———. "Response to Getty, Rittersporn and Zemskov." *American Historical Review*, June 1994.

———. "The Sober Monster." *New York Review of Books*, June 8, 1995.

———. "The Fugitive." *New Republic*, March 18, 1996.

———. "Terrorists." *New York Review of Books*, March 6, 1997.

"Conversation with Robert Conquest." *Humanities*, May–June 1993.

Cottrell, Robert. "Russia's Dream City." *New York Review of Books*, April 23, 1998.

"The Cracked Crystal Ball." *Newsweek*, November 19, 1979.

Crossman, Richard, ed. *The God That Failed.* New York: Harper, 1949.

Csepeli, Gyorgy, and Antal Orkeny. *Ideology and Political Beliefs in Hungary: The Twilight of State Socialism.* London: Pinter, 1992.

Dallin, Alexander. "Causes of the Collapse of the USSR." *Post-Soviet Affairs*, October–December 1992.

d'Encausse, Helen Carrere. *The End of the Soviet Empire: The Triumph of the Nations.* New York: Basic, 1993.

Dicks, Henry V. *Licensed Mass Murder: A Socio-Psychological Study of Some SS Killers.* New York: Basic, 1972.

Djilas, Milovan. *Fall of the New Class: A History of Communism's Self-Destruction.* New York: Knopf, 1998.

Dobrynin, Anatoly. *In Confidence.* New York: Random House, 1995.

Draper, Theodore. "Who Killed Soviet Communism?" *New York Review of Books*, June 11, 1992.

Dubcek, Alexander. *Hope Dies Last.* New York: Kodansha International, 1993.

Ehrenburg, Ilya. *Post-War Years, 1945–1954.* Cleveland: World Publishing Co., 1967.

Ekedahl, Carolyn McGiffert, and Melvin A. Goodman. *The Wars of Eduard Shevardnadze.* University Park: Pennsylvania State University Press, 1997.

Enzensberger, Hans Magnus. *The Consciousness Industry.* New York: Seabury Press, 1974.

Epstein, Julius. *Operation Keelhaul: The Story of Forced Repatriation from 1944 to the Present.* Old Greenwich, Conn.: Devin-Adair, 1973.

Erlanger, Steven. "Reform School." *New York Times Magazine*, November 29, 1992.

Fairbanks, Charles. "The Suicide of Soviet Communism." *Journal of Democracy*, Spring 1990.

———. "The Nature of the Beast." *National Interest*, Spring 1993.

Fantel, Hans. "I Once Admired Hitler." *New York Times*, op-ed, April 30, 1995.

Farkas, Vladimir. *Nincs Mentseg—Az AVH Alexredese Voltam* (No Excuse—I Was a Lt. Colonel in the AVH). Budapest: Interart Studio, 1988.

Fest, Joachim C. *The Face of the Third Reich: Portraits of the Nazi Leadership.* New York: Pantheon, 1970.

Festinger, Leon. *A Theory of Cognitive Dissonance.* Evanston, Ill.: Row, Peterson, 1957.

Figes, Orlando. "Communism: Two Autopsies." *New York Times Book Review*, March 19, 1995.

———. "Without a Fight." *New York Times Book Review*, September 3, 1995.

"For the Record." *National Review*, May 24, 1993.

Freedom Review, correspondence, July–August 1992.

Gaddis, John Lewis. *We Now Know: Rethinking Cold War History.* Oxford: Clarendon Press, 1997.

Genovese, Eugene D. "The Crimes of Communism." *Dissent*, Summer 1994.

Glebov, O., and J. Crowfoot, eds. *The Soviet Empire: Its Nations Speak Out.* London: Harwood, 1989.

Gong, Xiaoxia. "Repressive Movements and the Politics of Victimization." Ph.D. dissertation, Harvard University, 1995.

Gorbachev, Mikhail. *Perestroika: New Thinking for Our Country and the World.* New York: Harper and Row, 1987.

———. "No Time for Stereotypes." *New York Times*, op-ed, February 24, 1992.

———. *Memoirs.* New York: Doubleday, 1996.

Gorbachev, Raisa. *I Hope*. London: HarperCollin, 1991.

"Gorbachev and Hart on List of Admired Men." *New York Times*, January 10, 1988.

"Gorbachev-Yeltsin Session: 'Committed to Common Work.'" *New York Times*, September 7, 1991.

Greenhouse, Stephen. "French Communist Chief Attacked for Stance on Soviet Coup." *New York Times*, August 27, 1991.

Greenstein, Fred I. *Personality and Politics*. Chicago: Markham, 1969.

Grigorienko, Petro G. *Memoirs*. New York: Norton, 1982.

Grigoriev, Sergei. *The International Department of the CPSU Central Committee*. Cambridge: Kennedy School of Government, Harvard University, 1995.

Gromyko, Andrei. *Memoirs*. New York: Doubleday, 1990.

Handler, Andrew, and Susan V. Meschel, eds. *Red Star, Blue Star: The Lives of and Times of Hungarian Students in Communist Hungary (1948–1956)*. New York: Columbia University Press, 1997.

Hegedus, Andras. *A Tortenelem es a Hatalom Igezeteben* (Under the Spell of History and Power). Budapest: Kossuth, 1988.

Heller, Mikhail. *Cogs in the Wheel: The Formation of Soviet Man*. New York: Knopf, 1988.

Heller, Mikhail, and Alexander M. Nekrich. *Utopia in Power: The History of the Soviet Union from 1917 to the Present*. New York: Summit Books, 1986.

Herf, Jeffrey. "A Wolf in Sheep's Clothing?" *Tikkun*, July–August 1994.

Hobsbawn, Eric. *On History*. New York: Norton: 1997.

Hochschild, Adam. "The Secret of a Siberian River Bank." *New York Times Magazine*, March 28, 1993.

———. *The Unquiet Ghost: Russians Remember Stalin*. New York: Viking, 1994.

Hodos, George H. *Show Trials: Stalinist Purges in Eastern Europe, 1948–1954*. New York: Praeger, 1987.

Hollander, Paul. *Political Pilgrims: Travels of Western Intellectuals to the Soviet Union, China and Cuba, 1928–1978*. New York: Oxford University Press, 1981.

———. "Models of Behavior in Stalinist Literature." In Hollander, *Many Faces of Socialism*. New Brunswick, N.J.: Transaction, 1983.

———. "Socialist Prisons and Imprisoned Minds." *National Interest*, Winter 1987.

———. *The Survival of the Adversary Culture*. New Brunswick, N.J.: Transaction, 1988.

———. *Anti-Americanism: Critiques at Home and Abroad*. New York: Oxford University Press, 1992.

———. *Decline and Discontent: Communism and the West Today*. New Brunswick, N.J.: Transaction, 1992.

———. "Soviet Terror, American Amnesia." *National Review*, May 2, 1994.

———. "A Comparative Moral Reassessment of Nazism and Communism." *Partisan Review*, Fall 1995.

———. "Digesting the Collapse of Communism: Responses of Western Intellectuals." *Quadrant*, October 1995.

Horn, Gyula. *Colopok*. (Pillars) Budapest: Zenit, 1991.

Hruby, Peter. *Fools and Heroes: The Changing Role of Communist Intellectuals in Czechoslovakia*. New York: Pergamon Press, 1980.

Ignatieff, Michael. "In the Center of the Earthquake." *New York Review of Books,* June 12, 1997.

Johnson, Paul. *Modern Times.* New York: Harper and Row, 1983.

Jowitt, Ken. "Explaining the End of Soviet Power." *East European Constitutional Review,* Spring–Summer 1997.

Jurgens, Urda. *Raisa: The First Lady of the Soviet Union.* New York: Summit Books, 1990.

Kaiser, Robert. *Why Gorbachev Happened.* New York: Simon and Schuster, 1991.

Kalugin, Oleg. *The First Directorate: My Thirty-Two Years in Intelligence and Espionage Against the West.* New York: St. Martin's Press, 1994.

———. "In the New Russia." *New York Times Book Review,* April 2, 1995.

Kapusciniski, Riszard. *Imperium.* New York: Knopf, 1994.

Kasenkina, Oksana. *Leap to Freedom.* Philadelphia: Lippincott, 1949.

Keller, Bill. "Gorbachev Urges Minority States." *New York Times,* April 18, 1987.

———. "Moscow's Other Mastermind." *New York Times Magazine,* February 19, 1989.

———. "De Klerk's Gorbachev Problem." *New York Times Magazine,* January 31, 1993.

———. "The Art of the Possible." *New York Times Book Review,* October 20, 1996.

Kennan, George F. "The Gorbachev Prospect." *New York Review of Books,* January 21, 1988.

———. "The Buried Past." *New York Review of Books,* October 27, 1988.

———. "Witness to the Fall." *New York Review of Books,* November 16, 1995.

———. *At a Century's Ending: Reflections, 1982–1995.* New York: Norton, 1996.

Khoklov, Nikolai. *In the Name of Conscience.* New York: McKay, 1959.

Kinzer, Stephen. "Release of Honecker Is Drawing Fire in Germany." *New York Times,* January 24, 1993.

———. "Ex-East German Spymaster Finds Polishing His Image Is Hard." *New York Times,* December 8, 1995.

Kirkpatrick, Jeane J. *The Withering Away of the Totalitarian State and Other Surprises.* Washington, D.C.: American Enterprise Institute Press, 1990.

———. "The National Prospect" [symposium]. *Commentary,* November 1995.

Kissinger, Henry. "The Right to Be Right." *New York Times Book Review,* November 14, 1993.

Klehr, Harvey, and John Haynes. "The End." *New Republic,* March 23, 1992.

Klima, Ivan. *The Spirit of Prague and Other Essays.* New York: Granta Books, 1994.

Knight, Amy. *Beria: Stalin's First Lieutenant.* Princeton: Princeton University Press, 1993.

Koch, Stephen. *Double Lives.* New York: Free Press, 1995.

Koestler, Arthur. *The Yogi and the Commissar.* New York: Collier, 1945.

Kolakowski, Leszek. "Marxist Roots of Stalinism." In Robert C. Tucker, ed., *Stalinism: Essays in Historical Interpretation.* New York: Norton, 1977.

———. *Main Currents of Marxism.* Vol. 3. New York: Oxford University Press, 1978.

Konrad, Gyorgy. *Az Ujjaszuletes Melankoliaja* (The Melancholy of Rebirth). Budapest: Patria Books, 1991.

Konrad, Gyorgy, and Ivan Szelenyi. *Intellectuals on the Road to Class Power*. New York: Harcourt Brace Jovanovich, 1976.

Kopelev, Lev. *The Education of a True Believer*. New York: Harper and Row, 1980.

Kraditor, Aileen S. *"Jimmy Higgins": The Mental World of the American Rank and File Communist, 1930–1958*. New York: Greenwood Press, 1988.

Krasnov, Vladislav. *Soviet Defectors: The KGB Wanted List*. Stanford, Calif.: Hoover Institution Press, 1985.

Kravchenko, Victor. *I Chose Freedom*. New York: Scribners, 1946; New Brunswick, N.J.: Transaction, 1988.

Kristof, Nicholas D. "The Wounds of War: A Generation of Japanese Is Haunted by Its Past." *New York Times*, January 22, 1997.

Krivitsky, W. G. *In Stalin's Secret Service*. New York: Harper, 1940.

Kryuchkov, Vladimir. *Lichnoe Delo* (Personal Business). Moscow: Olimp, 1996.

Kuran, Timur. "The Inevitability of Future Revolutionary Surprises." *American Journal of Sociology*, May 1995.

———. *Private Truths, Public Lies: The Social Consequences of Preference Falsification*. Cambridge: Harvard University Press, 1995.

Laqueur, Walter. *The Dream That Failed: Reflections on the Soviet Union*. New York: Oxford University Press, 1994.

Larina, Anna. *This I Cannot Forget*. New York: Norton, 1993.

le Carré, John. "My New Friends in the New Russia: In Search of a Few Good Crooks, Cops and Former Agents." *New York Times Book Review*, February 19, 1995.

Leites, Nathan. *A Study of Bolshevism*. Glencoe, Ill.: Free Press, 1953.

Leonhard, Wolfgang. *Child of the Revolution*. Chicago: Regnery, 1958.

———. "Does Gorbachev Mean a Change?" *The East-West Papers*, no. 4, November 1986.

Levchenko, Stanislav. *On the Wrong Side: My Life in the KGB*. Washington: Pergamon-Brassey's, 1988.

Levitsky, Boris. *The Uses of Terror: The Soviet Secret Police, 1917–1970*. New York: Coward, 1972.

Levy, Alan. *Good Men Still Live! The Odyssey of a Professional Prisoner*. Chicago: O'Hara, 1974.

Lewin, Moshe. *The Gorbachev Phenomenon*. Berkeley: University of California Press, 1988.

Ligachev, Yegor. *Inside Gorbachev's Kremlin*. New York: Pantheon, 1993.

Lipset, Seymour Martin, and Gyorgy Bence. "Anticipations of the Failure of Communism." *Theory and Society*, no. 23, 1994.

Litvan, Gyorgy. "'Mi Kommunistak Kulonos Emberek Vagyunk . . .' A Stalinizmus Lelektana" (We Communists Are Special People: The Psychology of Stalinism). *Szazadveg* (Budapest), nos. 6–7, 1988.

Loebl, Eugene. *My Mind on Trial*. New York: Harcourt, 1976.

Lowenhardt, John. *The Reincarnation of Russia: Struggling with the Legacy of Communism, 1990–1994*. Durham, N.C.: Duke University Press, 1995.

Maier, Charles S. *Dissolution: The Crisis of Communism and the End of East Germany*. Princeton: Princeton University Press, 1997.

Malia, Martin. "A Fatal Logic." *National Interest*, Spring 1993.

———. *The Soviet Tragedy*. New York: Free Press, 1994.

Markov, Georgi. *The Truth That Killed*. New York: Ticknor and Fields, 1984.

"Markus Wolf: East Germany's Jewish Master Spy" [interview]. *Tikkun*, January–February 1994.

Matlock, Jack F., Jr. "The Go-Between." *New York Review of Books*, February 1, 1996.

———. "Gorbachev: Lingering Mysteries." *New York Review of Books*, December 19, 1996.

McMillan, Johnson Priscilla. "Cold Warmonger." *New York Times Book Review*, May 25, 1997.

Medvedev, Zhores. *Gorbachev*. New York: Norton, 1986.

Meray, Tibor. *Nagy Imre Elete es Halala* (The Life and Death of Imre Nagy). Munich: Ujvary/Griff Publishers, 1983.

Meyer, Frank S. *The Moulding of Communists*. New York: Harcourt Brace, 1961.

Miner, Steven Merritt. "Dark Prince of the Kremlin." *New York Times Book Review*, May 5, 1996.

———. "A Revolution Doomed from the Start." *New York Times Book Review*, March 9, 1997.

Mlynar, Zdenek. *Night Frost in Prague: The End of Humane Communism*. London: C. Hurst and Co., 1980.

———. *Can Gorbachev Change the Soviet Union?* Boulder, Colo.: Westview Press, 1990.

Montefiore, Simon S. "Eduard Shevardnadze." *New York Times Magazine*, December 26, 1993.

Moore, Barrington, Jr. *Authority and Inequality Under Capitalism and Socialism*. Oxford: Clarendon Press, 1987.

———. "Liberal Prospects Under Societ Socialism: A Comparative Historical Perspective." *The First Annual W. Averell Harriman Lecture* [pamphlet]. Columbia University, November 15, 1989.

Moroz, Valentyn. "A Report from the Beria Reserve." *Problems of Communism*, July 1968.

Morrison, John. *Boris Yeltsin: From Bolshevik to Democrat*. New York: Dutton, 1991.

Murphy, Kenneth. *Retreat from the Finland Station: Moral Odysseys in the Breakdown of Communism*. New York: Free Press, 1992.

Nagy, Imre. *On Communism: In Defense of the New Course*. New York: Praeger, 1957.

Oates, Joyce Carol. "Meeting with Gorbachev." *New York Times Magazine*, January 3, 1988.

Odom, William E. *The Collapse of the Soviet Military*. New Haven: Yale University Press, 1998.

Ollman, Bertell. "The Regency of the Proletariat in Crisis: A Job for Perestroika." *PS: Political Science and Politics*, September 1991.

"On with the Show." *New Yorker*, January 1993.

Orlov, Yuri. *Dangerous Thoughts*. New York: Morrow, 1991.

Palazchenko, Pavel. *My Years with Gorbachev and Shevardnadze*. University Park: Pennsylvania State University Press, 1997.

Paloczi-Horvath, George. *The Undefeated*. Boston: Little Brown, 1959.

Pareto, Vilfredo. *The Rise and Fall of Elites*. New Brunswick, N.J.: Transaction, 1991.

Perczel, Tamas. "Jar e Majd Orban Victor a Jozsef Nador Ter 1-be?" (Will Victor Orban Visit Joseph Nador Square No. 1?). *Elet es Irodalom* (Budapest), June 26, 1998.

"Perspectives on Obedience to Authority: The Legacy of the Milgram Experiments." *Journal of Social Issues*, Fall 1995.

Pipes, Richard. "Can the Soviet Union Reform?" *Foreign Affairs*, Fall 1984.

———. "Where Is the Glasnost?" *Wall Street Journal*, December 1, 1987.

———. "Misinterpreting the Cold War." *Foreign Affairs*, January–February 1988.

———. "The Toady." *New Republic*, October 19, 1992.

———. *Communism: The Vanished Specter*. Oslo: Scandinavian University Press; New York: Oxford University Press, 1994.

———. "Beltway Commissar." *New Republic*, November 27, 1995.

———. "The Seeds of His Own Destruction." *New York Times Book Review*, March 24, 1996.

———, ed. *The Unknown Lenin*. New Haven: Yale University Press, 1996.

Pirogov, Peter. *Why I Escaped*. New York: Duell, Sloan, and Pierce, 1950.

Posner, Vladimir. *Eyewitness*. New York: Random House, 1992.

Powers, Thomas. "Who Won the Cold War?" *New York Review of Books*, June 20, 1996.

Pryce-Jones, David. *The Strange Death of the Soviet Empire*. New York: Holt, 1995.

Puddington, Arch. "After the Fall." *Commentary*, May 1993.

Punkosti, Arpad. "Hoherkomedia" (The Comedy of the Executioner). *HVG* (Budapest), June 1, 1996.

———. *Rakosi a Csucson, 1948–1953* (Rakosi at the Top). Budapest: Europa, 1996.

Radu, Michael. "The Soviet Tragedy." *Orbis*, Winter 1995.

———. *Collapse or Decay? Cuba and the East European Transitions from Communism*. Washington, D.C.: Cuban-American Foundation, n.d.

Radzinsky, Edward. *Stalin*. New York: Doubleday, 1996.

Rainer, Janos M. *Nagy Imre: Politikai Eletrajz* (Imre Nagy: Political Biography). Budapest: Intezet, 1996.

Reagan, Nancy, with William Novak. *My Turn: The Memoirs of Nancy Reagan*. New York: Random House, 1989.

Remnick, David. "Thank You, Mr. Gorbachev." *New York Times*, December 4, 1987.

———. "Dead Souls." *New York Review of Books*, December 19, 1991.

———. "The Counterrevolutionary." *New York Times Review of Books*, March 25, 1993.

———. *Lenin's Tomb*. New York: Random House, 1993.

———. "Hammer, Sickle and Book." *New York Review of Books*, May 23, 1996.

———. "The War for the Kremlin." *New Yorker*, July 22, 1996.

———. "The First and the Last." *New Yorker*, November 18, 1996.

Resis, Albert, ed. *Molotov Remembers: Inside Kremlin Politics—Conversations with Felix Chuev*. Chicago: Ivan Deem, 1993.

Rosenberg, Tina. *The Haunted Land*. New York: Random House, 1995.

Rosenthal, A. M. "Naked in the Square." *New York Times*, December 13, 1996.

Rosenthal, Andrew. "A Soviet General's Second Thoughts." *New York Times*, September 21, 1989.

Rubinstein, Alvin Z. "Soviet Success Story: The Third World." *Orbis*, Fall 1995.

Ruge, Gerd. *Gorbachev: A Biography*. London: Chatto and Windus, 1991.

Rush, Myron. "Fortune and Fate." *National Interest*, Spring 1993.

Satter, David. *Age of Delirium: The Decline and Fall of the Soviet Union*. New York: Knopf, 1996.

Schlesinger, Arthur, Jr. "The Party Circuit." *New Republic*, May 29, 1995.

Schmemann, Serge. "From Comrade to Critic in Five Years." *New York Times Book Review*, February 21, 1993.

Schoenfield, Gabriel. "A Charming Communist." *Commentary*, December 1995.

Schuman, Frederick L. "Horrors of Bolshevism, Inc." *New Republic*, May 6, 1946.

Schweizer, Peter. *Victory: The Reagan Administration's Secret Strategy That Hastened the Collapse of the Soviet Union*. New York: Atlantic Monthly Press, 1994.

Sejna, Jan. *We Will Bury You*. London: Sidwick and Jackson, 1982.

Semprun, Jorge. *What a Beautiful Sunday!* New York: Harcourt Brace Jovanovich, 1980.

Serge, Victor. *Memoirs of a Revolutionary, 1901–1941*. London: Oxford University Press, 1963.

Shalin, Dmitri N., ed. *Russian Culture at the Crossroads*. Boulder, Colo.: Westview Press, 1996.

Shane, Cott. *Dismantling Utopia: How Information Ended the Soviet Union*. Chicago: Ivan R. Dee, 1994.

Sharansky, Natan. "As I See Gorbachev." *Commentary*, March 1988.

———. "Gorbachev Plays a Double Game." *New York Times*, January 4, 1997.

Shenon, Philip. "Vietnam Party Vows to Maintain Absolute Power." *New York Times*, June 25, 1991.

Shevardnadze, Eduard. *The Future Belongs to Freedom*. London: Sinclair and Stevenson, 1991.

Shevchenko, Arkady. *Breaking with Moscow*. New York: Ballentine, 1985.

Shipler, David. *Russia*. New York: Penguin, 1983.

Shlapentokh, V. *Soviet Intellectuals and Political Power—The Post-Stalin Era*. Princeton: Princeton University Press, 1990.

Simes, Dmitri K. "Confirmation Time." *National Interest*, Summer 1995.

Sinyavski, Andrei. *On Socialist Realism*. New York: Pantheon, 1960.

Skvorecky, Joseph. "Two Peas in a Pod: Why Nazis and Communists Sing the Same Songs." *Idler*, November 1986.

Smith, Andrew. *I Was a Soviet Worker*. London: Hale, 1937.

Sobchak, Anatoly. *For a New Russia*. New York: Free Press, 1992.

Solnick, Steven L. *Stealing the State: Control and Collapse in Soviet Institutions*. Cambridge: Harvard University Press, 1998.

Solovyov, Vladimir, and Elena Klepikova. *Boris Yeltsin: A Political Biography*. New York: Putnam, 1992.

Somin, Ilya. "Riddles, Mysteries and Enigmas: Unanswered Questions of Communism's Collapse." *Policy Review*, Fall 1994.

Souvarine, Boris. *Stalin: A Historical Survey of Bolshevism.* New York: Alliance Book Corp., 1939.

Spiegel, Irving. "Kravchenko Kills Himself Here; He Chose Freedom from Soviet." *New York Times,* February 26, 1966.

Stanley, Alessandra. "A Lament by America's Top Communist." *New York Times,* August 31, 1991.

———. "Gorbachev's New Battle: Overcoming His Legacy." *New York Times,* March 10, 1995.

———. "Dmitri Volkogonov, 76, Historian Who Debunked Heroes, Dies." *New York Times,* December 7, 1995.

———. "Stalin's Music Man Is a Kremlin Star Again." *New York Times,* February 1, 1996.

Steele, Jonathan. *Eternal Russia: Yeltsin, Gorbachev and the Mirage of Democracy.* Cambridge: Harvard University Press, '1994.

Steele, Shelby. "The New Sovereignty." *Harpers,* July 1992.

Sudetic, Chuck. "Bulgarian Communist Stalwart Says He'd Do It All Differently." *New York Times,* November 28, 1990.

Sudoplatov, Anatoli, and Pavel Sudoplatov. *Special Tasks.* Boston: Little, Brown, 1994.

Sukosd, Mihaly. "Nagy Imre Sorsa" (The Fate of Imre Nagy). *168 Ora* (Budapest), June 4, 1996.

Szasz, Bela. *Volunteers for the Gallows: Anatomy of a Show-Trial.* New York: Norton, 1971.

"Tales of a Master Spy from the Other Side." *Time Magazine,* November 25, 1991.

Tanenhaus, Sam. "What the Anti-Communists Knew." *Commentary,* July 1990.

Tatu, Michel. *Mikhail Gorbachev: The Origins of Perestroika.* Boulder, Colo.: East European Monographs; distributed by Columbia University Press, 1991.

Taubman, Philip. "Chernobyl Reconsidered." *New York Times,* April 26, 1986.

Thayer, Nate. "Day of Reckoning." *Far Eastern Economic Review,* October 30, 1997.

Tokes, Rudolf L. *Hungary's Negotiated Revolution.* New York: Cambridge University Press, 1996.

Tolstoy, Nicolai. *Victims of Yalta.* London: Hadden and Stoughton, 1977.

Toranska, Teresa. *"Them": Stalin's Polish Puppets.* New York: Harper and Row, 1987.

Trimble, Jeff. *Discussion Paper D-24.* Joan Shorenstein Center: Harvard University, February 1997.

Tyler, Patrick E. "A Ghost of Maoist Fervor Lingers On in Disgrace." *New York Times,* April 10, 1996.

Ulam, Adam. *The Communists.* New York: Scribners, 1992.

Unwin, Peter. *Voice in the Wilderness: Imre Nagy and the Hungarian Revolution.* London: MacDonald, 1991.

Urban, George R., ed. *Scaling the Wall.* Detroit, Mich.: Wayne State University Press, 1964.

Voinovich, Vladimir. *The Anti-Soviet Soviet Union.* New York: Harcourt Brace Jovanovich, 1985.

Volkogonov, Dmitri. *Gyozelem es Tragedia: Stalin Politikai Arckepe* (Victory and Tragedy: The Political Portrait of Stalin). Budapest: Zrinyi, 1990.

———. *Trotsky: The Eternal Revolutionary.* New York: Free Press, 1996.

Voslenshy, Michael. *Nomenklatura: The Soviet Ruling Class.* Garden City, N.Y.: Doubleday, 1984.

Washburn, Wilcomb E. "The Treason of Intellectuals." *Young America Foundation.* Herndon, Va., 1992.

Wat, Alexander. *My Century: The Odyssey of a Polish Intellectual.* Berkeley: University of California Press, 1988.

"We Weren't Following Orders but the Currents of the Cold War." *New York Times,* March 24, 1996.

"Who Is Markus Wolf?" *Tikkun,* July–August 1994.

Wisse, Ruth R. "By Their Own Hands." *New Republic,* February 3, 1997.

Wolf, Markus, "East Germany's Jewish Master Spy" [interview]. *Tikkun,* January–February 1994.

Wolf, Markus. *Man Without a Face.* New York: Random House, 1997.

Yakovlev, Alexander. *The Fate of Marxism in Russia.* New Haven: Yale University Press, 1993.

Yeltsin, Boris. *Against the Grain: An Autobiography.* New York: Summit Books, 1990.

Zinner, Tibor. "Az AVH-s Vezetok Sorsa" (The Fate of the AVH leaders). *Historia* (Budapest), November 3, 1996.

Zubok, Vladimir, and Constantine Pleshakov. *Inside the Kremlin's Cold War: From Stalin to Khrushchev.* Cambridge: Harvard University Press, 1996.

Index